WHEATON PUBLIC LIBRARY

3 5143 00940766 6

W9-BSQ-866

823.09 DOY

APR   2017

Sims, Michael, 1958- author

Arthur and Sherlock : Conan
Doyle and the creation of
Holmes   WITHDRAWN

WHEATON PUBLIC LIBRARY
226 N. CROSS
WHEATON, IL 60187
(630) 668-1374

Arthur and Sherlock

By the same author

Arthur and Sherlock

Conan Doyle and the Creation of Holmes

MICHAEL SIMS

BLOOMSBURY

NEW YORK · LONDON · OXFORD · NEW DELHI · SYDNEY

Bloomsbury USA
An imprint of Bloomsbury Publishing Plc

1385 Broadway	50 Bedford Square
New York	London
NY 10018	WC1B 3 DP
USA	UK

www.bloomsbury.com

BLOOMSBURY and the Diana logo are trademarks of Bloomsbury Publishing Plc

First published 2017

© Michael Sims, 2017

All rights reserved. No part of this publication may be
reproduced or transmitted in any form or by any means, electronic or
mechanical, including photocopying, recording, or any information storage
or retrieval system, without prior permission in writing from the publishers.

No responsibility for loss caused to any individual or organization acting on or
refraining from action as a result of the material in this publication can be
accepted by Bloomsbury or the author.

ISBN: HB: 978-1-63286-039-2
ePub: 978-1-63286-038-5

Library of Congress Cataloging-in-Publication Data is available.

4 6 8 10 9 7 5 3

Typeset by RefineCatch Limited, Bungay, Suffolk
Printed and bound in the U.S.A. by Berryville Graphics Inc., Berryville, Virginia

To find out more about our authors and books visit
www.bloomsbury.com. Here you will find extracts, author interviews,
details of forthcoming events, and the option to
sign up for our newsletters.

Bloomsbury books may be purchased for business or
promotional use. For information on bulk purchases please contact
Macmillan Corporate and Premium Sales Department at
specialmarkets@macmillan.com.

To
George Gibson
with admiration and affection

"What clue could you have as to his identity?"

"Only as much as we can deduce."

"From his hat?"

"Precisely."

"But you are joking. What can you gather from this old battered felt?"

"Here is my lens. You know my methods."

—SHERLOCK HOLMES AND DR. WATSON
IN "THE ADVENTURE OF THE BLUE CARBUNCLE"

Contents

Remembering

A shiny brass plate suspended from a wrought-iron railing along the street proclaimed

DR. CONAN DOYLE

SURGEON

Patients wishing to consult Arthur strode along Elm Grove until they were three doors from its west end, where it met King's Road. The sign stood before number 1, Bush Villas, the first of two narrow three-story houses squeezed between and sharing walls with other establishments. On the left, as seen from the street, rose the brick bell tower and elegant arching windows of the newly renovated Elm Grove Baptist Church. On the right stood the handsome curving façade of Bush Hotel, which advertised as both "Commercial and Family" and which boasted the largest billiard saloon in Southsea. Always preoccupied with sports and physical activity, broad-shouldered Arthur enjoyed playing billiards in the hotel and playing bowls on the broad green behind it.

The flat's large, square front windows faced almost due north and thus received strong light without glare. Patients entered through the arched entryway on the left, adjacent to the church, where the front door opened into a hall that led to a small waiting room and a consulting room on the ground floor. Stairs led up to the surgery and a private sitting room, and another flight climbed to a pair of bedrooms on the top floor, which patients never saw.

In early 1886, Arthur Conan Doyle was a few months shy of twenty-seven. For less than four years, he had operated—not always with success—a medical office in Southsea, a bustling residential section of Portsmouth,

England. Lacking the funds to buy into an established practice, he had resolved to build his own from scratch, and after a little research he decided upon Portsmouth as a promising setting. In local sporting circles and scientific societies, he was known for his sociability and his hearty, infectious laugh.

Four years after settling here, he was no longer so poor that he had to buy creaky chairs and a faded rug on credit to furnish the sitting room. He did not sleep in his ulster, as he had for the first couple of weeks at Bush Villas when he owned no bed linens. He did not have to cook bacon on a little platform rigged on a wall over the gas jet. He no longer borrowed money from his mother back home in Edinburgh. Gradually his income had climbed, but his fear of creditors had faded only when he married the petite and soft-spoken Louise Hawkins—nicknamed "Touie"—with whom he fell in love after caring for her younger brother during his last days. Patients still trickled in, but Arthur no longer peered anxiously down through the wooden blinds to count passersby who stopped to read his brass nameplate.

They were not rich, Touie and Arthur, but they were comfortable. The most important luxury that Arthur could now afford was more opportunity to write. Since moving to Southsea, he had spent as much time as possible at his desk, upstairs in the space to which patients were never admitted. He filled page after page with his neat, small script. Gazing thoughtfully out the window beyond his desk, he became so intimate with the view from his study window that later he wrote it into one of his novels—the sound of rain striking a dull note on fallen leaves and a clearer note on the gravel path, the pools that formed in the street and along the walkway, even a fringe of clear raindrops clinging to the underside of the bar atop the gleaming gate. With the windows open in warm weather, he could smell the damp earth.

Here Arthur wrote stories of mystery, adventure, and the supernatural, and rolled them up and inserted them into mailing tubes for the postman. Having once thought of these unsolicited writing efforts as returning quickly and reliably like carrier pigeons from the magazines and newspapers to which he sent them, he gradually met greater success. He also wrote articles about his hobby, photography, ranging from colorful accounts of steaming along the coast of Africa to technical advice on how to prepare lenses.

In the style of the time, however, most of his stories were printed anonymously, resulting in a growing reputation with editors while he remained unknown to the public. Finally he decided that he must write a novel. Only his name on the spine of a long work of fiction, he told himself, could begin to build readers' awareness of him. He had written one awkward little novel whose only copy had been lost in the mail, but he was determined to try again.

He was drawn to detective stories out of his own interest. He had long admired the logical mind of Edgar Allan Poe's unofficial detective C. Auguste Dupin. He had enjoyed the adventures of Émile Gaboriau's eagle-eyed police detective Monsieur Lecoq. The bold man-hunters of penny dreadfuls, Charles Dickens's Inspector Bucket from *Bleak House*, Wilkie Collins's Sergeant Cuff from *The Moonstone*, Anna Katharine Green's more recent New York policeman Ebenezer Gryce from *The Leavenworth Case*—many such detectives already cavorted in Arthur's imagination when he decided to create his own.

He had no experience with real-life detective work. As he turned over plot ideas in his mind, however, he recalled his years as a student at medical school in Edinburgh—his birthplace, to which he returned in 1876 at the age of seventeen, after boarding schools in England and Austria. And especially he thought about his favorite professor, a short, hawk-nosed wizard named Joseph Bell. A surgeon and a brilliant diagnostician, he had impressed his young student in many ways. Arthur had always admired Bell's oracular ability not only to diagnose illness but also to perceive details about patients' personal lives. Arthur thought of the professor's quirky habits—his intense gaze darting at fingertips and cuffs to read a patient's history of work and play, his attention to subtleties of accent, to mud splashes on boots. He recalled Bell's commanding way of speaking with such confidence that he won over every person who argued with him.

As a detective, Arthur thought, Joseph Bell would have approached crime-solving with systematic, modern knowledge. He would need practical experience in chemistry and forensic medicine, as well as encyclopedic knowledge of the history of crime. He must attend to the large implications of small details. Such a character would be a new development in crime fiction—a scientific detective.

In the late winter and early spring of 1886, at his window above Elm Grove, in his small office away from the scurry of marriage and medicine, among books and piles of papers, Arthur wrote page after page, sending his memory back almost a decade into the past.

Part 1

Dr. Bell and Mr. Doyle

The student must be taught first to observe carefully. To interest him in this kind of work we teachers find it useful to show the student how much a trained use of the observation can discover in ordinary matters such as the previous history, nationality, and occupation of a patient. . . . Physiognomy helps you to nationality, accent to district, and, to an educated ear, almost to county. Nearly every handicraft writes its sign-manual upon the hands. The scars of the miner differ from those of the quarryman. The carpenter's callosities are not those of the mason.

—JOSEPH BELL, M.D.

CHAPTER I

A Super-Man

So now behold me, a tall strongly-framed but half-formed young
man, fairly entered upon my five years' course of medical study.
—ARTHUR CONAN DOYLE, *MEMORIES AND ADVENTURES*

Arthur Doyle led the patient into a crowded gaslit amphitheater,
through a cluster of medical students surrounding Dr. Joseph Bell's
chair, and left him standing before the professor. The man's attitude
was respectful but not servile. He did not remove his hat. In a Scottish
accent, he explained that he had come to Edinburgh Royal Infirmary seeking
treatment for the early stages of elephantiasis.

As usual with patients, at first Dr. Bell showed no expression, in his
reserved way that seemed to young Arthur how a Red Indian in North America
might behave. From childhood Arthur had enjoyed tales of the American frontier, and such imagery leapt easily to mind. Bell pressed his fingertips together
as he leaned back in his chair, looked the patient over, and remarked for the
benefit of his students, "Well, my man, you've served in the army."

"Aye, sir."

"Not long discharged?"

"No, sir."

"A Highland regiment?" Although he spoke with the crisp accent called
"educated Edinburgh," Bell's high-pitched voice did not match the tanned,
muscular body that made him look younger than his forty years.

"Aye, sir."

"A non-com officer?"

"Aye, sir."

Then came what seemed a far-fetched guess: "Stationed at Barbados?"

"Aye, sir."

After the patient departed, Bell explained his inferences—that the man did not remove his hat because he had been in the military, that he had not been long out of service or he would have regained civilian habits, that his air of authority indicated he had been a noncommissioned officer rather than a common soldier. And obviously he was a Scot. "As to Barbados," he added, "his complaint is elephantiasis, which is West Indian and not British." The patient might have contracted the disease in other parts of the British Empire—India or Afghanistan as well as the West Indies—but apparently Bell's deduction was correct.

Bell had received no prior information about the man other than Arthur's note of his illness. Although he was an excellent surgeon and clinical teacher, as well as personal physician to Queen Victoria whenever she visited Scotland, Bell was most renowned for his diagnostic skills. He tended to begin an interview by deducing personal details about the patient's illness, profession, and life by flicking his gray-eyed gaze—half-critical and half-sardonic, Arthur thought—from hat to elbows to boots. He maintained that an observant man ought to learn a great deal before the patient spoke. Regarding female patients, he went so far as to claim that doctors ought to foresee which part of her body a woman was about to discuss by her posture and how she held her hands.

When he explained his reasoning, Bell was lecturing, not inviting discussion. Few professors and students mingled at Edinburgh University in the late 1870s; sometimes no words were exchanged with individual students. Many sat or stood before the students and delivered lectures, the salient points of which were to be recorded in notes scribbled by the array of silent young men in their dark coats and ties—some mustached or bearded, but many youthfully clean-shaven like Arthur. Arthur would pay his four guineas for anatomy lectures, for example, and would be expected thereafter to diligently attend class. However, Bell was more personable, more interested in his students, than most professors. He was known as an unusually kind figure, especially to women and children, as well as to students as long as they were prepared for class.

After teaching systematic and operative surgery for years, Bell was appointed senior surgeon to the infirmary in 1878. He was among the "extra-academical instructors," professors not directly employed by Edinburgh University whose classes were recognized as available for credit toward a degree. Bell's own mentor, the legendary James Syme, had led a campaign to recognize extramural instruction, which had finally been authorized in 1855, while Bell was a student. Under this program, which had long been flourishing by the time Arthur enrolled in 1876, students could study with surgeons and others at the internationally renowned infirmary, as well as with other small groups of medical professionals headquartered around Surgeons Square—Park Place School, Surgeons' Hall, Minto House School, and others. They could attend classes or other instruction at the Royal Public Dispensary, the Edinburgh Eye Infirmary, the Royal Maternity Hospital, the Sick Children's Hospital, and elsewhere in the city. They could also study for credit in Leipzig or Paris or other recognized medical universities.

Tired-looking young men in black coats or tweed, laden with books and notebooks, poured from the gates to the hospital, tapping their walking sticks against the stones and at times stepping aside to avoid a carriage clattering down the cobblestones. Among the many wards in the grand three-winged, U-shaped Royal Infirmary building, two housed patients whose ailments were considered instructive to the students who thronged the wide central staircase, often dodging pairs of nurses carrying a patient between them in a sedan chair. I WAS NAKED AND YE CLOTHED ME, read one of the signs between Ionic columns out front, and the other I WAS SICK AND YE VISITED ME. The charity infirmary was the culmination of a century and a half of donation and subscription—and where money was short, glassmakers had glazed windows without charge and joiners had donated sashes. Completed in 1741, the infirmary was proving inadequate to succor the hordes of suffering poor, and additional buildings were rising.

For the first time in his life, Arthur felt engaged by a course and a teacher. Eager to help his mother through financial straits—at least to keep her from having to contribute to his college costs—he was trying to cram each year's classes into a half year so that he might spend the rest of the year assisting a doctor, getting his expenses covered and gaining experience. Eager to excel and curious about almost everything, he scrawled countless notes. At times it seemed to Dr. Bell that Arthur wanted to transcribe every word he said. Often, after a patient left, the student asked the professor to repeat details so that he might get them correct.

Joe Bell—as students and friends affectionately called him—was Arthur's favorite professor. Rather short, with angular shoulders, an aquiline nose, and a weathered, ruddy face, he was an easily recognized sight around campus and town. Even at a distance, he was known by his twitchy, uneven walk—a brisk stride conquering a limp.

Working as clerk for the famed surgeon and teacher presented quite an opportunity for an ambitious student. Tall, broad-shouldered Arthur was quick-witted, forthright, and diligent; in his late teens, he was beginning to outgrow the rebellious temper of his early years. His eyes, with their unusual two tones of blue in the iris, were as busy as his professor's.

Arthur had admired Bell's theatrical diagnostic routine since before beginning work in the outpatient ward. Every six months, each surgeon appointed several dressers (assistants) to help him handle the traffic. Bell chose Arthur, along with a few other trusted dressers, from among many young men. Arthur did not think of himself as an outstanding student; he had earned grades of Satisfactory in all classes except for an S-minus in clinical surgery. But Bell came to consider him one of the most promising men who had studied under him—a youngster fascinated by all aspects of diagnosis and attentive to the large implications of small details. Surgical outpatients might walk in with any sort of complaint: wounds or chronic pain, ailments ranging from respiratory to gynecological. Bell demanded that students be prepared for whatever misfortune might appear. The new infirmary was completed in 1879, and during the next year fifteen thousand patients passed through its outpatient clinic.

Arthur and other efficient clerks interviewed patients in a side room and herded them quickly in and out of Bell's examination. He sorted as many as seventy or eighty per day, noted details about their complaint or injury, and then brought them in one by one for a consultation—during which he often thought Bell learned more with a glance than had Arthur with his queries. When Arthur began working as clerk, Bell warned him that outpatient interviews required familiarity with the uniquely Scottish slang employed by uneducated locals. Although his parents were Irish, Arthur had been born in Edinburgh—on Picardy Place, in a three-story house of modest but handsome flats near the Gothic Revival parapets of St. Paul's and St. George's Episcopal Church. He assured Bell that he was fluent in the local vernacular. Inevitably, one of the first patients Arthur asked about his ailment proved incomprehensible: he complained of a bealin' in his oxter. Bell was amused to have to explain to Arthur that the location of the pain was the armpit and the problem was an abscess.

"From close observation and deduction, gentlemen," Bell would declaim confidently, "you can make a correct diagnosis of any and every case." He was proud of his reputation as an intelligent observer. "However," he would add, "never neglect to ratify your deductions, to substantiate your diagnosis with the stethoscope—and by other recognized and everyday methods of diagnosis."

Bell would look over a patient and remark casually, "Cobbler, I see." Then came the explanation to students, the leap from a detail that not one of the young men had observed: a worn place on the inside of the knee of a patient's trousers. It was where a cobbler rested his lapstone, across which stretched the leather that was to be hammered into greater strength.

He pointed out to students other clues of profession that he insisted they ought to observe at a glance. Once he immediately identified a patient as either a slater or a cork-cutter: "If you will only use your eyes a moment you will be able to define a slight hardening—a regular callus, gentlemen—on one side of his forefinger, and a thickening on the outside of his thumb—a sure sign that he follows the one occupation or the other."

Once Bell's clerk brought in a mother and child. The doctor exchanged greetings with her and asked casually, "What sort o' crossing did ye have from Burntisland?"—a town in Fife, on the Firth.

"It was good," she answered.

"And had ye a good walk up Inverleith Row?"

"Yes."

"And what did ye do with the other wain?"

"I left him with my sister in Leith."

"And would ye still be working at the linoleum factory?"

"Yes, I am."

To students Bell explained his mutually supporting surmises: that the woman had a Fife accent, that Burntisland was the closest town in Fife, and that the fingers of the woman's right hand bore a dermatitis peculiar to workers in the Burntisland linoleum factory. "You notice the red clay on the edges of the soles of her shoes," he added pointedly, "and the only such clay within twenty miles of Edinburgh is the Botanical Gardens. Inverleith Row borders the gardens and is her nearest way here from Leith." And although she was carrying a coat with her, it was obviously too large for the boy accompanying her, so he must have an older sibling.

"Quite easy, gentlemen," remarked Bell on another occasion, "if you will only observe and put two and two together."

One of Arthur's predecessors as Bell's assistant, a student named A. L. Curor, had idolized Bell as Arthur did, and later called him "a super-man." Bell's family agreed with such students. When he traveled by train with his family, he entertained his children by observing details about their fellow passengers and, once the strangers had departed, by deducing their private lives from such clues. He would tell his children the occupations and habits of the strangers with whom he had exchanged nary a word, as well as their likely destination. Later his daughter remembered, "We thought him a magician."

CHAPTER 2

Your Powers of Deduction

It is no wonder that after the study of such a character, I used and
amplified his methods when in later life I tried to build up a scientific
detective who solved cases on his own merits and not through the
folly of the criminal.

—ARTHUR CONAN DOYLE, *MEMORIES AND ADVENTURES*

The kind of diagnostic clairvoyance that so impressed Arthur was not
limited to Joseph Bell. He was a member of a generation of observant, insightful European physicians who—with few diagnostic
tools and tests available beyond a talent for quick observation—were in
demand and lauded. Around the turn of the nineteenth century, medical
professionals began to emphasize careful observation of patients and to reject
traditional non-medical notions of the genesis of disease. Seldom since the
Hippocratics of the fifth century B.C.E., who sought to discover the mecha-
nistic processes by which disease invades a body—rather than to divine
which deity or spirit to blame for the attack—had medicine focused more on
careful observation as the key to diagnosis and treatment.

The Austrian physician and dermatologist Ferdinand von Hebra,
founder in the 1840s of the renowned Vienna School of Dermatology,
demonstrated similar perception, especially in observing bodily traces of
profession and personal history. To diagnostics he brought experience in
postmortem pathology and extensive work on scabies and eczema. Hebra's
mentor, the Bohemian clinician and pathologist Joseph Škoda—the first
professor to lecture in German rather than Latin at the University of

Vienna—guided Hebra into this formerly neglected and even disdained specialty. He thought the young man's aptitude for diagnostic observation and extrapolation, as well as his talent for lively fact-based lecturing, could contribute greatly.

Often Hebra asked not a single question before stating a patient's ailment, age, weight, region of birth, and recent activities. He advised students, when examining a skin eruption, to look for scratch marks rather than to merely ask the patient if the eruption itched. A callus on the ball of a thumb would tell Hebra that the patient was a hatter. Velvety skin and a pink nose signaled a drinker of brandy or beer. In grasping a patient's hands he would notice a pinprick-scarred forefinger and tell his students, "This man is a tailor."

Like Joseph Bell, Hebra was considered an entertaining professor as well as a knowledgeable one. One student not studying medicine remarked that he didn't "care a rap about dermatology" but that he found Hebra's lectures more entertaining than a show at Vienna's famed Theater an der Wien.

Once a patient limped in and sat down to unwind a bandage he had tied around his leg. Hebra announced to his students, "This man is a Croat, fifty-five years of age, has pulmonary tuberculosis—and is a tailor by occupation."

Students who recalled their professor's previous recognition of a tailor from finger scars knew that he had not yet touched this man's hands. They were skeptical this time.

"Wouldn't you know he was a tailor?" Hebra demanded. "Look at that little strip of drab cloth he has tied around the bandage. Tailors use that stuff for vest linings."

In an era in which tradesmen and laborers tended to wear predictable, almost uniform-like clothing and to work repetitively with their hands, such assessments required educated scrutiny but not second sight. In the early 1750s, in *The Rambler*, Samuel Johnson—one of Arthur Doyle's favorite historical figures, thanks to James Boswell's quirky biography—had employed this well-known characteristic in a beautiful analogy:

> As any action or posture, long continued, will distort and disfigure the limbs; so the mind likewise is crippled and contracted by perpetual application to the same set of ideas. It is easy to guess the trade of an artizan by his knees, his fingers, or his shoulders: and there are few among men of the more liberal professions, whose minds do not carry the brand of their calling, or whose conversation does not quickly discover to what class of the community they belong.

Johnson's observational skills were not entirely literary. He personally investigated the notorious Cock Lane Ghost, helping expose what Boswell called "the imposture" behind the scenes. A century after Johnson's remarks, and a decade after Arthur's birth, a Frenchman published an influential survey of the diagnostic value of stigma (visible characteristics of disease) resulting from occupational labor. Auguste Ambroise Tardieu, a French specialist in forensic medicine and toxicology, explored the topic at length in *A Study of the Physical and Chemical Changes Caused in Certain Parts of the Body by the Practice of Diverse Professions, to Assist in Medical-Legal Research of Identity.* Tardieu described other such perceptive diagnosticians. They included the Frenchman Jean-Nicolas Corvisart, a cardiology pioneer and personal physician to Napoleon; Corvisart's pupil Guillaume Dupuytren, an openly freethinking surgeon and anatomist so renowned that he inspired Honoré de Balzac's story "The Atheist's Mass" and was mentioned in Gustave Flaubert's novel *Madame Bovary*; and Armand Trousseau, a French internist who defined what came to be called Trousseau's early signs of malignancy from cancer—and who later diagnosed them in himself and soon died.

In medical school, Arthur attended the Friday clinics held in the infirmary's surgical amphitheater, in the attic of the main building. Semicircular tiers of benches surrounded the polished deal operating table, below which stood a tin tub filled with sawdust that could absorb blood. Not surprisingly, uncertain students cowered before Dr. Bell's authority and confident presence. They had witnessed his absolute control over both students and patients. When a prospective patient made it clear that he was unwilling to fraternize with common students while awaiting a chance to consult Bell, the doctor simply threw him out of the clinic.

Once, after a patient limped in and stood before the gathered students without taking off his coat, Bell turned to a nervous young man in the lecture audience and demanded, "What is the matter with this man, sir? Come down, sir, and look at him!"

The student walked hesitantly down to the patient.

"No!" squawked Bell. "You mustn't touch him!" He commanded the cowering student firmly, "Use your eyes, sir! Use your ears. Use your brain, your bump of perception," he added, invoking the already debunked "science" of phrenology. He returned to his usual theme: "And use your powers of deduction."

The young man warily looked the patient over and finally volunteered a diagnosis: "Hip-joint disease, sir!"

Bell leaned back in his chair and steepled his long, delicate fingers under his chin. "Hip-nothing!" he snorted derisively. "The man's limp is not from his hip, but from his foot—or rather from his feet. Were you to observe closely," he continued, "you would see that there are slits, cut by a knife, in those parts of the shoes where the pressure of the shoe is greatest against the foot. The man is a sufferer from corns, gentlemen, and has no hip trouble at all."

Then Bell went on to reveal that his first diagnosis was trivial compared to what else he had observed: "He has not come here to be treated for corns, gentlemen. We are not chiropodists. His trouble is of a much more serious nature. This is a case of chronic alcoholism, gentlemen." The patient must have been mortified as Bell enumerated details of his appearance: "The rubicund nose, the puffed, bloated face, the bloodshot eyes, the tremulous hands and twitching face muscles, with the quick, pulsating temporal arteries—all show this."

Slyly Bell reiterated his point about confirmation: "These deductions, gentlemen, must, however, be confirmed by absolute and concrete evidence." He pointed out that poking from the patient's right-hand coat pocket was the top of a whiskey bottle.

On another occasion, Bell read—and revealed to the class—the life of a student instead of a patient. A young man had failed dismally in his efforts to diagnose a patient's illness under the fierce eye of Dr. Bell, who then snapped, "Get out your notebook, man, and see whether you can't express your thoughts that way."

He turned to the amused class and invoked the biblical Isaiah and Matthew: "The gentleman has ears and he hears not, eyes and he sees not!"

Bell turned back to the student, who, in nervously taking a notebook from his pocket, had dislodged a letter. He tried and failed to hide it.

"You come from Wales, don't you, sir?" demanded Bell, a Scot himself, Edinburgh born and raised. "I thought so! A man who says *silling* for *shilling*, who rattles his *R*'s, who has a peculiar, rough, broad accent like yours, sir, is not a Scotchman. You are not an Irishman; you are not an Englishman. Your speech smacks of Wales."

He turned away from the squirming and blushing young man for a moment and addressed the other students, explaining that he had further confirmation of his deductions beyond the man's enunciation. He had observed that the dropped letter was addressed in a feminine hand to

"Mr. Edward Jones—that is his name, gentlemen"—and postmarked the day before at Cardiff. "Cardiff is in South Wales, and the name Jones proclaims our friend a Welshman."

To Arthur and his fellow students, Joe Bell seemed irresistibly colorful. He would roll up to a university entrance in his low barouche, with its double facing seats—behind them a half roof folded like a bellows, in front an elevated driver in livery calling to Bell's paired bay horses, whom his children had named Major and Minor. Old-timers at the hospital realized that, whether deliberately or unwittingly, Bell mimicked his own revered mentor, Professor James Syme, an innovative surgeon and renowned professor who had died in 1870. Bell stopped, however, before copying his teacher's yellow carriage with its gaudily painted C-spring suspension.

He also credited Syme with diagnostic acumen greater than his own, although few of Syme's other students later emphasized this trait. Bell liked to quote Syme's motto: "Try to learn the features of disease or injury as precisely as you know the features, the gait, the tricks of manner of your most intimate friend."

After graduating from Edinburgh University in 1859, the year of Arthur's birth, Bell had served as house physician under Syme at the Royal Infirmary. Syme had been a legend at the university, an exemplar of the genius and commitment of which the medical school liked to boast. Interested in chemistry from childhood, he discovered in his late teens that coal tar, the oily sludge resulting from coal processing, could be used to produce a solution of caoutchouc or india-rubber—and thus could be employed to waterproof textiles such as silk. Glasgow chemist Charles Macintosh patented a variation of this method and went on to produce a new kind of waterproof coat soon named after him.

Bell's positions at the university had included Hospital Surgeon, Demonstrator of Anatomy, and Surgeon to the Eye Infirmary, but he was acclaimed beyond Edinburgh. For several years, he had been editor of the respected *Edinburgh Medical Journal*, which was known throughout Europe and America. He was known for his influential textbook, *A Manual of the Operations of Surgery for the Use of Senior Students, House Surgeons, and Junior Practitioners* ("My aim has been to describe as simply as possible those operations which are most likely to prove useful, and especially those which, from their nature, admit of being practised on the dead body"). He came from a long line of Edinburgh physicians, including his grandfather Charles

Bell, who described what came to be called Bell's palsy. The Bell generations of sons alternated the names Benjamin and Joseph.

Nor had it taken Bell long to build this impressive résumé. At the age of twenty-one, he read a brilliant paper on epithelial cancer to the usually skeptical and contentious Royal Medical Society of Edinburgh, who responded with a standing ovation. William Turner, who had been a distinguished professor of anatomy since 1865, said of Bell's two-year tenure as Demonstrator of Anatomy early in his career, "Whilst discharging his duties he acted as my junior, and acquired a well-deserved popularity amongst the students from his powers of observation, his clearness of exposition, his capacity for taking trouble to help them in their difficulties, and by his words of encouragement."

Arthur too considered Bell kind and admirably conscientious with students and patients. The professor was sincere in his claim that he asked nothing of students that he had not already accomplished himself, and he taught compassion as much as diagnosis. Bell felt that commitment to his fellow human beings was a religious duty. A passionate naturalist, hunter, and gardener, he traced both his love of the world and his yearning to help humanity to his faith. Upon his marriage in 1865, his mother told his wife that he had been "dedicated to God in his cradle," and the newlyweds committed a tithe of their income to the church. His wife died in 1874. When Arthur met him two years later, Bell was still a silently grieving man with two young daughters and a son to raise. Despite his many commitments, he seldom missed a Sunday in church with them.

He had long been demonstrating his faith through deeds; both his high-pitched voice and his halting gait resulted from his own courage. In the early 1860s, as an overworked medical assistant, young Joe Bell had tended agonized and dying patients during numerous epidemics. The serpentine Water of Leith, which lazily bisected Edinburgh, might as well have been a sewer for all the filth it carried. During the preceding few years, Edinburghers had been brought down by cholera, typhoid, and smallpox, and early 1864 saw the exhausted city reeling from an even more devastating outbreak of diphtheria. Fate spared Arthur, who was not yet five years old.

Diphtheria was named from the Greek word for leather. Its effect was sadly memorialized in the nickname for Spain's epidemic year of 1613—El Año de los Garrotillos, "The Year of Strangulations." The disease produced gray mucus and a leathery membrane in the throat, resulting in choking as well as sore throat, swollen and inflamed tonsils, fever, and usually inflammation of the heart.

The University of Edinburgh's own Francis Home had described the appearance of diphtheria's choking gray membrane as "blankets of a bed that has been laid in." Home promoted the local slang word *croup*, an onomatopoeic term for a noise in the throat, into the official name of the respiratory illness that caused the noise—although diphtheria was more severe. A Berwickshire-born surgeon who served as the school's inaugural professor of *materia medica* (the origins, composition, and attributes of medicines), performed the world's first vaccination against measles, and even served as surgeon of dragoons in Flanders, Home was one of the titans to whom students such as Joe Bell feared they might never measure up.

The effects of the disease had been known for centuries, although only recently had physicians recognized that what they were now calling diphtheria was identical to illnesses known in the mid-eighteenth century as epidemic croup, malignant sore throat, and the terrifying name *morbus strangulatorius*. Speculations about its cause ranged from gases produced by decaying animals to cold weather, from a marshy atmosphere to the inevitable supernatural explanations. Fortunately, magic was no longer proposed as etiology. Moreover, the discovery in 1876, during Arthur's freshman year in medical school, of a microscopic bacterium that causes anthrax suggested that the cause of diphtheria might soon be found, after so many centuries of suffering.

In 1864, miserable with empathy for children choking from diphtheria's mucus, Bell yearned to devise a method for removing it. No one had yet been able to invent an implement that could efficiently suction out the mucus. Finally, by sucking on a pipette, he drew the infected mucus from the throat of a child on whom he was operating—an act that pulled some of it into his own mouth.

Afterward he suffered from the disease himself for many months. During his convalescence, when the pain was declining after three miserable weeks of a fiercely infected throat, friends observed for the first time a nasal twang in Bell's voice. He could feel a flapping membrane in his throat that seemed to disrupt enunciation. After three more weeks, he was almost mute and experiencing an alarming double vision. Although the pain in his throat lessened, swallowing became more difficult. Often part of a swallow of liquid came back into his nasal passages, requiring a pinch or two of snuff to clear his head. One leg almost ceased to function and he began to experience chest pain.

Prescribed rural bed rest by no less an authority than Syme himself, Bell retired to the family estate in Glendoick, north of Edinburgh on the river

Tay. After losing the ability to walk alone even with a cane, Bell finally surrendered to the need for someone to hold one of his arms—and then for two people, one on each side. Eventually he was able to swallow again. Gradually speech returned, but his voice remained high-pitched. It was a full four months after the onset of his own diphtheria before Bell felt he could walk with most of his old speed, and he never lost the limp. By January 1865, Bell was presenting a talk to the Medico-Chirurgical Society, which was later published in the *Journal* as an admirably calm and detailed third-person account of what readers gradually realized was an autobiographical drama.

Having long since triumphed over dangerous illness, Joseph Bell made it clear that compassion was as crucial to medicine as a clever diagnosis. Demonstrating that clues invisible to the untrained eye could quickly inform a keen observer of another person's character and history, he showed Arthur and other students that his diagnoses were not mere theater. He taught that experience must be buttressed by tireless study of the professional journals. Reinforcing these lessons through his indulgence of Arthur's questions about methods, Bell served as a model of both scientific intelligence and moral commitment. Arthur never forgot his mentor's demonstrations or their implications.

CHAPTER 3

Art in the Blood

"Art in the blood is liable to take the strangest forms."
—SHERLOCK HOLMES, IN ARTHUR CONAN DOYLE,
"THE GREEK INTERPRETER"

In a narrow cul-de-sac in Edinburgh lurked one of Arthur's most vivid memories of his childhood. Growing up poor, amid other rowdy boys sporting in the closes and wynds of the city, he had had to learn to fight. Always a feud simmered between boys on opposite sides of the street. Having battled his way to the top of his own group, as temporary king of the poor lads from the flats, one day he went up against the top rich boy from the villas across the way. They tackled each other in a villa garden. Evenly matched, they kept at it without declaring a winner until both were bloody and exhausted.

"Oh, Arthur," his mother exclaimed when she saw him, "what a dreadful eye you have got!"

"You just go across and look at Eddie Tulloch's eye!" replied her unrepentant son.

On another occasion, a bootmaker's lad on an errand, carrying a green baize bag, encroached upon the territory of Arthur and his chums. Arthur stepped up to fight him, and the boy responded by swinging the boot-filled bag against his head, knocking him almost unconscious.

He did not avoid fights on the street, but at home Arthur sought a quiet corner and a book. Born to an artistic legacy, he had been drawn to literature from his earliest memory, and from a young age he encountered writers. His father's side career as a painter and illustrator, as well as the greater reputation of other family members, had introduced Arthur and his siblings to notable writers and artists, some of whom came to call. The Edinburgh Doyles were not well off, unlike some other branches of the family, and at times Arthur squirmed with embarrassment when wealthier relatives and other strangers visited his parents' modest flat. One such visitor was a tall, smiling, prematurely white-haired man of about fifty. He seemed ancient to Arthur, who could not have been more than four, as he dandled the little boy on his knee. Later, as a young man, Arthur proudly recalled that he had once sat on the lap of William Makepeace Thackeray, author of *Pendennis* and *Vanity Fair*.

His father, Charles Altamont Doyle, was the brother of English-born Richard "Dickie" Doyle, a well-known *Punch* illustrator and creator of the magazine's famous logo of Punch and Judy. Charles and Dickie were the sons of Irish caricaturist and lithographer John Doyle, famous under the pen name "H.B." for his sedate political caricature that eschewed the kind of grotesque personification employed by predecessors such as Thomas Rowlandson.

Charles was himself a talented artist, but he had not achieved the skill or renown of his relatives. Elegant, bearded, witty, but a lover of drink, Charles was a hopelessly impractical man, creative but undisciplined—and haunted by personal demons. He had worked for decades as an architectural draftsman, one of several assistants to the prominent architect Robert Matheson. As Scotland's Clerk of Works, Matheson was known for his Italian Renaissance public buildings, including the New Register House in New Town, which he designed to complement Robert Adam's original eighteenth-century Register House.

Charles's most important work in Matheson's office was helping to design a fountain for Holyrood Palace. This was a commission from the young Queen Victoria, who wanted Holyrood to have a forecourt fountain reminiscent of one erected by James V in the early sixteenth century at Linlithgow Palace in West Lothian. When completed, the Holyrood fountain rose almost twenty feet above the cobblestones, sporting a rearing unicorn and a round-hatted piper above a ring of traditional lion heads pouring water into the surrounding moat. On the master sketch of this artifact, which Matheson described as "more in the class of a work of Art than ordinary Building work," Charles's signature appeared alongside Matheson's—an unusual degree of recognition under Matheson, who took most such credit for himself. Charles also submitted a design for one of the grand windows of the Glasgow Cathedral, but his name did not appear on the list of contributing artists.

Over the years, Charles Doyle had illustrated numerous books. In 1877 he still possessed enough skill to draw sixty fanciful, elegant pictures for *Our Trip to Blunderland* by "Jean Jambon," a pseudonym comically Gallicizing the first name and other initials of John Hay Athole Macdonald, Solicitor General for Scotland. Macdonald had amused himself during his off-hours by writing a nonsensical, pun-filled children's book so taken with Lewis Carroll's *Alice* tales that it cited them in the first paragraph.

But Charles's sporadic career was in decline. His earlier illustrations for London publishers were little known in Scotland. Rather than sell his infrequent watercolors and drawings, he sank to trading them for spirits, and thus one Edinburgh pub accumulated a private gallery of Doyle artwork. By the time that Arthur was three years old, his father was sometimes so drunk that he could neither recall his own name nor rise from a crawl on the floor. He was even caught drinking furniture varnish.

Charles might sneak any small item out of the house to exchange it for drink. His humiliated wife would find herself facing irate tradespeople who presented bills for goods she had never seen—only to learn that Charles had bought them on credit and sold them for secret cash. At times he resorted to burgling his children's coin boxes. To escape confinement in his room during one of his drinking bouts, Charles had been known to strip off his underwear, tie it together with bed linen, and risk his life and dignity using this cloth rope to climb out a window and scramble down a wall of the house.

Despite her frustrations and disappointments, Mary Doyle seems to have remained loyal toward and affectionate with Charles. "To know him was to love him," she said later. Arthur seems to have tightly closeted his father's secrets and discussed them little, if at all, with friends, alluding to them only obliquely in surviving letters to his mother.

For a quarter of a century, Charles labored in the Office of Works, a position he had held since the age of nineteen. At no point could his annual salary plus artwork fees have surpassed £300—too modest an income to house, feed, and educate a large family. As long ago as the early 1860s, barely thirty years old, Charles had been drinking so heavily and missing so many days that the Office of Works placed him on half pay for most of a year. His considerable talent and his amiable disposition endeared him to his superiors, Robert Matheson and Andrew Kerr, and the pair tolerated his flaws until they became unbearable. In June 1876, a few months before Arthur's return to Edinburgh, the office retired Charles during restructuring. He was only forty-four. The retirement report provided a sanitized public version: Charles Doyle had "discharged his duties with diligence and fidelity," and therefore he was granted an annual pension of £150.

Either Mary kept significant details from Arthur or he persisted in denying them. When she told him the retirement news in a letter, he asked innocently if his father had been unwell or if there might be some other reason for his retirement.

Thus most of the responsibility for the welfare of the children fell upon Arthur's lively, resourceful, gray-eyed mother, whom he adored and idealized. It was she who provided emotional stability and introduced him to a love of learning. She told Arthur about Gustave Flaubert and Théophile Gautier, about the Goncourt brothers. Mary was gently chaffed in the family for reading even while performing household chores. He always remembered her stirring porridge with a spurtle—a stick shaped to prevent lumps in the oats—in one hand while the other held the *Revue des Deux Mondes* close to her nearsighted eyes. In the *Revue*, with its familiar brownish-yellow cover, Arthur first glimpsed the mostly fictional Middle Ages of chivalry and derring-do that captured his imagination.

Such devotion to literature helped inspire her son. Arthur's skill with words improved rapidly when he read to his mother while she knitted. He first learned to read French by such independent means as laboriously spelling out and pronouncing the captions of illustrations in a volume of Jules Verne. Verne's first popular novel was *Cinq semaines en ballon* (*Five Weeks in a Balloon*), serialized in a magazine and then published in book form in 1863, when Arthur was four. During Arthur's early childhood, many of Verne's most popular works were published, including *The Adventures of Captain Hatteras*, *Journey to the Center of the Earth*, and *From the Earth to the Moon*. They whetted Arthur's appetite for adventure and helped hone his fluency in French.

Mary also developed an appreciation for the U.S. physician and essayist Oliver Wendell Holmes, author of such popular works as *The Autocrat of the Breakfast Table*, published the year before Arthur's birth. His vivid anecdotes about the triumph of modern medicine helped shape Arthur's views. The surname Holmes was spoken respectfully in the Doyle household.

Mary had an entire flock to worry over. When Arthur returned to Edinburgh from boarding school at the age of seventeen, his older sister, Anne Mary Frances Conan, called Tottie and later Annette, was barely twenty but already working as a governess in Portugal. She sent home every penny she could spare. Constance Amelia Monica (Conny) was twelve, and Caroline Mary Burton (Lottie) was ten. Arthur's only brother, John Frances Innes Hay, nicknamed Duff, was three and a half. Jane Adelaide Rose, called Ida, was only one, and during Arthur's first year of medical school his mother gave birth to another girl, Bryan Mary Julia Josephine, soon nicknamed Dodo.

The Doyle family's financial straits, especially following Charles's loss of his Office of Works position, had finally led Mary to resort to running a boardinghouse. Perhaps this development felt like closing a circle for Arthur's parents. Around 1850, when Charles Doyle first came to Edinburgh, he had found lodging with a widow, whose daughter, the alluring Mary, soon caught his eye. But Arthur was ashamed of this situation, which he regarded as a fall from grace, and as the eldest son, he felt the burden of his siblings' and parents' expectation that he would rescue the family.

CHAPTER 4

Seven Weary Steps

Stonyhurst, that grand mediaeval dwelling house . . . Year by year, then, I see myself climbing those seven weary steps and passing through as many stages of my boyhood.

—ARTHUR CONAN DOYLE, *MEMORIES AND ADVENTURES*

Despite the hard work in his college medical studies with Joe Bell, Arthur was much happier than he had been during his early childhood at Newington Academy in Edinburgh—his last extended experience of the city prior to eight years of boarding school. As a child he had walked only a couple of blocks, to Salisbury Place, for this first immersion in school, where the one-eyed, pockmarked headmaster, Patrick Wilson, wielded his tawse—a leather thong with slits and tails—with sadistic glee.

Life was a little better during two years under gentler Father Francis Cassidy at Hodder Place down in Lancashire in northern England, but the other teachers were not so kind. And Hodder, where Arthur spent two long years bare of holidays except for six weeks each summer, was the preparatory school for nearby Stonyhurst. At the renowned Jesuit school, masters punished infractions with fierce blows across the hand from a boot-sole-size strip of india-rubber called a tolley. Afterward, Arthur could not use his battered, throbbing hand even to turn a door handle and leave the room. The next morning, he would find it difficult even to grasp his portion of dry bread and watered milk in the incongruously elegant, marble-tiled dining room.

Proud, defiant Arthur yearned for respect and affection, but he refused to bow to bullying by supposed educators. He not only tried to bear punishment with a stoic lack of expression; he sought opportunities for mischief to prove that his spirit remained unbroken. Gradually, Arthur realized that he was more often beaten than many of his classmates, but he seems to have assessed this ratio as proof of his independence. Again and again he needed to prove himself—to others and to himself.

Fellow students learned that Arthur was a born storyteller who could enliven a rainy half-holiday (Wednesday and Saturday afternoons) with tales of heroic derring-do. Rapt students sat or squatted on the floor, resting chin in hand, and gazed at Arthur perched atop a desk. Although sometimes he demanded his payment of tarts before he would begin, and even though he might stall in midscene until a snack of apples reignited his narrative, the students applauded his storytelling. Gradually, he began to yearn for a more prominent and lasting venue.

Although only one friendship remained after Stonyhurst days, with a student named Jimmy Ryan, Arthur got along well with most other students, such as classmate Patrick Sherlock, who was a distant relative of Arthur's Irish aunt Jane Doyle. Probably young Patrick reminded Arthur of William Sherlock, the controversial divine who wound up dean of St. Paul's Cathedral in London in the late 1600s; Arthur's favorite historian, Thomas Babington Macaulay, featured Sherlock prominently in his *History of England*. Arthur often ran across this surname. Resentfully immersed in theology at Stonyhurst, the increasingly freethinking young man also may have been familiar with the writings of William Sherlock's son. Thomas Sherlock's defense of Christian doctrine regarding miracles was said to have helped inspire the philosopher David Hume—one of Edinburgh's legendary sons, and a luminary in the Scottish Enlightenment—to write his determinedly rational "Of Miracles," a notorious chapter in his 1748 *Inquiry Concerning Human Understanding*. And 1868, the year that Arthur turned nine, saw publication of *A Lost Name*, a novel by the Irish ghost story writer and Gothic novelist Sheridan Le Fanu, which featured a character named Carmel Sherlock.

Arthur also resented the endless drilling in Latin and Greek and mathematics. He disliked Homer in his native tongue and he disliked Euclid in any language. Yet, between Hodder and Stonyhurst, he plodded through the seven classes, one concentrated in each year: elements, figures, rudiments, grammar, syntax, poetry, and rhetoric. His weakest subject was chemistry—Stonyhurst was advanced enough to have recently constructed a chemistry laboratory—but nonetheless Arthur wrote home threatening to frighten his siblings with chemical experiments.

At Stonyhurst Arthur discovered in himself a previously unrealized store of talent and imagination. In 1874, the year he turned fifteen, he watched other boys suffer loudly over an assignment to write poetry on the theme of Moses and the parting of the Red Sea. Arthur, in contrast, having loved verse as far back as he could remember, jumped into the task with glee: "Like pallid daisies in a grassy wood, / So round the sward the tents of Israel stood . . ."

The next year he edited Stonyhurst's college magazine, wrote a lot of poetry, and astonished himself by passing the matriculation exam of the University of London, the usual ending of the Stonyhurst curriculum, with honors—and Arthur's surprised friends carried him around a playground in celebration. His view of his own prospects was changing. He had begun to feel that he had potential.

Not all his masters were impressed, however. Arthur had too long balked at the restrictions of school. When he told one professor that he was considering becoming a civil engineer, the blunt reply was "Well, Doyle, you may be an engineer, but I don't think you will ever be a civil one."

Despite being surrounded by the grim Church of Scotland, the Irish Doyles—originally the Anglo-Norman name D'Oil—had remained Catholic. Arthur's father was fervent, his mother sincere while compassionately rejecting the concept of eternal hellfire. Yet, when Stonyhurst offered to remit Arthur's tuition fees if his parents committed him as a Jesuit, his mother refused. Arthur was grateful. As a child, of course, he had accepted his parents' religion without question. But gradually the judgmental ferocity and narrow-mindedness of his professors, along with his reading of philosophical and scientific books and articles, helped steer Arthur away from Catholicism. When he heard a prominent priest proclaim that everyone outside the Church was damned for eternity, he found himself horrified and disgusted. Gradually he was turning away from organized religion's claustrophobic and newly minted cosmos, from its many doctrines he considered irrational and unfair. He could admire some of the church's hallowed traditions, its incense and music, its role in ethics and upholding orderly behavior. But he could not embrace its dogma.

There followed a year at another Jesuit school, Stella Matutina, near Feldkirch, in the beautiful Vorarlberg province of western Austria, amid the snow-capped Tyrolese Alps high above the Bodensee. A measure of kindness from masters at Feldkirch began to help tame Arthur's rebellion and anger. Here he read German until, as he told his mother jokingly, he stopped reading English books. True, when speaking quickly he might accidentally modify a neuter noun with a feminine adjective, but he progressed rapidly.

Students were required to walk three abreast during their semiweekly hikes, with every foreigner accompanied by two Germans to encourage learning the language; by the spring of 1876, Arthur found that he could make himself understood during a three-hour ambulatory chat. He claimed in a letter to his mother that he had read an eight-hundred-page German history of Europe. While stumbling often, he found himself fluent enough to perceive the occasional error in this tome—such as when the author split Admiral Hyde Parker into two admirals, one named Hyde and one named Parker.

In the school band, Arthur proved strong enough and strong-winded enough to play the bombardon, a bass tuba so large that his classmates once stuffed his pillow and sheets into its throat. Rejoicing in outdoor activity, as always, he hiked forty-two miles in the Alps with a heavy iron-tipped alpenstock on his shoulder. Back indoors, he founded and edited a handwritten school "newspaper" he titled *The Feldkirchian Gazette*, which he wrote in his own school notebooks in violet ink. Onto these ambitious pages he slapped the bold motto "Fear not, and put it in print," but immediately he learned the consequences of such ambition. Thanks to his scrawled editorial protesting that the masters often read students' letters before distributing them, the school banned Arthur's first venture into periodicals after only two issues.

Arthur had always been not only a reader but also a writer. By the age of five, he was writing a thirty-six-word saga in large childish letters in his foolscap notebook—illustrated with marginal scrawls by the author— recounting a battle between a tiger and a man. It ended badly for the latter. A surviving fragment of this scrawled story indicates how well Arthur armed his characters: "each man carring a knife gun pistle." The family liked to quote Arthur's remark upon finding his protagonist vanquished so quickly: "It is very easy to get people into scrapes, and very hard to get them out again."

On the way home in August 1876, after glimpses of Strasbourg and Basel and elsewhere, Arthur stopped in Paris. He arrived with twopence in his pocket and immediately spent one of them on a reviving drink of licorice and water. Unable to afford a cab, he left his trunk at the train station and tramped the hot summer streets along the stinking Seine toward the home of his great-uncle and godfather, Michael Conan, from whom he had inherited a middle name and a love of learning. At the foot of the Champs-Élysées, he saw the Arc de Triomphe some distance away, oriented himself, and walked until he found his uncle's flat on the Avenue de Wagram.

Although they had never met, Michael had encouraged Arthur for years. "I shall look to his development with great interest," Michael had written to his sister before her precocious boy had even reached his fifth birthday. He advised her to teach Arthur multiplication, division, maps, and geography before sending him to school. "As to Arthur's future development, that, apart from Nature's endowments, will much depend upon the mother who cherishes him and at once secures his love and respect." Following his eighth birthday, Michael had sent Arthur a children's history of France—enlivened with color illustrations of queens and kings in their grand robes and crowns—and assured him that, with his mother's fluency in the language, he would soon be reading the book's text. It had sparked the boy's imagination.

Michael Conan turned out to be a fiery, broad-shouldered Irish intellectual, a former editor of the *Art Journal*, who spent the sweltering summer days in his shirtsleeves. He and Arthur got along famously. Conan encouraged his obviously intelligent grandnephew to read the American short-story writer Edgar Allan Poe, who had died in 1849 at the age of forty. Apparently he didn't know that Arthur had admired Poe since boyhood and had kept a copy of his *Tales of Mystery and Imagination* at Feldkirch. In fact, back home in Edinburgh in September, Arthur was taking breaks from pre-enrollment medical study with a tutor to read Poe aloud and terrify his younger siblings.

CHAPTER 5

Athens of the North

Travellers who have searched the whole world round have found no fairer view.

—ARTHUR CONAN DOYLE, *THE FIRM OF GIRDLESTONE*

Arthur turned seventeen in the summer of 1876, about the time he returned to the picturesque city of his childhood. Edinburgh nested atop three hills in the narrow valley between the Pentlands to the south and the Firth of Forth two miles to the north and east. It was rich in adjectives for the winds that bedeviled it—*scowthering* and *blae*, *nirly* and *snell*. From some vantage points, a watcher gazing northeast across the Firth, toward where it opened into the German Ocean (as locals called the North Sea), could glimpse a beacon from the Gothic tower of a lighthouse five miles off on the Isle of May. Warning shipmasters since 1816, it had been updated twenty years later with a refractor lens that made its flame visible from afar.

Dawn mists rose from the valley until they dwindled to a plume above medieval Edinburgh Castle. Perched on a craggy basalt cliff, the castle rose several stories from the summit, which towered four hundred feet above the base. On the inland side rose a turret from whose crown of lancet windows archers had rained arrows upon besieging armies since the twelfth century.

The castle was so high that its time gun could be heard far in every direction. This civic reminder had been fired at one P.M. every day but Sundays since early 1861, before Arthur turned two, alerting Leith ship captains and New Town shop owners to set their clocks, while every man on

Princes Street reached for a waistcoat pocket to check his watch. The sound carried so far from the castle that its instigator, Charles Piazzi Smyth, Scotland's Astronomer Royal, prepared a concentric map showing the number of seconds it took the gun's boom to reach each distance, for even more accurate timekeeping.

Prior to the invention of modern cannon, this fortress had been considered almost impregnable—and because it controlled Edinburgh, and thus Scotland, it had weathered many a siege. The castle stood so high that shepherds in Fife to the north could turn from shearing to glimpse it like a mirage on the horizon. Mariners sailing in from the northeast could peer up at its battlements long before they reached the shore. It provided an unparalleled view of the region—northward to the jagged peaks of the Grampians, eastward across a thousand dirty rooftops toward the storied height of Arthur's Seat, southward to the Pentlands. A travel guide to Scotland published in 1859 boasted that the view from the castle combined "in one vast expanse the richest elements of the beautiful and the sublime." The view of the city from the sea, the mountainous terrain, and Greek Revival architecture had earned Edinburgh the nickname "Athens of the North."

The castle cast its royal shadow across a bustling market down in the city. The drum and bugle accompanying a changing of the guard could be heard above the clatter of carriage wheels, the taunts of street urchins, the rumble of passing trains. Dense with public houses and shops, bristling with turnpike stairs and crow-stepped gables, the Grassmarket had been a public site since the fifteenth century. In Arthur's time it was still renowned for its cattle and horse trading. The venerable White Hart Inn was there, and the Black Bull, with its marble relief columns framing the entrance, and above them the words SPIRIT J. WILKINSON MERCHANT. Next door stood the Carriers Warehouse, where one-horse wagons clustered out front, piled with goods covered in tightly stretched tarpaulins against the frequent rain. To proclaim that their wares had traveled from exotic climes, the Tobacco & Snuff Manufactory featured above its sign a bust of a turbaned man, perhaps formerly the figurehead on a ship's prow. Beneath it, wagons uncoupled from their horses projected handy rails on which loungers could lean to smoke and gossip.

The Grassmarket had once been home to Edinburgh's public executions, including most famously that of a fishwife named Maggie Dickinson. Hanged in 1724 for murdering her own baby, she woke during transportation of her body home. Her attendants were astonished to realize that she had passed out rather than died. Judged to have served her sentence—and possibly to have been rescued by God—she was freed. Afterward, however, hanging sentences in Scotland were revised to read "until dead."

With the town reduced to ashes more than once, only the castle itself, and Holyrood Palace at the other end of the slanting ridge now called the Royal Mile, had withstood the flames—to be plundered later by Cromwell's army. By the late 1870s, as Arthur attended his classes, Holyrood's crumbled abbey stood amid gasworks and breweries, as if its Gothic entrance fronted a stage set across which the red-uniformed guard paced mechanically back and forth.

Between the Castle and the University, in hilltop Greyfriars Kirkyard, orange-breasted robins and a clowder of plump cats wove among the chiseled names of Scottish history and the iron mortsafes that had protected graves from "resurrection men" such as William Burke and William Hare, who robbed graves and murdered the poor back in the 1820s.

Clustered below and east of the castle, the dark streets of Old Town sprawled in medieval disarray—poorly bracketed upper stories bulging above greasy streets so narrow that a man walking could stretch out his arms and touch a grimy wall on either side. Once Edinburgh's tall buildings had housed aristocracy, until crowding and plague had driven them to the suburbs. By the 1870s, however, soot-flecked washing fluttered on clothes poles jutting from the windows of once proud houses that bore above their door a scutcheon with a tarnished coat of arms.

The view from many windows was a dreary prospect of slate roofs topped with red chimneys spouting eye-smarting clouds of smoke—with now and then the rooftop scrabble of a blackened urchin sweeping a chimney. Not surprisingly, the city had held on to its Middle Scots nickname, "Auld Reekie" (Old Smokey). Not only the smoke stank. So did the foul breath of tanneries and glue factories, and the effluvia from chamber pots emptied into street carts or into the streets themselves. At least the winds that buffeted the high elevation helped to dispel the stench.

There was so little space for the city to sprawl horizontally that it had instead climbed vertically. After their social betters fled, the poor were crowded into stacks of filthy flats—on the lower floors, sometimes two abreast with pigsties or stables. By the time Arthur first toddled down the cobblestones beside his mother, many of the former slums—tottering buildings locally called *lands*—had fallen. The Great Fire in 1824 had burned for five days, gutting or bringing to the ground such monuments as Old Assembly Hall, as well as more than two dozen tenements—some as tall as fourteen stories, said to be the tallest in Europe—from the High Street to Borthwick's Close, including the birthplace of James Boswell in Parliament Close. Many hovels and tenements were torn down and replaced with safer and cleaner modern housing, but poverty and crowding still defined the Old Town.

He could stand high on the wind-plagued North Bridge, which joined Old Town to the cleaner streets and neoclassical buildings of New Town, and see the monuments to civic progress and mercantile ambition that had helped turn Edinburgh into a world-renowned center of intellectual labor. He was studying medicine in part because the university boasted one of the finest medical departments in the world. In the eighteenth century, the Scottish Enlightenment had flowered in this center of research and publishing—philosopher and mathematician Dugald Stewart, economist Adam Smith, geologist James Hutton, and many others. Walter Scott, Arthur's favorite novelist in his later youth, had been born in College Wynd, by the Cowgate, not far from Arthur's own birthplace; had lived in George Square by the university that Arthur attended every day; and had died only a generation before Arthur's birth. Ambition and artistry were in the very air of Edinburgh.

But Edinburgh was not a refuge in which Arthur could forget his troubles. His father's financial unreliability and the end of his career at the Office of Works placed an ever greater financial burden upon Mary. Finally, considering the limited alternatives available to a genteel woman, she decided to take in boarders. In 1875, a twenty-two-year-old medical student who was in the last half of his senior year had rented a room. Literary, poetic, but practical enough to study medicine, Bryan Charles Waller came from a respectable family in Yorkshire. He was only six years Arthur's senior, but he seems to have soon developed a curious relationship with Mary Doyle—one about which family records later remained silent. At first Arthur liked him, and "Dr. Waller," as Arthur called him, advised the eager young man to pursue medicine. By May 1876, just before Arthur left Feldkirch, he was telling his mother that surely Dr. Waller would agree that Arthur would have "hard work getting up the subjects" for medical school, considering his ignorance of trigonometry and the later books of Euclid. But a tutor was found and Arthur was accepted at the university.

When Arthur returned to Edinburgh in September, fresh from his last year of boarding school and eager to see his beloved Mam, he learned that she was not going to be at home. Mary would be visiting at Massongill House, Bryan Waller's family manse in Yorkshire. Arthur was either too innocent to consider the implications or too private to mention them to anyone. For reasons that remain mysterious, it wasn't long before Waller rose above the level of lodger to the point of paying the entire Doyle family's rent.

Meanwhile, facing a forced retirement, Charles tried sporadically to create artwork. In 1876 he painted one of his more cheerful (and least bizarre) works: a watercolor of many colorful skaters on the frozen white Duddingston Loch. Situated under the steep southern promontory of Arthur's Seat, the loch offered boating among swans in summer and skating by torchlight at dusk in winter. Scotland was said to be the home of ice skating as a sport, and the Edinburgh Skating Club was already over a century old. Arthur enjoyed the Edinburgh region's football and golf, hills to be climbed, trails to be hiked, and lochs on which to curl and slide and skate. When Arthur learned from his mother that his father had left the Office of Works, he remarked that perhaps this change would permit Charles to complete his skating picture soon. But if the family had dreams of a rise in Charles's artistic reputation following this change, they were disappointed.

CHAPTER 6

No Man of Flesh and Blood

I do not think that life has any joy to offer so complete, so soul-filling as that which comes upon the imaginative lad, whose spare time is limited, but who is able to snuggle down into a corner with his book knowing that the next hour is all his own.

—ARTHUR CONAN DOYLE, "JUVENILIA"

Daily, on his way to classes and the clinic, Arthur walked past a den of temptation at 54 and 55 South Bridge, in the shadow of the university: James Thin, Bookseller. Although Thin sold new books as well, the majority of his many rooms were devoted to the diverse plunder of auctions and estate sales—shelf after groaning shelf boasting the kind of serious volumes that Thin's tradition-minded, classically trained scholars sought or were pleased to stumble upon. Only strict organization could prevent chaos among such plenty. Thus one entire room was devoted to medicine, another to theology, another to law. Thin sold few novels.

An Edinburgh institution since 1848, Thin's shop had seen Macaulay and Carlyle browse and gossip. Diminutive, skittish Thomas de Quincey had prowled its shelves, mostly after sunset, his opium-ravaged teeth looking caved in and making his lower lip jut when he spoke with his usual fine manners. The university's eccentric Professor John Stuart Blackie would dash across Bridge Street to inquire about books, weaving between carriages and shoppers, his black gown flapping around his knees.

The intent expressions and occasional exclamations of delight from Thin's patrons—often whiskery old men tottering atop ladders, from which they browsed fat arcane volumes—reminded one observer of Dominie Sampson, a schoolmaster in Walter Scott's 1815 novel *Guy Mannering, or The Astrologer*. Scholarship was revered in Edinburgh. The fictional Sampson was one of sixty-plus figures capering on the two-hundred-foot-tall Scott Monument, whose Gothic Revival excesses on Princes Street celebrated Edinburgh's favorite contemporary writer.

James Thin's siren call to impecunious Arthur was a window card informing him that for threepence he could purchase any volume in the large tub beneath the sign. Thruppence was precisely his daily budget for a midday meal and beer. As he neared the bookshop on his way for food, Arthur wrestled with two kinds of hunger, and most days his body bested his mind. About once a week, however, he skipped lunch and stopped at the tub of books.

Unable to even aspire to fine editions, he would happily sort through these volumes, which had been evicted from more valuable real estate within the shop. Patiently he exhumed logarithmic tables, deceased almanacs, and the annotated navel-gazing of Scottish theologians, setting each book aside, digging deeper in the hope of treasure. Often he found some. One day he would take home Jonathan Swift's dense satire on Christianity, *Tale of a Tub*, and the next Alain-René Lesage's picaresque novel *Gil Blas*—tomes whose thick leather bindings and faded gilt recalled better days in the library of a gentleman.

One day he picked out a stubby volume armored in dour brown leather: a treatise on warfare, written in Latin. He opened the front page and found on the flyleaf, in a firm angular hand, a signature that had faded to yellow— *Ex libris Guilielmi Whyte 1672*—from an era that had already captured his imagination, and in a handwriting that seemed to begin writing a story in his mind. The past seemed deliriously romantic to him. He bought the book. In general, however, despite his endless drilling in Latin and Greek at Stonyhurst and before, he felt that an English translation was an irresistible shortcut to ancient greatness. To that end, in this tub Arthur found all four volumes of Thomas Gordon's acclaimed edition of the Roman historian Tacitus, battered but no less readable.

He ran across the essays of Joseph Addison, who founded an age of literate journalism when he launched *The Spectator* in 1711 with Joseph Steele. Further fueling his passion for British history, Arthur read the classic account of the English Civil War by Edward Hyde, the first Earl of Clarendon. He enjoyed the poems of the seventeenth-century courtier George Villiers, the second Duke of Buckingham, and those of the eighteenth-century satirist Charles Churchill. Although he ranged widely, he turned most often to the writers of Scotland, Ireland, and England for his instruction and entertainment.

Arthur's appetite for books had begun at an early age. However much he fought other boys during his rambles on the streets, at home in the evenings and on weekends he dived into books as a refuge. As a child he read so quickly that the nearby library informed his mother that he would not be allowed to borrow more than two books per day.

In 1874, at the age of fifteen, Arthur had spent his three-week Christmas holiday with relatives in London, where he saw the renowned actor Henry Irving play Hamlet and where he admired the glittering swords in the armory of the Tower. Foremost on his pilgrimage, however, was Westminster Abbey. Despite his passion for British history, Arthur first sought out not the gilt-bronze supine Edward III on his sarcophagus, not the marble effigy of Mary, Queen of Scots with her white hands eerily raised in prayer, but the South Transept, nicknamed "Poets' Corner." There, below the grand rose window, near the grave of Chaucer and the bust of Milton, he paid his respects to the mortal remains of Thomas Babington Macaulay. "His body is buried in peace," read the gravestone, "but his name liveth for evermore." It was the kind of antique diction and heroic sentiment that quickened Arthur's pulse.

The Scottish historian and politician had, for Arthur, opened a window in the formerly opaque wall of history. For years, moving from school to school, Arthur had packed in his luggage a tired copy of Macaulay's 1843 collection *Critical and Historical Essays*. These diverse writings had first appeared in the Whig journal *Edinburgh Review*. Macaulay was typical of the *Review*'s commitment to a serious and stylish engagement with literature and history in longer, more thoughtful essays.

Macaulay had long since become Arthur's favorite writer. At the bookshop's discount bin, forgoing lunch one day, he found a newer but still tattered and lovingly read copy of the *Essays*. With its dramatic big-brush portraits of figures such as Machiavelli and Frederick the Great, Francis Bacon and John Bunyan, the collection fed Arthur's appetite for history but also sparked a yearning to imitate Macaulay's grandeur and sweep. Although some critics complained about Macaulay's smug patriotism, especially in his somewhat fictionalized history of England, as a young man Arthur admired Macaulay's authoritative tone and his curiosity about different levels of society. The adolescent boy had lingered particularly over his idol's grand flourishes, provocative asides, and vivid attention to the texture that brought a scene to life. Later Arthur agreed with the criticisms.

But other writers also appealed to his imagination. Before he could even understand them as a child, Arthur was given a set of Walter Scott's novels bound in olive-green cloth. Later, despite his mother's advice that he ought to sleep instead, he read them in bed by candlelight, unable to tear himself away from the heroics. He admired Scott's adventurous tales so much that his first copy of the author's 1820 novel *Ivanhoe* suffered an untimely demise. Carrying it about with him as a boy, Arthur absentmindedly left it on a grassy creek bank and found it days later downstream—washed ashore like a drowning victim, muddy and bloated.

Critics such as John Ruskin and Thomas Carlyle argued that *Ivanhoe*, set at the end of the twelfth century, inspired the revival of English interest in medieval history that still flourished during Arthur's time. It also established a mental image of the fabled Robin Hood, appearing for the first time in this novel under the name Locksley, as a merry outlaw so adept with a bow that he can split another's arrow. "This must be the devil, and no man of flesh and blood," whisper the yeomen; "such archery was never seen since a bow was first bent in Britain." Arthur thrilled at such scenes.

From an early age, he was aware that Scott could be long-winded and discursive, but Arthur thought that once he turned his attention to the action at hand, he conjured scenes like a sorcerer—the texture of everyday life in Elizabethan England in *Kenilworth*, the treacherous rivalries of the Byzantine Empire during the First Crusade in *Count Robert of Paris*. Only a few years before Arthur discovered Scott, a commentator had praised the national icon, "whose novels have not only refreshed and embellished the incidents of history, but have conferred on many a spot, formerly unknown to fame, a reputation as enduring as the annals of history itself." Since these early days of reading, Arthur had sometimes wished that Scott had turned his imagination to the figures of his own time rather than spent so many years conjuring the past.

Arthur also loved martial poetry. He found nothing more inspiring than a vision of a stout-hearted soldier marching into battle against the odds. He admired valor the way he loved all things that struck him as manly—boxing, patriotism, hunting. At Stonyhurst he had finally succeeded in memorizing all seventy eight-line stanzas of Macaulay's heroic lay "Horatius," which opened with a driving meter that Arthur found irresistible:

Lars Porsena of Clusium
　By the Nine Gods he swore

That the great house of Tarquin
   Should suffer wrong no more.
By the Nine Gods he swore it,
   And named a trysting day,
And bade his messengers ride forth,
   East and west and south and north,
To summon his array.

He loved reading about adventures as much as he loved adventuring. As a young child, he admired above all other writers the Irish American novelist Mayne Reid, especially such works as his 1851 dime novel *The Scalp Hunters: A Romance of the Plain*. Its opening words helped conjure Arthur's romantic view of the American West:

> Unroll the world's map, and look upon the great northern continent of America. Away to the wild west, away toward the setting sun, away beyond many a far meridian, let your eyes wander. Rest them where golden rivers rise among peaks that carry the eternal snow. Rest them there.
>
> You are looking upon a land whose features are un-furrowed by human hands, still bearing the marks of the Almighty mould, as upon the morning of creation; a region whose every object wears the impress of God's image . . .
>
> Follow me, with the eye of your mind, through scenes of wild beauty, of savage sublimity.

After several pages of ecstatic description, Reid exclaimed, "These are the Rocky Mountains, the American Andes, the colossal vertebræ of the continent!"

Immersed in such books ever since he had learned to read, Arthur as a boy spent his time imagining hand-to-hand combat with fierce Red Indian braves and finding his wounds nursed by a charming squaw. Having mentally voyaged from Hudson Bay to Cape Horn, he knew how to behave aboard a ship. In his mind he carried a long-barreled Kentucky rifle and was sure he understood how to elude pursuers by running down a brook to throw bloodhounds off his scent. He still bore with him these stirring tales—and a vision of himself as an adventurer—when he strode along Edinburgh's hilly streets toward the university.

CHAPTER 7

Ode to Opium

The healthy skepticism which medical training induces, the desire to prove every fact, and only to reason from such proved facts—these are the finest foundations for all thought.

—ARTHUR CONAN DOYLE, "THE ROMANCE OF MEDICINE"

By the time Arthur enrolled in 1876, the University of Edinburgh was a renowned center of medical education. The Royal College of Surgeons was founded in 1505, during the reign of James IV, its "Seill of Cause" granted in response to a bill of supplication presented by "Surrgeanis and Barbouris within the Burgh of Edinburgh." At the time, alongside scourges and hanging, other royally approved public torture included vise-pinching noses, boring holes through tongues, and nailing ears to a log. In the 1870s the College of Surgeons looked back respectfully on the temerity and foresight of its founders—who, in the school's genesis myth, dared to found an enclave of learning amid barbarism.

Youngest of the Scottish universities, Edinburgh had been teaching surgery and anatomy since early in the sixteenth century. The notion of a qualified professional physician, however, was relatively recent. Not until 1858, the year before Arthur's birth, did the British medical establishment publish a register of accredited medical men. The profession had been advancing dramatically throughout the first half of the century, and all around Arthur were the recent fruits of research and experimentation. Shedding the cobwebs of the past, the largely progressive university was defining itself in opposition to more conservative Anglican institutions such as Oxford and Cambridge, where many influential faculty members still opposed such flourishing new ideas as Darwinian natural selection.

Like astronomy and geology and biology, medicine was growing in its understanding and in its technologies. Since their infancy in the seventeenth century, microscopes had become more advanced, enabling the detailed study of cellular structure, from tree xylem to human blood. The idea of inoculation—the introduction of smallpox virus into individuals who were not immune—had been explored earlier in China, Africa, and India, but not until 1796 did Englishman Edward Jenner effectively demonstrate the value and methods of inoculation in ways that the European medical community could no longer mock. In the 1840s a steel hypodermic syringe was first used to administer a subcutaneous injection—physicians having overcome two centuries of opposition to the method after early attempts had sometimes been fatal.

One of the great names in Edinburgh University's recent history was James Young Simpson, who announced the anesthetic virtues of chloroform in 1847, sixteen years after its discovery. The new painkilling tool was quickly adopted in many areas. In the mid-1840s, dentist Horace Wells revived a notion originally proposed half a century earlier by the great chemist Humphrey Davy: the inhalation of nitrous oxide for pain relief. A colleague administered the so-called laughing gas to Wells while another colleague extracted one of his teeth without causing great pain. About the same time, a patient requesting to be mesmerized before surgery on his ulcerated tooth instead found himself inhaling sulfuric ether—one of many new weapons in the ancient struggle against pain.

Joseph Bell was not the only Edinburgh professor who inspired Arthur with the thrill and the modern relevance of medicine. For example, the renowned Charles Wyville Thomson, a professor of natural history in his mid-forties, taught zoology. In 1876 he returned from serving as Chief Scientist aboard HMS *Challenger*, having persuaded the Royal Society to fund adaptation of a naval vessel into a floating laboratory for study of the world's barely known ocean life.

William Rutherford was the professor of physiology after serving as Fullerian Professor of Chemistry. He was short but broad-shouldered, and his enormous barrel chest projected a stentorian voice not softened by a beard that reminded Arthur of Assyrian bas-reliefs. He turned forty about the time Arthur met him. Having grown up in the tiny village of Ancrum

Craig, in rural Roxburghshire on the southeastern coast of Scotland, and
gone on to study in Vienna, Paris, and Berlin, Rutherford spoke with a
curious accent. Dissecting a frog, he would exclaim, "Ach, these Jarman
frags!" He had the presence and authority to cope with winter class sizes—
250 students in his practical physiology course and twice as many in systematic physiology. He was famously adept at combining lecturing and
demonstration. Often Rutherford began almost shouting his lecture from
the hall, before reaching the classroom and his desk, not yet visible when he
began, "There are valves in the veins . . ."

Arthur studied chemistry under Alexander Crum Brown, whose many
contributions to science included a system of diagramming chemical
compounds by denoting atoms with their symbols inside circles linked to the
nucleus with a dashed line. Brown was known for his kindness and his
unflappable manner. When a chemistry experiment that was supposed to
result in a fire or explosion failed to do so, some men in the class were guar-
anteed to supply a shout of "Boom!" Brown would emerge from where he
had taken refuge against the expected blast, calmly say, "Really, gentlemen!"
and proceed with the class.

Henry Littlejohn was in his late forties when Arthur enrolled. Like Joe
Bell, he was Edinburgh born and an alumnus of the university and of the
Royal College of Surgeons. He had also studied at the Sorbonne. In 1854
the Royal College of Surgeons elected him a fellow and the Edinburgh Town
Council appointed him Police Surgeon. The next year, he presented his first
lecture in the School of Medicine and soon became known for his theatrical
persona at the lectern. Gesturing dramatically, he presented with clarity and
startling wit his perspective on topics ranging from the hygiene of slum
dwellers to the drainage system of ancient Rome. Soon he was lecturing on
forensic medicine. In 1861, following the collapse of a tenement that resulted
in thirty-five deaths and countless injuries, the Edinburgh Town Council
appointed Littlejohn as Edinburgh's first Medical Officer of Health. His
career partnered science and law enforcement.

Some professors influenced Arthur more by reputation than by presence.
Robert Christison, for example, retired in 1877, but his legacy haunted the
classrooms. He studied in Paris with the chemist Pierre Jean Robiquet and the
Minorcan-born French toxicologist Mathieu J. B. Orfila, who was renowned
for his studies of arsenic poisoning. Christison began teaching by following
criminal investigations and trials in Scotland's *State Trials*, informed by the
best French texts. He first became known to the general public for his role in
the 1828 trials of William Burke and William Hare—the notorious grave

robbers who turned murderers to supply anatomists' need for corpses at a time, prior to the Anatomy Act of 1832, when only executed criminals were available for dissection. Christison served as a medical witness in the trial; later, as medical advisor to the crown for Scotland, he formulated guidelines for the examination of corpses. Beginning on the side of prisoners in the Justiciary Court, sought by king's counsel seeking loopholes for their clients, he was soon retained as a regular counsel across the aisle, on behalf of His Majesty's courts.

Christison was legendary by the time Arthur entered his realm. Besides serving often as a forensic witness, he had extended and surpassed Orfila's pioneer work in toxicology. And, like his colleague Joseph Bell, Christison had not hesitated to gamble his health—even his life—on research. After reading accounts of traditional "ordeal by poisoning" rituals among the natives of Old Calabar, a British colony along the Niger River on the south-western coast of Africa, Christison experimented with the so-called Calabar ordeal-bean. In response to overwhelming evidence of the legume's toxicity, including eyewitness accounts of grisly deaths, Christison prevailed upon his colleagues, including Syme, to cultivate it and supply him with fresh beans. He first tested the poison on animals, including a rabbit, every detail of whose death within five minutes he noted, and he recorded that slugs who nibbled the first fleshy cotyledons that pushed up through the soil from the vegetating bean were dead within twenty-four hours.

Despite noting that "this poison is one of great intensity of action," Christison ingested some of it himself, and when he experienced few symptoms he increased the dosage. He compared the sensations' progress with his previous experience of Indian hemp, opium, and morphia. "Being now quite satisfied that I had got hold of a very energetic poison," he told the assembled members of the Royal Society of Edinburgh in 1855, "I took immediate means for getting quit of it, by swallowing the shaving water I had just been using, by which the stomach was effectually emptied." Arthur paid close attention to such stories of scientific daring.

While he studied with these eminent men, most of Arthur's energy was concentrated on lectures, textbooks, and medical articles. One of his most frequently consulted texts was *The Essentials of Materia Medica and Therapeutics* by Alfred Baring Garrod, an English physician who taught those topics at University College London, where he had also founded a museum of materia medica. Most physicians concocted and dispensed their own medications. It was essential to understand the therapeutic properties of an ever-growing arsenal, as well as to appreciate modern reassessments of traditional treatments that had emerged from sources such as medieval physick gardens. Thus Garrod had issued revised editions every few years since the acclaimed first in 1865.

Arthur bought the sixth edition in 1878. A fellow of the Royal Society, Garrod was renowned for promoting lithium to treat gout, because he discovered that it dissolved crystals of uric acid—elevated percentages of which he found in the urine of gout patients—and for naming and describing rheumatic arthritis. Arthur signed the flyleaf and began annotating the book throughout. He pored over the encyclopedic volume, underlining items and making notes on almost every page, summarizing sections in marginal notes. He noted that hemorrhoids ought to be treated with "Ointment of Galls and Opium" and included details about how to treat "a bad gonorrhoea." He turned to the back and wrote on the endpapers his own abbreviated recipes for concocting medications. Directions for making opium included "Evaporate excess Colour between Calico."

The back pages and other parts of the book wound up scribbled over with accounts of how patients might respond to particular drugs. Many of these notes Arthur composed in jaunty mnemonics and initialed *ACD*. He devoted fourteen rhyming lines, for example, to "Corrosive Sublimate as a Poison." In his "Ode to Opium," scribbled on an inside page, he rose to a gritty lyricism while still amusing himself:

> I'll tell you a most serious fact
> > That opium dries a mucous tract
> And constipates and causes thirst
> > And stimulates the heart at first
> And then allows its strength to fall
> > Relaxing the capillary wall.
> The cerebrum is first affected,
> > Contracted pupils are detected
> On tetanus you mustn't bet
> > Secretions gone except the sweat
> Lungs and sexuals don't forget.

CHAPTER 8

Drinking Poison

Several times in my life I have done utterly reckless things with so little motive that I have found it difficult to explain them to myself afterwards.

—ARTHUR CONAN DOYLE, *MEMORIES AND ADVENTURES*

Knowing the measure of his own ignorance, Arthur ran an advertisement for work during his time off from actual medical classes: "Third year's student, desiring experience rather than remuneration, offers his services." In the summer of 1878, he worked with Dr. Charles Sidney Richardson, who attended the poor in Sheffield, in Yorkshire, England. This position lasted only three weeks; later Arthur stated that he and Richardson parted "by mutual consent." He wrote of Yorkshire, "No woods, little grass, spouting chimneys, slate-coloured streams, sloping mounds of coke and slag, topped by the great wheels and pumps of the mines."

From dismal Sheffield he escaped to spend a few weeks with Doyle relatives in Maida Vale, amid the bustle and grandeur of London. He was so poor, and apparently so disappointed by the short-lived position with Richardson, that he seriously considered the offers of military recruiting sergeants who were set up in Trafalgar Square looking for burly, dejected young men. They offered the traditional earnest payment of one shilling. This exchange—a practice discontinued the following year—was equivalent to a handshake, and would have been followed by a visit to a magistrate and further payment for enlistment.

But Arthur resisted. He reminded himself that his mother had worked hard to provide him with a promising future. Still, he volunteered to serve as a medical dresser on ambulances in Turkey during the Russian War, but the latest in a long history of bloody conflicts was over before he could be shipped out.

The next answer to his advertisement arrived grandly postmarked Ruyton-of-the-Eleven-Towns, a village in Shropshire smaller than its name, where he worked with Dr. Henry Francis Elliot. Arthur didn't mind laboring hard, even from dawn to midnight, but he found that he hated the unsuspected loneliness of serving as a medical assistant. After he wandered into his employer's drawing room now and then, to speak to Mrs. Elliot where she sat with her baby, the doctor informed him sharply that he was defying custom: the assistant was to keep to himself and not socialize with the physician or his family. At one point Arthur wrote to his mother that he had worked three months without a chat with anyone, beyond an occasional word when he was invited into Elliot's company for "a smoke."

This temporary position was also memorable for the way it tested Arthur's nerve. During a celebration at a historic site, a cannon's fuse was lit. Instead of firing, however, it exploded, raining shrapnel onto a bystander. A frantic messenger raced to Elliot's house, only to return with his inexperienced young assistant instead. Arthur found himself gazing at a lump of iron projecting from the head of a man who lay in bed. He had to decide immediately. He grasped the projecting iron near the man's hair and tugged it out. When he did so, below the blood he could see clean white bone, which told him that the iron had not reached the man's brain. He stitched the wound. Arthur's decisive response inspired new confidence in himself—and, he noted, in those around him.

The next year Arthur's summer position with Dr. Reginald Hoare in England's Midlands was paid—a token £2 per month. Arthur was still raw, but learning as quickly as he could. He liked Hoare. His luxuriant beard and country lad's shoulders belied a canny professional who could turn three-shilling treatments and one-shilling prescriptions, eked from the paupers of Aston in central Birmingham, into an annual income of £3,000.

Doing his part, however, kept Arthur scurrying day and night. Some evenings, already exhausted, he would be handed a scribbled list of as many as a hundred medicaments to weigh, measure, stir, and package in their boxes and phials. Try as he might, he made mistakes. He was known, for example, to occasionally prepare detailed directions for a patient's pill box that, when opened, proved empty.

* * *

During his busy first few weeks with Dr. Hoare in Birmingham in June 1879, Arthur risked his life in a dangerous experiment. Sometime earlier, while suffering from neuralgia, he had given himself several doses of an alkaloid pain depressant called gelseminum. It was derived from the plant *Gelseminum* (later *Gelsemium*) *sempervirens*, a twining yellow-blossomed vine native to tropical and subtropical American woodlands, called variously evening trumpet flower or yellow jasmine. Many parts of the plant were saturated with toxic alkaloids of the strychnine family. Arthur's pain continued unabated at first, so he exceeded the prescribed dosage—and observed no ill effects.

Alfred Baring Garrod addressed gelseminum at length in his *Materia Medica*. Under the heading *Tinctura Gelsemii* in his copy, Arthur underlined key parts of Garrod's description: "It has been employed in various forms of neuralgia, rheumatism, and muscular spasm, as a sedative . . . Death results from apnoea, due to paralysis of the respiratory muscles." To the ailments it would treat, Arthur scrawled the marginal addendum "also for Chorea and inflammation."

Underneath these notes he wrote "Fraser" and underlined it. Formerly Robert Christison's assistant, Thomas Richard Fraser assumed the position of professor of materia medica upon his mentor's retirement in 1877. Like Christison, Fraser was known for his adventurous and personal approach to pharmacology. It had been launched with his gold-medal-winning thesis on the ordeal-bean of Calabar, a further examination of the poison with which Christison had experimented. By Arthur's time, Fraser was a prominent figure. The year he became professor of materia medica, he was invited to join the Royal Society, and in 1878 he became dean of the medical faculty. Arthur studied with him during his second year.

"Though much used in America," Garrod said of gelseminum, "it has hitherto been little investigated in this country." In the United States, physicians often prescribed gelseminum for pain accompanying a variety of ailments, including influenza, ague, and menstrual cramps. Gelseminum was less accepted throughout Europe—and not approved for the British pharmacopoeia—because its confirmed dangers outweighed its possible virtues. Arthur must have known that no medical professional doubted its threat. In an 1832 article, the U.S. physician William Tully was already warning of the dangers of exceeding recommended dosages: "If a quantity larger than is barely necessary . . . is administered, it produces . . . ultimately even stupor, coma, and death."

During the late 1870s, several medical scientists devoted extensive research to gelseminum. For example, *The Lancet* had been publishing a series of well-researched articles on it by Sydney Ringer, a professor of thera-peutics at Garrod's own University College, and William Murrell, a demon-strator of physiology at the same institution. Founded by surgeon and reformer Thomas Wakley in 1823, *The Lancet* had become an indispensable organ of British medicine, and as an ambitious student Arthur would have been expected to follow each issue closely.

Thus he could not have missed the series by Ringer and Murrell. Reporting research on frogs, cats, rabbits, guinea pigs, and a poodle, they concluded, "In all these experiments, death appears to have resulted from asphyxia." In the spring of 1876, Ringer and Murrell reported administering gelseminum to six human beings on seventeen occasions, "in doses sufficient to produce decided toxic effects." Patients described a predictable succession of symptoms: brow pain, giddiness, eyeball pain, dimming of sight, double vision, drooping eyelids, and restricted movement of the eyeball. "The patient next complains of weakness of the legs, and we have never pushed the drug beyond the production of this symptom." They analyzed the effect on respiration and circulation, body temperature, mental faculties, and other phenomena. A physician reported that in 1866 he took gelseminum "through mistake," reporting that his most frightening symptom was almost total blindness for several hours.

In June 1878 *The Lancet* concluded its gelseminum series with two arti-cles on it "as a toxicological agent." Because of the drug's unpopularity in Britain, most of the material for this survey derived from U.S. sources. Standards there were so lax that one U.S. physician ordered a patient to take a dose of gelseminum tincture and declared that if she held up a finger and saw only one—thus not yet experiencing double vision—she could risk another dose. Physicians reported many deaths—a pregnant woman who overdosed on gelseminum, a woman who died after receiving it as a painkiller following an abortion, and sailors who plundered a barrel of what they mistakenly thought to be alcohol but was actually tincture of gelseminum. One doctor had witnessed the deaths of three children from overdose.

Yet Arthur boldly imitated the dangerous exploits of Robert Christison and Thomas Fraser with the calabar bean. Tincture of gelseminum was created by mixing dried gelseminum roots and rhizomes, which were avail-able as gelseminum powder, with standard percentages of alcohol and water. Arthur measured his dosage of the milky yellow fluid in minims. The minim had been introduced in 1809 as a more precise unit than a drop, formerly the standard measure. Apothecaries had long known that viscosity and other factors caused the size of a drop to vary, so finally they standardized a minim as equaling 1/60th of a fluid drachm or 1/480th of a fluid ounce. Arthur employed a graduated glass pipette called a minimometer to measure out his self-poisoning. He administered gelseminum to himself in increasing dosages and monitored its effects, in order to determine which amounts might truly constitute an overdose—and what his symptoms might be during the process. During this time he denied himself tobacco because he feared it might skew his results.

Rather than increase his dosage in increments, he quickly escalated it as he took gelseminum at roughly the same hour each day. He started on a Monday morning at 10:30 by swallowing forty minims of the bitter liquid with no apparent effect, and on Tuesday sixty minims also seemed harmless. Wednesday's dose was ninety—already exceeding the limit established as fatal. Twenty minutes after he took it, Arthur rose from his chair and found himself giddy. His limbs felt weak. He checked his pulse and found it thready but not frightening. Soon the symptoms faded away.

He soldiered on. Thursday morning found him swallowing 120 minims. Soon he felt giddy again, but not as severely as on Wednesday. He felt almost normal until he walked outdoors at about one o'clock, when slowly he realized that he was having difficulty seeing distant scenes. To focus his eyes, he had to concentrate and squint. Nonetheless, on Friday he administered to himself 150 minims—double the supposedly fatal dosage. He found that at this advanced level his giddiness all but disappeared. In its place, however, he gradually developed barely surmountable lethargy and an agonizing frontal headache. Severe diarrhea kept him running to the chamber pot—which surely prevented his being available to assist Dr. Hoare.

Despite these frightening symptoms, despite his body's many ways of warning that it was greatly agitated by the poison, the weekend found Arthur raising his bet against fate. On both Saturday and Sunday morning he took 200 minims of gelseminum—over a third of an ounce. The headache returned with a vengeance. Diarrhea became so constant and severe on Sunday that he resolved to end the experiment. Despite feeling overwhelmingly depressed, despite a hammering headache, he made a note of the dosage and counted his pulse. It was weak but steady.

Against the odds, Arthur survived. He wrote up his experiment and sent it to the *British Medical Journal.* He carefully described his symptoms and summarized his conclusions. "A healthy adult may take as much as 90 minims with perfect immunity," he declared flatly, failing to mention that he was a robust young man whose body was used to being pushed to its limits in boxing, hiking, and other rigorous activities. "I feel convinced that I could have taken as much as half an ounce of the tincture," he remarked, "had it not been for the extreme diarrhœa it brought on."

His account appeared as a letter to the editor in the issue of September 20, 1879, titled simply "Gelseminum as a Poison." He signed it "A.C.D.," and included Dr. Hoare's address: Clifton House, Aston Road, Birmingham. It was his first publication about medicine. In its bodily risk, it was worthy of Christison's and Fraser's example. Whether a form of bravado or despair, of professional hero worship or personal self-torture, this antic verged on the suicidal—and wound up a public statement of reckless disregard for danger that would soon find other expressions.

CHAPTER 9

Intemperance

I walked ever among pitfalls and I thank all ministering angels that I came through, while I have a soft heart for those who did not.
—ARTHUR CONAN DOYLE, *MEMORIES AND ADVENTURES*

"Would you care to start next week for a whaling cruise?" asked Claud Currie, a friend and fellow student. In his senior year, Arthur had been wearily studying for an examination when Currie approached. It was February 1880, and beyond Arthur's books and papers the window showed a blustery raw day. Students at Edinburgh University were much freer than those in English universities, and, like others, Arthur rented his own room off campus.

It was common practice for a whaling ship to take along a medical student as a poorly paid doctor in search of experience. Currie had served in such a capacity once before and had been invited again. "I find at this last moment that I can't go," he explained, "and I want to get a man to take my place." The *Hope*, departing from Peterhead on the northeastern coast of Scotland, was heading for the Arctic. "You'll be surgeon. Two pound ten a month and three shillings a ton oil money."

It was decent pay, although going on the expedition would require that Arthur drop out of school for several months. With no expenses aboard, he could save money—and his imagination yearned for escape, for new horizons. Exhausted by the scholarly grind, Arthur postponed finishing medical school.

He departed Shetland on a cold day in March. A three-master with a steam screw, the *Hope* stood out among the Peterhead whaling fleet—once

proud but declining after its predations had helped reduce the whale population to a fraction of its former glory. Only forty-five feet long from iron-
reinforced bow to stern, and twenty-eight feet wide amidships with a
seventeen-foot depth, the *Hope* was fortified with iron inside the double
planking at the waterline. She could shove her way through Arctic ice floes.

Arthur's role was hardly burdensome. Save on those rare occasions when
he was called upon for medical assistance, he served as clerk—one day
compiling a list of hosiery, the next dispensing tobacco. Like Charles Darwin
when he sailed as naturalist aboard the *Beagle* with Captain Robert FitzRoy
in the 1830s, Arthur was intended to be captain's companion as much as
anything else. The captain dined with officers, not with crew, who supped
with their own class. But Arthur found that he enjoyed the company of the
mates as much as that of the captain. He was drawn to their strapping
vitality and wild ways. Neither classed nor bunked among the mates, he did
not think of himself as one of them, but after boxing with the steward, he
found that the latter's black eye raised the crew's estimation of their college-
educated medico.

Although he drank a lot himself, the drunkenness aboard ship shocked
Arthur. In his journal he noted that one drunkard was clearly suffering with
delirium tremens—a topic he knew personally from experience with his
father—and he felt that the man ought to have been taken to the infirmary
rather than the brig.

Many dangers awaited Arthur at sea in the Arctic. Frequently he even
found himself in the water. He fell off the slippery decks or icy floes often
enough that the sardonic captain nicknamed him the "Great Northern
Diver," after the fishing bird known in North America as the common loon.
As the medical man and an educated young gentleman, he was not expected
to participate in hunts. Eager for adventure and fond of blood sports,
however, he rowed out to whales in impossibly tiny, tossing boats, and
looked a dying whale in the eye. He bludgeoned and skinned seals and shot
walrus. He sent occasional reports home to his mother, telling her more
details than most mothers would want to know, as if teasing her with the
dangers and risk of this work he did not have to do—but which he had
embraced. Piercing cold, strangely lit nights, and alien creatures crept into
his imagination. He had proved himself with common men and officers, had
faced the cold and darkness and grown stronger. The Arctic cowed him no
more than the poison with which he had dosed himself the year before.

* * *

The *Hope* docked in Peterhead in September 1880. In early 1881 he visited family in Ireland for an extended stay. There, hundreds of miles from other family and from college, Arthur became infatuated with a succession of young women, but his flirtations seldom amounted to much, and he complained about several women in letters. He wrote to a friend that he had met a nineteen-year-old who placed first in her class in the most difficult examination open to women at Trinity College—where she was a bursar, as Scots called students on scholarship—but that she did not talk to him at the dinner table, did not like to dance, would not play accompaniment to a song, and generally showed herself "an addle-headed womanly fool." On this same trip, however, Arthur met a young woman named Elmore "Elmo" Welden. After a week of flirting, he wrote to his mother that he would happily marry Miss Welden, but that there were also other girls he longed, at least in passing, to marry. Little came of any of these flirtations and brief romances.

In August 1881, delayed by a year largely because of the whaling voyage, Arthur was awarded his degrees of Bachelor of Medicine and Master of Surgery at a ceremony in Edinburgh. In a letter he sketched himself waving the diploma aloft, above the caption "Licensed to Kill." He attended the funeral of a family friend. With his wide-ranging enthusiasm for outdoor activities, he had adopted photography as a hobby, and soon he was off to the Isle of May to photograph birds among friends who were hunting, hoping to record the trip and write it up for the *British Journal of Photography*. They accepted it. "After Cormorants with a Camera" appeared in two October installments of the flourishing weekly, and Arthur added another periodical to his résumé. Later the same year it was reprinted in *Anthony's Photographic Bulletin* in the United States—his first writing published there.

He used a folding Meagher camera, with a bellows body and a half dozen backs that would hold the plate but permit it to be fully withdrawn. He became something of an encyclopedia about every new interest. Although he already carried an ash tripod, he fashioned for himself a monopod, a walking staff with an iron spike at one end and an adjustable ball-and-socket joint for the camera base at the other. The spike enabled the one-legged camera stand to penetrate four inches into soil and thus become as steady as a tripod without the trouble and weight. In his growing enthusiasm for photography, Arthur didn't hesitate to advise other photographers in his first article.

Charles Doyle, Arthur's father, left almost no written traces in his first few years after retirement in 1876. Friends had long urged Mary Doyle to have her volatile, drunken husband removed from their home and placed in professional care, insisting that it was the only way to save his life—and to restore some calm and order to her own. Yet she hesitated.

Finally she relented. Perhaps she saw this advertisement:

INTEMPERANCE—Home for Gentlemen in Country House in the North of Scotland. Of very old standing. Home Comforts. Good Shooting, Trout-Fishing and Cricket. HIGHEST REFER-ENCES. Apply MR. D FORBES, BLAIRERNO HOUSE, DRUM-LITHIE, FORDOUN, KINCARDINESHIRE.

It appeared, among many notices under the heading "Homes for the Intemperate," in the comprehensive annual *Medical Directory*, which claimed to include "statistical and general information respecting the universities, colleges, schools, hospitals, dispensaries, societies, poor-law service, asylums for the insane, public services, &c, &c." Over the years it had featured advertisements for everything from "pure and healthy leaches" to the Equilibrium Carrying Chair for transporting invalids on staircases. Such institutions as Blairerno House were one of the era's attempts to help both alcoholics and their families, trying to rise above the abuse that previous generations had heaped upon both. Drumlithie was on the coast north of Dundee, almost to Aberdeen—roughly a hundred miles from Edinburgh.

In early 1881 at the latest, if not before, Blairerno House gained a new inmate. Although Charles Doyle had behaved with notorious disregard for others, he seems to have avoided criminal charges, and he had not been violent. Thus he must have agreed to his own incarceration. In Scotland, the Habitual Drunkards Act of 1879 defined institutions described as licensed retreats for inebriates, and required that the patient submit a signed and witnessed letter admitting to habitual drunkenness as defined by the law.

In the foothills of the Grampian Mountains, Blairerno was a house of only two stories, with thick stone walls, and surrounded by numerous outbuildings. Specializing in treating alcoholics, David Forbes, the director of Blairerno House, lived on-site, supported by an all-female ménage: wife, daughter, two sisters, and five servants. The eighteen male inmates—who included a music teacher, a medical student, two accountants, a tobacco manufacturer, a retired military officer, a "landed proprietor," and now Mr. Doyle, "architect and artist"—were a genteel lot who apparently inspired few worries. That shooting was an option indicates a lack of fear on the part of the staff. Nonetheless,

Charles tried to escape numerous times and developed a reputation as an amiable but troublesome patient.

Arthur described the event with glib euphemisms in a letter to his sister Lottie. "We have packed papa off to a health resort," he wrote on April 9, 1881. Otherwise, he seems to have maintained a tight-lipped silence about intimate misfortunes. In letters to his family and friends, Arthur complained at times about money and magazine publishers and other topics, but he had become adept at keeping his darker worries to himself—or at least out of his written records. Later he occasionally wrote about these issues in fictional terms, but he barely alluded to the realities.

Arthur was the man of the family now. In September 1881 his sister Lottie, only fifteen and a half years old, traveled to join their older sister Annette in Portugal, to also work as a governess. Lonely, hardworking Annette had been there for years, living on as little as possible and sending the rest home. Lottie began the same kind of life. Arthur felt increasing urgency in his desire to contribute, and he daydreamed about rescuing his mother from work, his sisters from their own faraway labors. Except for rare holidays, not since his early childhood had the Doyle family all been together under the same roof.

In October 1881, Arthur was twenty-two. Wondering about his future, needing any kind of steady income, he went to sea again. He served for three months as medical man aboard the *Mayumba*, a decrepit steamer that creakingly purveyed cargo and passengers between Liverpool and the western coast of Africa. The voyage was fraught with danger from the first. The *Mayumba* barely remained afloat during a hurricane just after it departed Liverpool— the storm that sank the SS *Clan Macduff*, whose loss received considerable attention in the British newspapers. Later Arthur realized that during the hurricane the *Mayumba* must have passed near the sinking *Clan Macduff*. While he attended frightened and sick female passengers, Arthur's own cabin was flooded, but his camera equipment remained dry in a tight deal box.

Not until Madeira was the weather calm enough to permit photography. The peak of Tenerife proved annoyingly fog-shrouded, but there were many other opportunities for memorable photographs during the voyage. A week of calm sea off Sierra Leone gave Arthur time to lie under an awning and admire the flying fish "as they flickered, like bars of silver, over the crests of the waves." At Fernando Po (the island of Bioko), he photographed a horrific former slave barracoon and a shark that circled the ship just below the surface. At Old Calabar, the British colony sixty miles up the Calabar River from the coast—the region associated with the poison experiments of Robert Christison and William Fraser—he photographed a personage he described as "a native prince," who complained that the image did not resemble him. Many men were struck down with fever, and at least one died of it, on Christmas Eve. At Lagos, Nigeria, Arthur succumbed, and he lost several days to delirium. But his remarkably tough body triumphed and he found himself back on deck, barely able to stand but feeling that he had won another battle.

Despite the misfortunes dealt to the voyage, Arthur further tempted fate. While the *Mayumba* was near the Cape Coast Castle, one of the former slave forts on the Gold Coast, he dived into the water and swam alongside the hull. Shortly afterward, as he sat drying himself on deck, he spied a shark's fin cutting the surface of the water. Once again he had understood the risks and ignored them—just as he had done with gelseminum and while whaling in the Arctic. He realized that he often acted out of bravado, dismissing the likelihood of peril, but he seemed unable to predict in advance when he might again feel the urge to prove himself.

Aboard the ship Arthur met the renowned U.S. minister and orator Henry Highland Garnet. Born a slave in Maryland in 1815, Garnet had been a powerful force in the abolitionist movement, but eventually founded the African Civilization Society in the hope of repatriating former slaves and their descendants back to Africa. After the Civil War, he became the first black minister to preach to the U.S. House of Representatives. Recently President James A. Garfield had appointed Garnet as Minister and Consul-General to Liberia. On the western coast of Africa, the Republic of Liberia had been founded in 1847 by people of African ancestry fleeing oppression in the United States. Although he arrived successfully in Liberia, Garnet died a few weeks after this voyage.

Arthur greatly enjoyed conversing with Garnet aboard ship. He had become desperate for literate conversation, and he and Garnet discussed writers such as George Bancroft, author of *History of the United States of America, from the Discovery of the American Continent* and other works, and John Lothrop Motley, author of *Causes of the Civil War in America* and many other volumes of history. At one point, conversing learnedly with an accomplished black man, Arthur realized that Garnet himself must once have been a slave. "This negro gentleman did me good," wrote Arthur later, "for a man's brain is an organ for the formation of his own thoughts and also for the digestion of other people's, and it needs fresh fodder."

The *Mayumba* returned to Liverpool in mid-January 1882. Arthur wasted no time in quickly turning experience into writing. In March and April the *British Journal of Photography* published his two-part article, "On the Slave Coast with a Camera." While describing photographic experiences, he fleshed out his account with vivid glimpses, literary snapshots of action, and snippets of witty dialogue. Mostly he played his discomforts and fears for comedy, but he closed by saying, "Better a week in the Welsh mountains with a light camera and a good companion than all the lights and shades of fever-haunted gorilla-land." And he had opened the article by saying that to anyone considering travel to the west coast of Africa, he offered *Punch's* memorable advice regarding marriage: "Don't." To his mother he said flatly that he did not intend to continue as a shipboard medico, that he could make more money in the same amount of time with his pen.

CHAPTER 10

Dr. Conan Doyle, Surgeon

I had everything to gain and nothing in the whole wide world to lose.
And I had youth and strength and energy, and the whole science of
medicine packed in between my two ears. I felt as exultant as though
I were going to take over some practice which lay ready for me.

—ARTHUR CONAN DOYLE, *THE STARK MUNRO LETTERS*

Whatever tensions in the Doyle family may have swirled earlier around Bryan Waller, the former tenant who had grown into Mary's financial helper and possibly more, they came to a head in early 1882. Surviving letters reveal no other details, but in April Arthur wrote to his sister Lottie that he "nearly frightened the immortal soul" out of Waller and that the other man "utterly refused to fight." Arthur liked to brag to his family, and often exaggerated in letters (at times comically), which explains his claim to Lottie that when he was finished with Waller the fellow did not leave his house for twenty-three days. He told his sister that although he and Waller had since managed a "nominal reconciliation"—which seems unlikely had they actually stooped to fisticuffs—Waller had left Edinburgh.

Meanwhile, also in early 1882, Arthur applied for every sort of medical position he found listed and was rejected each time. Desperate, he accepted an unrealistically promising offer from a former fellow student. Capricious and volatile Dr. George Budd—who had been only a year ahead of Arthur in medical school—had harried his schoolmate into accepting a position with him in Plymouth, on the coast of Devon. Yet six weeks later Budd withdrew it. Later Arthur learned that Budd had read his letters to and from his mother and learned of his complaints about Budd's presumptuousness and volatility; and Arthur had to admit that Budd's own complaints about Arthur's bohemian disarray were justified. His promised job ended as suddenly as it had begun.

With hardly a spare shilling in the pocket of his tweeds, Arthur decided he needed to regain momentum. His research indicated that Portsmouth, a shipping and military port between Plymouth and Brighton, across the Channel from Normandy, offered a range of potential patients and no surplus of doctors. Barely twenty-three years old, already a veteran of medical school, of Arctic and African voyages, and of apprenticeship work, Arthur was eager to launch an independent career as a medical man. Unable to buy into an established practice, he would have to build his own from scratch.

He arrived in June. Old fortified Portsmouth struck him as gray and drear, but he liked the holiday atmosphere, the piers and hotels and promenades, in the prosperous neighborhood of Southsea. Portsmouth was guarded by the Isle of Wight and was in fact an island itself, with the city containing all of low-lying Portsea Island, which stood between Langstone Channel to the east and Portsmouth Harbor to the west. Southsea faced southward into Spithead, the western end of the Solent, the strait that separated the Isle of Wight from the Hampshire coast and which bustled with yachts and men-of-war parading before its three round forts.

Arthur bought a map and strolled to his hotel through unfamiliar streets. He carried only his ulster, probably a tin box for the top hat that was de rigueur for a young professional man, and a bulky leather portmanteau. The bag was heavy with photographic equipment and glass plates, clothing, books, and a large brass sign that he had had made in Plymouth—DR. CONAN DOYLE, SURGEON.

Filthy urchins scuttled by on bare feet. Frequently Arthur stepped over tracks for the horse-drawn tram system whose bustling terminus was at Clarence Pier, where his steamer had docked at the jetty with its view of Victoria Barracks and the broad green parade ground. Around him dozens of boxy tram cars clattered on miles of track, with passengers comfortable behind windows but the driver exposed to rain on a chariot-like platform behind the two horses. Bath chairs, like baby perambulators for adults, were also available to push tourists in rickety comfort.

Arthur needed at once to make sense of the city's labyrinthine streets. He must rent a house, ideally some distance from other doctors' establishments. Like most cities in England, Portsmouth needed more doctors. Over the last three decades, the town had cleaned itself up a bit, but it was still dirty and unhealthy. Robert Rawlinson, one of the first health inspectors appointed under England's urgently needed Public Health Act in 1848, had visited Portsmouth and written at length about its sad state. Tiny houses were packed with too many occupants. Behind each ran an open sewer, which helped create ideal conditions for the cholera epidemic that killed a thousand people the next year. Inspecting the barracks area that Arthur later walked past upon his arrival, Rawlinson wrote, "At present the soldiers' wives and families inhabit one of the most wretched, crowded and unhealthy quarters of the town; and the usual haunts of the sailor, when on shore, are dens so vile and degraded that language cannot describe them." Conditions had improved by the time Arthur arrived, but even basic sanitation was little known among the lower classes.

Arthur spent his first week locating and examining unoccupied houses that fit his needs. Then he chose one and moved into his new headquarters: number 1, Bush Villas, on a bustling tree-lined street named Elm Grove. The rent was £40 per annum. Living on desperate optimism, Arthur worried that the estate agent would demand a deposit, but nothing further was required once he invoked the name of his famous uncle Dickie, the cartoonist.

A wrought-iron railing helped distinguish his building from the Elm Grove Baptist Church on the left and the Bush Hotel on the right. The church had been renovated during the last few years, its face opened up with more windows to compensate for the shading block of villas across the street. By the time Arthur arrived, its grand brick façade and arched windows dominated the neighborhood, with the weathervane atop its spire obeying the winds from more than a hundred feet above Elm Grove. Nearby were bustling shops. The trees for which the street was named offered inviting shade and softened the boulevard's commercial air.

At a sale in Portsea, Arthur bought a tired old bed and trickled away a few precious pounds on basic furniture for the sitting room—a table, three chairs, and a small rug. On tick (credit, from "on ticket") he bought a red lamp, England's universal symbol of a physician, and placed it in a front window. Arthur slept several nights wrapped in his ulster before his reliable mother sent blankets. The portmanteau, in the back room with nothing but a stool beside it, became his pantry and table. With no other furniture in his bedroom upstairs, he sat on the bed and ate from a tin of corned beef. Gradually he improved the furnishings—hanging white curtains in the downstairs front room, for example, to improve his office's appearance from the street. He asked his mother to send knickknacks, as well as Poe's poems and Bret Harte's stories.

*　*　*

At first he could not afford to have the gas turned on, but soon it was available in his bedroom and kitchen and hall; downstairs the consulting room was fitted for gas but the waiting room was not. Once it was on, Arthur rigged a platform above the jet on the wall so that it would support a small pan. He cooked many a slice of bacon this way, and felt that with tea and bread it made a quite acceptable meal. Now and then he splurged on a saveloy, a spicy sausage originally made from pig brains. Preoccupied with language, history, and medicine, he probably knew that the word *saveloy* had descended from the Latin word *cerebellum*.

Desperate to attract patients, Arthur peered down at the street through wooden Venetian blinds, counting passersby who stopped to read the brass nameplate he had hung on the railing before his entryway. One day twenty-eight people paused in twenty-five minutes, the next day twenty-four in only fifteen. He put up a second plate, this one confiding that he offered free consulting hours from ten to one on Mondays, Wednesdays, and Fridays—"to get," he wrote to his mother, "the good will of the poor."

It wasn't long, however, before he discovered that few patients dropped in during free hours. And he worried that offering such a discount might lower his professional status in the neighborhood. A friendly fellow physician nearby, William Roylston Pike, advised Arthur—perhaps self-servingly—to take down the sign, arguing that such a ploy might prove helpful in some areas but that it could be counterproductive in an exclusive neighborhood such as Southsea.

Arthur also became friends with Dr. William Henry Kirton, a young dentist whose office was across the street, and Kirton recommended him to patients. Fledgling dentists had an easier time attracting business because, unlike physicians, they were legally permitted to advertise. One Southsea dentist paid every week to have his name run in large type along the margins of the local directory's advertisement pages. Arthur could not employ such lures. He had been at Bush Villas for six days before his first patient appeared—a woman seeking a vaccination. He spent two shillings and sixpence purchasing the requested vaccine from London, but the woman could pay only one and six. Realizing the irony in this transaction, he confided to a family friend that many more such patients would result in his selling his newly acquired furniture.

On his first evening in Southsea, Arthur had been out strolling when he came upon a rough lout kicking a woman. Arthur intervened and later reported that he "emerged from the fray without much damage." To his surprise, one of his first patients was this man, who clearly did not recognize his former opponent. Arthur doctored him, charged him a pittance, and sent him on his way.

Gradually other patients trickled in. The first were either too poor to pay their usual doctor or simply curious about the newcomer. Most physicians earned a high percentage of their income by selling drugs to patients, and Arthur counted upon this tradition. From shelves in the back room, stocked with medicaments bought wholesale on tick, he dispensed enough to pay for his groceries—if not enough to contribute substantially to his rent.

At times patients fell into his lap. "A man had the good taste to fall off his horse the other day just in front of the window," he wrote his mother, "and the intelligent animal rolled on him." He quickly doctored the victim, and soon the story was in the local papers—a useful flurry of free advertising.

Usually confident, even cocky, Arthur was discovering in himself a talent for self-promotion, and he knew that most of all he needed to get into the community and let his prospective patients see him as their neighbor. He enjoyed meeting new people. Fond of colorful characters—and quick to turn them into anecdotes for his letters and even fictional characters for the stories he was beginning to write—he came to know many of the local oddballs.

One tall old neighbor whose haughty scowl reminded Arthur of a horse would sit grandly in her window, as still as a cameo, until one of her unpredictable fits inspired her to skim a china plate out the window at an innocent passerby on the street. Whenever she experienced one of these outbursts, she would bestow some of her prized pottery upon Arthur—only to demand it back when she calmed down. Once he kept a pottery jug for his troubles, although she complained. With other neighbors he sometimes bartered medical care for food. Arthur felt guilty knowing that when the epileptic grocer had a new seizure, it meant afternoon tea and butter for Dr. Conan Doyle.

Arthur also faced many sad experiences as a young doctor. Once a poor woman begged him to tend her daughter, whom he found lying on a rickety cot in their modest sitting room. Holding a candle, he bent over the bed, shocked to find by the flickering light that the patient was a young woman—she turned out to be nineteen—with pained brown eyes and tormented-looking, unnaturally thin arms and legs.

"Oh, if God would only take her!" moaned her mother.

Arthur later recalled how such painful experiences helped turn him away from the traditional religion of his upbringing and boarding school. He lost any sense that life in this world is a spiritual obstacle course leading to the next, and as a result, he found himself no longer able to believe the hoary old stories about a benevolent God.

CHAPTER 11

A Wealth of Youth and Pluck

I found that I could live quite easily and well on less than a shilling per day, so I could hold out for a long period.
—ARTHUR CONAN DOYLE, *MEMORIES AND ADVENTURES*

Arthur's brother, Innes, arrived in mid-July 1882, traveling with the rolled-up carpet that Mary Doyle had sent to smarten up her elder son's bare consulting room. Only nine years old, dark-haired, clad in knickers, Innes lit up the eight-room house with energy and enthusiasm. Arthur had invited him, offering to take over the cost of supporting him, with the idea that his little brother would help around the house and office. Eager to circumvent his mother's doubts, Arthur assured her that Portsmouth was a "far healthier town" than Edinburgh.

He had first requested that his mother send his fourteen-year-old sister Constance. He agreed with the common idea that a physician lost face with patients if he answered the office door himself, and he was eager to assign this task to one of his siblings. When Mary Doyle vetoed the idea of sending her young daughter, Arthur badgered her into sending Innes instead. Although he was fond of his siblings and hoped to reduce his mother's financial burden, he also wanted help in presenting himself from the first as a successful physician. Always sensitive to how others perceived him, he didn't even want to be seen polishing his own brass nameplate out front, so he sneaked out to do it late at night. Hoping to look older and more impressive, he had grown a mustache.

The morning after the boy's arrival, while Arthur got the teakettle boiling over a reluctant fire and prepared cold salmon and bread with butter and marmalade, Innes rushed out to buy a newspaper. The government of Egypt was in turmoil and Britain had dispatched troops to guard the Suez Canal, which had connected the Red Sea and the Mediterranean since its decade of construction was completed in 1869. Perhaps imitating his big brother, Innes was already preoccupied with the fortunes of Britain's sprawling empire. Some days they waited outside a newspaper office for the day's issue, with its fresh news of the bombardment of Alexandria. Innes found the parading soldiers at the Victoria Barracks stirring and inspiring. Some days he wandered down to the beach on his own, volunteering to help fishermen on their boats.

Arthur enjoyed the company of his siblings, and of children in general. In the summer of 1877, he had taken his sisters Lottie and Conny along on a holiday ramble with his Stonyhurst friend Jimmy Ryan to the Isle of Arran, in the Firth of Clyde on the western coast of Scotland. There he was surprised to encounter, of all people, Dr. Joe Bell from Edinburgh. Two years later, while working in the Midlands as assistant to Dr. Reginald Hoare, he had spent his spare time entertaining the physician's six- and ten-year-old children by making paper cutouts of French Zouave soldiers—distinctive and colorful in baggy trousers and short jackets—and the more familiar English Guardsmen with their sashes and tall fur hats. His imagination leapt quickly to military images. At Hodder at the age of nine, he had mailed home toy French foot soldiers as gifts for his sisters.

Arthur and Innes had a good time together. "I am very happy to know that I have a little brother," Arthur had written home from Stonyhurst, at the age of fourteen, in response to his mother's letter about Innes's birth, and he had grown ever more fond of the boy's company. Most evenings in Southsea, the beautiful warm weather lured Arthur and Innes outdoors. Arthur led treks for miles down winding streets, along docks where foreign ships' oddly colored flags snapped in the wind, past both recent artillery fortifications and antique long-barreled cannon called sulverin. The military history of Britain cast its shadow over the island—and, to Arthur's patriotic and imaginative eyes, lent it glamour. Founded in the twelfth century by a Norman merchant, Portsmouth had grown slowly for three centuries. Then Southsea had grown up around, and been named for, one of Henry VIII's "device forts," built in the mid-1500s to protect the southern coast, like Pendennis Castle in Cornwall or Yarmouth guarding the western end of the Solent on the sloping shores of the nearby Isle of Wight. For centuries Portsmouth had been a center of royal shipbuilding. Everywhere Arthur and Innes turned, history flavored the town.

Arthur enrolled Innes at Hope House Day School in Green Road, under master Thomas Henry Vickery. Rudyard Kipling, who was six years

Arthur's junior, had attended the same institution, which he later described as "a terrible little dayschool." But the good-humored lad settled into his new routine. Whenever he was home from school, Innes brought life and humor into the house. From the beach he brought home crabs that scuttled from room to room until Arthur or Innes didn't see one and accidentally stepped on it with a sickening crunch.

Although it seems to have had little effect on his energy, Innes arrived with a lump in his neck along his throat. Probably a temporary glandular problem, it quickly improved. Arthur thought that spending much of his time outdoors—the boy soon glowed with ruddy health—contributed more to Innes's recovery than did the doses Arthur administered of syrupus ferri iodidi, a greenish iron-rich medicament that physicians and druggists concocted for a variety of ailments.

By the middle of August, Innes was writing to their mother, "We have vaxenated a baby and got hold of a man with consumtion." He also recounted how a Gypsy pulled his cart, loaded with chairs and baskets, up to their door and began urgently ringing the bell. Later Arthur thought that this farcical experience epitomized his chaotic early days in Southsea.

"Go away!" Arthur shouted downstairs toward the door, but the man kept ringing.

Innes went to the door, lifted up the flap of the letter box, and yelled out a repetition of Arthur's command.

The man swore at Innes and demanded to see the doctor.

Innes ran upstairs to tell Arthur that the Gypsy was a patient. Abruptly changing his tone, Arthur hurried downstairs to open the door. It turned out that the poor man was so determined because his child was suffering from measles.

"We got sixpence out of them," Innes wrote to his mother.

Under the circumstances, Innes naturally absorbed his older brother's preoccupation with money. Always looking over his shoulder at creditors, Arthur kept careful tallies of income and expenses; in letters to his mother he often itemized his parsimonious budgeting. Sometimes, when Mary Doyle tried to send money, Arthur refused, once writing, "Lord knows I am as poor as Job but have a wealth of youth and pluck." During the same time, he confidently declared to her, "There is nothing I put my mind to do that I have not done most completely."

Despite his swagger, often he accepted her contributions or even requested help. Prior to his arrival in Portsmouth, he had insisted that she lend him £5 by return mail, but he was optimistic that soon he would not need to beg for help. He prophesied that within five years his annual income would rise to £1,000. During his first difficult months in Southsea, however, he went so far as to answer an advertisement he saw for a physician who would be willing to move to the Terai, in Nepal south of the Himalayas.

Ashamed of his poverty, and still a volatile young man, Arthur was quick to turn shame into anger when presented with a bill—as when he swore at a clothes cleaner and threw money at him. To his mother he confessed that his indignation at being dunned was exceeded only by his outrage when a patient dared to object to his own demand for prompt payment. Once he ended a letter to a friend by remarking that he saw a "taxgatherer" coming and needed to bid her farewell so that he could hide under a table.

During his first year in Southsea, Arthur earned only £154, too little to even require a tax payment, as he noted on a form to the government. The form was returned with a scrawled commentary: *Most unsatisfactory.* Arthur wrote underneath those words *I entirely agree* and mailed it back. Inevitably such cheek led to an audit, but Arthur's scribbled ledger of evidence resulted in a draw, and he departed on good terms with the laughing auditors.

However low his income, Arthur had to have access to books, so he joined a circulating library. Libraries had come a long way since the chained tomes of Renaissance Oxford. By the 1880s many kinds of libraries had sprouted to meet the growing demand during a century of rising literacy: subscription libraries, reading societies, circulating libraries, collections for medical schools and botanical gardens, book clubs devoted to poetry or fiction. Arthur read a great deal of history and science—not limited to medicine— but he also had an almost insatiable appetite for fiction.

After centuries in which poetry had represented the summit of literary achievement, fiction had climbed in the nineteenth century to a position as the most popular form of literature. It was also ever more critically esteemed, especially after the publication of such monumental works as Leo Tolstoy's *War and Peace* in 1869, George Eliot's *Middlemarch* a couple of years later, and Anthony Trollope's *The Way We Live Now* in 1875. "We have become a novel-reading people, from the Prime Minister down to the last-appointed scullery maid," Trollope had observed in 1870, at a lecture in Edinburgh. "Poetry we also read and history, biography and the social and political news of the day. But all our other reading put together hardly amounts to what we read in novels."

By Arthur's time, all but the wealthiest readers joined libraries and borrowed novels rather than purchased them. Earlier major writers such as Charles Dickens and his primary rival, William Makepeace Thackeray, had issued most of their novels in monthly (or sometimes weekly) installments, and Trollope's angry and satirical *The Way We Live Now* had been one of the last significant publications in that form. Periodical publication also had its faults. But most British writers of book-length fiction in the 1880s targeted the market dominated by Charles Edward Mudie and his vastly popular Mudie's Lending Library and Mudie's Subscription Library. The library trade was dominated by what had long been known as "three-decker" novels, after the three decks of seventeenth-century warships. The preceding century had seen popular novels such as Oliver Goldsmith's *The Vicar of Wakefield* issued in two volumes and Samuel Richardson's *Clarissa* in seven. But such variety had been boxed into uniformity by the powerful libraries, which now all but insisted upon the three-volume format that had dominated the fiction market throughout Arthur's youth.

Digressions and subplots proliferated not because of a particular taste for literary corpulence but out of authors' need to fill the space that Mudie demanded. Many novelists conceived and planned their tales with the requisite format in mind. When *Far from the Madding Crowd*, Thomas Hardy's fourth novel and first commercial success, was published in 1874, the American novelist and critic Henry James complained, "The work has been distended to its rather formidable dimensions by the infusion of a large amount of conversational and descriptive padding." In a private letter, Charles Reade, the author of Arthur's favorite novel, *The Cloister and the Hearth*, had complained of the "childish egotism" motivating writers such as "the Tri-Volumniors."

Arthur worked hard but was not entirely deprived of a social life. He joined the Literary and Scientific Society and attended its meetings and dances. He played cricket. Friends who visited included Claud Currie, whose inability to ship out on the *Hope* had opened the door for Arthur's great Arctic adventure a couple of years earlier. One friend pronounced number 1, Bush Villas, to be "palatial" and "charming," and called the consulting room "swagger"; another was surprised by the shortage of cutlery but impressed with the site's potential as a medical practice.

As he settled into a new routine in Southsea, Arthur began to concentrate spare time on writing. Late into the night he scrawled stories—imitative at first, clearly beginner's work, but stories. Carefully he copied them onto fresh foolscap, rolled them up, inserted them into mailing cylinders, and entrusted them to the postal service, which promptly returned them—like, he thought, paper boomerangs. Still, now and then he tasted success, enough to encourage him. He crafted some stories to order—one about a Derby sweepstakes, which he wrote in imitation of the style of the popular Welsh writer Rhoda Broughton, author of novels such as *Not Wisely, but Too Well* and the popular supernatural story "The Truth, the Whole Truth, and Nothing but the Truth."

Arthur sent a brief story called "That Veteran" to *All the Year Round.* This legendary weekly could still honestly run atop every double-page spread of its two-column pages the heading *Conducted by | Charles Dickens*, twelve years after the beloved author's death, because his son, Charles Junior, had inherited the editorship. Finally, after months of waiting, Arthur received a check for £2.50, about half what he expected. Even after all this time, the magazine postdated the check by four days—a practice, a bank clerk informed Arthur when he went to deposit it, not only illegal but also a howling alarm of bad credit. It did not seem a good omen for his writing career.

CHAPTER 12

The Circular Tour

After ten years of such work I was as unknown as if I had never
dipped a pen into an ink bottle.

—ARTHUR CONAN DOYLE, *MEMORIES AND ADVENTURES*

During his first few months at Bush Villas, Arthur turned his imagination to his whaling voyage two years earlier. The dramatic scenes
of the Arctic, its ethereal beauty, and the romantic melancholy it
inspired had remained with him, and he drew upon vivid memories to write
a ghost story, "The Captain of the 'Pole-Star,'" which he sold to *Temple Bar*
for a satisfying ten guineas. It showed no great originality in his conception
of a ship captain haunted by the ghost of his former love, who lures him onto
an ice floe, where he dies. But the setting was vivid, the atmosphere forbidding, and Arthur conjured a dramatic sense of tragic fate. Turning toward
his own experience for background, resurrecting scenes he had witnessed—
he even made the narrator a young ship's doctor—he soon rose above his first
tales situated in exotic but poorly imagined settings such as the Australian
gold fields or the North American frontier.

During 1883, continuing to harvest his seafaring memories, he wrote
"J. Habakuk Jephson's Statement" and began sending it to magazines. Arthur
was fascinated by the already legendary fate of a British merchant brigantine
named the *Mary Celeste*. He had been reading about it for more than a decade.
In early December 1872, when Arthur was thirteen, the 282-ton ship was
found derelict four hundred miles east of the Azores, with its cargo of seventeen hundred barrels of industrial alcohol still in the hold but threatened by

three feet of sloshing water. The ship had been at sea for a month, its last log entry dated November 25. Unmanned but still under full sail, it was drifting toward Gibraltar. Its captain, his wife, their young daughter, and seven crewmen had vanished—along with the ship's single lifeboat. One of her pumps had been disassembled, but there was no sign of violence or accident to explain the absence of people. Pirates would have looted; a storm would have wrecked. During the intervening decade, despite government investigations and idle speculation, no trace of the family or crew had been found.

For some reason, Arthur changed the name of the ship from *Mary Celeste* to *Marie Celeste*, while keeping the real name of the captain and even of the rescue ship, the *Dei Gratia*. Most of his account was fictional. To make his own story more eerie, for example, Arthur claimed that both of the ship's lifeboats were present. He added the supernatural-sounding detail that the ship, despite its abandonment, had remained so becalmed that a thread bobbin had not even rolled off the sewing machine.

In the summer of 1883, Arthur was delighted when "J. Habakuk Jephson's Statement" was accepted by James Payn, editor of *The Cornhill*, probably the most distinguished publisher of short fiction in Britain. The esteemed monthly—to whose pages Arthur had long aspired—had been founded in 1859 by the since legendary editor George Murray Smith. He was the son of George Smith, cofounder of the publishing firm Smith, Elder & Co., which was known for the high quality of its offerings, ranging from Charles Darwin's scientific travelogue, *Zoology of the Voyage of the Beagle*, to Charlotte Brontë's novel *Jane Eyre*. To steer *The Cornhill*, the primary rival of Dickens's monthly *All the Year Round*, Smith hired William Makepeace Thackeray, Dickens's primary rival as a novelist. *The Cornhill*'s status was such that Queen Victoria chose it to serialize her *Leaves from the Journal of Our Life in the Highlands*.

James Payn was a writer himself, author of moderately popular novels such as *Lost Sir Massingberd* and *Richard Arbour, or The Family Scapegrace*. He had written many stories before venturing to tackle a novel. After more than a decade editing Edinburgh's own *Chambers's Journal*, he had become editor of *The Cornhill* as recently as 1883, when Leslie Stephen, the former editor, stepped down.

When Arthur got his hands on a copy of the January 1884 issue, there was his story, the lead, with half the first page taken up by a striking illustration of a half-naked black African. To Arthur's delight, his story did not disappear into the void. A year later the *Boston Herald* reprinted it, apparently construing it as a factual account.

Meanwhile, Arthur's 1882 *London Society* story "Bones, or, The April Fool of Harvey's Sluice" had been reprinted in 1885 by the U.S. publisher Dodd, Mead in volume four of its anthology *Tales from Many Sources*. Therein Arthur and other young British authors such as Thomas Hardy stood amid their better-known colleagues—Wilkie Collins, popular children's author Juliana H. Ewing, James Payn, and Charles Reade. It was Arthur's first appearance between book covers.

A second soon followed. In October 1887 the editor George Redway included "J. Habakuk Jephson's Statement" in his prominent three-volume anthology *Dreamland and Ghostland: Strange Stories of Coincidence and Ghostly Adventure*, which bore the misleading extended subtitle *Embracing Remarkable Dreams, Presentiments, and Coincidences, Records of Singular Personal Experience by Various Writers, Startling Stories from Individual and Family History, Mysterious Incidents from the Lips of Living Narrators, and Some Psychological Studies, Grave and Gay*. Redway chose a couple of Arthur's other stories as well, but only those narrated in the first person in a manner that might be interpreted as factual. Thus Arthur's imagined details, including the newly French-sounding name *Marie Celeste*, soon became part of the ship's myth.

"Have you seen what they say about your *Cornhill* story?" a friend called to Arthur on a Portsmouth street one winter day in early 1884. He was waving a London evening newspaper.

Eager for praise but cautiously donning a modest expression, Arthur peered over his friend's shoulder as the man turned to the column and read aloud: "*The Cornhill* this month has a story in it which would have made Thackeray turn in his grave."

Arthur said later that the alleged friend escaped assault only because there were witnesses nearby on the street.

This incident reminded Arthur of the rare benefits of anonymity. Mostly, like other writers, he experienced only the frustrations attending anonymous publication. Soon, however, praise helped balance the scales. More than one reviewer speculated that the author of "J. Habakuk Jephson's Statement" was Robert Louis Stevenson. This mistake was flattering—Arthur admired the work of his fellow Scot—but it did nothing to enhance Arthur's own reputation, except with editors. Distant critical applause could not be heard at Arthur's upstairs desk in Southsea.

But Stevenson himself suffered the same questions of identity when he published shorter tales rather than novels. Less than two years earlier, Arthur had picked up a two-year-old issue of *The Cornhill*, dated September–October 1880, and with excitement read a long story, "The Pavilion on the Links." Not until later that year did he, along with many other readers, confirm the authorship of this story—and of others he had enjoyed—when they appeared together in *New Arabian Nights*, under the byline of Robert Louis Stevenson.

Such speculation was rampant in publishing. Most fiction published in periodicals at the time was unsigned. Political journalists earlier in the century had worn anonymity as their armor, and afterward it remained in fashion. Although his editorship drew readers, Charles Dickens had used writers' anonymity to mask the extent of his own contributions to his periodicals *Household Words* and *All the Year Round*. Dickens felt that such intrusive editing lent his periodical a unified voice, an overall house style, but many contributors considered it an erasure of their individuality. By Arthur's time, anonymous publishing was slowly expiring but not yet dead. Publishers had realized that a famous author's name on the cover or masthead would lure subscribers, and that anonymity had at times disguised slanderers and other irresponsible writers. And writers were increasingly eager to gain credit for their labors.

Gradually the ambitious Arthur decided that only with publication of a novel could he draw attention to his work. In 1883 he wrote his first novel, a rather awkward and static tale with the bland title *The Narrative of John Smith*. In it Arthur gazed into a mirror and wrote about a medico who yearned to write fiction. Arthur made an effort to step outside himself by making the narrator twice his own age and handicapped with gout, thus forced to narrow his focus onto a stack of blank paper, but it was an unconvincing personation. He speculated on the origins of religion, on the urge to write, on politics, on women, on life in general. The book was more a series of sketches and miniature essays than a novel.

Finally Arthur sent out the manuscript—only to have it lost in the mail. It was never received by the publisher and never returned to the author. To his inquiries, the post office replied on its standard blue forms that they had no record of it. Arthur tried rewriting it from memory, but he seems to have given up in frustration or simply lost interest, perhaps because this freshman project went stale as he outgrew it. He never finished the rewrite.

Summoning his usual determination, he tried again. During 1884 and 1885, Arthur wrote a novel entitled *The Firm of Girdlestone*. The melodramatic plot somewhat resembled that of *A Lost Name*, an 1868 novel by Sheridan Le Fanu, the celebrated Irish master of ghost stories and Gothic thrillers. Stepping considerably outside his own experience this time, Arthur told the story of the escalating chicanery perpetrated by John Girdlestone, founder of the London firm of Girdlestone and Company, and his son Ezra, in their desperate attempts to hide the financial ruin caused by the elder Girdlestone's speculations. Arthur moved from a static structure for *The Narrative of John Smith* to a frenetic one for *The Firm of Girdlestone*. He told his sister that his book abounded in exciting murder scenes, and added, "I would need a private graveyard to plant all my characters in."

Arthur didn't try to hide his contempt for the Scrooge-like financiers. When three crew members die on one of the firm's ships, the younger Girdlestone remarks mercilessly, "We know very well what that means. Three women, each with an armful of brats, besieging the office and clamouring for a pension."

From the beginning, Arthur realized that the novel was derivative and uninspired. To his mother he described it as "fairly good as light literature goes nowadays." But he kept sending it out. Publishers just as reliably returned it, in what Arthur later described as "the circular tour" that manuscripts take from writer to editor and back to writer like homing pigeons. Privately sharing their opinion, he felt that he couldn't blame publishers for not snapping up *Girdlestone*.

CHAPTER 13

The Unseen World

There is great promise, I think, in the faces of the dead. They say it is but the post-mortem relaxation of the muscles, but it is one of the points on which I would like to see science wrong.

—ARTHUR CONAN DOYLE, *THE STARK MUNRO LETTERS*

In December 1883, Arthur's lighthearted short story "Selecting a Ghost" appeared in *London Society*, which over the preceding couple of years had also published "The American's Tale," "The Gully of Bluemansdyke," and others of his stories. This time, rather than trafficking in spooks of his own, Arthur mocked the claims of spiritualist mediums that they could summon ghosts on demand. The narrator, Silas D'Odd, has grown wealthy in the grocery business and as a consequence has bought a castle, Goresthorpe Grange, but he is shocked to learn that the moldering corridors lack a ghost: "As the presence of a kennel presupposes that of a dog, so I imagined that it was impossible that such desirable quarters should be untenanted by one or more restless shades."

D'Odd and his wife turn to her cousin, who has already furnished the castle with a crest and fake family portraits. Eventually, under the influence of a drug, D'Odd finds several ghosts applying to him for work at Goresthorpe. "I am the invisible nonentity," sighs one. "I am electric, magnetic, and spiritualistic. I am the great ethereal sigh-heaver." Other ghosts appear—an old woman who says, "Sir Walter was partial to me"; a cavalier who boasts, "There is a blood stain over my heart . . . I am patronised by many old Conservative families"; a vague presence who quavers, "I snatch letters and place invisible hands on people's wrists." Finally a horrific vision of rotting bones in a shroud murmurs, "I am the embodiment of Edgar Allan Poe . . . I am a low-caste spirit-subduing spectre . . . Work with grave-clothes, a coffin-lid, and a galvanic battery." In the end Silas D'Odd discovers that he was hallucinating under the influence of chloral.

Arthur may have been mocking himself in part, because during this time he began to explore spiritualism, the belief that after death disembodied spirits can communicate with the living. During his years in Southsea, Arthur read dozens of books about spiritualism, which in its alleged physical manifes-tations claimed to provide demonstrable evidence—rather than demanding a leap of faith—that the human spirit survives death. His earliest memory was the sight of his dead maternal grandmother in June 1862, before his fourth birthday. In 1881, while still in Edinburgh, he had attended a spiritualist lecture entitled "Does Death End All?" Now, in Southsea, he thought obses-sively about this topic. In 1876, the great naturalist Alfred Russel Wallace, who had recognized the importance of natural selection at the same time as Charles Darwin, published a collection of three long essays about spiritualism, *On Miracles and Modern Spiritualism*. Arthur read this book attentively, along with dozens of other volumes exploring the question of whether some part of a human being's personality and character—some essence or distillation—might survive and even transcend the death of its vehicle.

In early 1885, a Southsea colleague and friend, Dr. William Roylston Pike, consulted with Arthur about a patient—a young man named John (inevi-tably nicknamed Jack) Hawkins, who suffered from seizures that seemed to be growing steadily worse. Arthur accompanied Pike and examined the pale and feeble patient, who was twenty-five, only a month older than himself. Sadly, he confirmed the older doctor's diagnosis of the seizures' cause—cerebral meningitis, an inflammation of the tissues surrounding the brain. Usually it was fatal.

When examining Jack, Arthur met the rest of the Hawkins family. A Gloucestershire widow, Emily Hawkins had moved to Southsea only a few months earlier with her son Jack and her daughter Mary Louisa. Nicknamed "Touie," Jack's sister was almost twenty-eight. The family rented a terraced flat not far away, overlooking the sea and Southsea Common. Soon Jack grew worse, and apparently because of conflicts at their lodging, Arthur offered his own spare bedroom at Bush Villas to Jack. This way he could attend the boy himself at a moment's notice. Emily Hawkins already had one son in a Gloucester mental asylum, and naturally preferred that Jack not go to a hospital—the last resort for the sick because of the mortality rate in such institutions.

Although it was a generous and romantic gesture, apparently Arthur expected to also get paid for this on-site medical work. In his autobiographical novel *The Stark Munro Letters*, the patient's family asks the narrator to recommend lodging and Munro offers his own house. "Both ladies thanked me a very great deal more than I deserved," he remarks; "for after all it was a business matter, and a resident patient was the very thing I needed." When he offered to take in Jack Hawkins, Arthur was in financial straits. Again unable to meet his bills in Southsea, he had recently forwarded some to his faithful mother, knowing that she would pay them, as she had in the past.

Jack's condition had been steadily worsening, and he died on the twenty-fifth of March, only a few days after moving into Arthur's house. Two days later, Arthur rode with the Hawkins family as Jack's coffin was conveyed from Bush Villas—a hearse parked outside must have been a poor advertisement for a physician—to the relatively new Highland Road Cemetery. During this time 40 percent of the burials at Highland Road were of children. Many had not dodged illness and accident to reach adulthood, and their small gravestones stood in solemn rows with the larger stones of their kin as Arthur's patient was laid to rest.

Hardly had Arthur returned to Bush Villas when a policeman arrived to interrogate him about Jack's death. There was a question about whether anyone might profit from it, especially this little-known young physician, in whose house the patient had quickly expired. Fortunately, Dr. Pike had examined Jack, at Arthur's request, only the night before his death. Pike's professional opinion of the case, along with his established reputation, freed Arthur from suspicion.

Arthur found the death of his young patient traumatic, professionally and personally. But there were larger philosophical implications. For some years, Arthur had described himself as an agnostic and skeptic. Gradually, however, he had begun to yearn for greater spiritual satisfaction than he found in a materialist's view of life. Now and then he even attended a table-rapping session, in which a medium in a darkened parlor claimed to communicate with the spirits of those who had "crossed to the other side," as spiritualists liked to say. Arthur struggled to accept the mediums' oracular ambiguity and theatrical table-rapping as evidence. The death of Jack Hawkins prompted further speculation along these lines.

* * *

Arthur's father was not dead, but his absence from the family was almost as final. In early 1885 Charles Doyle, while still an inmate at Blairerno, somehow got his hands on a bottle and, furiously drunk yet again, began to believe that God was ordering him to escape. In struggling to obey, he broke a window. When he tried to leave, staff restrained him, and he fought back, striking everyone within reach.

As a consequence, in May, Charles left the facility aimed at helping peaceable alcoholics. He was moved to where a professional staff was better prepared to deal with volatile behavior—not far south, to the Royal Lunatic Asylum in the village of Hillside, north of Montrose. Founded in 1781 as the Montrose Lunatic Asylum, Infirmary & Dispensary, largely through local private subscription, it had received its first royal charter in 1810, and was the oldest such institution in Scotland. It had grown in both quality of treatment and accommodations for inmates during its century of existence. In 1858 new buildings were built on nearby Sunnyside Farm, primarily a long three-story hospital in the Tudor revival style. Locally the entire institution came to be called Sunnyside. The old buildings remained part of the hospital, and it was in these that a befuddled Charles found himself.

His behavior at Blairerno had been so alarming that the authorities took action even before notifying Mary or Arthur. Admission of a patient on an emergency basis, according to the lunacy laws in Scotland, required examination by two physicians, both of whom had to submit their medical evaluation to a sheriff. Charles was quick to supply Sunnyside with just cause. Immediately he informed one of the doctors, James Ironside, that he was receiving messages "from the unseen world." With his growing interest in spiritualism, Arthur may have been impressed by this remark. When the other doctor, James Duffus, began questioning Charles, the patient began swearing and calling the doctor and his staff devils.

Charles also maintained that he had been to Sunnyside before, which was untrue, and claimed first that his brother was dead and then that he was living. He was unable to summon the names of his children. Both doctors certified Charles's inability to function on his own, and the sheriff authorized his incarceration. Charles joined the five hundred or so patients at Sunnyside, the great majority of whom were paupers cared for out of charity, with about eighty patients whose family paid their way.

Charles seemed to be in good overall physical health. But Dr. Duffus wrote of the new patient, "Has been weak minded & nervous from his youth, and from his own account took refuge in alcoholics very early to give him courage &c. . . . Is, or was a clever draughtsman, & is the brother of the

Doyle connected with *Punch* in its early days." Charles also confessed to Duffus that while drunk he had attacked a servant girl at Blairerno.

Apparently the Doyle family accepted the admitting physicians' assessment of Charles, for he remained at Sunnyside. Mary began to worry that if Charles were free he would quickly kill himself with drink, and possibly harm someone else along the way. However sad it was for Arthur that his father was institutionalized, Sunnyside was an alternative that the family could contemplate without shame. Dr. James Howden, the superintending physician, rejected the barbarism of the past and wanted his institution to remain in the vanguard of compassionate treatment. "We must not . . . lose sight of the great principle of non-restraint . . . which has revolutionised the treatment of the insane," he wrote, "so that the modern asylum has the character and aims of a Hospital and a Sanitorium rather than of a Prison or a Poorhouse." Reform in such arenas was a growing movement. Novelist Charles Reade had also written *Hard Cash*, an exposé of the abuse and exploitation of inmates housed in private insane asylums—a novel that, like the crusading works of Charles Dickens, Harriet Beecher Stowe, and others, had effected real change in the world.

Thus Sunnyside was not a place of punishment. Entertainments ranged from magic lantern shows to picnics and dances. The constantly touring D'Oyly Carte Opera Company, a collaboration between theater impresario Richard D'Oyly Carte and the comic opera team of lyricist W. S. Gilbert and composer Arthur Sullivan, even brought its troupe to Sunnyside.

At first Charles was so confused he didn't understand where he was or how he had gotten there. "Does not remember in the afternoon," wrote one physician of him, "whether he was out in the morning." In mid-July a physician at Sunnyside wrote that during the preceding week Charles had been weak and confused, complaining "of an overpowering presentiment that he was going to die, that he would die in 48 hours." Charles consulted twice with a priest, prayed often, and read his prayer book. From Blairerno, David Forbes informed the Sunnyside physician that Charles had often behaved in this way. More than once, Forbes had seen Charles lie down as if to die, only to gradually "come to life again."

Although he was generally considered an equable patient, his troubles grew worse rather than better. In mid-November, an attending physician wrote of Charles, "This morning took an epileptic attack of general convulsions, the first fits we have known him have." There had been no record of epilepsy before, but the disease sometimes had been known to follow other traumatic damage to the body—such as toxic levels of drink. Afterward

Charles did not recall the seizure. Gradually such attacks occurred more frequently, and his memory declined until he could not be expected to recall even the most recent events. He was hidden away from society and family. For Charles, it was not the afterlife so much as his own daily life that became the unseen world.

The next year, in his story "John Barrington Cowles," which was published in *Cassel's Saturday Journal*, Arthur described a character with telling details: "As I supported him towards his lodgings I could see that he was not only suffering from the effects of a recent debauch, but that a long course of intemperance had affected his nerves and his brain."

The death of Jack Hawkins at Bush Villas naturally precipitated a greater intimacy between the Hawkins family and Arthur. Even as they grieved, Touie and her mother felt guilty that Arthur had unwittingly invited such trauma into his life. Soon Arthur found himself drawn to the quiet but amusing Touie. Petite, with childishly small hands and feet, Touie radiated quiet poise. She had a glint in her eye suggesting that she was ready for humor, but she refused to laugh at insults or at jokes performed at someone else's expense. Quickly their interest blossomed into romance. Although there is no record of dramatic passion on either side, Arthur confessed later that quiet little Touie inspired his most protective masculine urges.

On the sixth of August, four and a half months after Jack's death, the Reverend S. R. Stable united Arthur and Touie as husband and wife in the Thornton-in-Lonsdale parish church, in Yorkshire—near Bryan Waller's estate at Masongill, where Arthur's mother had been living since about 1883, paying a nominal rent to Waller.

A. Conan Doyle, MD, wrote Arthur precisely on the register. The license noted that he was the son of Charles Doyle, artist. Touie signed as *Louise Hawkins*, revising as usual her birth name, Mary Louisa. She would have still been mourning the death of her brother, and probably there were few guests. Although Arthur may not have been happy about it, Bryan Waller was present; he signed as witness to Touie's signature. Arthur's sister Conny, home from Portugal, was present, as was Innes, now a rambunctious twelve-year-old.

Several of Touie's siblings had died already, and as a consequence she received a larger share of her father's estate than otherwise would have been the case. For one thing, she received a greater percentage of profits from businesses and rents from properties. Her father's will had also insisted upon no hearse to convey his coffin but rather that it be carried to the gravesite on the shoulders of honest, sober workingmen, each of whom was to be paid £1.

With no family money of his own to add to the equation, soon Arthur responsibly signed up for life insurance policies. But his new legal situation meant that thenceforth he would be in charge of Touie's income, which came to £100 per year. Thus from the date of their wedding he faced fewer worries about money. Arthur wrote little in his letters and elsewhere about the early days of the marriage, and at first it seems to have had little overall effect on his life. During their honeymoon in Ireland, he often played cricket.

Gradually, as he settled into marriage, and as he accepted Touie's legacy as a part of their combined income, Arthur began to devote more time to writing. His short stories had built up a small reputation within the publishing world, but he needed to write a novel. He thought he had a good idea for a book-length adventure in the flourishing genre of detective stories. He began to imagine how a mind such as Dr. Joseph Bell's would sparkle if turned to the solving of crimes.

Part 2

Prophets and Police

Every writer is imitative at first. I think that is an absolute rule; though sometimes he throws back on some model which is not easily traced.

—ARTHUR CONAN DOYLE, *MEMORIES AND ADVENTURES*

CHAPTER 14

The Method of Zadig

Voltaire taught us the method of Zadig, and every good teacher of medicine or surgery exemplifies every day in his teaching and practice the method and its results.

—JOSEPH BELL

When Arthur sat down to create a scientific detective, he was not only joining the flourishing genre of crime fiction; he was also conjuring the latest incarnation of a persistent ideal in literature. Now and then across the millennia, amid the chaos and unfairness of society, a writer had imagined a just, rational hero whose eagle eye and respect for evidence enabled him to stride boldly free of bias and preconception. As Arthur well knew, Edgar Allan Poe was not the first writer to imagine the critical observation and rational analysis of evidence. Poe consciously sent Dupin following in the footsteps of distinguished predecessors, particularly a biblical prophet and a supercilious philosopher.

The biblical book of Daniel, dated by modern scholars to the second or third century B.C.E., comprises both legendary Aramaic court tales and visions of apocalypse. One of the former stories about Daniel—lion tamer, dragon killer, and prophet—describes his investigation of a crime. A man of noble heritage, Daniel is among the Hebrews exiled in Babylon. Like "The Murders in the Rue Morgue," one of the Daniel stories is a locked-room mystery.

"Why do you not worship Bel?" demands the Persian king Cyrus of Daniel. The name Bel was actually a title, meaning roughly "master" or "lord," and among the Hebrews it seems to have been associated particularly with Marduk, a Mesopotamian deity who later became the patron god of Babylon.

"Because I do not revere idols made with hands," replies Daniel, "but only the living God who made heaven and earth and has dominion over all flesh."

"You do not think Bel is a living god? Do you not see how much he eats and drinks every day?" Each evening twelve measures of flour, forty sheep, and six containers of wine were placed as offerings before the holy statue of Bel.

"Do not be deceived, O king," Daniel says with a smirk and a laugh. "It is only clay inside and bronze outside; it has never eaten or drunk anything."

The furious Cyrus calls for his seventy priests of Bel and offers an ultimatum: "Unless you tell me who it is who consumes these provisions, you shall die. But if you can show that Bel consumes them, Daniel shall die for blaspheming Bel."

Daniel shrugs. "Let it be as you say."

The priests make their preparations and inform Cyrus that they are leaving for the night. "You, O king, set out the food and prepare the wine. Then shut the door and seal it with your ring. If you do not find that Bel has eaten it all when you return in the morning, we are to die. Otherwise Daniel shall die for his lies against us."

The priests depart. Cyrus places his offerings before the statue of Bel. With only the king beside him, Daniel instructs his servants to bring ashes from fires and to spread them across the floor inside the temple. Only then do they leave, with the king using his signet ring to seal the door behind them.

The next morning the king returns with Daniel, sees the unbroken seal, and asks rhetorically, "Are the seals unbroken, Daniel?"

"They are unbroken, O king."

Cyrus himself opens the door and peers in at the now empty table that the night before had groaned with offerings, and he praises his god. "You are great, O Bel. There is no deceit in you."

But Daniel won't yet permit Cyrus to enter the room. From the doorway he indicates the dusting of ashes on the floor. "Look at the floor, and consider whose footprints these are."

"I see the footprints of men, women, and children!" says the king.

Daniel examines the footprints and shows Cyrus that the priests were using a secret entrance under the offering table. Each night they had been entering the temple, with their wives and children, to feast upon the offerings. The furious king rounds up all his priests, who show Cyrus the secret door. He orders them all killed. Furious and disappointed, he turns the statue of Bel—indeed, the entire temple—over to the proto-detective. Daniel destroys them.

In his revelation of what actually happened behind the scenes, Daniel provides the kind of narrative satisfaction that would later draw readers such as Arthur Conan Doyle to this kind of story—a reconfiguring of the reader's assumptions, the replacement of what seems to have happened with what actually happened. He also proves the value of diligent attention to physical clues.

More than two millennia later, in the late 1740s, the French philosopher and satirist François-Marie Arouet, who wrote under the nom de plume Voltaire, published *Zadig, or, The Book of Fate*. Although Voltaire presented Zadig as a Babylonian philosopher, the author's satire was aimed straight at the inequalities and trumpery of mid-eighteenth-century Europe. In a life as engineered for rhetorical points as that of Candide, Voltaire's later creation, Zadig encounters every kind of misfortune, from war to thwarted love. He remains strictly rational, so attentive to the overlooked clues around him that he seems to possess supernatural insight.

In Voltaire's account, Zadig is strolling outdoors when he is accosted by a royal eunuch, who with his attendants is searching the thickets and fields. "Young man, have not you seen, pray, her majesty's dog?"

"You mean her bitch, I presume," replies Zadig with the kind of omniscient smugness that Edgar Allan Poe would later assign to Dupin.

"You are very right, sir, 'tis a spaniel bitch indeed."

"And very small," Zadig remarks. "She has had puppies too lately. She's a little lame with her left forefoot and has long ears."

The eunuch asks, naturally, which way the dog ran.

But Zadig replies that he hasn't seen her, and that he didn't even know the queen had such a dog until the eunuch mentioned it.

This comic routine plays out again when the king's favorite horse escapes its groom and the huntsman asks Zadig if he has glimpsed it.

"No horse ever galloped smoother," replies our hero. "He is about five foot high. His hoofs are very small. His tail is about three foot six inches long. The studs of his bit are of pure gold, about twenty-three carats. And his shoes are of silver, about eleven pennyweight apiece."

"Whereabouts is he?" asks the relieved huntsman.

"I never set eyes on him."

Naturally the eunuch and the huntsman think that Zadig is lying, for some obscure reason, because clearly he has seen both animals. They drag Zadig before a judge, who condemns him to be whipped. Before the sentence can be executed, both the dog and horse are found and returned to the king.

Clearly Zadig is innocent. The judges rescind the whipping but charge Zadig with lying and fine him four hundred ounces of gold.

Zadig relents and divulges his detective-style observational method. First he noticed a small dog's footprints in sand that showed a streaked pattern between them wherever the sand rose, indicating that it was a bitch with pendant teats, thus mother of a recent litter of pups. Slight brushings alongside the front paw prints suggested the presence of long ears. One consistently faint paw print indicated lameness. As for the horse, Zadig noticed its tracks in the road were equidistant, indicating that they were made by a trained galloper. In a lane only seven feet wide, the horse's tail had brushed dust off each side, so its tail must be at least three and a half feet long. The philosopher saw leaves knocked off a tree at a height of five feet. The golden bridle and silver shoes had left marks on different kinds of stone.

The resulting notoriety attracts so much adoring attention that Zadig resolves to keep his mouth shut in the future.

Nine years before Voltaire died in 1778, Jean Léopold Nicolas Frédéric Cuvier was born in France. He became one of the great zoologists, well known to Arthur as Baron Cuvier. Although he vehemently opposed the evolutionary ideas of Lamarck and others, who maintained that animals had changed slowly over time in response to their environment, Cuvier demonstrated that extinction had occurred—a revelation that dealt a major philosophical blow to the ecclesiastical view of a static and perfect nature.

In Arthur's time Cuvier was honored mostly for his extensive work in the comparative anatomy of animals, living and extinct. One of his most influential contributions to natural philosophy was his discovery that to an educated eye a single bone can reveal much about the structure and behavior of the creature that once possessed it, because of the predictable correlation between various parts of animals' bodies. Unearthing fossils in every direction, scientists used Cuvier's discovery as the cornerstone of paleontology, and such similarities were part of what Darwin later reinterpreted as evidence of kinship.

"Today," wrote Cuvier, "someone who sees the print of a cloven hoof can conclude that the animal which left the print was a ruminative one, and this conclusion is as certain as any that can be made in physics or moral philosophy." Then he evoked Voltaire's contribution to his thinking about scientific detective work: "This single track therefore tells the observer about the kind of teeth, the kind of jaws, the haunches, the shoulder, and the pelvis of the animal which has passed: it is more certain evidence than all of Zadig's clues."

CHAPTER 15

The Footmarks of Poe

Edgar Allan Poe, who, in his carelessly prodigal fashion, threw out
the seeds from which so many of our present forms of literature have
sprung, was the father of the detective tale, and covered its limits so
completely that I fail to see how his followers can find any fresh
ground which they can confidently call their own. For the secret
of the thinness and also of the intensity of the detective story is, that
the writer is left with only one quality, that of intellectual acuteness,
with which to endow his hero. . . . On this narrow path the writer
must walk, and he sees the footmarks of Poe always in front of him.

—ARTHUR CONAN DOYLE

Before the evolution of detective stories into a genre that would draw
Arthur's attention and ambition in the 1880s, fictional detectives first
had to appear in other literary landscapes. Originally most such
protagonists were not actual detectives, either official or private. An investi-
gating amateur of the time was likely an innocent victim of a conspiracy or
someone otherwise caught in a crime, one who pursued justice or revenge
without recourse to official law and its enforcers.

This was the approach taken, for example, by English radical William
Godwin in his scandalous 1794 novel *Things as They Are, or, The Adventures
of Caleb Williams*. In Godwin's tangled philosophical novel—a dramatiza-
tion of some of the ideas he had expressed a year earlier in his *Enquiry
Concerning Political Justice and Its Influence on Morals and Happiness*—he
intended to show the ways in which innocent victims suffer from the

byzantine mazes of an unjust society. With a talent for mishap worthy of Zadig, whose adventures had appeared half a century earlier, Caleb Williams works with all the resolve of a detective, but primarily to save himself from the threat of violence and undeserved prosecution. He does not decipher clues à la Poe's later detective Auguste Dupin.

Edward Bulwer-Lytton moved further along the road toward an actual detective story in his 1828 novel *Pelham: or, The Adventures of a Gentleman*. Henry Pelham, however, is a snobbish young dandy who strives to liberate a friend unjustly arrested for murder. Legal shenanigans, atmospheric settings, menacing strangers, obscure clues, misleading circumstantial evidence—all the elements were there. Rising above his disdainful upbringing, Pelham collaborates with felons, masks himself as a priest, and ultimately triumphs. But he remains an avenging friend, a devoted amateur, not a detective.

Often such stories were also shrouded in Gothic trappings that distracted from the case and distinguished them from what Arthur came to think of as a detective story. Other writers approached the genre—including the German fabulist E. T. A. Hoffmann, for example, in his story "Mademoiselle Scuderi." The bloody Inquisition brings death to Mademoiselle Scuderi's door, and she responds courageously and intelligently. However, she is not an investigator—not a trained professional such as Inspector Bucket, not a miraculously gifted amateur such as Auguste Dupin. Her methods could not be described as an organized investigation. For a long time, few talented writers crossed the Rubicon into constructing their narratives around the solving of a crime.

Born in Boston in 1809 to itinerant actors who died during his early childhood, Edgar Poe was adopted by the Allan family of Richmond, Virginia. They sent him to boarding schools in England, but he was back home by the age of eleven. In 1826 he enrolled in the University of Virginia and soon built up gambling debts that prompted him to leave college and join the army. Every move in his life was accompanied by trouble with demons such as alcohol and gambling. At the age of twenty-seven he married his thirteen-year-old first cousin, Virginia Clemm, with whom he adopted the kind of life his parents had lived, following work from city to city, first to Philadelphia, then Baltimore and New York City.

Poe was still in his teens when his first book was published—*Tamerlane and Other Poems*. Although he was a writer of great individuality, Poe—born only a few years after the close of the eighteenth century—was rooted in

Gothic melodrama. Upon his death in 1849 at the age of forty, he bequeathed literature a legacy that haunted the following decades with its seductive reek of depravity. Readers found it hard to forget the plague of the Red Death or William Wilson facing his doppelgänger. After closing a volume of Poe, the horrible crimes in the stories remained all too vivid—Montresor walling up Fortunato in a dank vault, a dead man's heart that beats on in the ears of his murderer, the vengeful shriek of a black cat entombed with its murdered mistress. In stories about the glories and dangers of balloon travel, mesmerism, and voyages to the moon, Poe explored the possibilities of scientific (and pseudoscientific) discovery, joining a tradition that dated back to tales such as *Icaromenippus*, Lucian's satirical second-century account of a flight to the moon. In Arthur's youth this tradition had been rejuvenated by his favorite French adventure novelist, Jules Verne. His knowledge of science was apparent in his essay "Eureka: A Prose Poem," which lyrically explored astronomers' puzzlement over the question of why the night sky is black if space boasts an infinite number of stars. Other essays ranged from "The Philosophy of Furniture" to "The Rationale of Verse."

Aside from Poe's tales of fantasy and the macabre, crime fiction was also never the same after he contributed a few stories to the genre. Arthur particularly enjoyed Poe's detective stories about an eccentric Frenchman named Monsieur C. Auguste Dupin, who showed off his ratiocinative skills in three cases. Poe's offhand innovations included bringing back his detective protagonist for further adventures.

Two months after Poe became editor of the flourishing young Philadelphia periodical *Graham's*, readers of the April 1, 1841, issue turned to page 165 and found, filling the lower half of the page, a poem entitled "Comparisons" by Charles West Thomson. An ordinary, safe poem of its time, it sprinkled a few obvious analogies between human life and that of ephemeral natural phenomena, opening with

> A leaf upon the stream,
>   When the brook is rushing by
> In its glorious summer dream,—
>   Such am I.—

Then, turning the page, unsuspecting readers encountered a story different from the usual magazine fare represented by Thomson's poem—a story so different, in fact, that it would soon be acclaimed as founding a new genre. There, in capitals near the top of page 166, appeared

THE MURDERS IN THE RUE MORGUE.
BY EDGAR A. POE.

Its opening read like a philosophical essay: "It is not improbable that a few farther steps in phrenological science will lead to a belief in the existence, if not to the actual discovery and location of an organ of *analysis*." For later editions, Poe removed the opening reference to phrenology, with its vision of a corporeal seat for analytical thought. But he retained his overall theme of the sensual delight in deciphering puzzles:

> The mental features discoursed of as the analytical are, in them-selves, but little susceptible of analysis. We appreciate them only in their effects. . . . As the strong man exults in his physical ability, delighting in such exercises as call his muscles into action, so glories the analyst in that moral activity which disentangles. He derives pleasure from even the most trivial occupations that bring his talent into play. He is fond of enigmas, of conundrums, of hieroglyphics, exhibiting in his solutions of each a degree of acumen which appears to the ordinary apprehension preternatural.

Readers who kept going soon found themselves not in a philosophical discussion but in the presence of a new kind of story: the account of an investigation, an unraveling of a puzzle by means of reason and observation. The criminal as folk hero fighting an unjust society and royal whim—a staple of popular literature from the ballads of Robin Hood to Henry Fielding's 1743 fictionalized account of the real-life criminal Jonathan Wild and beyond—had suddenly been joined by the intellectual crime-fighter as hero. And soon Poe's readers were wandering in the dark alleyways of the penny newspapers, illuminated by a brilliant mind and a vivid writing style. Originally Poe had titled the story "The Murders in the Rue Trianon." The change to "Rue Morgue" was a wise decision, adding a chilling whiff of death from the first page.

Poe's surprised readers did not know how to think of this curious character Dupin. With London's metropolitan police force having been founded as recently as 1829, only twelve years before Poe's story, the notion of a detective—professional or amateur, official or private—was unknown to most readers. In the story Poe did not even use the word *detective*, which had not yet been employed in this context.

Thus reviewers turned to other analogies to describe Dupin's talent. "The reader is disposed to believe that this must be the actual observation of some experienced criminal lawyer," wrote a commentator in the *Pennsylvania Inquirer*, in response to Dupin's debut, "the chain of evidence is so wonderfully maintained through so many intricacies, and the connexion of cause and effect so irresistibly demonstrated." The *Ladies' National Magazine* said flatly, "Mr. Poe is a man of genius . . . 'The Murders in the Rue Morgue' is one of the most intensely interesting tales that has appeared for years."

None of Poe's work was more influential than this clever and revolutionary tale that, however outrageous its premise of murder by ape, eschews the supernatural in deciphering the mystery at its core. Poe brought Dupin back for two further adventures. He appeared next in "The Mystery of Marie Rogêt," published in *Snowden's Ladies' Companion* in installments that appeared in late 1842 and early 1843. It was inspired by the real-life murder in New York of an American woman named Mary Cecelia Rogers, but Poe moved the story to Dupin's Paris and Gallicized the victim's name. Many other details he borrowed with little change from newspaper accounts. While pretending to show how Dupin "unravelled the mystery of Marie's assassination," Poe later bragged, "I, in fact, enter into a very vigorous analysis of the real tragedy in New York." Such long-winded analysis weakened the story. With little action or dialogue, it was more of an essay, analyzing the popular evidence regarding a brutal crime that had obsessed the popular press in both Europe and the United States.

In December 1844, a third and final Dupin case appeared in a publication called *The Gift: A Christmas and New Year's Present for 1845*. "The Purloined Letter" was decidedly a detective story, and one that emphasized Dupin's skill as an armchair puzzle solver. In the 1840s Poe wrote other stories that addressed investigative techniques and the unraveling of tangled clues, launching a number of ideas that soon became characteristic of the genre. He wrote the first story in which a detective springs a surprise on a murderer to elicit a confession ("Thou Art the Man"), and the first in which a detective shadows a suspect through urban throngs ("The Man of the Crowd"). "The Gold-Bug" featured a Dupin-like logician named William Legrand—another impoverished aristocrat, but this time in New Orleans rather than Paris—and centered on a treasure hunt and the deciphering of a coded message.

Planning "Rue Morgue" so carefully—later he described it as "written backwards"—Poe was taking to its limit his notion of the need for unity of effect in fiction. He well understood that, knowing his solution before setting pen to paper, he wrote like a magician whose first job was to misdirect the viewer's eye. "These tales of ratiocination owe most of their popularity to being something in a new key," Poe wrote to the American poet Phillip Pendleton Cook. "I do not mean to say that they are not ingenious—but people think them more ingenious than they are. In the 'Murders in the Rue Morgue,' for instance, where is the ingenuity of unravelling a web which you yourself (the author) have woven for the express purpose of unravelling?"

Poe was writing only a few decades after Baron Cuvier explained his discoveries regarding the correlation of body parts in animals. In "Rue Morgue," the detective hands a volume of scientific writings to the narrator and says, "Read now this passage from Cuvier." Dupin consults the great zoologist in part because they have similar methods—the reconstruction of a full scene from a few pieces of evidence.

In "The Murders in the Rue Morgue," the bodies of a young woman and her mother, Mademoiselle Camille L'Espanaye and Madame L'Espanaye, are found inside a locked apartment on the fourth floor of a house in the Rue Morgue in the Quartier St. Roch in Paris. They have been the victims of a brutal murder. Wild cries in the night draw a crowd and gendarmes. They find the daughter's still-warm body stuffed inside the fireplace's chimney, and the mother's sprawled in a paved courtyard behind the building—her throat slashed so viciously that, when the gendarmes try to raise the body, her head falls off.

Dupin informs the narrator that he knows G——, the prefect of police, who will grant permission for the amateur puzzle lover to examine the scene of the crime. Dupin resembles a Gothic protagonist in taste and mannerisms, but he strolls through Poe's bloody story like the embodiment of reason. The narrator of "Rue Morgue" serves primarily as audience for a disquisition, and—despite the bloodshed—the case remains for Dupin an intellectual exercise.

In time Dupin unravels the mystery and reveals that the murderer was an orangutan who had escaped from his owner, an irresponsible mariner. Frightened by the women's response to him, the ape acted blindly and killed Madame L'Espanaye—readers eventually learn—by holding the razor and mimicking gestures he had seen his master perform at a shaving mirror. Dupin places an advertisement in *Le Monde*, a paper known for its shipping news, claiming to have captured on the morning of the murder "a very large, tawny Ourang-Outang of the Bornese species." The sailor snaps at the bait— and, captured by Dupin and his Boswell, he confesses all in a manner that became a common denouement in detective stories.

Naturally Poe was himself drawing upon much that he had read. Just as his 1839 doppelgänger story "William Wilson" had been inspired in part by a similar idea in Washington Irving's little-known story "An Unwritten Drama of Lord Byron," so did his detective story have roots in many sources. Even his villain was not conjured purely out of his own arabesque imagination. The American poet and soldier David Humphreys was known for his late eighteenth-century satirical poem "The Monkey Who Shaved Himself and His Friends." The titular primate, Jacko, imitates his barber master's gestures with a razor. After wounding a dog and cat, Jacko tries to carry out an action he has often watched his master perform—shaving himself. But of course the monkey doesn't understand the danger. In the end he "drew razor swift as he could pull it, / And cut, from ear to ear, his gullet."

Mischievous simians had cavorted in European fiction since before Voltaire's Candide mistook two women's monkey paramours for attackers. Poe's choice of a particular animal villain—an orangutan—had a more direct ancestor in the work of another writer close to Arthur's heart. Walter Scott's 1832 novel *Count Robert of Paris*, the master's penultimate book and one of which Arthur was quite fond, featured a homicidal "Ourang Outang." Scott described it as having "a strange chuckling hoarse voice," and later it emits "a deep wailing and melancholy cry, having in it something human, which excited compassion."

Poe's murderer also emits terrifying cries. In the first newspaper account of the murders, Dupin reads that "the inhabitants of the Quartier St. Roch were aroused from sleep by a succession of terrific shrieks." The gendarme reports loud and drawn-out screams. He hears a gruff Frenchman and also a shrill voice, "that of a foreigner." Poe had fun with the witnesses. A Frenchman thinks the shrill voice is that of an Italian; a Dutchman is certain it was French; possibly German, says an Englishman; undoubtedly English, insists a Spaniard. But of course it is an orangutan, screaming like Walter Scott's orangutan but waving a razor like David Humphreys's monkey.

Poe imitated other aspects of Scott's orangutan's behavior. "Something then, of very great size, in the form of a human being," wrote Scott, "jumped down from the trap-door, though that height must be above fourteen feet." Eventually the ape kills a man who is in the midst of a speech professing his lack of belief in God. Poe's orangutan enters and departs through a high window, then murders the two women—the mother by cutting her throat: "With one determined sweep of its muscular arm it nearly severed her head from her body."

For Poe, as for many of his contemporaries, apes represented the dark side of humanity—not fallen angels so much as the devils of our lesser nature. In his later story "Hop-Frog" (originally subtitled "The Eight Chained Ourangoutangs"), he brought back this alarming creature—that is, he has the titular dwarf persuade the vicious king and his companions to dress as orangutans before he sets them on fire in revenge for their torment of him and the innocent Trippetta. The villains' dressing as apes was equivalent to confessing their low character.

The kind of horrific story represented by "The Murders in the Rue Morgue" was not uncommon in the penny press of Poe's day. Sensational "true" accounts of crimes sold newspapers and magazines. What Poe brought to the field was a new character and a new approach—a story centered not on the brutality of the crime itself, although he provided buckets of blood, but on the discovery of its perpetrator, which required a focus upon the intelligence and methods of the investigator. This was not a species of fiction that could have existed prior to notions of the value of evidence instead of divination, investigation instead of accusation, trial instead of torture—all working within a justice system that at least made gestures toward fairness. The fictional detective was a modern character for a busily changing era, a kind of scientist relying upon reason as a guide through the age-old battles of violence and crime.

CHAPTER 16

How Do You Know That?

As to work which is unconsciously imitative, it is not to be expected
that a man's style and mode of treatment should spring fully formed
from his own brain.

—ARTHUR CONAN DOYLE, "PREFACE,"
THE ADVENTURES OF SHERLOCK HOLMES

Between "The Murders in the Rue Morgue" and Arthur's decision to
write a detective story, other writers followed Poe in the footsteps of
the prophet Daniel and the philosopher Zadig. Some followed Poe's
lead into a new kind of crime story. But one, like Voltaire and the unnamed
author of the biblical saga, wrote a similarly observant character into a
different kind of tale.

Alexandre Dumas *père* did not write detective stories. After beginning his
career as a dramatist, he wrote a series of novels about Marie Antoinette, many
other novels, essays and articles on contemporary topics, an encyclopedia of
gastronomy, and volumes recounting his travels to Florence, Switzerland, and
elsewhere. By Arthur's time, however, his most renowned contribution to
literature was the trilogy nicknamed the d'Artagnan Romances.

The first of these rousing adventure novels set in sixteenth-century
France, *The Three Musketeers*, appeared in 1844, and a sequel, *Twenty Years
After*, was published the following year. Then, a century after Voltaire put
the observant Zadig through his adventures in observation and deduction,
Dumas assigned the same role to d'Artagnan. A mammoth, 268-chapter
third installment, titled *The Vicomte of Bragelonne: Ten Years Later*, appeared

in installments between 1847 and 1850. The sprawling narrative included the entire adventure later entitled *The Man in the Iron Mask*. And it featured memorable scenes of d'Artagnan working as a detective.

For the creation of his most famous Musketeer, Dumas had been inspired by the adventures of the real-life Charles Ogier de Batz de Castelmore, the actual Comte d'Artagnan—or rather by the version of d'Artagnan who swaggered through a semi-fictional memoir published in 1700. Although Dumas was interested in the real-life crime and intrigue surrounding him in mid-nineteenth-century France, in writing some scenes of *The Vicomte of Bragelonne* he was clearly paying tribute to his revered Voltaire. Zadig's example hovers over d'Artagnan's every move.

In his scenes of d'Artagnan as detective, moreover, Dumas may have been influenced by Auguste Dupin. In 1846, the year before *The Vicomte* began monthly serialization, a French translation of Poe's "Murders in the Rue Morgue" was published in three installments in the Paris newspaper *La Quotidienne*. "Un meurtre sans exemple dans les fastes de la justice" ("A murder unprecedented in the records of justice") appeared anonymously, with not only a new title but both place and character names altered—and with Auguste Dupin transformed into Henry Bernier. But substantially the story was the same. There were no international copyright laws, so translating an American story without crediting its original author was not illegal.

Indeed, four months later a rival newspaper, *Le Commerce*, ran a separate anonymous translation, much shorter than the first, entitled "Une sanglante énigma" ("A bloody mystery"). When the author of the latter story was accused of plagiarizing the former, he replied, "It is not in *La Quotidienne* but in the stories of E. Poe, an American scholar, that I took . . . the central idea of the story." One result of this piracy was a great deal more notice for Poe than would have been the case otherwise. Following this flurry of attention, however, Poe did not become truly well-known in France until after the poet Charles Baudelaire began translating stories and a few poems in 1848, with the majority following after 1852.

In the later pages of Dumas's *Vicomte de Bragelonne*, the arrogant swordsman d'Artagnan performs his detective work when sent by Louis XIV to confirm or refute a minister's account of an alleged hunting accident. "You will, therefore, go there, and will examine the locality very carefully," commands the king. "A man has been wounded there, and you will find a horse lying dead. You will tell me what your opinion is upon the whole affair."

When d'Artagnan reports to the king after his investigation, he resurrects the participants' actions in preternatural detail. "The weather was very well adapted for investigations of the character I have just made," he reports, "it has been raining this evening, and the roads were wet and muddy—"

"Well, the result, M. d'Artagnan?"

The specifics d'Artagnan reveals naturally impress the king with his perception: "One of the riders was more impatient than the other, for the footprints of the one were invariably in advance of the other about half a horse's length . . . His horse pawed the ground, which proves that his attention was so taken up by listening that he let the bridle fall from his hand . . . The one who had remained stationary traversed the Rond-point at a gallop, about two-thirds of its length, thinking that by this means he would gain upon his opponent; but the latter had followed the circumference of the wood."

Some particulars Dumas drew straight from Voltaire.

"He who followed the circumference of the wood was mounted on a black horse."

"How do you know that?" demands the king.

"I found a few hairs of his tail among the brambles which bordered the sides of the ditch . . . The horse of the cavalier who rode at full speed was killed on the spot."

"How do you know that?"

"The cavalier had not time even to throw himself off his horse, and so fell with it. I observed the impression of his leg, which, with a great effort, he was enabled to extricate from under the horse. The spur, pressed down by the weight of the animal, had plowed up the ground . . . Sire, while the dismounted rider was extricating himself from his horse, the other was reloading his pistol. Only, he was much agitated while he was loading it, and his hand trembled greatly."

"How do you know that?"

"Half the charge fell to the ground, and he threw the ramrod aside, not having time to replace it in the pistol."

"Monsieur d'Artagnan, this is marvellous you tell me."

"It is only close observation, sire, and the commonest highwayman could tell as much."

During Arthur's youth, Daniel, Zadig, and d'Artagnan were well-known figures in the popular imagination. The Bible was still the primary source of European society's accepted myths; Voltaire was read by most literate Europeans; and Dumas was one of the most popular novelists of the nineteenth century. Thus, in 1880, when Arthur was nearing the end of medical school and adventuring aboard the *Hope*, the August issue of *Popular Science Monthly* ran a thoughtful essay by Thomas Huxley entitled "On the Method of Zadig: Retrospective Prophecy as a Function of Science," and expected that its readers would understand the analogy and the reason for it.

Arthur admired Huxley. A renowned natural scientist and educator who had earned the nickname of "Darwin's Bulldog" for his eloquent defense of his friend Charles Darwin's ideas about natural selection and nature's slow change over time, Huxley explored in this essay the idea that scientists were, in a sense, prophets looking into the past rather than the future. Their methods might at first make their deductions look as mysterious as soothsaying—but only until those methods were explained and the evidence examined. "The foreteller," Huxley argued,

> asserts that, at some future time, a properly situated observer will witness certain events; the clairvoyant declares that, at this present time, certain things are to be witnessed a thousand miles away; the retrospective prophet (would that there were such a word as "backteller"!) affirms that, so many hours or years ago, such and such things were to be seen. In all these cases it is only the relation to time which alters—the process of divination beyond the limits of possible direct knowledge remains the same.

Born in 1859, the year that finally saw publication of Charles Darwin's long-gestated masterpiece, *On the Origin of Species*, Arthur had grown up amid the nineteenth century's revolutionary scientific thinking about the interpretation of nature—that the earth itself hoarded hard evidence that defied and ultimately might supplant written revelation. At the University of Edinburgh he had been surrounded by respectful discussion of such evidence-based thinking. Although Joseph Bell was a devout Christian, his teaching of diagnostics had relied entirely upon the interpretation of factual clues.

In Arthur's imagination, Bell's legacy fit in well with such figures as Zadig, d'Artagnan, and Dupin. But Bell possessed a trait that the others did not. He was dramatic, theatrical proof that seeming clairvoyance beyond the limits of direct knowledge was possible in the real world. It was not fantasy. And unlike Daniel and Zadig, Dr. Bell had practiced his wizardry not on kings but on ordinary human beings—soldiers, fishwives, street urchins—and, like the retrospective prophets of science, he had divined their past, their recent actions, even their character. Arthur had witnessed it with his own eyes.

CHAPTER 17

Games of Chess, Played with Live Pieces

These games of chess, played with live pieces, are played before small audiences, and are chronicled nowhere. The interest of the game supports the player. Its results are enough for justice.

—CHARLES DICKENS, "THE DETECTIVE POLICE"

Although Poe wrote detective stories as logical fantasies, he was conjuring his detective in a new era. Unlike ancient biblical prophets and fictional Babylonian philosophers, Dupin deciphered clues amid an established network of metropolitan police. During the century prior to Arthur's birth, the complex task of keeping the civil peace may have evolved more slowly than some other aspects of the social contract, but it did see a halting progression forward. The royal promise of relative security that had once been known in England as the "king's peace" had long since failed to meet the needs of a burgeoning society. Efficient policing required that both officers and detectives earn the trust of the public. Partnership between police and citizenry could evolve only through familiarity and some measure of respect.

Before the mid-eighteenth century, victims of misdeeds in England had recourse to few methods of justice or recompense. People accused of a crime might find themselves pursued by a bounty hunter, a fierce professional perhaps paid by bail bondsmen. Inhabiting the shadow of the law alongside bounty hunters were characters called thief-takers, who were usually in the employ of those few victims who could afford to pay for pursuit or retribution. Naturally such an arrangement lent itself to chicanery. Some thief-takers, for example, acted clandestinely as go-betweens, returning to their owner goods that had been stolen by the thief-taker's own secret partner.

In 1749, real-life crime detection and literature began the collaboration whose fruits surrounded Arthur as he turned his hand to detective fiction. In that year, almost a century before Poe's "Murders in the Rue Morgue," Englishman Henry Fielding saw publication of his picaresque novel *Tom Jones*. An ambitious and industrious man who worked from a Bow Street office rather than an ivory tower, Fielding was also chief magistrate of London. In the same year he launched an organization soon called the Bow Street Runners.

Although in some respects the Runners were more like private detectives than like police officers, they were in many ways the first modern police force. They were paid out of allocated government funds, for example, a kind of salary that divided them from their juridical ancestors. Originally there were only eight. Dashing about with official backing, they arrested offenders, served subpoenas and other writs, tracked bail jumpers. Attracting both favorable and critical attention in the press, the Runners helped prepare the English public for the idea of an organized metropolitan police.

What was needed was an official police department—despite such an institution's own fertile ground for corruption—to respond to crimes and to capture criminals. Not until a third of the way through the next century, however, did a new law create a metropolitan police force. In 1829, eight years before Victoria became queen and thirty years before the birth of Arthur Conan Doyle, the popular Home Secretary Robert Peel succeeded in getting Parliamentary approval for his proposed Metropolitan Police Act. He insisted that if Parliament wanted him to prevent crime rather than to merely track perpetrators, they must support this innovation. A guarantee of arrest, he argued, was a stronger crime preventive than severity of punishment—on, he might have added, those rare occasions when arrest actually followed. The police act replaced the antique plexus of watchmen, parish constables, thief-takers, and Bow Street Runners with a reasonably organized force.

Robert Peel's new police officers were nicknamed "bobbies" in England and "peelers" in Ireland. Peel had earned his reputation while launching the Royal Irish Constabulary during his tenure as Chief Secretary for Ireland, in which his job was to maintain "order"—as defined by the English occupying force. Within a decade of the bobbies' founding, the Bow Street Runners were gone.

Another factor nudging fiction writers toward detective stories were the popular tales and books claiming to be memoirs of real-life investigators. In 1811 Eugène François Vidocq, a French criminal turned policeman, founded the Brigade de la Sûreté, a civil police and detective bureau. Soon Napoleon Bonaparte turned the Sûreté into a national police force. A tireless self-promoter, Vidocq starred in ghosted memoirs detailing his adventures, beginning in 1828, then in openly fictionalized accounts capitalizing upon his notoriety. The public thrilled to his pursuit of criminals, his undercover operations in disguise, and his accounts of training other agents who, like himself, wanted to leave behind a life of crime and embrace law enforcement.

But Vidocq's secret-police activities and sometimes violent methods resulted in scandal, a reorganization of the Sûreté, and ultimately his own resignation. In 1833 he founded the first known private inquiry agency, which also provided bodyguards and other security officers. Meanwhile, the books about him had inspired authors such as Honoré de Balzac and Victor Hugo, both of whom wrote often about criminal activities, and would later serve as models for Émile Gaboriau in France and Anna Katharine Green in the United States.

Soon London saw a bold new figure striding down the street. These officers were a tough-looking lot—tall, sturdy, dressed in blue top hat and tailcoat. This modest uniform was intended to make them look as different as possible from the red-coated and metal-helmeted soldiers who had often served as military police on the streets. Bobbies were armed with only a wooden truncheon and a pair of handcuffs. At first they carried a wooden rattle to summon other officers, but it turned out to be too cumbersome and not loud enough. A whistle replaced it.

But bobbies were there to prevent crimes or to respond to them immediately, not to decipher clues and investigate the crimes discovered or interrupted by uniformed officers. Not until the 1830s, after uniformed bobbies began patrolling streets, did the word *detective* even appear. The English word *detect*, meaning to catch or discover someone in the act of committing a crime, dates from the first half of the fifteenth century in English, and derived from the Latin *detegere*, meaning "to uncover." The new meaning described a new job. A centralized police force, charged with preventing and responding to crime, required a division assigned to solve crimes and hunt down their perpetrators—a detective bureau, including plainclothes detectives who could operate in disguise or at least without uniforms announcing their identity before they could even strike up a conversation with a wary publican.

The department's need to work incognito at times inspired fears that in reality this new creation, the detective, was merely a government spy authorized to mingle with and entrap respectable citizens. Vidocq's reputation for secret-police activity had accompanied his reputation for crime-solving across the Channel, and English newspaper readers were quite familiar with the genuine risks of government spying. Not until 1842, following the public outcry over a scandalous case in London that helped create a more welcoming political atmosphere for it, did Scotland Yard create the Criminal Investigation Department. At first it comprised only two inspectors and six sergeants.

Not surprisingly, intelligence of the logical, deductive, fictional kind was not the most eagerly sought trait for detectives in the real world. When police administrators surveyed the uniformed ranks for potential detectives, they first looked for courage, strength, and fortitude. They demanded familiarity with the dark city streets and their teeming crowds—from the hardworking ironmongers, haberdashers, and other shop owners to the "swell mob" of dandified pickpockets, the skilled cracksmen, the bludgers, the squealers and finks, the opportunistic mutcher lifting tuppence from a drunk. Arthur knew enough about the world, and had read enough real-life accounts of crime, to know that his intellectual detective would need extensive experience of the criminal underworld.

The first officers to sign up for detective work included an enterprising young man named Charles Field, who soon rose through the ranks to become inspector at the Woolwich Dockyards and finally chief of the Detective Branch before he retired in 1852. The English journalist George Augustus Sala described Field as "clean-shaven, farmer-like." His ordinariness in dress and mien were calculated professional attributes.

Charles Dickens, at the height of his fame and influence, met and admired Field and soon wrote articles about him for his periodical *Household Words*—articles that helped promote the concept of vigilant police detectives in the public imagination, including a vivid and atmospheric tribute entitled "On Duty with Inspector Field." The word *detective* was still unfamiliar enough in 1850 for Dickens to wrap it in quotation marks in the title of his first article on these innovators, "Three 'Detective' Anecdotes." But soon the term flourished in the thriving daily, weekly, and monthly periodicals.

In an essay, "The Detective Police," Dickens, with typical enthusiasm and impatience for change, apostrophized the new detectives by contrasting his vision of them with his memory of their predecessors. "We are not by any means devout believers in the old Bow Street Police," he wrote, despite his comical but rather admiring portrait of them in his second novel, *Oliver Twist*.

> To say the truth, we think there was a vast amount of humbug about those worthies. Apart from many of them being men of very indifferent character, and far too much in the habit of consorting with thieves and the like, they never lost a public occasion of jobbing and trading in mystery and making the most of themselves. Continually puffed besides by incompetent magistrates anxious to conceal their own deficiencies, and hand-in-glove with the penny-a-liners of that time, they became a sort of superstition. Although as a Preventive Police they were utterly ineffective, and as a Detective Police were very loose and uncertain in their operations, they remain with some people a superstition to the present day.
>
> On the other hand, the Detective Force organised since the establishment of the existing Police, is so well chosen and trained, proceeds so systematically and quietly, does its business in such a workmanlike manner, and is always so calmly and steadily engaged in the service of the public, that the public really do not know enough of it, to know a tithe of its usefulness . . .
>
> Such are the curious coincidences and such is the peculiar ability, always sharpening and being improved by practice, and always adapting itself to every variety of circumstances, and opposing itself to every new device that perverted ingenuity can invent, for which this important social branch of the public service is remarkable! For ever on the watch, with their wits stretched to the utmost, these officers have, from day to day and year to year, to set themselves against every novelty of trickery and dexterity that the combined imaginations of all the lawless rascals in England can devise, and to keep pace with every such invention that comes out . . .

A frequent writer for *Household Words*, George Augustus Sala, remembered in his autobiography that Dickens was seldom heard discussing higher literature or indeed intellectually ambitious art of any kind. "What he liked to talk about was the latest new piece at the theatres, the latest exciting trial or police case, the latest social craze or social swindle, and especially the latest murder and the newest thing in ghosts." Dickens's worshipful applause for detectives did not escape Sala's notice. "Dickens had a curious and almost morbid partiality for communing with and entertaining police officers," he wrote. This public approbation may have also had a pleasing incidental effect. "Any of the Detective men will do anything for me," Dickens wrote to Bulwer Lytton in 1851.

One of Charles Field's colleagues, Inspector Jonathan "Jack" Whicher, became even better known. (Dickens disguised him as Witchem in some admiring articles, in which he referred to Field as Wield.) Among the first eight members of the new Detective Branch that Scotland Yard formed in 1842, Whicher soon earned the respect of his colleagues, one of whom later dubbed him "the prince of detectives." Like most successful detectives, he strove for near invisibility. His smallpox scars did not make him stand out because many people wore such a visible medical history.

Whicher achieved renown, and helped the public begin to accept the notion of professional investigators making their way through the populace without uniforms. Although he was criticized at times, he was applauded, and steadily promoted, for his successes—from capturing the valet who stole Leonardo da Vinci's *Virgin and Child* and other paintings in 1856 to the scandalous murder at Road Hill House in 1860. The always bloodthirsty national press kept hounding the police to solve the brutal killing of a small boy, Francis Saville Kent, whose corpse was found in a privy just outside his family home with his throat slashed. Against public opinion and departmental doubts—both of which helped to damage his reputation for some time—Whicher persisted in his conclusion that the boy had been murdered by his sixteen-year-old half sister, Constance Kent. Eventually she confessed and Whicher was vindicated, leading to a growing conviction that he was all but infallible.

Apparently Dickens's assistant editor on the monthly periodical *Household Words*, Henry Wills, wrote the first public description of an actual police detective. In an article entitled "The Modern Science of Thief-Taking," Wills described Whicher—in his first appearance under the alias Witchem—as he first met him on the stairs at a public gathering, during which the detective witnessed dismay on the faces of those miscreants who recognized their official nemesis despite his undistinguished face.

"On the mat at the stair-foot there stands a plain, honest-looking fellow, with nothing formidable in his appearance, or dreadful in his countenance; but the effect of this apparition . . . is remarkable . . . You never saw such a change as he causes, when he places his knuckles on the edge of the table, and looks at the diners *seriatim*." With cautious mutual respect, Whicher and the thieves recognized each other.

Whicher calmly ordered a Frenchmen and three others to leave London. They agreed immediately to do so, and he accompanied them to the train station. Afterward, as Wills walked on the platform with him, Whicher explained that the criminals were members of "a crack school of swell-mobsmen," meaning a gang of petty thieves—pickpockets and burglars.

From its title to its closing, Wills's article furthered detectives' growing reputation as heroic figures who acquired power over criminals through detailed knowledge of them. Reinvented as modern and scientific, thief-taking was presented as a combination of observation, evidence, and courage—an idealized image of science in the pursuit of justice.

Dickens and Wills were quick to praise the virtues of these new public servants, and then quick to exploit their encounters with them. As a consequence of his acquaintance with Dickens, Inspector Field helped inspire the first detective in a literary novel—Inspector Bucket, "a detective officer," in Dickens's 1852 novel *Bleak House*. Built around a long-running legal battle over discrepancies in conflicting wills—the case of Jarndyce and Jarndyce progressing with glacial slowness through the Courts of Chancery—the novel is saturated with images of fog and muck. Within the depraved cosmos of *Bleak House*, the kindhearted Inspector Bucket serves as a moral figure, almost heroic, as he searches for a murderer and then for the missing Lady Dedlock. Dickens also employed his detective as a narrative wild card—a man who may reenter the story at any point, and who will materialize in a room without even a creak in the floorboards. Omniscient as well as omnipresent, he has Dickens's own legendary photographic gaze: "He looks at Mr. Snagsby as if he were going to take his portrait."

Some years after Dickens invented Inspector Bucket, his friend and colleague Wilkie Collins made a detective one of the major characters in his 1868 novel *The Moonstone*. Ever since his 1859 success *The Woman in White*, Collins had been almost as famous as Dickens. Other popular books had followed—*No Name, Armadale,* and then *The Moonstone*. Many more works came from his busy pen. Collins also wrote a memorable story that served as a transition between earlier forms of fiction and detective stories. Usually republished as "Anne Rodway's Diary," but originally published in 1856 under a different title as part of a series, it featured a smart and resourceful young woman who must investigate injustice.

Collins's writing demonstrated unusual sympathy for female characters and also for the poor, even the drug-addicted poor. His account in *The Moonstone* of the delusory effects of opium grew out of his personal experience. He became addicted to laudanum to lessen the pain of his "rheumatic gout," a form of arthritis, and even wrote of his own paranoid hallucinations, including the existence of a "ghost Wilkie" who at times shadowed his every move.

The Moonstone, however, was more than a sensation novel. Intelligent, witty, complexly plotted, narrated by several different characters with varying perceptions of the events they had witnessed, it proved hugely successful. The plot revolves around the titular gem, a diamond stolen in India—long before the story opens—from the head of a sacred statue of Chandra, the Hindu god of the moon. In a supernatural story, the god would have exacted revenge upon the heathens. In a story of suspense and detection, however, the guilty human beings torment themselves and others without divine intervention.

Like Dickens, Collins indicated his detective's perception with a scientific gaze. He made Sergeant Cuff a less intimidating character overall than Inspector Bucket, although one who had a distinctly forbidding demeanor when meeting strangers:

> When the time came for the Sergeant's arrival, I went down to the gate to look out for him.
>
> A fly from the railway drove up as I reached the lodge; and out got a grizzled, elderly man, so miserably lean that he looked as if he had not got an ounce of flesh on his bones in any part of him. He was dressed all in decent black, with a white cravat round his neck. His face was as sharp as a hatchet, and the skin of it was as yellow and dry and withered as an autumn leaf. His eyes, of a steely light grey, had a very disconcerting trick, when they encountered your eyes, of looking as if they expected something more from you than you were aware of yourself. His walk was soft; his voice was melancholy; his long lanky fingers were hooked like claws. He might have been a parson, or an undertaker—or anything else you like, except what he really was. A . . . less comforting officer to look at, for a family in distress, I defy you to discover, search where you may.

Inspired by actual police officers they had known, Charles Dickens and Wilkie Collins used the factual to help them conjure the fictional. Eccentric and observant men themselves, they showered quirks and insight upon their imaginary detectives, and in doing so made them memorable beyond the boundaries of *Bleak House* and *The Moonstone.* But they did not assign either Inspector Bucket or Sergeant Cuff central roles in their respective novels. The first novelist to make a logical, attentive detective into his central character was a Frenchman who had been inspired in part by a fictional Frenchman created by an American writer. As Arthur liked to point out, many roads in the development of crime fiction lead back to Edgar Allan Poe.

Poe's expeditions into fantasy and the macabre drew more attention than his detective puzzles, perhaps in part because supernatural stories were the oldest form of fiction and detective stories the newest. For a quarter century after "The Murders in the Rue Morgue" appeared in 1841, in fact, what Poe called his "tales of ratiocination" seems to have inspired few disciples in the crime genre. But eventually one writer responded enthusiastically to Poe's stories about an eagle-eyed amateur detective: the Frenchman Émile Gaboriau. Inspired also by the real-life policeman Vidocq, as well as by the novels of his countrymen Honoré de Balzac and Victor Hugo—which often dealt with crime and criminals—Gaboriau introduced a policeman referred to by his colleagues as Monsieur Lecoq, who appeared in several subsequent novels. In his modest debut in 1866, when Arthur was seven, Lecoq appeared as a relatively minor character in *L'Affaire Lerouge* (usually translated into English as *The Widow Lerouge* or *The Lerouge Case*), which featured an amateur detective named Père Tabaret. Lecoq rose to the starring role six years later with a novel named after him. Promoted all over Paris with mysterious posters bearing only the title to build up advance interest, *Monsieur Lecoq* was an immediate sensation, and soon Gaboriau was a household name. Gaboriau knew how to keep readers turning pages, and he knew how to promote his work. Arthur greatly enjoyed the adventures of Monsieur Lecoq, noting later, "Gaboriau had rather attracted me by the neat dovetailing of his plots."

After years in the French cavalry, Gaboriau began the best possible training for a thriller writer. He served as secretary to the dramatist and novelist Paul Féval, who wrote everything from swashbucklers to vampire stories. Féval kept Gaboriau researching forensic details in morgues and among the offices of the Sûreté. In an odd tribute, Gaboriau later swiped the nickname of the villain in one of Féval's novels, Lecoq (the Rooster), and gave it to his own protagonist—himself a criminal turned policeman, like Eugène François Vidocq.

Although he was one of many writers influenced by the "memoirs" of Vidocq, Gaboriau was too good a writer to merely imitate Vidocq, Poe, or anyone else. His stylish and entertaining novels helped create the police procedural and influenced many later writers such as Anna Katharine Green. Gaboriau excelled at planting clues and strewing red herrings, but he was just as interested in the investigative routine employed by his police detectives. He admired patient legwork and careful interrogation. He also spent more time than many of his later colleagues in bringing his characters to life, fleshing them out as individuals—rich in quirks and contradictions—and in conjuring the boulevards and countryside of France through which they make their cautious way. His dialogue was lively and his descriptions sparkled. He conjured rural fields and police stations, backstreet pubs and palaces.

Gaboriau tended to bifurcate his novels into detective story and Gothic family drama. In the first part a crime is discovered, an investigation carried out, and a culprit revealed; in the second part, the detective tends to vanish for a time while the author reveals the tangled history of mistakes and cruelties that led to the murder. At times they read like two related books joined together, not always the most compelling of structures. Anna Katharine Green, whose books clearly show Gaboriau's influence, sometimes used this approach. Arthur enjoyed this kind of two-part story and absorbed it as a standard approach to writing thrillers.

All around Arthur, in medical school and in his wide-ranging extracurricular reading, in newspapers and magazines and books, he saw evidence that scientists were a kind of detective. Detective-minded Joe Bell was a scientist to the core. But only Gaboriau had demonstrated that a detective—busily noting and analyzing details, as well as building a mental and physical library of criminal cases—needs to be a kind of scientist.

Part 3

Mr. Holmes and Dr. Watson

No writer is ever absolutely original. He always joins at some point on to that old tree of which he is a branch.

—ARTHUR CONAN DOYLE, *MEMORIES AND ADVENTURES*W

CHAPTER 18

Dr. Sacker and Mr. Hope

His results, brought about by the very soul and essence of method, have, in truth, the whole air of intuition.

—EDGAR ALLAN POE, "THE MURDERS IN THE RUE MORGUE"

A *tangled skein,*" Arthur scribbled in one of his cheap red marbled notebooks. He was considering possible titles and images for the detective novel that had begun to grow in his imagination. For this note he may have been recalling a prominent image in Émile Gaboriau's 1867 novel *The Mystery of Orcival*, featuring Monsieur Lecoq. In one passage Gaboriau describes an investigator's thoughts: "The difficulty is to seize at the beginning, in the entangled skein, the main thread, which must lead to the truth through all the mazes, the ruses, silence, falsehoods of the guilty." It had been translated into English in 1871, only two years before Gaboriau's death; Arthur was twelve at the time.

Later Arthur crossed out *A Tangled Skein* and replaced it with the title *A Study in Scarlet*, which he explained in Chapter 4. "I must thank you for it all," says Holmes to Watson, who persuaded him to look into the mystery. "I might not have gone but for you, and so have missed the finest study I ever came across: a study in scarlet, eh? Why shouldn't we use a little art jargon. There's the scarlet thread of murder running through the colourless skein of life, and our duty is to unravel it, and isolate it, and expose every inch of it."

Holmes's remark still echoed Gaboriau. In setting this new title above his melodrama, however, Arthur seemed to be aiming for a more artistic tone than the usual blood and thunder of the thriller field. A study was an artist's preliminary sketch, or in literature a thoughtful survey. In using the term in a finished work, united with a particular color, Arthur aligned himself with the Aesthetic movement—with writers and critics such as Walter Pater and the young Oscar Wilde. Pater's 1873 *Studies in the History of the Renaissance* was considered a sacred text of Aestheticism, and the notoriously decadent Algernon Charles Swinburne had published in 1880 a book entitled *Studies in Song*. *L'art pour l'art* was the unofficial group's motto, "art for art's sake," implying that art was divorced from the burden of moral education that had bowed its back through centuries. One of the best-known painters among the Aesthetics was James Abbott McNeill Whistler, American-born but long settled in London, who was famous for works such as his 1862 painting "Symphony in White, No. 1: The White Girl," and his 1871 portrait of his mother titled "Arrangement in Grey and Black, No. 1." Thus the title *A Study in Scarlet* lent Arthur's novel an artsy frisson of vice.

From the very first, Arthur thought in scenes. Under the title he wrote in his notes,

> *The terrified woman rushing up to the cabman. The two going in search of a policeman. John Reeves had been 7 years in the force, John Reeves went back with them.*

Soon memories of Joe Bell at Edinburgh played like a stage drama across Arthur's imagination. He remembered his aquiline face, his sharp, perceptive gaze. He imagined that if a keen observer à la Dr. Bell applied himself to crime instead of to medicine, he would represent an almost invincible combination of perception and knowledge—at least in the stage-managed world of popular fiction.

Real-world crime detection was more haphazard and erratic. Forensics encountered resistance from tradition, like the rest of science. One of the most dramatic advances in criminal investigation—the detection of previously overlooked fingerprints and their value as a form of identification—had been initiated in India in the 1850s. But a systematic approach for it had been proposed only as recently as 1880, by a Scottish surgeon named Henry Faulds. In 1886, the year that Arthur wrote *A Study in Scarlet*, Faulds presented his idea to London's police department—which dismissed it as far-fetched and impractical.

But as yet Arthur had little interest in actual criminal investigation. Instead he began to envision his detective as a kind of awe-inspiring genius who dazzled a befuddled world with his insight. Such an omniscient character would sound insufferably smug narrating his own triumphs, however, and with access to his thoughts a reader might too soon perceive the puzzle pieces coming together. Thus, like Poe's Dupin, he would need a Boswell. Arthur was transforming the doctor who inspired him into a detective, and he made this assistant into a physician. The scientific training and humanitarian outlook of medicine shaped Arthur's outlook on many topics.

On another page he wrote at the top, *Study in Scarlet*. Below this new title he listed his main characters, beginning with a name for the physician who would narrate: *Ormond Sacker* [or Secker]—*from Sudan*. The given name Ormond probably occurred to Arthur because of the Great Ormond Street Hospital, near the British Museum in Bloomsbury. Founded in the early 1850s as the Hospital for Sick Children—the first such institution in England—it had grown from a mere ten beds to a major center well-known to physicians and medical students across the nation. Charles Dickens was an important early promoter.

The surname Sacker or Secker may have come from a small lane called Secker Street behind St. John's Church near London's other important center for helping the unprotected: Royal Waterloo Hospital for Children and Women. Perhaps Arthur picked up several names for his novel from a single glance at a London map or a stroll around this neighborhood; at times he visited relatives and friends in the city and always happily explored. On the other side of the Royal Waterloo from Secker Street was Stamford Street, and a young man named Stamford became the second person to show up in the novel.

Arthur was a passionate walker and often tramped the streets of Southsea or farther across Portsmouth, with or without his brother, Innes. Only a block from his home on Elm Grove was the parallel Belmont Street, and therein lived one William Rance. Arthur may well have known Rance or seen his name, because he assigned this uncommon name to the police constable who had originally appeared in his notes as John Reeves. Other names in *A Study in Scarlet* may have derived from neighborhood strolls. Madame Charpentier, proprietor of a boardinghouse in the novel, may have owed her name to Arthur's neighbor Ernest G. Charpentier. Farther down Elm Grove from Bush Villas was Sunnyside, the home of one James Cowper, whose surname would adorn a Mormon character.

Arthur gave one of the police inspectors a French surname that was quite uncommon in England—Lestrade. This name appears not once in London directories of the period. Probably Arthur was remembering Joseph Alexandre Lestrade, a fellow alumnus of both Stonyhurst and the University of Edinburgh, who received his Bachelor of Medicine and Master of Surgery degrees in 1883; they would have had many reasons to know each other at university.

He assigned a less unusual name, Gregson, to the other inspector, perhaps derived from a crusading missionary and temperance advocate, the Reverend J. Gelsen Gregson, who was a distinguished member of the Baptist church in Elm Grove, close by Arthur's flat in Bush Villas. In 1882, the year that Arthur moved to Southsea, Gregson published a memoir of his missionary work in the Afghan War, *Through the Khyber Pass to Sherpore Camp and Cabul*; its preface was dated from Southsea. It was precisely the kind of book to which Arthur was drawn. Gregson, the optimistic founder of the Soldiers' Total Abstinence Association, retired to Southsea in 1886, the year that Arthur wrote *A Study in Scarlet*.

In identifying his detective, Arthur did not want to use a Dickensian kind of moniker that implied character—not "Mr. Sharps or Mr. Ferrets," he said later. Yet he yearned for something unusual. He scrawled lists, considering various combinations of given names and surnames, including Sherrington Hope.

Finally he settled upon Holmes as his detective's surname, likely because of his and his family's fondness for the writings of Oliver Wendell Holmes. But Holmes was also a name one often saw around England. It was particularly associated with London in the minds of many, because of the popular volume *Holmes's Great Metropolis: or, Views and History of London in the Nineteenth Century*, published in 1851, the year of the Crystal Palace exhibition. Sherrington evolved into Sherrinford, and Arthur's new hero was to be Sherrinford Holmes.

Reserved, wrote Arthur about his protagonist in his red notebook. —*Sleepy eyed young man—philosopher*. He assigned him a trait reminiscent of a Poe character: *collector of rare Violins*, adding, *An Amati*, designating the Italian family of violin-makers considered to rank with the Stradivari and Bergonzi families.

Thinking of Dr. Bell, Arthur gave Holmes "sharp and piercing" gray eyes and a thin nose that lent his face an aquiline vigilance. There, however, the physical resemblance ended. Arthur envisioned a hero more physically impressive than short, limping Bell—a square-jawed, dark-browed man, over six feet tall and lean as a whippet. In the novel, he radiates confidence and vigor. When Watson meets him, Holmes's hands, stained with ink and laboratory chemicals, offer a surprisingly strong handshake. But they can manipulate scientific instruments with a delicate touch.

Arthur thought of another useful detail—he had a store of such mental images from his medical school days in Edinburgh—and wrote "chemical laboratory." As for "young man," Arthur thought of both Watson and Holmes as roughly his own age. He was twenty-seven in early 1886.

But the given name Sherrinford did not satisfy Arthur. He considered others. Besides his Stonyhurst classmate Patrick Sherlock, and the William Sherlock who cavorted through Macaulay's *History of England*, and fictional characters such as Carmel Sherlock in Sheridan Le Fanu's novel *A Lost Name*, Arthur must have also encountered the name Sherlock in the context of crime-solving. During his time in medical school in Edinburgh, London's metropolitan police force already included one Chief Inspector William Sherlock of Division L in Lambeth, who was often mentioned in British newspapers amid their extensive reports of crime and investigations. The adventures of Sherlock were reported in *The Times* and *The Home Chronicler*, as well as in other periodicals. The 1881 census listed Inspector Sherlock as stationed at Kennington Road in Lambeth. In February 1881, *The Portsmouth Evening News* reported a rowdy inquest into a murder that had occurred at Chatham in northern Kent. Chief Inspector Sherlock had been sent from London to assist the Chatham authorities in their investigation.

Beginning in 1882, as he settled in Southsea, Arthur read *The Portsmouth Evening News* and other papers religiously, with his usual appetite for news wed to a fresh desire to situate himself within an unknown community. In January 1883, the newspaper reported that a brawl at the Anchor Inn on crime-ridden York Street had resulted in arrests. As a consequence, the paper noted, Inspector Sherlock was in court at Westminster, the area of central London around Parliament on the northern bank of the Thames. In the same week *The Times* reported another of Sherlock's exploits.

The 1881 post office directory listed a second Sherlock in the London police department—a Chief Inspector James Sherlock of Division B in Rochester Row. There was even an Inspector Thomas Holmes—and, in coincidence's nod to Gaboriau, an Inspector John Le Cocq. Arthur may well have consulted this directory. He set his crime scene at "3, Lauriston Gardens, off the Brixton Road," a neighborhood within Division L, and thus under the jurisdiction of Chief Inspector William Sherlock. Although the Brixton Road was a real London thoroughfare, probably Arthur invented Lauriston Gardens as a tribute to his hometown. He could not have walked around Edinburgh without treading Lauriston Street, Lauriston Place, or Lauriston Park.

For reasons that can never be known for certain, the name Sherlock occurred to Arthur as a replacement for Sherrinford. He kept the beloved surname and named his detective Sherlock Holmes.

Along with memorably christening his genius of a detective, Arthur changed the name of his narrator from the dandified-sounding Ormond Sacker to a more prosaic John Watson. For this name, he may have been recalling Dr. Patrick Heron Watson in Edinburgh, or his friend James Watson who lived in Southsea (though he may have met James Watson after creating Holmes). The Conservative solicitor and senior Scottish legal figure William Watson, Baron Watson, received considerable attention in the press, having served as Lord Advocate throughout Arthur's time in Edinburgh, and afterward as Lord of Appeal in Ordinary. Or perhaps Arthur was influenced by the fame of Sir Thomas Watson, whose death in late 1882 drew adulatory attention to the ninety-year-old doctor. A former president of the Royal College of Physicians, as well as physician-in-ordinary to Queen Victoria, Watson was considered a noble embodiment of Arthur's profession. Arthur may have heard of Watson as early as his medical school days, because the famed physician had also studied in Edinburgh. And Arthur could not have missed laudatory obituaries for Watson in the *British Medical Journal*, *The Lancet*, and numerous newspapers, including *The Times*, which called Watson "eminent." Clearly Arthur had read Sir Thomas Watson's writings. In a later Sherlock Holmes story, he borrowed a memorable image from the 1843 tome *Lectures on the Principles and Practice of Physic*, in which the real-life Watson remembered an old man who was said to be able to chalk a billiard cue with his gouty knuckles. Wherever he got the name, Arthur's point seems to have been that "John Watson" sounded like an ordinary Englishman. He would provide a mundane, level-headed, John Bull view of the detective's genius and foibles.

Poe had revealed almost nothing about his nameless narrator, who exists primarily to marvel over Dupin's abilities and quirks; and in Gaboriau's novels, Lecoq's mentor and occasional companion Père Tabaret did not narrate the events. Arthur had bigger plans for his detective's sidekick. Eventually he even parenthetically subtitled *A Study in Scarlet* "Being a Reprint from the Reminiscences of John H. Watson, M.D., Late of the Army Medical Department," and began it with a brief sketch of Dr. Watson's life prior to the fateful meeting with Mr. Holmes.

Arthur would have read often in Garrod's *Materia* about University College in London. Known earlier as London University and later as the

University of London, it was where Garrod taught. It was also where Ringer and Murrell, authors of the gelseminum series in *The Lancet* that seems to have prompted Arthur's dangerous self-poisoning in 1879, worked as well. Such associations may have inspired him to associate Dr. Watson with this institution. Arthur wrote that Watson was awarded his Doctor of Medicine degree at University College in 1878, at which time his creator was halfway through medical school. Clearly Arthur envisioned Watson as close to his own age.

Reconsidering Watson's likely military history, Arthur crossed out "Sudan" and wrote "Afghanistan" in his notebook. Although he himself had never served in the military, he envisioned Watson as a wounded veteran, a man likely to be brave and resourceful. The final English defeat of Napoleon at Waterloo in 1815 had left the far-reaching British Empire with no powerful international rivals beyond Russia. Some members of the English military elite worried—unrealistically, it soon turned out—that Russian troops in Asia were inching toward India, which the English famously considered the "jewel in the crown" of the ill-gotten British Empire. The first Afghan War, from 1838 to 1842, had been the opening move in a bloody international chess game between England and Russia to control central Asia. A combined force of British and Indian soldiers invaded Afghanistan in 1838, but during a three-year war were unable to maintain a puppet government and were defeated. From 1878 to 1880, during Arthur's time in medical school, the English again invaded Afghanistan. Despite extensive fighting and attempts at treaties, Afghan troops were ultimately able to repel the aggressors.

Arthur decided to have Watson serve in Candahar, the capital of Afghanistan, with the Fifth Northumberland Fusiliers, a real British infantry regiment. Watson says that he fought in the Battle of Maiwand with the Berkshires, officially called Princess Charlotte of Wales's (Berkshire) Regiment. A village fifty miles northwest of Candahar, Maiwand had been the site of the bloody and mortifying final British defeat in 1880. Arthur was weaving recent history and revived public interest into his story. In 1886, as he wrote *A Study in Scarlet*, a gigantic iron statue of a lion was erected in Reading, Berkshire, the regimental home of the 66th Foot, as a tribute to British soldiers who died at Maiwand.

At the time of the battle, the Berkshires had actually still been called the 66th Foot; like the Northumberlands, they underwent a name change the following year. But Arthur didn't worry about such details. Never one to fret over what he considered irrelevant minutiae, Arthur dashed his pen across the page, summoning idea after idea that he did not bother to confirm as accurate. He assigned Watson the title of assistant surgeon, for example, unaware that it had been eliminated in 1872. In the real British army, in the late 1870s Watson would have been an acting surgeon, within a lieutenant's pay grade. Later Arthur also had Holmes refer offhandedly to "that little thing of Chopin's" that he once heard the Moravian violinist Wilma Norman-Neruda play very well, and he adds, "Tra-la-la-lira-lira-lay." Never mind that Chopin composed no pieces for solo violin and there was no record of Madame Norman-Neruda having ever played Chopin. This was, after all, fiction.

Watson remarks that he has "neither kith nor kin in England, and was therefore as free as air." He "naturally gravitated to London," he says, "that great cesspool into which all the loungers and idlers of the Empire are irresistibly drained." In this attitude too Arthur was echoing Poe's narrator, who remarks, "With sickness of heart, the wanderer will flee back to the polluted Paris as to a less odious because less incongruous sink of pollution." Arthur was still heavily under the influence of his literary ancestor.

Born in 1859 in Edinburgh, Scotland, young Arthur Doyle returned here after boarding school and attended medical school, where he met Joseph Bell—who would, a decade later, serve as Arthur's real-life inspiration for Sherlock Holmes. Here the twelfth-century Castle towers above the Grassmarket, which had been a public trading site for centuries.
UNIVERSITY OF ABERDEEN

Arthur revered and idolized his mother, Irish-born Mary Foley Doyle, who read to the family often and introduced Arthur to French literature. Her husband's intemperance (and later his incarceration) left Mary in charge of the family during Arthur's childhood and early adulthood. This portrait is by her husband's brother, Richard "Dickie" Doyle, an illustrator who achieved greater success than his brother Charles.

Arthur with his father, Charles Doyle. Charles's chaotic drinking lost him his career with Scotland's public Office of Works, his career as an artist, and his role in the Doyle family. Many of Arthur's later stories and novels would feature uncontrollable drunks and men suffering from similar demons. GETTY IMAGES

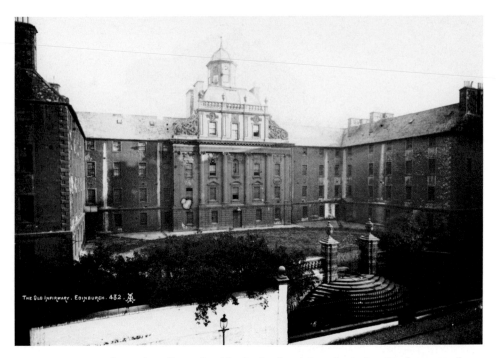

In 1876, upon completing boarding school in England and Austria, Arthur Doyle returned to his hometown and enrolled in medical school at the University of Edinburgh. Some of the classes were held in other venues, such as the Royal Infirmary, where Arthur studied with Joseph Bell. CITY OF EDINBURGH COUNCIL — EDINBURGH LIBRARIES

Joseph Bell, M.D., turned forty in 1877, the year that young Arthur Doyle met him and became his devoted acolyte. Later Bell recalled that Arthur paid close attention to his professor's demonstrations of deduction from small clues, often staying afterward to ask for details and writing them in his notebook.

Arthur Conan Doyle as a young doctor, turning from medical school at the University of Edinburgh toward his own medical practice in England. With his father in institutions for the intemperate and later for the mentally unstable, Arthur keenly felt the family's expectations about his financial prospects. CONAN DOYLE ESTATE LTD.

Bush Villa - Southsea

Arthur standing before his flat at number 1, Bush Villas in Southsea, a residential suburb of Portsmouth, England, on the Channel coast. Here he began his medical practice in 1882 and here he began his serious career as a writer, culminating in his writing of *A Study in Scarlet* in early 1886.

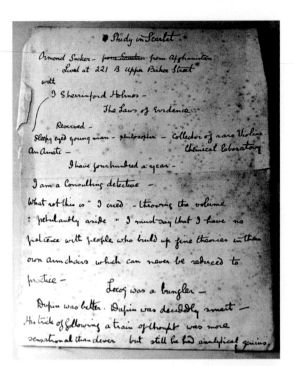

A surviving page of Doyle's early notes, in the planning stage of *A Study in Scarlet*. At this point, he had not yet hit upon the names Sherlock Holmes and John Watson. His characters were Sherrinford Holmes and Ormond Sacker.
GETTY IMAGES

D. H. Friston's dramatic illustration for the cover of the December 1887 issue of *Beeton's Christmas Annual*, which included the debut of Sherlock Holmes, who strode confidently through *A Study in Scarlet*.
BEETON'S CHRISTMAS ANNUAL, MAGAZINE (DECEMBER 1887)

" He examined with his glass the word upon the wall, going over every letter of it with the most minute exactness." (*Page 23.*)

From this first published image of Sherlock Holmes, by D. H. Friston, the "unofficial consulting detective" appears with magnifying glass in hand, scientifically evaluating clues invisible even to police detectives. Four years later, Sidney Paget made Holmes's figure familiar in households across England—and soon throughout the rest of the world—often featuring the now iconic deerstalker.
BEETON'S CHRISTMAS ANNUAL, MAGAZINE (DECEMBER 1887)

"THE SINGLE, GRIM, MOTIONLESS FIGURE WHICH LAY STRETCHED UPON THE BOARDS." (Page 31.)

One of Charles Doyle's awkward, even amateurish, drawings for the first independent book publication of his son's novel *A Study in Scarlet*. Arthur failed in his attempt to secure respectable payment for his father's contribution, which probably he himself requested.

that you have been getting yourself very wet lately, and that you have a most clumsy and careless servant girl?"

"My dear Holmes," said I, "this is too much. You would certainly have been burned, had you lived a few centuries ago. It is true that I had a country walk on Thursday and came home in a dreadful mess; but, as I have changed my clothes, I can't imagine how you deduce it. As to Mary Jane, she is incorrigible, and my wife has given her notice; but there again I fail to see how you work it out."

He chuckled to himself and rubbed his long nervous hands together.

"It is simplicity itself," said he; "my eyes tell me that on the inside of your left shoe, just where the firelight strikes it, the leather is scored by six almost parallel cuts. Obviously they have been caused by someone who has very carelessly scraped round the edges of the sole in order to remove crusted mud from it. Hence, you see, my double deduction that you had been out in vile weather, and that you had a particularly malignant boot-slitting specimen of the London slavey. As to your practice, if a gentleman walks into my rooms smelling of iodoform, with a black mark of nitrate of silver upon his right fore-finger, and a bulge on the side of his top-hat to show where he has secreted his stethoscope, I must be dull indeed, if I do not pronounce him to be an active member of the medical profession."

I could not help laughing at the ease with which he explained his process of deduction. "When I hear you give your reasons," I remarked, "the thing always appears to me to be so ridiculously simple that I could easily do it myself, though at

"THEN HE STOOD BEFORE THE FIRE."

each successive instance of your reasoning I am baffled, until you explain your process. And yet I believe that my eyes are as good as yours."

"Quite so," he answered, lighting a cigarette, and throwing himself down into an armchair. "You see, but you do not observe. The distinction is clear. For example, you have frequently seen the steps which lead up from the hall to this room."

"Frequently."

"How often?"

"Well, some hundreds of times."

"Then how many are there?"

"How many! I don't know."

"Quite so! You have not observed.

The Strand paid professional illustrators well, and in doing so produced an immediately recognizable—and soon hugely influential—magazine. This is Sidney Paget's first published portrayal of Sherlock Holmes and Dr. Watson, at 221B Baker Street, in "A Scandal in Bohemia," the first in *The Strand*'s series of Sherlock Holmes stories, published in the July 1891 issue.

STRAND MAGAZINE, VOL. II (AUGUST 1891)

Capitalizing upon the extraordinary popularity of their suddenly famous author, *The Strand* ran a profile of Arthur Conan Doyle in the August 1892 issue, showing him in the first flush of fame. STRAND MAGAZINE, VOL. IV. (AUGUST 1892)

The same issue of *The Strand* featured a photo of Arthur and Touie enjoying the hot new trend of tandem tricycles. Throughout his life, Arthur was restless and energetic, indulging in vigorous outdoor sports, including cross-country biking and skiing. STRAND MAGAZINE, VOL. IV. (AUGUST 1892)

"HOLMES WAS WORKING HARD OVER A CHEMICAL INVESTIGATION."

The legacy of Arthur Conan Doyle's study with Dr. Joseph Bell influenced his creation of Sherlock Holmes in many ways. Some of them are reflected in Sidney Paget's now iconic illustrations for *The Strand*, as in this scene from "A Scandal in Bohemia," the first story and the beginning of global fame for the character and his creator. GETTY IMAGES

CHAPTER 19

Bohemians in Baker Street

Sherlock Holmes [is] a bastard between Joe Bell and Poe's Monsieur
Dupin (much diluted).

— ARTHUR CONAN DOYLE, IN A LETTER TO
ROBERT LOUIS STEVENSON

*L*ived at 221 B Upper Baker Street, wrote Arthur in his notebook, under
his narrator's name. Like Poe, Arthur was careful to locate the hero's
headquarters quite specifically. Dupin lives—and is consulted by the
gendarmerie—at number 33, Rue Dunot, in the aristocratic and artistic Left
Bank neighborhood of the Faubourg St. Germain, in Paris. Arthur's choice
of Upper Baker Street was in Westminster, London—the locale of the real
Inspector Sherlock.

At the time of his writing, Baker Street was not more than a quarter of
a mile long. North of where Marylebone Road crossed it, it divided into
Upper Baker Street, where house numbers continued upward to include 221.
Later, however, Arthur crossed out *Upper* and situated his heroes in the
southern end of Baker Street, thus making the address 221 purely fictional.

Baker Street was dense with London history. During the eighteenth
century, William Pitt the Elder, twice prime minister, had lived in Upper
Baker Street, beside Regent's Park. The street had known the home of the
glamorous Sarah Siddons, the Welsh tragedienne renowned for her haunting
portrayal of Lady Macbeth, and the birthplace of novelist Edward Bulwer,
later Lord Lytton. Madame Tussaud opened her first waxwork exhibition at
the Baker Street Bazaar in 1835.

Poe's Dupin is an indolent aristocrat who resides with the narrator in a "time-eaten and grotesque mansion," because his family's impoverishment has reduced him to frugality—but not to industry that might overcome the need for it. The more modern Arthur, in contrast, placed Holmes and Watson in a shared second-story (first floor, in British usage) flat on a busy urban thoroughfare near Regent's Park. The *B* in the street number indicated that their flat was on the second floor within a larger building, which Arthur probably envisioned as one of the eighty or so flat-fronted, four-story Georgian terraces in this desirable neighborhood. Some London addresses used *bis* after a street number, a common French term referring to a house that had formerly been a single residence but was later divided into flats, and at times *bis* was shortened to merely *B*.

In the published book, Dr. Watson and Sherlock Holmes settle down in their new chambers and launch a memorable partnership:

> We met next day as he had arranged, and inspected the rooms at No. 221B, Baker Street, of which he had spoken at our meeting. They consisted of a couple of comfortable bed-rooms and a single large airy sitting-room, cheerfully furnished, and illuminated by two broad windows. So desirable in every way were the apartments, and so moderate did the terms seem when divided between us, that the bargain was concluded upon the spot, and we at once entered into possession. That very evening I moved my things round from the hotel, and on the following morning Sherlock Holmes followed me with several boxes and portmanteaus. For a day or two we were busily employed in unpacking and laying out our property to the best advantage. That done, we gradually began to settle down and to accommodate ourselves to our new surroundings.

Arthur employed a reliable literary method of bringing a fictional character to life and building suspense on the page: he permitted Dr. Watson to puzzle over Sherlock Holmes's paradoxes, and to become preoccupied with the enigma of his new roommate's personality and character. From the moment they move into Baker Street together, each day of their acquaintance brings Dr. Watson a new glimpse of Holmes's mysterious ways.

"The reader may set me down as a hopeless busybody," says Watson, when I confess how much this man stimulated my curiosity, and how often I endeavoured to break through the reticence which he showed on all that concerned himself. Before pronouncing judgment, however, be it remembered, how objectless was my life, and how little there was to engage my attention. My health forbade me from venturing out unless the weather was exceptionally genial, and I had no friends who would call upon me and break the monotony of my daily existence. Under these circumstances, I eagerly hailed the little mystery which hung around my companion, and spent much of my time in endeavouring to unravel it.

Watson takes a sheet of paper and catalogues the quirks of his new housemate, under the heading "Sherlock Holmes—his limits." Drawing upon memories of Joe Bell, Arthur had Watson note that Holmes's knowledge of geology is "practical, but limited. Tells at a glance different soils from each other. After walks has shown me splashes upon his trousers, and told me by their colour and consistency in what part of London he had received them." Arthur assigned Holmes a similarly specialized knowledge of botany, rather like his own. "Well up in belladonna, opium, and poisons generally," writes Watson. "Knows nothing of practical gardening." He notes that Holmes's understanding of chemistry, in contrast, is "profound."

The young doctor's mysterious new acquaintance seems to understand British law on a practical basis rather than a theoretical one, and knows anatomy in the same way. He can box, play the violin, and handle a sword and a singlestick (cudgel). At first, Watson sees Holmes as shockingly ignorant of literature, astronomy, and philosophy, yet Holmes soon turns out to be a ready encyclopedia of sensational literature: "He appears to know every detail of every horror perpetrated in the century."

Not surprisingly, Watson is preoccupied with a simple question: What does Holmes do for a living? There is no hint of inherited money paying his bills. He spends many hours away from Baker Street, in chemical laboratories and dissection rooms and on unexplained adventures, yet he confirms Stamford's statement that he is not a medical student. He does not seem to be reading for a degree in any of the sciences.

"Yet his zeal for certain studies was remarkable," observes Watson, "and within eccentric limits his knowledge was so extraordinarily ample and minute that his observations have fairly astounded me." Why, Watson keeps asking himself, would a man pursue such obscure knowledge? "No man burdens his mind with small matters unless he has some very good reason for doing so."

Arthur assigned Holmes an intriguing trait that seems to have been based upon his own character: "Nothing could exceed his energy when the working fit was upon him; but now and again a reaction would seize him, and for days on end he would lie upon the sofa in the sitting-room, hardly uttering a word or moving a muscle from morning to night." At times Watson suspects that Holmes may be addicted to some kind of drug, which in the second Holmes novel would prove to be the case: He takes cocaine when he feels benumbed by the routine of everyday life—that is, when no criminal puzzle presents itself. But no drug shows up in *A Study in Scarlet*.

By unconsciously pouring into Holmes some of his creator's personal inconsistencies and inchoate rebellion, Arthur painted him as a hero who was larger-than-life but believably complex. Like protagonists such as d'Artagnan, Holmes is both intelligent and fearless. Many thriller writers had created their protagonist as a kind of heroic alter ego. Physical courage came so naturally to Arthur, however, that he did not have to imagine a contempt for danger and bestow it upon Sherlock Holmes. He merely drew upon his own casual bravery in the face of poison overdoses, thrashing whales, boxing sailors, and circling sharks.

From the first, however, Arthur envisioned his detective as outside the predictable loyalties of earlier heroes, naturally above bourgeois morality. In mocking the functionaries of law and order, Holmes can even sound like Robin Hood or other laughing rogues. Disdain for the established police force—and especially for detectives who strode through society without an identifying uniform—had alternated, since its founding, with optimistic respect for the new kind of policing.

Not one to fall into slavish hero worship himself, Arthur gave Watson a skeptical eye for his new friend's arrogance, vanity, and other foibles. This narrative ploy permitted him to round out the relationship and raise it above the worshipful acolyte role played by Poe's narrator. Watson misses, however, what the reader perceives, which is that sometimes Holmes is pulling his roommate's leg. He claims, for example, to have no idea who Thomas Carlyle may be. He absurdly pretends ignorance of the heliocentric cosmos of Copernicus—and gullible Watson swallows the bait, at least at first.

"You appear to be astonished," remarks Holmes about Watson's response to his claimed ignorance of astronomy. "Now that I do know it I shall do my best to forget it."

"To forget it!" exclaims Watson.

"You see, I consider that a man's brain originally is like a little empty attic, and you have to stock it with such furniture as you choose. . . . It is of the highest importance, therefore, not to have useless facts elbowing out the useful ones."

"But the Solar System!"

"What the deuce is it to me?" Holmes exclaims; "you say that we go round the sun. If we went round the moon it would not make a pennyworth of difference to me or to my work."

But Holmes, playing his game, does not describe what his work may be.

Sometimes the inconsistencies in Holmes's character resulted from Arthur's own slapdash, devil-may-care approach to writing. He didn't worry about details and apparently considered internal consistency a minor virtue in fiction—not one on which he was going to lavish much attention. Soon Holmes reveals that, like his creator, he is quite knowledgeable about history and science. As the novel unfolds, Watson discovers that Holmes can casually cite obscure passages in the scientific writings of Darwin, such as the great scientist's idea that human beings' appreciation for the rhythms of music may have predated spoken language. A walking encyclopedia of the history of crime and detection, Holmes maintains an extensive scrapbook/catalogue of criminal references. Arthur may have recalled a scene from the 1871 novel *A Terrible Temptation*, by one of his favorite writers, Charles Reade. In it a character maintains a vast personal filing system:

> Underneath the table was a formidable array of note-books, standing upright, and labelled on their backs. There were about twenty large folios, of classified facts, ideas, and pictures; for the very wood-cuts were all indexed and classified on the plan of a tradesman's ledger; there was also the receipt-book of the year, treated on the same plan. . . . Then there was a collection of solid quartos, and of smaller folio guard-books called Indexes. . . . By the side of the table were six or seven thick pasteboard cards, each about the size of a large portfolio, and on these the author's notes and extracts were collected from all his repertories into something like a focus, for a present purpose.

Despite his patriotism and fierce ambition and commitment to a medical career, despite his preoccupation with money and his devotion to family, Arthur liked to think of himself as bohemian. The term derived not from inhabitants of the actual Kingdom of Bohemia—which, in 1867, had become part of the Austro-Hungarian Empire—but from *bohémien*, originally the French term for Romany people often described in English with the word *Gypsy*. A decade before Arthur's birth, in the satirical novel *Vanity Fair*, William Makepeace Thackeray—who later dandled Arthur on his knee in Edinburgh—expressed the bourgeois view when he wrote of Becky Sharp as she wandered Europe, "She became a perfect Bohemian ere long, herding with people whom it would make your hair stand on end to meet."

In 1863, an anonymous essayist in *The Westminster Review* had written,

> As the phrase "Egyptian" was once generally used in our own country to describe a vagrant of any clime or tribe, so the term "Bohemian" has come to be very commonly accepted in our day as the description of a certain kind of literary gipsy, no matter in what language he speaks, or what city he inhabits . . . A Bohemian is simply an artist or littérateur who, consciously or unconsciously, secedes from conventionality in life or in art. In its essence, Bohemia is, or was, a protest against the subjection of human life to money-making, and of human intellect to conventional rule.

Looking back later, Arthur thought that at sixteen, in 1874, he had been too Bohemian for his relatives in London. In *A Study in Scarlet*, in a scene of almost marital domesticity, he even had Watson smoke his pipe and keep awake for Holmes's return from a late-night jaunt by reading Henri Murger's *Scènes de la Vie de Bohème*, the semi-autobiographical story cycle about starving artists in Paris that had created the current international image of bohemianism. Such themes suited Arthur's title, with its echoes of the decadent Aesthetic movement.

But Holmes, not Watson, best demonstrated Arthur's own resistance to conventionality. Working for himself, bragging about his genius, at times sleeping all day and tracking miscreants by night, disdaining money, snubbing Scotland Yard detectives and other representatives of authority and convention, mapping a world without the supernatural, demonstrating the potential of sheer intellect—Holmes was a revolutionary combination of attributes. Arthur had merged the characters he met in real life and in fiction, embodied his own reckless bravery and burgeoning passion for justice, and married a Romantic vision of science to the myth of the heroic adventurer. At the age of twenty-seven, he had conjured a new kind of hero.

CHAPTER 20

A Little Too Scientific

The fatal mistake which the ordinary policeman makes is this, that he gets his theory first, and then makes the facts fit it, instead of getting his facts first of all and making all his little observations and deductions until he is driven irresistibly by them into an elucidation in a direction he may never have originally anticipated.

—JOSEPH BELL

Arthur's admiration for Edgar Allan Poe and Émile Gaboriau, which had begun in his boyhood, flowered into his own incarnation of a smug, brilliant detective. Thus he imagined Dr. Watson comparing his new roommate's talents to those of both Monsieur Lecoq and Auguste Dupin—only to meet with a dismissive response. In his early notes for *A Study in Scarlet*, Arthur wrote down snatches of dialogue as if taking dictation: "Lecoq was a bungler—Dupin was better. Dupin was decidedly smart. His trick of following a train of thought was more sensational than clever but still he had analytical genius."

Despite his amateur status, Dupin is known to the gendarmerie. He undertakes the case in "The Purloined Letter" at the behest of his acquaintance "Monsieur G——, the Prefect of the Parisian Police." Neither Dupin nor his companion is impressed with G——'s intelligence. "We gave him a hearty welcome," says the narrator; "for there was nearly half as much of the entertaining as of the contemptible about the man, and we had not seen him for several years." G—— "had a fashion of calling everything odd that was beyond his comprehension, and thus lived amid an absolute legion of oddities."

Arthur gave his detective a similar contempt for the official police force in *A Study in Scarlet*: "There is no crime to detect, or, at most, some bungling villainy with a motive so transparent that even a Scotland Yard official can see through it." Of the two official detectives in *Scarlet*, Holmes remarks, "Gregson is the smartest of the Scotland Yarders; he and Lestrade are the pick of a bad lot."

Dupin was an amateur with a talent for logic. Holmes, in contrast, while not a policeman, was also not a layman. By dint of burning the midnight oil in library and laboratory, as well as extensive experience in the real world, he had turned his passion for observation and minutiae into a position as consulting detective. While it was unlikely that any actual police detectives had ever begged a private inquiry agent to assist them, as Gregson beseeched Watson's new roommate, at least Holmes was a young professional with a growing reputation.

Holmes often echoes Dupin and Gaboriau in other ways. "Experience has shown, and a true philosophy will always show," says Dupin in "The Mystery of Marie Rogêt," "that a vast, perhaps the larger portion of the truth arises from the seemingly irrelevant." And Monsieur Lecoq remarks, "This is one of those vulgar details whose very insignificance makes them terrible, when they are attended by certain circumstances." In a later Holmes story, the detective remarks to Watson about a clue, "It is, of course, a trifle, but there is nothing so important as trifles."

Arthur was not one to deny his influences—and perhaps he foresaw that readers could not miss his debts. In the published book, Watson remarks to Holmes, "You remind me of Edgar Allan Poe's Dupin. I had no idea that such individuals did exist outside of stories."

But Arthur had no intention of making his fictional detective speak generously of forebears. Just as Poe placed a critique of the criminal-turned-detective Vidocq into the mouth of Dupin, so did Arthur have Holmes mock Dupin. "Now, in my opinion," scoffs Holmes, puffing at his pipe, "Dupin was a very inferior fellow . . . He had some analytical genius, no doubt; but he was by no means such a phenomenon as Poe appeared to imagine."

Watson asks about Lecoq.

"Lecoq was a miserable bungler," fumes Holmes in reply; "he had only one thing to recommend him, and that was his energy. That book made me positively ill. The question was how to identify an unknown prisoner. I could have done it in twenty-four hours. Lecoq took six months or so." Clearly Holmes is referring to Gaboriau's *Monsieur Lecoq*. "It might be made a textbook for detectives to teach them what to avoid."

* * *

One notable contrast between Arthur's detective duo and Poe's is exemplified by how they meet. Dupin and his narrator bump into each other while seeking "the same very rare and very remarkable volume" in "an obscure library in the Rue Montmartre." The two men are barely in and of the world. Despite Dupin's emphasis on reason and evidence, they exist in a murky, candlelit landscape familiar to readers of Poe's *Tales of the Grotesque and Arabesque.*

In contrast, Arthur opened Chapter 1 of *A Study in Scarlet* with Dr. Watson seeking affordable lodgings. Young, wounded, exhausted, and of a naturally modest disposition, he seems to stride out of the real world in a way that Poe characters never manage.

Poe was born in 1809 and died at the age of forty, a decade before Arthur's birth. His natural bent was Romantic and Gothic. In Edinburgh half a century down the literary road, Arthur grew up reading Mayne Reid melodramas of the American western frontier—and reading Edgar Allan Poe. Later, as he sat at his Southsea desk in the mid-1880s and conjured Sherlock Holmes and Dr. Watson, his imagination naturally returned to the work of one of his favorite writers, and to the analytical detective who had intrigued him since boyhood. By this time, however, Arthur was influenced by plainspoken, more realistic adventure writers who eschewed Poe's cobwebs. He admired, for example, his fellow Scot Robert Louis Stevenson and the American Bret Harte. And his admiration showed in his work; in 1884 at least one *Cornhill* reader had attributed Arthur's own "J. Habakuk Jephson's Statement" to Stevenson, and Arthur had written stories such as "The American's Tale" in imitation of Harte's tales of gold rush mining towns on the American frontier.

In creating his own detective, Arthur would naturally recast Dupin's influence in his own later, less Romantic era. He also drew from the real-world inspiration of Dr. Bell, who strode among suffering patients, noting their occupational scars and mud-splashed boots—and weaving from such seemingly unrelated clues a narrative of their lives. Poe was knowledgeable about the natural and theoretical sciences, as his wide-ranging essay "Eureka" and other works demonstrate, but he did not endow his detective with a scientific approach to crime-solving. Borrowing from Voltaire, he gave Dupin a playful kind of observant genius that lends itself to the logical deciphering of puzzles.

Poe had not had the good fortune to study with Joseph Bell. He could assign Dupin a theory of observation, and he could detonate verbal fireworks about logic. But apparently Poe himself did not have the trained observational skills to bestow upon his brainchild. Arthur did. He was no detective himself, but he had witnessed such talents at work. Years of training with one of the most acclaimed diagnosticians of his time had left Arthur aware that such insight was not only possible but an art and science that one could cultivate.

Sherlock Holmes, in contrast to Dupin, embodies Arthur's faith in science as both an instrument of progress and an intellectual adventure. In *A Study in Scarlet*, Watson runs into his old friend Stamford, who had been a surgeon's assistant under him at St. Bartholomew's Hospital Medical College—the oldest continuously operating hospital in Britain, dating back to the twelfth century. Like so many others, this link may have been inspired by Arthur's real life. Sir Thomas Watson, the Dr. Watson whose death received so much attention a few years before Arthur wrote his first detective novel, was involved with the hospital popularly known as Bart's.

Young Stamford mentions that an acquaintance named Sherlock Holmes is also seeking a roommate. "He is a little queer in his ideas," warns Stamford, "—an enthusiast in some branches of science."

"A medical student, I suppose?" asks Watson.

"No—I have no idea what he intends to go in for. I believe he is well up in anatomy, and he is a first-class chemist; but, as far as I know, he has never taken out any systematic medical classes. His studies are very desultory and eccentric, but he has amassed a lot of out-of-the-way knowledge which would astonish his professors."

Stamford hesitates about explaining further until Watson worries that this Holmes character may have some terrible flaw. "Is this fellow's temper so formidable, or what is it?" he demands.

"It's not easy to express the inexpressible," protests Stamford. "Holmes is a little too scientific for my taste—it approaches to cold-bloodedness."

Arthur saw himself as brave and indomitable, and he wanted to convey the same traits in Holmes—before Dr. Watson even meets him. In Stamford's ensuing description of young Holmes's character, Arthur drew from his own experience, including his dangerous experimentation with overdoses of gelseminum seven years earlier. "I could imagine his giving a friend a little pinch of the latest vegetable alkaloid," Stamford says cheerily of Holmes, "not out of malevolence, you understand, but simply out of a spirit of inquiry in order to have an accurate idea of the effects."

Many plants naturally produce alkaloids, including hyacinth, ragwort, periwinkle, and hemlock. Morphine was the first to be isolated by scientists, from the opium poppy, in the first decade of the nineteenth century. Other alkaloid toxins include strychnine, cocaine, nicotine, and even caffeine. Thanks in part to his heavily underlined copy of Alfred Baring Garrod's textbook from medical school, Arthur knew his materia medica. He must have smiled as he put in Stamford's mouth further words about Holmes's commitment to science: "To do him justice, I think he would take it himself with the same readiness."

"Very right, too," says Watson.

"Yes, but it may be pushed to excess." Then Arthur brought in memories of the reputation of figures such as Robert Christison at medical school: "When it comes to beating the subjects in the dissecting-rooms with a stick, it is certainly taking rather a bizarre shape."

"Beating the subjects!"

"Yes, to verify how far bruises may be produced after death."

In a high-ceilinged chemical laboratory, amid the flickering blue flames of Bunsen lamps and worktables glittering with test tubes and retorts, Stamford introduces them: "Dr. Watson, Mr. Sherlock Holmes."

The tall young man offers a surprisingly firm handshake and remarks casually, "You have been in Afghanistan, I perceive."

As they depart later, Watson asks Stamford, "How the deuce did he know that I had come from Afghanistan?"

"That's just his little peculiarity," replies Stamford with a smile. "A good many people have wanted to know how he finds things out."

After devoting much of "The Murders in the Rue Morgue" to a reprint of the newspaper account of the tragedy, Poe later has Dupin hold forth at great length about what he deduced from the contradictory statements of witnesses quoted therein and from what he himself observed in his examination of the crime scene. But Poe actually devotes only a small paragraph to the examination itself, and only a single sentence to how his detective behaved: "Dupin scrutinized everything—not excepting the bodies of the victims."

In contrast to Poe's omission of Dupin's actual methods, in Gaboriau's 1867 Lecoq novel *The Mystery of Orcival*, the French author described the young policeman's ardor for the overlooked physical evidence of a crime scene:

They ascended to the room in question, and M. Lecoq, forgetting his part of a haberdasher, and regardless of his clothes, went down flat on his stomach, alternately scrutinizing the hatchet—

which was a heavy, terrible weapon—and the slippery and well-waxed oaken floor. . . .

"When the assassin threw the hatchet, it first fell on the edge—hence this sharp cut; then it fell over on one side and the flat, or hammer end left this mark here, under my finger. Therefore, it was thrown with such violence that it turned over itself and that its edge a second time cut the floor, where you see it now." . . .

He knelt down and studied the sand on the path, the stagnant water, and the reeds and water-plants. Then going along a little distance, he threw a stone, approaching again to see the effect produced on the mud. He next returned to the house, and came back again under the willows, crossing the lawn, where were still clearly visible traces of a heavy burden having been dragged over it. Without the least respect for his pantaloons, he crossed the lawn on all-fours, scrutinizing the smallest blades of grass, pulling away the thick tufts to see the earth better, and minutely observing the direction of the broken stems.

Following in the muddy footsteps of Lecoq rather than Dupin, blood-hound Sherlock Holmes trusts to the value of his prey's spoor—the traces, all but invisible to untrained and less gifted eyes, that enable him to reconstruct the tragedy.

As he spoke, he whipped a tape measure and a large round magnifying glass from his pocket. With these two implements he trotted noiselessly about the room, sometimes stopping, occasionally kneeling, and once lying flat upon his face . . . For twenty minutes or more he continued his researches, measuring with the most exact care the distance between marks which were entirely invisible to me, and occasionally applying his tape to the walls in an equally incomprehensible manner. . . .

"They say that genius is an infinite capacity for taking pains," he remarked with a smile. "It's a very bad definition, but it does apply to detective work."

In "The Murders in the Rue Morgue," Auguste Dupin and his narrator stroll Parisian streets—always at night, because at dawn they close the shutters and read and sleep by "the ghastliest and feeblest of rays" from candles. During one of these nocturnal rambles, Dupin reveals how he appears to have read the thoughts of his companion—one of the moments that Sherlock Holmes later mocks. When Dupin explains, his train of observation and reasoning is painfully unconvincing. "He boasted to me, with a low chuckling laugh," remarks the narrator, "that most men, in respect to himself, wore windows in their bosoms, and was wont to follow up such assertions by direct and very startling proofs of his intimate knowledge of my own."

Yet Poe did not substantiate this claim by providing the reader with examples of Dupin's insight into the narrator's character. Instead he described a behavior that strikes an almost ridiculous Gothic note: "His manner at these moments was frigid and abstract; his eyes were vacant in expression; while his voice, usually a rich tenor, rose into a treble which would have sounded petulantly but for the deliberateness and entire distinctness of the enunciation."

Arthur, in contrast, felt that his hero ought to demonstrate his genius, not merely proclaim it. When reading detective stories, he found it annoying that the hero often triumphed through luck or through methods that were never explained to the reader. Thus, after he has examined the crime scene in Chapter 3, Holmes explains to skeptical police inspectors, "There has been murder done, and the murderer was a man. He was more than six feet high, was in the prime of life, had small feet for his height, wore coarse, square-toed boots and smoked a Trichinopoly cigar. He came here with his victim in a four-wheeled cab, which was drawn by a horse with three old shoes and one new one on his off fore leg. In all probability the murderer had a florid face, and the finger-nails of his right hand were remarkably long. These are only a few indications, but they may assist you."

Holmes's approach is evidence-based. For example, in one instance he remarks, "There is no branch of detective science which is so important and so much neglected as the art of tracing footsteps. Happily, I have always laid great stress upon it, and much practice has made it second nature to me." Holmes not only discerns that two men had been present before the horde of constables merged to investigate the crime, he even estimates the height of one from his stride, and imagines the fashionable dress of the other from impressions of his elegant boots.

Readers could overcome their skepticism about Holmes's extraordinary abilities because Watson was there first—wondering aloud, demanding explanations. This narrative point of view also permitted the detective to hold forth.

"You appeared to be surprised," remarks Holmes, "when I told you, on our first meeting, that you had come from Afghanistan."

"You were told, no doubt," replies Watson.

At this point, sitting at his desk in Bush Villas only six years after completing his studies in Edinburgh, Arthur again conjured specific demonstrations of Joseph Bell's insight that he himself had witnessed. The memories were still fresh.

"I *knew* you came from Afghanistan," insists Holmes. "From long habit the train of thoughts ran so swiftly through my mind, that I arrived at the conclusion without being conscious of intermediate steps. There were such steps, however. The train of reasoning ran, 'Here is a gentleman of a medical type, but with the air of a military man. Clearly an army doctor, then. He has just come from the tropics, for his face is dark, and that is not the natural tint of his skin, for his wrists are fair.'" (Indeed, Stamford told Watson that he looked "as thin as a lath and as brown as a nut.") "He has undergone hardship and sickness, as his haggard face says clearly," Holmes continues. "His left arm has been injured. He holds it in a stiff and unnatural manner. Where in the tropics could an English army doctor have seen much hardship and got his arm wounded? Clearly in Afghanistan."

CHAPTER 21

The Book of Life

I began to think of turning scientific methods, as it were, onto the work of detection . . . I thought to myself, "If a scientific man like Bell was to come into the detective business, he wouldn't do these things by chance. He'd get the thing by building it up scientifically." So, having once conceived that line of thought, you can well imagine that I had, as it were, a new idea of the detective—and one which it interested me to work out.

—ARTHUR CONAN DOYLE, IN AN INTERVIEW

Early in the process of planning his detective novel, scribbling in his notebook and drawing upon his memories of Dr. Bell, Arthur imagined Holmes having written an article about his scientific method of detection—and foresaw Watson's impatient response to it:

"What rot this is" I cried—throwing the volume petulantly aside "I must say that I have no patience with people who build up fine theories in their own armchairs which can never be reduced to practice—"

Arthur kept this idea in the final version. In the second chapter of the published book, after they settle into their rooms at 221B Baker Street, Watson runs across an unsigned article, "The Book of Life," in a magazine. Its author claims that, through the systematic observation of seemingly minor details, one could deduce a great deal of personal information about a stranger.

From a drop of water, a logician could infer the possibility of an Atlantic or a Niagara without having seen or heard of one or the other. So all life is a great chain, the nature of which is known whenever we are shown a single link of it. Like all other arts, the Science of Deduction and Analysis is one which can only be acquired by long and patient study nor is life long enough to allow any mortal to attain the highest possible perfection in it. Before turning to those moral and mental aspects of the matter which present the greatest difficulties, let the enquirer begin by mastering more elementary problems. Let him, on meeting a fellow-mortal, learn at a glance to distinguish the history of the man, and the trade or profession to which he belongs. Puerile as such an exercise may seem, it sharpens the faculties of observation, and teaches one where to look and what to look for. By a man's finger nails, by his coat-sleeve, by his boot, by his trouser knees, by the callosities of his forefinger and thumb, by his expression, by his shirt cuffs—by each of these things a man's calling is plainly revealed. That all united should fail to enlighten the competent enquirer in any case is almost inconceivable.

"What ineffable twaddle!" exclaims Watson in this version. "I never read such rubbish in my life."

Holmes reveals that he wrote the article himself. "I have a turn both for observation and for deduction," he says with rare understatement. "The theories which I have expressed there, and which appear to you to be so chimerical are really extremely practical—so practical that I depend upon them for my bread and cheese."

Soon comes Holmes's revelation that will subvert Watson's goal of a relaxed convalescence after his wounding at Maiwand: "I am a consulting detective, if you can understand what that is. Here in London we have lots of Government detectives and lots of private ones. When these fellows are at fault they come to me, and I manage to put them on the right scent. They lay all the evidence before me, and I am generally able, by the help of my knowledge of the history of crime, to set them straight. There is a strong family resemblance about misdeeds, and if you have all the details of a thousand at your finger ends, it is odd if you can't unravel the thousand and first."

Always Holmes demonstrates that his experience is informed by extensive reading. For example, "the forcible administration of poison," he tells Watson, "is by no means a new thing in criminal annals. The cases of Dolsky in Odessa, and of Leturier in Montpellier, will occur at once to any toxicologist."

In the essay that Watson derides, Holmes uses the term *deduction* instead of *induction* in the way that many English speakers commonly did during the nineteenth century—as almost a synonym for *inference*. He even refers to his own "rules of deduction." Technically, as well-educated Arthur probably knew, *deduction* means reasoning from the general to the particular, as in "All human beings are mortal. Queen Victoria is a human being. Therefore Queen Victoria is mortal." Certainly Holmes employs this kind of thinking as well. He propounds a theory and then sets out to test it, like any good scientific thinker—often disproving his original theory through discovery of new information. But most of his method was based upon induction. He reasoned from the particular to the general, as in "This man's footprints are very far apart. Only tall men can manage such a stride. Therefore this man is tall." *Deduction*, however, had also been one of Joseph Bell's favorite words, so naturally Arthur placed it in the mouth of his Bell-inspired detective.

In conjuring Holmes's scientific approach, Arthur was not only echoing Zadig and Dupin; he was also exploring the concepts of Francis Bacon, who by Arthur's time had come to be considered the patron saint of rational inquiry. At times he invoked Bacon explicitly. "One's ideas must be as broad as Nature if they are to interpret Nature," remarks Holmes to Dr. Watson. Even the phrase *to interpret nature* was associated, in the minds of the nineteenth-century educated class, with Bacon. His 1620 magnum opus, *Novum Organum*, had been subtitled *True Suggestions for the Interpretation of Nature*. Originally titled *Novum Organum Scientiarum* ("New instrument of science"), it was Bacon's manifesto on the foundations of what would later be called the scientific method.

Bacon argued against excessive respect for traditional text-revering approaches and in favor of evidence-based research. In doing so, he embodied, clarified, and furthered the philosophical yearning of his age—for greater knowledge and understanding of those matters that might reasonably be expected to fall within the human ken. In fact, Bacon explicitly defined "inductive history" as "historical matters consequentially deduced from phenomena, facts, observations, experiments, arts, and the active sciences."

Arthur almost certainly read the long biographical and critical essay on Bacon by Thomas Babington Macaulay, one of his favorite writers. Macaulay (who employed the term *induction* correctly) misrepresented Bacon's primary method as one in which the observer gathers details without a preconceived theory with which to unite them—the idea that induction can only follow informed observation. Macaulay summarized what he considered Bacon's tiresome obviousness with his notorious pie analogy: "'I ate minced pies on Monday and Wednesday, and I was kept awake by indigestion all night . . . I did not eat any on Tuesday and Friday, and I was quite well.'"

Arthur portrayed Bacon's theme of the everyday demonstration of observation by turning Dr. Bell into Mr. Holmes. And even the confidence that Holmes's prescience inspires in others was echoed in one of Bell's later remarks: "The patient, too, is likely to be impressed by your ability to cure him in the future if he sees you, at a glance, know much of the past. And the whole trick is much easier than it appears at first."

One of Watson's first compliments to his roommate proved how much he has been won over by Holmes's demonstrations of his technique: "You have brought detection as near an exact science as it ever will be brought in this world."

And Arthur placed in Watson's observation a telling glimpse of Holmes's human side: "My companion flushed up with pleasure at my words, and the earnest way in which I uttered them. I had already observed that he was as sensitive to flattery on the score of his art as any girl could be of her beauty."

CHAPTER 22

A Basilisk in the Desert

I had written in *A Study in Scarlet* a rather sensational and overcoloured
picture of the Danite episodes which formed a passing stain in the early
history of Utah.

—ARTHUR CONAN DOYLE, *OUR SECOND AMERICAN ADVENTURE*

Not all of Émile Gaboriau's books featured the police detective
Monsieur Lecoq. He was prominent, however, in the 1867 novel
The Mystery of Orcival, which was translated into English in 1871,
when Arthur was twelve. Gaboriau divided this tale into two parts. The first
recounted the detective's brilliant investigation of a violent murder and the
second included a flashback tracing events leading to the murder and to the
perpetrator's flight.

Arthur employed this structure, which was not unique to Gaboriau, in
writing *A Study in Scarlet*. After only seven lively and amusing chapters, he
left Holmes and Watson in London and whisked readers across the Atlantic
to North America—and back in time to 1847. Arthur had never visited the
New World, but like adventure writers from Homer to Robert Louis
Stevenson, he instinctively turned toward underexplored regions as exotic
settings. As early as "The American's Tale," an awkwardly slangy story
published in *London Society* in 1880, he had employed the violent U.S. frontier in this way. That he would inevitably get many details wrong didn't
worry him. He was quick to subordinate facts to story.

He ended Part 1 with Holmes capturing Jefferson Hope, the killer of
Enoch Drebber at 3, Lauriston Gardens. Then came Part 2, "The Country of

the Saints," which provided the history of the incidents that led to the murder. Arthur wrote Hope's story in the third person.

In seeking appropriate villains for his melodrama, Arthur settled upon a group often excoriated in the English press at this time: Mormons. It was a canny ploy. Adherents of the Church of Jesus Christ of Latter-day Saints had been controversial ever since Mormonism's founding in the late 1820s in upstate New York by convicted confidence artist Joseph Smith. In 1830 Smith published the Book of Mormon, written in awkward imitation of the style of the King James Bible. Smith claimed that he had translated ancient golden plates written in the "Reformed Egyptian Alphabet," and that their buried location—and translation key—had been revealed to him by an angel named Moroni. Amid religious and civil controversy, including violent clashes with locals and eventually with the federal government, Mormon groups gradually migrated from New York to Ohio, then to Illinois and Missouri—ever westward, toward the less-governed, less-observed frontier.

Joseph Smith became embroiled in many contentious relationships within his own church, and in 1844 he was killed by a mob that attacked the jail where he was being held for trial. A new leader, Brigham Young, rose to prominence and led the migration farther westward. The Mormons finally settled in the Salt Lake Valley region of Alta California, Mexico, which in 1850 became what it still was when Arthur wrote *A Study in Scarlet*: the U.S. territory of Utah.

Arthur saw zealous—and often quite successful—Mormon mission-aries around him in English society. During the single decade of the 1850s, they baptized forty-three thousand English converts into their church. Although polygamy had been forbidden in England since the Bigamy Act of 1603, many poor people seem to have weighed the risks of a new faith against the narrow avenues and high walls of the English class system—and opted for change.

The Book of Mormon forbade polygamy, but among elders Smith encouraged it. In 1876 the Doctrine's prohibition against it was removed. Soon novelists began exploiting this controversial practice, in part through accounts of virtuous women described as having resisted indoctrination and thus escaped the life of sin planned for them. At times the heroine's virtue was threatened in titillating detail. Readers could absolve their lapse into prurience, however, through the piety with which victims condemned their tormentors. Church leaders were portrayed as licentious and vain, their followers as bovine and fainthearted. Drink, forbidden by Mormon doctrine, was presented as commonplace.

Stories about evil Mormons had been popular throughout Arthur's life. His childhood favorite author, Captain Mayne Reid, wrote one, *The Wild Huntress*, published in 1861, when Arthur was two years old. In Maria Ward's didactic 1855 novel *Female Life Among the Mormons*, the heroine, Ellen, recounts how Joseph Smith personally sabotaged her betrothal and how she fell under his spell. "His presence was that of the basilisk," she recalls. "He exerted a mystical magical influence over me—a sort of sorcery that deprived me of the unrestricted exercise of free will."

In 1885, the year before Arthur wrote *A Study in Scarlet*, one of his favorite writers, Robert Louis Stevenson—collaborating with his wife, Fanny Van de Grift Stevenson—published a sequel to his popular 1882 story collection *New Arabian Nights*.

Arthur greatly admired Stevenson's writing and found himself trying to emulate his friendly, vivid style. Also an Edinburgh native, Stevenson was nine years Arthur's elder and a fellow alumnus of Edinburgh University— where he had also taken classes with Joseph Bell. Stevenson was born into a family of engineers who specialized in lighthouse design. In the first decade of the nineteenth century, his grandfather, the renowned Robert Stevenson, built the Bell Rock lighthouse on the reef of Inchcape, the notorious grave-yard of ships off the southwest coast of Angus. But the young Stevenson had abandoned engineering for literature. His first great success, *Treasure Island*, had appeared in 1883, to wide acclaim. Two years later, just before Arthur began writing *A Study in Scarlet*, saw publication of Stevenson's novel *Prince Otto*, a fanciful but politically charged adventure story.

More New Arabian Nights: The Dynamiter comprised a series of stories within stories, narrated by various characters, with titles such as "Story of the Fair Cuban" and "Narrative of the Spirited Old Lady." The Stevensons set their first framed story, "The Destroying Angel," in Utah among violent Mormons. The Stevensons portrayed the Danites, their titular "angels," as a network of spies and assassins spanning the globe, imposing the will of Brigham Young on both apostates and "Gentiles" (non-Mormons). These were not uncommon ideas. A novel published only eight years before Arthur wrote *A Study in Scarlet* bore the subtitle "A Terrible Tale of the Danites of Mormon Land."

The Danites were founded as a secret vigilante group in 1838 while the Mormons were headquartered in Missouri. Four years earlier, Joseph Smith had started a private militia he called the Armies of Israel, and this may have been the origin of the Danites. Persistent rumors of a band of Mormon assassins emerged from Utah, but the church denied that such a group existed after the tumultuous early days in Missouri.

In the Stevensons' story, a family is threatened by the all-spying church that wants their money and their daughter. Terrified, they try to flee under cover of darkness, only to find the symbol of the Mormon Eye, which they had been taught to associate with church omniscience, drawn on a rock face. They turn back. The father is killed and the mother submits to an assisted suicide, leaving the narrating daughter in the hands of a manipulative old man who has long been secretly arranging a marriage with her. At the end of her story, the person to whom she recounts this saga doubts its truth—permitting the authors to exploit anti-Mormon sentiments without committing to them.

Seldom hesitating to borrow from other writers, Arthur incorporated generous helpings of *The Dynamiter* into *A Study in Scarlet*. He could not resist the dramatic potential of the evil Danites, whom he dubbed "Avenging Angels" instead of "Destroying Angels," the term used by Stevenson and others. He titled Chapter 5 of Part 2 "The Avenging Angels." Arthur gave the girl (and later young woman) in his story the name of the mother in the Stevenson tale, Lucy. Early in Part 2, a band of Mormons rescues a man named John Ferrier and the orphaned Lucy, whom Ferrier then adopts.

Like the Stevensons and many other writers, Arthur created an innocent young woman whose virtue is threatened by the conniving elders. But he trumped the Stevensons by making his villain Brigham Young himself, who had died less than a decade before Arthur began writing his novel. At one point, Young comes to Ferrier to ask why he has no wives, and to proclaim of Lucy, "She has grown to be the flower of Utah, and has found favour in the eyes of many who are high in the land."

But Lucy has fallen in love with Jefferson Hope, a man outside the faith—a forbidden love. Two young men, the ungentlemanly and threatening Enoch Drebber and Joseph Stangerson, visit Ferrier to insist upon Lucy's hand in marriage. He throws them out, which results in their threats of both human and divine reprisal. Ferrier urgently begs help from Hope. Ferrier winds up killed by Stangerson, and afterward Lucy is forced to marry Drebber. She dies a month later, and Jefferson Hope swears vengeance upon the killers. Unlike other writers about Mormons, Arthur did not indulge in sexual titillation; the marriage and death of Lucy occur offstage.

After years away, Hope returns in search of his enemies, only to find that they have fled the Mormons. He tracks them across the United States and eventually to England. In recounting his story to Holmes and Watson, Hope describes how he got a job driving a hansom cab in London in order to search for Drebber and Stangerson. The hansom was a two-wheeled vehicle that seated a pair of passengers behind a low double door that guarded their shoes and clothes from mud and excrement flung up by the horse's rear hooves; the top-hatted driver stood outside at the back, holding the reins through a loop on the roof.

Hope watched and waited. In the revelatory last chapter of *A Study in Scarlet*, Hope admits that he returned to the scene of his crime, searching for his lost ring, only to find the house surrounded by police. He evaded them by acting drunk, thus deliberately attracting attention instead of trying to avoid it. In this ploy too, Arthur was imitating Gaboriau. The murderer in *Monsieur Lecoq* attracts attention the same way, in order to get himself jailed alongside an already arrested accomplice.

A fan since boyhood of stories about the American frontier, Arthur admired Mark Twain's writing and is unlikely to have missed Twain's amusing and vivid 1872 book *Roughing It*, which recounted Twain's embroidered adventures in the western United States, including run-ins with Mormons. Twain sketched one brute reputed to be one of the Destroying Angels, whom Twain defined as "Latter-day Saints who are set apart by the Church to conduct permanent disappearances of obnoxious citizens."

Arthur's magpie mind seems to have plucked a term from Twain's account that appeared in no other contemporary book or article about the Latter-day Saints. "They may be darned sharp," says Jefferson Hope about his Mormon pursuers, "but they're not quite sharp enough to catch a Washoe hunter." The Washoe were a tribe of Native Americans long established in the region of Lake Tahoe; one of the Nevada Territory's nine original counties was named Washoe. Twain remarks that "Washoe is a pet nickname for Nevada," and employs it many times within his passages set in Utah and Nevada. But apparently the term was otherwise unknown until Arthur used it.

The overwrought historical background story was not equal in quality to the rest of *A Study in Scarlet*, lacking the texture and style of the Sherlock Holmes scenes, as well as the personal warmth of Dr. Watson as narrator. But it provided Holmes with an interesting opponent and allowed Arthur to stretch his wings as a writer.

And naturally the story ended with the triumph of this brilliant new detective. When Sherlock Holmes lures him into a trap, Jefferson Hope surrenders and remarks admiringly, "If there's a vacant place for a chief of the police, I reckon you are the man for it. The way you kept on my trail was a caution." It was the end of his trail. Hope turns out to be suffering from "an aortic aneurism," as Watson diagnoses it, and dies in his cell without appearing before a magistrate.

After Père Tabaret, the amateur private detective in Gaboriau's *The Widow Lerouge*, solves the case, he thinks about his primary rival on the police force: "This investigation will bring him honor, when all the credit is due me." In *A Study in Scarlet*, after Holmes explains final details of his deductions to Watson, they read in *The Echo*:

> It is an open secret that the credit of this smart capture belongs entirely to the well-known Scotland Yard officials, Messrs. Lestrade and Gregson. The man was apprehended, it appears, in the rooms of a certain Mr. Sherlock Holmes, who has himself, as an amateur, shown some talent in the detective line, and who, with such instructors, may hope in time to attain to some degree of their skill. It is expected that a testimonial of some sort will be presented to the two officers in fitting recognition of their services.

Upon reading this passage, Sherlock Holmes bursts out laughing. "Didn't I tell you so when we started? That's the result of all our Study in Scarlet: to get them a testimonial!"

"Never mind, I have all the facts in my journal," murmurs Watson, "and the public shall know them."

Rather than end on Watson's prophetic words, Arthur could not resist echoing Edgar Allan Poe one more time. Poe garnished many of his innovative stories with old-fashioned trappings, including quotations in other languages. He introduced "The Purloined Letter" with a Latin epigraph by the first-century Roman philosopher Seneca, closed "The Murders in the Rue Morgue" with a line in French from Jean-Jacques Rousseau's 1761 epistolary novel *Julie, or the New Héloise*. In context, the Rousseau quotation—Dupin's final words in the last sentence of the story—becomes a sarcastic commentary upon the bureaucratic incompetence of the official police force. Of G——, the prefect of police, Dupin remarks that "he has '*de nier ce qui est, et d'expliquer ce qui n'est pas*'": "to deny what is and to explain what is not."

In the closing paragraph of *A Study in Scarlet*, Arthur invoked the classics with a quotation spoken by Sherlock Holmes, whom Watson had first imagined to be ignorant of most literature: "In the meantime you must make yourself contented by the consciousness of success, like the Roman miser— '*Populus me sibilat, at mihi plaudo / Ipse domi simul ac nummos contemplor in arca.*'" The line, from Horace's *Satires*, translates, "The public hisses at me, but I am pleased with myself in private when I look at the money in my box."

It was not a particularly apt remark when proclaimed by a young man who had no client and had earned no fee during the investigation of the Lauriston Gardens murder. Not surprisingly in a novel written in only six weeks, the closing quotation reads like a last-minute touch with little thought behind it. Perhaps Arthur felt that he owed one last payment to Edgar Allan Poe, who had lent him so much capital to invest in the creation of Sherlock Holmes.

CHAPTER 23

A Born Novelist

If the secret history of literature could be written, the blighted hopes, the heart-sickening disappointment, the weary waiting, the wasted labor, it would be the saddest record ever penned.
—ARTHUR CONAN DOYLE, *THE NARRATIVE OF JOHN SMITH*

"Arthur has written another book," Touie Doyle was soon writing to Arthur's sister Lottie, "a little novel about 200 pages long, called A Study in Scarlet."

But no one seemed eager to publish Arthur's new book. Laboriously, he made a fair copy of the manuscript in his neat round hand, rolled it up and inserted it into one of the standard mailing tubes, and sent it out to publishers. He had not been surprised when publishers refused to gamble on *The Firm of Girdlestone*. But he was disappointed to find *A Study in Scarlet* making the same old circular tour. He considered this new novel superior to its predecessor.

Optimistically, he sent the manuscript to James Payn at *Cornhill*, who had published "J. Habakuk Jephson's Statement." Arthur hoped for serialization in that magazine. Payn replied that he liked the tale but that it was too short for a novel and too long for a story. Arthur agreed. And clearly *A Study in Scarlet* would never be picked up by the lending libraries, even if he could sell it as a magazine serial, for Mudie's seldom gambled on one-volume debut novels.

Nonetheless, in May 1886 Arthur sent the manuscript to J. W. Arrowsmith, a publisher situated in Bristol. It was a reasonable bet. In 1877

Arrowsmith had renamed the firm after succeeding its founder, printer William Browne, and had experienced growing success, especially since founding *Arrowsmith's Annual* in the early 1880s.

Yet in July Arrowsmith returned *A Study in Scarlet*. Determined not to give up, Arthur mailed it to a couple of other publishers. Each rejected it. Finally he thought to send it to Ward, Lock & Company, which specialized in sensational popular novels.

While Arthur was trying to sell *A Study in Scarlet*, a detective novel by the New Zealand novelist Fergus Hume demonstrated just how much commercial potential this field offered to hardworking (and lucky) authors. Hume first self-published *The Mystery of the Hansom Cab* and soon sold the copyright for £50—which he must have regretted, because the novel eventually sold a hundred thousand copies in Australia and half a million through the widely distributed Jarrold edition from London.

In the Australian gold rush era, Melbourne police assign the working-class detective Gorby to unravel the story of a corpse found in a hansom. Hume's debt to Gaboriau was so obvious that an 1888 parody was entitled *The Mystery of a Wheelbarrow, or Gaboriau Gaborooed, an Idealistic Story of a Great and Rising Colony*. Like Arthur, however, Hume was quick to reference his own genealogy, even having characters cite earlier detective story writers, from Poe to Anna Katharine Green. To keep the reader acquainted with Gorby's thought processes during the investigation, Hume gave him a curious habit: "Being a detective, and of an extremely reticent disposition, he never talked outside about his business, or made a confidant of anyone. When he did want to unbosom himself, he retired to his bedroom and talked to his reflection in the mirror." After Poe, Dickens, Collins, Gaboriau, and Hume, readers expected detectives to be eccentric.

In Ward, Lock's offices in Salisbury Square—the publisher had outgrown its birthplace in Fleet Street—Arthur's mailing tube crossed the desk of George Thomas Bettany. A former professor of botany and biology at Cambridge, Bettany edited several of Ward, Lock's series, including Popular Library for Literary Treasures, Science Primers for the People, and the Minerva Library of Famous Books. He was also the London editor of the distinguished U.S. periodical *Lippincott's*.

Overworked, like most editors, Bettany thought this little novel, *A Study in Scarlet*, might be outside his area of expertise. He took it home to his wife, the former Mary Jean Hickling Gwynne, who had studied medicine and who wrote fiction herself under the name Jeanie Gwynne Bettany. Her novel *The House of Rimmon* had been published by Remington in 1885, and Ward, Lock was publishing *Two Legacies* in 1886.

"I should be glad if you would look through this," Bettany recalled saying, "and tell me whether I ought to read it."

She read through the pages and enthusiastically reported back to her husband, "This is, I feel sure, by a doctor—there is internal evidence to that effect. But in any case, the writer is a born novelist. I am enthusiastic about the book, and believe it will be a great success."

In late October Arthur received Ward, Lock's reply.

Dear Sir,

We have read your story A Study in Scarlet, and are pleased with it. We could not publish it this year, as the market is flooded at present with cheap fiction, but if you do not object to its being held over until next year we will give you £25/–/– (Twenty-five Pounds) for the copyright.

We are,
Dear Sir,
Yours faithfully,
Ward, Lock & Co.

30 October 1886

Disheartened by this less-than-enthusiastic—and only modestly remunerative—response, Arthur replied immediately, on the first of November, with a request that Ward, Lock pay him royalties instead of purchasing the copyright in its entirety.

The English mail was efficient, as usual. "We regret to say," replied Ward, Lock on the following day, "that we shall be unable to retain a percentage on the sale of your work as it might give rise to some confusion. The tale may have to be inserted with some other, in one of our annuals, therefore we must adhere to our original offer of for [*sic*] the complete copyright."

Arthur agonized over his next decision. He was offended by the contract offered, but he also hated to think of his latest creation stagnating in a drawer for months or years instead of garnering his career a little more of the attention he felt he was beginning to deserve. Finally he agreed to Ward, Lock's terms.

A few weeks later, he wrote a painful letter concluding the bargain:

> November 20th 1886
>
> In consideration of the sum of Twenty-Five Pounds paid by them to me I hereby assign to Messrs. Ward, Lock & Co., of Warwick House, Salisbury Square, E.C. Publishers the Copyright and all my interest in the book written by me entitled A STUDY IN SCARLET.
>
> A. Conan Doyle, MD
>
> Bush Villa, Southsea

Eventually publication was scheduled for more than a year later, in the 1887 issue of *Beeton's Christmas Annual*.

In 1852 an English publisher named Samuel Orchart Beeton, barely in his twenties, made his name by gambling on publication of an incendiary anti-slavery novel, *Uncle Tom's Cabin*, by an American woman named Harriet Beecher Stowe. The same year, he launched a pioneering periodical, *The Englishwoman's Domestic Magazine*. The son of a Cheapside publican, Beeton yearned to pursue a more ambitious profession.

In 1856 he married a smart and enterprising young woman, Isabella Mary Mayson, who soon became renowned in her own right as the mage of practical domesticity, Mrs. Beeton. The couple made themselves a household name by publishing many diverse volumes, such as *Beeton's Dictionary of Useful Information, Beeton's Historian, Beeton's Book of Birds, Beeton's Book of Chemistry*, even *Beeton's Book of Jokes and Jests*. The Beetons first published *Mrs Beeton's Book of Household Management* in 1861, with sequels and related volumes snatched up by an eager public. Beeton founded an equally original and successful periodical for children, *Boy's Own Magazine*.

When Mrs. Beeton died in 1865, her devoted husband was all but crippled by grief. Already they had lost three children. The following year, however, fate dealt Beeton another blow. Following a banking collapse in May, many businesses closed. Beeton's only path to escaping bankruptcy lay in selling the copyrights of all his publications. The publisher Ward, Lock and Tyler bought them, retaining the experienced Beeton at a handsome salary. The company had been known as Ward and Lock until a third partner named Tyler joined in 1865. When Tyler departed in 1873 it reverted to its earlier name, so that by the time Arthur submitted the rolled manuscript of his brief novel in 1886, the firm was again merely Ward, Lock & Company.

By this time *Beeton's Christmas Annual* was a small-format magazine, of the size known in publishing as demy octavo, roughly eight and a half inches tall by five and a half inches wide. Some version of this holiday issue had appeared every winter since 1860. During its first decade, it had remained blandly noncommittal about contemporary affairs, but in 1872 and 1873 Beeton turned in a new direction and included political satire. Ward, Lock complained, despite the high sales and newspaper attention the satire drew, and Beeton lost his job. He died of tuberculosis in 1877, twelve years after his wife. Immediately the publisher changed the format of *Beeton's* annual Christmas issue to feature short stories—including three by Mark Twain in the first new issue—and plays intended for home performance.

Arthur had seen his stories in Christmas issues of several magazines. He had published one in the *Boy's Own Paper*, for example, every Christmas since 1883, beginning with his own holiday story, "An Exciting Christmas Eve; or, My Lecture on Dynamite." In 1886 "Cyprian Overbeck Wells. A Literary Mosaic" appeared. By Arthur's time, the *Beeton's* annual miniature anthology was so popular that a contemporary review described it as "an old institution, and as regularly looked for as the holly and the mistletoe." Thus Arthur was pleased to learn from Ward, Lock that his novel would appear in the 1887 issue of *Beeton's Christmas Annual*—the entire short novel in the December issue, not serialized, and in a venue likely to attract notice.

He was not the only family member contributing to periodicals. Back home in Scotland, near the coast north of Edinburgh, in Montrose Royal Asylum, a small in-house magazine had been launched, ambitiously titled *The Sunnyside Chronicle*. Arthur's anxious, capricious, talented father soon channeled his frustrated creativity into writing and drawing for it.

In mid-October 1886, two weeks before Ward, Lock offered to buy the copyright of *A Study in Scarlet*, Joseph Bell retired from the Edinburgh Infirmary. As Bell himself later wrote, for thirty-two years he had "never willingly spent a day in Edinburgh without entering its gates." He was forty-nine, and was leaving only because the Infirmary's bylaws specified limits to various positions, including his role as senior surgeon. He had been on the full-time staff for fifteen years.

"Lord," he wrote in his diary, "comfort me I pray thee in my sadness in parting from my dear Wards and dear friends and nurses."

With Florence Nightingale as one of the organizers and a primary contributor of funds, a subscription began to honor Bell's service to medicine and in particular to nursing. A few months later, in January 1887, a group called upon him at his home on Melville Crescent—a body of nurses and other staff and faculty representing not only the Royal Infirmary but also the Royal Hospital for Sick Children, the Princes Street Training Institution, and the Hospital for Incurables. They brought him enough tributes to furnish a new office, carrying in a pair of silver candelabra, a brass pen and inkwell set, a paperweight—and, as a setting for these, a beautiful oak writing table and chair.

Not that Joe Bell was going to retire from medicine. He was writing a textbook for nurses and remained editor of the *Edinburgh Medical Journal*. The Royal College of Surgeons of Edinburgh elected him president. And in May, a ceremony in the Hall of the Royal College of Surgeons presented Bell with a large portrait of himself and a raft of testimonials from colleagues. "Mr. Bell's whole career has been distinguished by the most honorable attention to his duties," proclaimed his colleague Henry Littlejohn on behalf of the Infirmary,

> whether as a teacher of systematic surgery in the Medical School, or as a teacher of clinical surgery in the Infirmary, whether as regards the patients committed to his charge, the nurses on his staff, or the students who thronged his classrooms and wards. An accomplished and dexterous surgeon, he secured the confidence of his patients and the public. His teaching powers were freely devoted to the nursing establishment of the Infirmary, while to the students he endeared himself by the practical character of his teaching and his frank and sympathizing manner.

In November 1887 the Royal Hospital for Sick Children appointed Bell surgeon to the children's ward, where almost half the cases were already attended by him because of his legendary way with young people. Herds of diseased, handicapped, and wounded children swarmed through the hospital. There were fractures and contusions resulting from falls on Salisbury Crag or from tenement windows, broken limbs from tram and carriage accidents. Birth defects of every kind were rampant: harelip, cleft palate, clubfoot, spina bifida. Neglect especially angered Bell. Frequently he treated small children who suffered from starvation, frostbite, eczema, ulcers, burns, and even genital injuries. He worked to both rescue the children and punish their alleged caretakers. A testament to scientific knowledge guided by compassion, the man who had served as Arthur's model for Sherlock Holmes was flourishing.

CHAPTER 24

The Preternatural Sagacity of a Scientific Detective

I never at any time received another penny for it.
—ARTHUR CONAN DOYLE, ABOUT *A STUDY IN SCARLET*

In July 1887, during the busy summer while Arthur was waiting for *A Study in Scarlet* to appear in *Beeton's Christmas Annual*, a brief letter of his was published in the spiritualist periodical *Light: A Journal of Psychical, Occult, and Mystical Research*. He wrote about his readings of Major General Alfred Wilks Drayson, Alfred Russel Wallace, and others, and added a curious assertion: "After weighing the evidence, I could no more doubt the existence of the phenomena than I could doubt the existence of lions in Africa, though I have been to that continent and have never chanced to see one."

Recently Arthur had been, he claimed, debating whether to buy Leigh Hunt's book *Comic Dramatists of the Restoration* for research on a writing project, and he insisted that he had mentioned this thought to no one. Then he attended his first séance with a professional medium, who, claiming to be inhabited by a spirit, wrote a message for Arthur in pencil: "This gentleman is a healer. Tell him from me not to read Leigh Hunt's book."

"Above all," Arthur exhorted in this first public admission of his spiritualist leanings, "let every inquirer bear in mind that phenomena are only a means to an end, of no value at all of themselves, and simply useful as giving us assurance of an after existence for which we are to prepare by refining away our grosser animal feelings and cultivating our higher, nobler impulses."

* * *

In November, the month in which Joseph Bell went to work as surgeon to the Royal Hospital for Sick Children, Arthur finally saw his Sherlock Holmes novel in *Beeton's Christmas Annual*. The periodical title ran across the top in relatively small black letters on a yellow band, and below it in much larger type appeared each year's issue title. In 1887 the lower band bore in bright red type, occupying a third of the cover, the words *A Study in Scarlet*. In the well-drawn illustration, a man in a frock coat was shown from behind, rising from a low-backed Windsor chair, his right hand grasping the chair's curving arm and his left reaching up toward a candle suspended in a holder from the *S* in *Study*. His tense posture implied shock and possibly fear; like Arthur's title, however, the cover illustration revealed nothing about the story within.

The issue went on sale in November for one shilling. Like most magazines, *Beeton's* was primarily a vehicle for commerce, and atop the early pages ran the heading *Beeton's Christmas Annual Advertiser*. The text and illustrations were black-and-white, but a few advertisers had paid for a three-color tipped-in insert on poorer-quality paper. Advertisements filled the first fourteen pages—announcements for everything from Sir James Murray's Pure Fluid Magnesia ("an excellent Remedy in cases of Acidity, Indigestion, Heartburn, Gravel, and Gout") to Darlow's magnetic Lung Invigorator. Plaudits and promises for Steiner's Vermin Paste jostled those for Southall's Sanitary Towels for Ladies and the Patent Thermo Safeguard Feeding Bottle (designed to rescue "Thousands of Infants who are now being Ruined in Health"). The back cover of the magazine bore a full-page advertisement for Beecham's Pills, "A Marvelous Antidote" for everything from "Wind and Pain in the Stomach" to "Disturbed Sleep, Frightful Dreams, and All Nervous and Trembling Sensations, &c."

After marching through this carnival of industry, Arthur found that the title page, opposite half-page advertisements for both Irish cambric pocket handkerchiefs and electrical treatments at Pulvermacher's Galvanic Establishment in Regent Street, bore, below a vestigial *A*, the words *STUDY IN SCARLET* in huge capitals, with *By A. Conan Doyle* prominent underneath. The other works in the 170-page volume—clearly minor by comparison, if allocated title page real estate was any clue—were described as "Two Original Plays for Home Performance," a popular form of party entertainment.

This title page masked considerable real-life drama. The author and illustrator of the first play, *Food for Powder: A Vaudeville for the Drawing Room*, which began on page 96, was listed as R. André. This was the second tightly guarded pseudonym for William Roger Snow, a fifty-three-year-old outcast member of a prominent London family. His indiscretions with an Irish actress had wrecked both his military career and his marriage, resulting in the need to write for money under pen names unknown to both the military and his wife. Before hiding behind the name Richard André, Snow had disguised himself as Clifford Merton. Wildly prolific, under each nom de plume he was popular as both a writer and an illustrator for adults and children. He garnished the *Beeton's* edition of his farce with whimsical sketches of the characters.

The Four-Leaved Shamrock started on page 115, where it bore the informative subtitle *A Drawing-Room Comedietta in Three Acts*, as well as the performance note "May also be acted as a Charade to the word 'Stoppage.'" Its author hid not a secret past but merely her gender behind a pen name. Catherine Jane—writing as C. J.—Hamilton had published three of her five novels, including *Marriage Bonds: Or, Christian Hazell's Married Life*, with Ward, Lock. She had also published some stories and her novel *Hedged with Thorns* under the pseudonym Retlaw Spring. Although born in England, Hamilton moved to Ireland after the death of her father, an Anglican vicar, and wrote from there. Later she was also known for her literate and celebratory nonfiction series *Women Writers: Their Works and Ways*. Hamilton's play was adorned with a few character portraits by the popular illustrator Matt Stretch, who portrayed the antics in a satirical mode reminiscent of illustrations for early Dickens by Hablot K. Browne (Phiz).

Then came another page of advertisements and the contents page, followed by seventeen more commercial pages, many of them featuring blurbs for books such as *The World's Inhabitants: Mankind, Animals, and Plants* and John Forster's *Life of Goldsmith*. When readers finally reached the official page 1, they could at least see ahead an expanse of text uninterrupted except by illustrations. Arthur's novella filled the next ninety-five pages.

Arthur was twenty-eight. Eight years had passed since the publication of his first story, "The Mystery of Sasassa Valley," in *Chambers's Journal*.

Beeton's commissioned D. H. Friston to illustrate the work. Friston set the stage with a frontispiece portraying the moment when Sherlock Holmes peers through a large magnifying glass at the word *Rache* scrawled upon the wall of the murder scene at 3, Lauriston Gardens. Clad in bowler hat and a belted, caped Inverness—a Scottish style of cloak only recently adopted in England—Holmes may have looked more stylish than Arthur intended. With a receding lower lip and chin, however, Holmes lacks the forceful demeanor he presents in Arthur's novel. But Friston furnished him with an appropriately aquiline nose, equipped him with a magnifying glass, and portrayed him towering over the police detectives.

The second illustration doesn't even show Holmes's face. While Gregson and Lestrade argue, Holmes is bent over the corpse in the room at Lauriston Gardens, the caption reading, "As he spoke, his nimble fingers were flying here, there, and everywhere." No other illustrations appear until Part 2, when John Ferrier awakens in the desert to find himself and the little girl Lucy rescued by Mormons. Friston showed two men helping the ragged and worn Ferrier stumble along, while another man carries Lucy on his shoulders. For his final illustration, Friston captured the moment when Jefferson Hope comes to the besieged Ferrier family and offers to help spirit them away during the night.

In his mid-sixties, David Henry Friston was a well-known artist. After his first wife's death in 1854, with seven children to support, he worked prolifically. His paintings had been exhibited at the Royal Academy, British Institution, and Royal Society of British Artists, but he was better known for his illustration work. Between 1871 and 1872, he illustrated the serial publication of Joseph Sheridan Le Fanu's sensuous vampire novella *Carmilla* in the short-lived London literary magazine *The Dark Blue*. His numerous illustrations for books had included at least two published by Ward, Lock. Like Matt Stretch and the pseudonymous Richard André, Friston had been providing drawings for *Beeton's* since 1885.

A Study in Scarlet was not the first work of Arthur's that Friston had been commissioned to illustrate. Working often at this time for *London Society*, he had illustrated four of Arthur's short stories during the last few years. For the Christmas 1881 issue, he illustrated both "That Little Square Box" and "The Gully of Bluemansdyke." The next year's Christmas issue saw Friston's drawings adorning Arthur's story "My Friend the Murderer." And in December 1885, only weeks before Arthur began writing *A Study in Scarlet*, he saw that his *London Society* story "Elias B. Hopkins—The Parson of Jackman's Gulch" had been illustrated by Friston.

Ward, Lock advertised the forthcoming *Beeton's Christmas Annual* in the November 1 issue of *The Publishers' Circular*, the fortnightly organ of the publishing and bookselling trade that had been founded half a century earlier, twenty years ahead of its current rival, *The Bookseller*. After exploiting their new author's urgent desire for publication, Ward, Lock added insult to injury by misspelling his name.

JUST READY, IN PICTURE COVERS, ONE SHILLING, BEETON'S CHRISTMAS ANNUAL, 28th Season, the leading feature of which is an original thrilling Story entitled

A STUDY IN SCARLET

By A. Condon Doyle.

This story will be found remarkable for the skilful presentation of a supremely ingenious detective, whose performances, while based on the most rational principles, outshine any hitherto depicted. The surprises are most cleverly and yet most naturally managed, and at each stage the reader's attention is kept fascinated and eager for the next event. The sketches of the "Wild West" in its former barren and trackless condition, and of the terrible position of the starving traveller with his pretty charge, are most vivid and artistic. Indeed, the entire section of the story that deals with early events in the Mormon settlement is most stirring, and intense pathos is brought out in some of the scenes. The publishers have great satisfaction in assuring the Trade that no annual for some years has equalled the one which they now offer for *naturalness, truth, skill, and exciting interest.* It is certain to be read, not once, but twice by every reader; and the person who can take it up and lay it down again unfinished must be one of those people who are neither impressionable nor curious. *A Study in Scarlet* should be the talk of every Christmas gathering throughout the land.

Then Ward, Lock placed at least a few advertisements in newspapers. An illustrated weekly, *The Graphic*, had garnered respect and influence in the world of European art since its founding eight years earlier, by the artist William Luson Thomas, as a more accomplished rival of the popular *Illustrated London News*, which was known for its sensationalism rather than for a commitment to serious visual artists. Thus the advertisement that appeared in the Saturday, November 26, issue would be seen by a variety of readers, many of them culturally sophisticated. It simply quoted from the earlier announcement in *The Publishers' Circular*—including the misspelling of Arthur's name.

Ward, Lock's staff also mailed notices about their latest holiday *Beeton's* to various newspapers. Many columnists would announce the publication of a book or periodical even if they lacked space or time (or desire) to review it. Several papers took brief notice of Arthur's first published novel. One such note—with Arthur's name spelled correctly this time—appeared in *Lloyd's Weekly Newspaper*, another rival of *The Illustrated London News*. Published every Sunday morning, *Lloyd's* had been flourishing ever since the repeal of the stamp tax in 1860 had permitted the publisher to lower the cost to a penny per issue.

"Beeton's Christmas Annual (Ward, Lock & Company)," read the notice in *Lloyd's* "Literature" column, "has for leading subject 'A Study in Scarlet' by A. Conan Doyle, a tale replete with stirring incidents, and described as a reprint of reminiscences of Army-surgeon Watson. The number also contains two original drawing room plays."

The 1887 *Annual* sold out of its tens of thousands of copies within a few weeks. When *The Graphic* published its review of the issue on the tenth of December, the reviewer omitted Arthur's name entirely, describing the author as anonymous and dismissing the book's originality. "It is not at all a bad imitation," puffed the reviewer on a more positive note, and then added perceptively, "but it would never have been written but for Poe, Gaboriau, and Mr. R. L. Stevenson. The hero of the tale is simply the hero of 'The Murder [*sic*] in the Rue Morgue.' Those who like detective stories, and have not read the great originals, will find the tale full of interest. It hangs together well, and finishes ingeniously."

Next, on the seventeenth of December, a review appeared in *The Glasgow Herald*, ranking Holmes much higher in relation to his ancestors—though this first laudatory review also misspelled Arthur's name. "The *piece de resistance*" of the current issue of *Beeton's*, the reviewer proclaimed, was

> a story by A. Conair Doyle entitled "A Study in Scarlet." It is the story of a murder, and of the preternatural sagacity of a scientific detective, to whom Edgar Allan Poe's Dupin was a trifler, and Gaboriau's Lecoq a child. He is a wonderful man is Mr Sherlock Holmes, but one gets so wonderfully interested in his cleverness and in the mysterious murder which he unravels that one cannot lay down the narrative until the end is reached. What that end is wild horses shall not make us divulge.

Two days later, a reviewer in *The Scotsman* gave Arthur's book unstinting praise:

> The chief piece in "Beeton's Christmas Annual" is a detective story by Mr A. Conan Doyle, *A Study in Scarlet*. This is as

entrancing a tale of ingenuity in tracing out crime as has been written since the time of Edgar Allan Poe. The author shows genius. He has not trodden in the well-worn paths of literature, but has shown how the true detective should work by observation and deduction.

This review ended with a prediction for Arthur: "His book is bound to have many readers."

CHAPTER 25

Truth as Death

His brush was concerned not only with fairies and delicate themes of the kind, but with wild and fearsome subjects, so that his work had a very peculiar style of its own, mitigated by great natural humour. He was more terrible than Blake and less morbid than Wiertz.

—ARTHUR CONAN DOYLE, ON HIS FATHER'S ARTWORK

In the last half of the 1880s, during his years at Sunnyside asylum, Charles Doyle often sat outside on the grounds, with the breeze tugging at his sketchbook, and drew and painted. When he focused on the world around him, he produced impressively realistic work, including sketches of his fellows on a picnic. He painted a lyrical watercolor of a man and woman peacefully strolling on a lawn near Sunnyside's handsome stone buildings with their crow-stepped gables and chimney pots. Through a window, Charles sketched a couple of the bare-faced rooks that socialized on the lawn. When one caught a worm and offered it to another, he asked underneath his drawing of this act, "Could unselfishness go further?"

Captivated by the elegant purple-and-green coleus adorning a Sunnyside dining table, Charles immortalized it in watercolor. He admired a curly-haired young housemaid on her hands and knees, polishing a floor, with her reflection visible below her—and sketched her in ink, tinting the result with watercolors. The young woman blushed and asked for a copy of the drawing, and Charles gave her one. Apparently his agreeable charm survived. He seems to have employed his artwork as a method of interacting with the staff and with other inmates; he posed for one group photograph with a large sketchbook firmly in hand.

Often Charles also drew images that none of his fellow inmates could see in the world around them. He conjured, for example, a giant squirrel carrying a bonneted human baby. Sometimes, like his famous brother Dickie, Charles drew fairies—tiny figures avoiding rain under a mushroom umbrella, peering from behind Christmas holly leaves and berries, riding on the back of an exotic fowl. Fairies were something of a family preoccupation. Once Charles turned the sketchbook sideways and painted a tall, beautifully moonlit scene of the Sunnyside buildings at night, with a pageant of pale spirits, including ethereal horses, cascading down from the clouds to the lawn.

Charles portrayed himself interacting with a sphinx in various ways—kissing it, riding it, fleeing its attack. In one drawing, labeled "Busting Out," he seems to be tearing his way through a piece of paper, squeezing through the rip he created, and dancing with joy after his escape. A fully dressed and long-bearded Charles shakes hands with a shrouded skeleton that claps him familiarly on the shoulder—while behind Charles a barely sketched-in angel reaches as if to grasp his left hand. But although he readily shakes the skeleton's bony hand with his right, Charles's left hand is firmly in his pocket and not available to angels. In the lower right corner, Charles titled this drawing "Truth as Death."

No doubt Charles missed Mary, from whom he had been apart for years—since he first went to Dr. Forbes's establishment for inebriates at Blairerno in 1881 (if not earlier). One scene in his Sunnyside sketchbook Charles conjured from memory or from yearning. In 1886 a home rule campaign was launched to set up a Scottish Parliament in Edinburgh, following a similar movement in Ireland. Irish himself and having lived in Scotland for decades, Charles was concerned about the extent to which England would permit greater autonomy within the rest of the United Kingdom. Prime Minister William E. Gladstone's support for Irish home rule was dividing the Liberal Party and helping erode its influence. During this time, Charles turned to plain India ink to portray himself, long-bearded and bespectacled, seated at the feet of his beloved Mary, intertwining his fingers around his knees and gazing adoringly at his smiling wife as she sews. Underneath he wrote affectionately, "Mary, my ideal home ruler. No repeal of the union proposed in this case."

On October 6, 1887, Charles told a physician that he had encountered his wife on the Sunnyside grounds. He had, he claimed, talked with her for a long time. It was fiction.

* * *

Arthur had long admired his father's talent and ambition, and he was pain-fully aware that it was wasting away in secret. He tried to help Charles by bringing him aboard his new novel. In early 1888, Ward, Lock proposed to republish *A Study in Scarlet* as a stand-alone volume. Owning the copyright, the publisher did not require Arthur's permission, but sought his coopera-tion. Whether Ward, Lock proposed the idea as a marketing ploy or Arthur hatched the plan out of filial affection, he approached his father about drawing illustrations for it.

At this time Charles was worrying often about death. In March 1888 an attendant at Montrose noted that Charles spent at least half of one day in prayer, kneeling in the billiard room with devotional in hand. "Has no memory for anything recent," the record noted, "but remembers well things he learnt and people he knew years ago."

Whatever his emotional state, Charles produced six drawings for Ward, Lock. Not one, however, demonstrated the grace or imagination visible in his previous work, or even the level of skill that he could still summon on occasion for his sketchbook. When he received the first two from his father, in a package without any accompanying note, Arthur wrote to his mother that neither drawing was bad, although they were "somewhat unfinished." Arthur thanked his father. Somehow Charles found the energy and focus to send a gracious note in reply, including kind wishes for Touie. When recounting this experience to his mother, Arthur added a hopeful if unrealistic postscript: "Papa in his letter seemed fairly contented with his lot."

Clearly Charles did not pose his fellow inmates or asylum staff as models for the drawings, any more than he paid attention to his son's descriptions of the setting and characters. Arthur may have been surprised that Ward, Lock even accepted them for publication. The first drawing portrayed the moment when Inspector Lestrade opens the door at 3, Lauriston Gardens, ushering Sherlock Holmes and Dr. Watson into the pres-ence of the corpse of Enoch Drebber. The awkward figures, barely delineated in a cartoon outline unworthy even of *Punch*, show a bearded Dr. Watson towering over a scrawny, shoulderless figure that bears no resemblance to Arthur's description of Holmes. The single professional policeman present—a goateed Lestrade—raises his hand in what Charles presumably meant to be a gesture of horror. With a shapeless hat pulled low over a broad forehead, above a simian face with sharpened chin, Holmes seems the least impressive person in the room. Ironically, the liveliest figure is the staring corpse of Drebber, whose unnatural sprawl fills the foreground.

The other drawings were no less amateurish. Holmes appeared in three of the six. In one, a figure—which not only ignored Arthur's description of Holmes but even failed to resemble Charles's other two representations of him—sits behind a desk, pointing a finger and lecturing the ragtag band of urchins whom Watson describes as "half a dozen of the dirtiest and most ragged street Arabs that ever I clapped eyes on." Holmes explains them to Watson: "It's the Baker Street division of the detective police force . . . There's more work to be got out of one of those little beggars than out of a dozen of the force. The mere sight of an official-looking person seals men's lips. These youngsters, however, go everywhere and hear everything." Later he dubbed the urchins the Baker Street Irregulars. Charles's representation of these boys is barely sketched in; they could be ten years old or forty—as could the figure of Holmes. Seated nearby, the bearded Watson looks, as he does in the crime scene illustration, rather like Charles Doyle himself.

Loyally, however, Arthur promoted the drawings to Ward, Lock. Soon he was informing Lottie that he had come to terms with the publisher "for Papa's drawings for the Study." Apparently a friend of Arthur's in Southsea, the architect Henry Ball, had agreed to create wood engravings from Charles's drawings.

But actually Ward, Lock tried to talk Arthur down on the already modest price that he had proposed for Charles's work. They offered only three guineas for the six blocks and Ball's tracings of them. Still a little-known writer with no sway in the publishing world, Arthur wrote Ward, Lock a humiliating letter explaining that normally Charles Doyle received £5 per page for his work, but that, because Arthur was interested in the success of this edition of his novel, he had determined to make the drawings available to them for £3 per page. He said flatly that their alternative offer seemed so incredible he could only assume that it was an error of some kind. "Ward & Lock are perfect Jews," he fumed to his mother. He insisted that he would rather burn the blocks than accede to such robbery.

In July 1888, Ward, Lock published the first stand-alone edition of Arthur's novel in their innovative shilling paperback series. The cover was cheap heavy paper, white, with *A Study in Scarlet* filling the top half with letters apparently intended to look exotically Eastern, and *By Conan Doyle* at an angle below.

Charles Doyle's drawing of the murder scene at Lauriston Gardens, with Holmes, Watson, and Lestrade in the doorway, appeared as frontispiece. The caption read, "The single, grim, motionless figure which lay stretched upon the boards. (Page 31)." The other five drawings also occupied full pages.

Commenting upon this "story of thrilling interest," a publisher's preface mistakenly assured the reader that the Mormon subplot was as accurate as it was enthralling. It also proclaimed that "the unraveling of the apparently unfathomable mystery by the cool shrewdness of Mr. Sherlock Holmes" was fully equal to the "sustained interest and gratified expectation" of such recent best sellers as Archibald Clavering Gunter's romantic adventure *Mr. Barnes of New York* and Lawrence L. Lynch's Chicago detective novel *Shadowed by Three*. Rather than praise Charles's feeble drawings, the preface cited his pedigree:

> The work has a valuable advantage in the shape of illustrations by the author's father, MR. CHARLES DOYLE, a younger brother of the late MR. RICHARD DOYLE, the eminent colleague of JOHN LEECH, in the pages of *Punch*, and son of the eminent caricaturist whose political sketches, signed "H.B.," were a feature in London half-a-century ago.

Apparently the tightfisted company never paid Arthur what he asked. In November Ward, Lock sent him a letter stating flatly that they owed him nothing beyond the amount they had already sent. Nor did the book ever make it into the railway stalls of bookseller W. H. Smith, a prized venue that may have been held out to Arthur as a lure to encourage his participation, perhaps because Ward, Lock had bought the rights to publish *Smith's Select Library of Fiction* in 1885.

He earned no more money for *A Study in Scarlet*, but here at last was a book with his name on the spine.

Not yet part of the larger publishing community, Arthur probably did not know about a recent precedent that cast Ward, Lock's no-royalties contract with him in an even harsher light. The Bristol firm of J. Arrowsmith—to which house Arthur had submitted *A Study in Scarlet*, to no avail—published its own Christmas annual, available for sixpence. In 1883 the third such featured a novella by Hugh Conway, the pseudonym for a lyricist, poet, and author of supernatural and mystery stories named Frederick John Fargus.

Conway sold outright to Arrowsmith, for £80, the copyright to his romantic thriller *Called Back*, a melodramatic, coincidence-driven saga of amnesia, cured blindness, and second sight. He must have thought this a savvy transaction when *Arrowsmith's Christmas Annual* sold only half of its six-thousand-copy issue.

Early in 1884, however, the publisher issued the slim novel for a shilling in its paper-covered series, Arrowsmith's Bristol Library. Within a couple of months, thirty thousand copies had leapt from the train station bookstalls to distract commuters from rattle and soot. Arrowsmith behaved honorably, canceling its original contract with Conway and signing a new one to pay him a royalty for six years. Meanwhile, Conway collaborated on a dramatic adaption of his novel with J. Comyns Carr, an influential art critic, gallery director, theater manager, and playwright, known for his promotion of avant-garde painters such as the Pre-Raphaelites.

Thus by 1887, when Ward, Lock published Arthur's novel, Arrowsmith had sold more than 350,000 copies of the British edition of *Called Back*. Everyone seemed to be talking about it. It was also widely translated—as well as published, without payment, in the United States. During a flurry of popularity in Amherst, Massachusetts, for example, *Called Back* caught the attention of a little-known poet named Emily Dickinson. She admired Conway's book and wrote a poem with the title "Called Back." When she died a few days later, her gravestone read "Called Back, May 15, 1886." Conway himself had died suddenly of typhoid the year before.

While the behind-the-scenes history of Conway's novel did not inspire Ward, Lock to pay Arthur royalties for *A Study in Scarlet*, its success did demonstrate the commercial potential of adventurous thrillers.

Despite these setbacks and reminders of his shaky literary status, during 1887 Arthur had completed his ambitious novel *Micah Clarke*, set in late seventeenth-century England, amid the Protestant rebellion to overthrow the Catholic James II following the death of his brother, Charles II. Arthur seems to have chosen as his models in this historical outing three favorites—Alexandre Dumas, Robert Louis Stevenson, and Charles Reade. During 1886, Stevenson's novel *Kidnapped* had been serialized in the weekly children's magazine *Young Folks' Paper*, which had also seen first publication of *Treasure Island* and *The Black Arrow*. *Blackwood's* responded favorably to the first half of Arthur's manuscript of *Micah Clarke*, but after reading the second and third Arthur's cherished magazine did not buy the book. He all but begged them to reconsider, but they resisted his entreaties. Soon he sent it elsewhere.

In 1888 Arthur adapted the second half of *A Study in Scarlet* into a three-act play. And on the thirtieth of August of that year, he went to the Langham Hotel in Marylebone to dine with Joseph Marshall (usually known as J. M.) Stoddart, who was in London from Philadelphia, where he edited *Lippincott's Monthly Magazine of Popular Literature and Science.*

They dined in a room with gold-and-scarlet mosaic marble floors and towering plaster relief ceilings. Since the Langham's completion in 1865, the neo-Gothic grand hotel, with its several stories featuring long rows of elegant windows—arched, mullioned, traceried—had become one of the most renowned lodgings in Europe, offering not only an electrically illuminated entrance but also the first hydraulic lifts in the country, called "rising rooms." The Prince of Wales had attended the grand opening, and the deposed Louis Napoleon III had spent much of his exile there.

Stoddart was known for seeking out authors he admired. He had invited two other guests—Thomas Patrick Gill, an Irish Member of Parliament, and the Irish writer Oscar Wilde, who was already a famous apostle of Aestheticism. Five years Arthur's senior, Wilde had recently published *The Happy Prince and Other Fables*—five fairy tales—but he was better known for his poetry, which had won Oxford's Newdigate Prize, and for plays such as *The Duchess of Padua.*

Arthur found Wilde charming and impressive. He liked his refined wit and his way of emphasizing rhetorical points with subtle gestures. When the quartet discussed how wars might be fought in the future, Wilde turned his face and raised a hand in a way that lent gravity to his single remark: "A chemist on each side will approach the frontier with a bottle."

Conservative and supported by the Lippincott publishing firm in Philadelphia, committed to quality and handsomely printed on good paper, *Lippincott's* had grown steadily in reputation and influence since its debut in 1868—although it had never achieved financial independence. From the first issue, with its editorial guarantee of good pay for writers ("It is no part of the publishers' plan to ask anyone to do something for nothing"), the magazine had been able to feature popular authors. Manuscripts arrived from all over the nation—from Frank R. Stockton in New England, from the pseudonymous Octave Thanet out west, from William Gilmore Simms in the South. The hugely popular mystery writer Anna Katharine Green, author of *The Leavenworth Case*, appeared in the pages of *Lippincott's*. Novelist Henry James, in his literary journalism mode, helped the magazine maintain a reputation for featuring some of the era's best travel writing.

Lippincott's set out to follow *The Atlantic's* policy of printing serials only by American authors, but soon broke its rule with an Anthony Trollope novel and followed by publishing whichever English-language writers appealed to the editors and the readers. Still, it could not catch up with the nation's two great literary magazines, *Harper's* and *Century*, both published in New York City. In 1886 *Lippincott's* moved from the more common two-column page to a single column, simpler to set and print. In 1887, the year before Stoddart met with Arthur, *Lippincott's* initiated a policy of publishing an entire novel in a single issue rather than serializing chapters. To squeeze between the covers of a single magazine issue, the novels had to be brief—"novelettes," the editors called them.

J. M. Stoddart wined and dined his trio. By the end of the evening, Oscar Wilde had agreed to produce a novel, which became *The Picture of Dorian Gray*, and Arthur had committed to write a second novel about Sherlock Holmes.

It was a heady time. During September 1888, four weekly issues of *The Pall Mall Gazette* published Arthur's brief novel *The Mystery of Cloomber*, an antic adventure built around the occult powers of Indian mystics. "In our opinion," enthused *The Portsmouth Evening News*, "the construction of this story is an improvement upon that of 'The Study in Scarlet,' which, although deservedly popular, lacks dramatic sequence, and it will add materially to the growing reputation of Dr. Doyle."

CHAPTER 26

Watson's Brother's Watch

"It has long been an axiom of mine that the little things are infinitely the most important."

—SHERLOCK HOLMES, IN "A CASE OF IDENTITY"

S teadied by his marriage and book contracts, Arthur was writing more than ever. Following the meeting with J. M. Stoddart, Arthur wrote a second Sherlock Holmes novel, *The Sign of Four*. He even used the Langham Hotel as a setting for one scene. From the first page, the more experienced Arthur was in control of the story in ways that he did not manage with *A Study in Scarlet*. He opened the novel with a shocking and decadent image that confirmed his indications in the first Holmes novel that the masterful detective and his Boswell were bohemians. Holmes sprawls in a velvet armchair, injecting a cocaine solution into his arm. Afterward he sighs blissfully and picks up an antique book. It is a moment worthy of Poe, but Arthur wrote it with a modern sense of pacing and immediacy, raising the curtain on a new drama about his eccentrics.

"Which is it today, morphine or cocaine?" asks Watson.

"It is cocaine, a seven-percent solution. Would you care to try it?"

"No, indeed," replies Watson, and begins to argue with Holmes's nonchalant attitude toward the drugs. "Count the cost!" he exclaims. "Why should you, for a mere passing pleasure, risk the loss of those great powers with which you have been endowed?"

"My mind rebels at stagnation," explains Holmes pompously. "Give me problems, give me work, give me the most abstruse cryptogram, or the most intricate analysis, and I am in my own proper atmosphere. I can dispense then with artificial stimulants."

Arthur gave this second Holmes novel greater emotional resonance than the first by sketching in more background for his characters—and by creating tension between them. Holmes demonstrates his methods by observing a particular reddish mud upon Watson's boots, which he knows to be unique to the region around the Wigmore Street post office, and because he knows that Watson has not written a letter he deduces that he went to the post office to dispatch a telegram.

Impressed, Watson nonetheless demands a more severe test. He hands over a watch, which he says has only recently come into his possession, and asks Holmes to observe and deduce. Without thinking of the artifact's possible emotional significance for Watson, Holmes delivers a shocking assessment. The initial *W.* suggests that it was from Watson's family, and since he acquired it only recently although his father has been dead for many years, it must have been in the possession of his elder brother. Then Holmes casually adds, "He was a man of untidy habits,—very untidy and careless. He was left with good prospects, but he threw away his chances, lived for some time in poverty with occasional short intervals of prosperity, and finally, taking to drink, he died. That is all I can gather."

Shaken, Watson accuses Holmes of charlatanry, and the detective must explain the clues—dents in the casing, pawnbrokers' numbers scrawled inside. Once again Arthur lent a story emotional depth by bringing in alcoholism, with a description of a watch that may have been in his own possession:

> "Finally, I ask you to look at the inner plate, which contains the key-hole. Look at the thousands of scratches all round the hole,— marks where the key has slipped. What sober man's key could have scored those grooves? But you will never see a drunkard's watch without them. He winds it at night, and he leaves these traces of his unsteady hand."

Holmes reveals that he has written technical monographs on attending to what Watson calls his "extraordinary genius for minutiae"—on distinguishing between tobacco varieties, on tracing footprints. In fact, Arthur reveals in this second novel that both his protagonists are authors. He has made Watson into the detective's biographer or memoirist, as he hinted in the closing pages of *A Study in Scarlet.* He even has Watson refer to his "little brochure" about the Jefferson Hope case, and Holmes says, "I glanced over it. Honestly, I cannot congratulate you upon it." By presenting the stories as actual case records, and Watson as a reporting participant, Arthur added an exciting sense of immediacy and reader participation to the series.

"Detection is, or ought to be," complains Holmes, "an exact science and should be treated in the same cold and unemotional manner. You have attempted to tinge it with romanticism, which produces much the same effect as if you worked a love-story or an elopement into the fifth proposition of Euclid."

This was a sly setup, because Arthur saturated *The Sign of Four* with not only romanticism but actual romance. Watson is smitten with Holmes's pretty young client, Miss Mary Morstan, from the moment she walks through the door at Baker Street.

> She was a blonde young lady, small, dainty, well gloved, and dressed in the most perfect taste. There was, however, a plainness and simplicity about her costume which bore with it a suggestion of limited means. The dress was a sombre greyish beige, untrimmed and unbraided, and she wore a small turban of the same dull hue, relieved only by a suspicion of white feather in the side. Her face had neither regularity of feature nor beauty of complexion, but her expression was sweet and amiable, and her large blue eyes were singularly spiritual and sympathetic.

Oddly, Watson also refers to "the years that I had lived with him in Baker Street," although *A Study in Scarlet* takes place only a few months after the two meet and clearly it is the only preceding case about which Watson writes. In *The Sign of Four* Arthur assigned Holmes a rather questionable motto that soon became famous. "How often have I said to you," the detective asks Watson, "that when you have eliminated the impossible, whatever remains, however improbable, must be the truth?" Arthur had employed almost the same phrasing some years earlier, in his story "The Fate of the *Evangeline*." After being rejected by such periodicals as *Blackwood's*, the story had appeared in the *Boy's Own Paper* in December 1885, only a couple of months before Arthur began writing the text of *A Study in Scarlet* and probably while he was plotting it. In the story, the narrator cites a fictional article from *The Scotsman* criticizing reckless opinions about the disappearance of the titular ship:

"It would be well," the "Scotsman" concluded, "if those who express opinions upon such subjects would bear in mind those simple rules as to the analysis of evidence laid down by Auguste Dupin. 'Exclude the impossible,' he remarks in one of Poe's immortal stories, 'and what is left, however improbable, must be the truth.' "

Perhaps Arthur was deliberately satirizing such articles by introducing a spurious quotation, but probably he was merely following his usual practice of writing quickly without bothering to check facts. No such sentence, nor even one similar to it, appears in Poe's Dupin stories. Whether or not during the intervening years a reader had pointed out this error to Arthur, in his second Sherlock Holmes novel he resurrected the concept and even its wording and gave it to his own creation.

Throughout *The Sign of Four*, Arthur wrote like a professional who was master of his melodramatic story and its colorful characters. "The Science of Deduction," he called the first chapter, echoing Holmes's phrase in his article "The Book of Life," which Watson had mocked in the early pages of *A Study in Scarlet*. From the first, Arthur was proclaiming his new creation a scientific detective, and readers quickly learned that Holmes was a busy working professional.

Mary Morstan consults Holmes—and Watson, whom she invites to stay and listen to her statement of the case—to decipher the mystery of her father's disappearance ten years earlier, in 1878. He left behind mostly "curiosities from the Andaman Islands." For the last six years, Miss Morstan has been receiving once each year an anonymous package containing "a very large lustrous pearl." She consults Holmes after receiving an anonymous letter that offers to explain her mysterious situation. Holmes and his eager sidekick agree to help. After Miss Morstan departs, Watson exclaims, "What a very attractive woman!" and Holmes replies, "Is she? . . . A client is to me a mere unit, a factor in a problem."

In conjuring atmosphere for his story, Arthur wrote lyrically of London. After stating in the previous chapter that the story took place in July, he carelessly described a September evening—an error that he would write to J. M. Stoddart to correct only after he had submitted the novel to *Lippincott's*, although it seems to have never been corrected in subsequent editions.

It was a September evening and not yet seven o'clock, but the day had been a dreary one, and a dense drizzly fog lay low upon the great city. Mud-coloured clouds drooped sadly over the muddy streets. Down the Strand lamps were but misty splotches of diffused light which threw a feeble circular glimmer upon the slimy pavement. The yellow glare from the shop-windows streamed out into the steamy, vaporous air and threw a murky, shifting radiance across the crowded thoroughfare. There was, to my mind, something eerie and ghostlike in the endless procession of faces which flitted across these narrow bars of light—sad faces and glad, haggard and merry. Like all humankind, they flitted from the gloom into the light and so back into the gloom once more.

Soon a four-wheeler cab carries them further into the mystery, to the home of Thaddeus Sholto, a bald young man so fearful he visibly trembles. He reveals that Miss Morstan's father is dead. Then he recounts the story of his own father's involvement with Captain Morstan. Major Sholto claimed that while they both served in the Thirty-fourth Bombay Infantry, he and Captain Morstan "came into possession of a considerable treasure," and that when they disagreed over its division, back home in England, Morstan died of a sudden heart attack. Remorseful about not sharing the treasure with the young Miss Morstan after her father's death, Major Sholto is in the act of telling his sons where the treasure is hidden when he dies while staring at a fearsome vision at the window: "It was a bearded, hairy face, with wild cruel eyes and an expression of concentrated malevolence."

As he had turned earlier to the Mormons of exotic Utah, Arthur now employed myths and stereotypes about the aboriginal pygmies of the Andaman Islands, an archipelago in the Bay of Bengal between India and Burma. Although he worked with several Englishmen, the actual murderer of Morstan and Sholto turned out to be a pygmy whom Watson describes with fear and revulsion: "There was movement in the huddled bundle upon the deck. It straightened itself into a little black man—the smallest I have ever seen—with a great, misshapen head and a shock of tangled, dishevelled hair. Holmes had already drawn his revolver, and I whipped out mine at the sight of this savage, distorted creature." The pygmy tries to fight Holmes and Watson with the blowgun that has been his silent murder weapon all along, and they shoot him.

Arthur conjured memorable and dramatic adventures for his duo, from tracking creosote-scented footprints across London with a dog named

Toby—"an ugly, long-haired, lop-eared creature, half spaniel and half lurcher"—to a rousing boat chase down the Thames at night. At the end of the exciting story, Arthur again turned to a flashback to reveal the saga prior to Holmes's involvement, but in *The Sign of Four* he devoted only one long chapter to it, rather than a substantial section of the narrative, as he had done with *A Study in Scarlet*. At the end, Holmes, fearing boredom again, turns back to his seven percent solution of cocaine.

Before long, Arthur found his first Sherlock Holmes novel compared to those of Hugh Conway and Émile Gaboriau. In January 1889, Andrew Lang, literary editor of the relatively youthful *Longman's Magazine* (the successor to *Fraser's Magazine for Town and Country*), wrote a candid assessment of Holmes's debut in his "At the Sign of the Ship" column for that periodical. His phrase "the horrors of recent months" referred to the brutal murders of several women, only a few months earlier, by an unidentified killer dubbed Jack the Ripper.

> For a railway story, to beguile the way, few things have been so good, of late, as Mr Conan Doyle's *Study in Scarlet*. It is a shilling story about a murder, unluckily, for the horrors of recent months do not dispose one to take pleasure in the romance of assassinations. However, granting the subject, this is an extremely clever narrative, rich in surprises, indeed I never was more surprised by any story than when it came to the cabman. To say more would be "telling," but one may admit that the weak place in the tale, as in most of Gaboriau's, is the explanation, the part of the story which gives the "reason why" of the mystery. However, with this deduction, Mr Conan Doyle comes nearer to the true Hugh Conway than any writer since the regretted death of the author of *Called Back*.

Arthur and Touie had even more exciting news at home than in the review papers. In January, Arthur delivered at home their first child, a daughter. Afterward he wrote to his mother that Touie was doing well and that Mary Louise Conan Doyle had arrived without luggage, naked, and bald, which required immediate effort to address each problem.

The next month, on February 25, 1889, the book division of Longman published a one-thousand-copy first edition of *Micah Clarke*. Andrew Lang had encouraged purchase of the novel, and gratifying response from the press began on publication day. "It is a fullgrown book," enthused the *Evening News*, "and contains some scenes and characters which will, we believe, be thought worthy of Scott." A few days later the same periodical stated flatly, "Dr. A. Conan Doyle has gone at one stride into the front rank of novelists." The reviewer insisted *Micah Clarke* was not only Arthur's finest work to date but "*the* best historical novel that has been published for years." *The Scotsman* said that it was a fine book for boys but much more. "Very interesting and very readable," declared *The Manchester Guardian*, and the reviewer pronounced himself eager for Arthur's next novel. One critic argued that Arthur had been too harsh in his treatment of the Puritans, another that he clearly had a bias in their favor. Soon the book appeared in the United States and throughout the Commonwealth, with reviewers from the *Brooklyn Daily Eagle* to the *Otago (New Zealand) Daily Times* praising it. Arthur wrote to many friends, asking them to order his new novel.

Andrew Lang was not the only person closely following Arthur's career as a writer. Either a family member was sending copies of favorable reviews to Charles Doyle or he was finding them in the Sunnyside library. In early 1889, after *Micah Clarke* was published, he devoted half a sketchbook page to notes about some of them:

> Arthur's Novel "Micha [*sic*] Clarke"
>   Reviewed on Scotsman 4th March 1889
> Highly favourable,
>   "Glasgow Herald" 19th March 1889
> "Mystery of Cloomber" Literary World 11th January 1889,
>   as follows—

He proceeded to summarize the latter review. Then, crowding his sketchbook pages as usual, Charles drew below his tribute to his son's success a three-leaved sprig of clover, scribbled for it a skinny body in knickers and swallowtail coat, and wrote, "There is an Irish lilt in this shamrock."

Although apparently happy for his son's taste of success, Charles was not content to have his own talent wither in darkness. He also kept thinking of his failure to provide for Annette and Lottie, both of whom had worked as governesses and sent home money to help support their mother. In the summer of 1889, Charles complained at length to his diary:

I am certain if my many Vols of, well, I'll say of not serious Work, were organised into some form submittable to the Public they would tickle the taste of innumerable men like myself—and be the Source of much Money which I should like to bestow on my Daughters, but Imprisoned under most depressing restrictions, what can I do?—

. . . my claim for Sanity is not best made by Enlarging on my common sence [*sic*]—as in the possession of a Certain Class of ability demonstrated in this Book and proved by 30 years of Official Public Life, tho' unfortunately not seen by certain Members of my own Family.

But his family had reason to believe that Charles could not survive outside the asylum. At about the same time as these private complaints to his journal, he became restless and excited. He claimed in the presence of attendants that he had already died and that the asylum was hell and the people around him were devils.

CHAPTER 27

Dread of Madhouses

I was now once more at a crossroads of my life.

—ARTHUR CONAN DOYLE, *MEMORIES AND ADVENTURES*

In late 1889 a young Englishman named John Coulson Kernahan had joined Ward, Lock & Co. as a junior editor. The author of a quirky meditation on mortality in the form of a novel, *A Dead Man's Diary: Written After His Decease*, Kernahan was helping Frederick Locker-Lampson edit a new edition of his popular anthology *Lyra Elegantiarum: A Collection of Some of the Best Social and Occasional Verse by Deceased English Authors*, and would go on to write popular novels such as *The Child, the Wise Man, and the Devil*, as well as a fictional prediction of coming war with Russia, *The Red Peril*.

As junior editor at Ward, Lock, he quickly had ideas. Kernahan was also assistant editor of the U.K. edition of *Lippincott's*, and the February 1890 issue, which was about to go on sale, would feature the complete text of *The Sign of Four*, commissioned the year before by J. M. Stoddart. Later Kernahan said that he found the issue of *Beeton's* in which *A Study in Scarlet* had appeared barely more than a year earlier, and took the red-yellow-and-black volume to the managing director, James Bowden.

"Is there anything being done with this?" Kernahan asked.

Bowden shook his head. "It served its purpose, and did respectably as the *Annual*." He pointed out that the sales of the first book edition the year before were not impressive, however. "And few reviewers had anything to say of it."

"No," Kernahan admitted, "so many books appear at Christmas that reviewers are not likely to write at length, or even to notice the contents of one of the many Christmas annuals."

A Study in Scarlet, however, had been the work of an unknown writer. Times had changed, Kernahan insisted. This man Doyle had since published a historical novel, *Micah Clarke*, and here *Lippincott's* was about to publish a second Sherlock Holmes novel. "I am as sure as one can humanly be," Kernahan claimed that he insisted, "that there is a great future for stories in which Sherlock Holmes figures. As you have *A Study in Scarlet*, the very first story about Sherlock Holmes, I suggest that you reissue it as a book, by itself, attractively produced, and attractively illustrated." He made a prediction: "I believe it will have a huge sale, and go on selling for years."

Finally the director agreed.

The Sign of Four appeared in England and the United States simultaneously, in both editions of the February 1890 issue of *Lippincott's*. In England Arthur's contract with *Lippincott's* gave the magazine three months of exclusivity. After that period expired, the novel was reprinted in various English periodicals, beginning with the *Bristol Observer* from May to July, followed by the *Hampshire Telegraph and Sussex Chronicle*, the *Birmingham Weekly Mercury*, and others. On the seventh of June, and again on the fourteenth, the *Bristol Observer* printed unsigned illustrations of the novel that portrayed Sherlock Holmes wearing a deerstalker hat. In his text Arthur had not mentioned such a hat, but the illustrator was not afraid to take liberties; he also adorned Holmes with a small dark mustache.

The deerstalker, made of tweed with a bill in both front and back, had been nicknamed the "fore-and-aft cap." Deer stalking was not quite the same as deer hunting, which in England referred to unarmed gentry riding after trained deer hounds. *Stalking* was the term for more solitary armed hunting, especially for selective culling of herds of fallow, roe, and other deer for game management. A new *Handbook of Deer-Stalking* had been published as recently as 1880. The deerstalker's design not only shielded both the face and the back of the neck; most variations also had flaps that could be pulled down to cover the ears. It was strictly rural headgear. The *Bristol Observer* artist, however, portrayed Holmes wearing the hat in Westminster and along the Thames.

* * *

"A most interesting man to talk to," one of Charles Doyle's asylum attendants noted on January 20, 1890. Charles seems to have never lost his charm. But the same medical record noted that Charles was not sketching as often as he had formerly, and that the quality of his drawings had greatly deteriorated.

Three days later, Charles was transferred to the Royal Edinburgh Asylum. He had been in Montrose for almost five years. Institutions often transferred patients after a few years, partly in the hope that they might find a change of staff and setting invigorating. The General Board of Lunacy described Charles's condition as "relieved," and stated that he was suffering not only from alcoholism but also from epilepsy and deteriorating memory.

The Royal Edinburgh was on an estate in Morningside, in southwestern Edinburgh. In a way, Charles was going back home, but his family was scattered far afield, so Charles was no less alone than he had been at Montrose. His new setting was much larger, with twice as many patients. Under director Thomas Clouston, the Edinburgh Royal Asylum was expanding and modernizing. Originally opened in 1813 as the Edinburgh Lunatic Asylum, it had been launched with parliamentary funds derived from punitive fines from the 1745 Jacobite rebellion. There was a large building for charity patients as well, but Charles's family could afford his £42 annual fee. After he was examined at the new facility and the staff realized how poor his memory was for recent events in his life, Charles was admitted with a new diagnosis: "epileptic insanity."

Geographically, Charles was a long way from Arthur's busy life in Southsea, but he was often on Arthur's mind. The son suffered a tumult of emotions about his father—love, pity, shame, anger—and they showed up in his fiction. In December 1890, each weekly issue of *Chambers's Journal* carried an installment of Arthur's long story "The Surgeon of Gaster Fell." In it the narrator suspects his neighbor, a surgeon, of trapping an elderly man in a cage, apparently for the sake of some dark experiment. But the story turns out to be the sad narrative of a family looking after their troubled father; the cage was an alternative to a fate the old man would have considered worse. "He has an intense dread of madhouses," revealed the surgeon in the story's closing note, "and in his sane intervals would beg and pray so piteously not to be condemned to one, that I could never find the heart to resist him." When this story was reprinted years later, Arthur deleted this too-revealing remark, but he left the fictional date of the story as 1885—the year that Charles Doyle had turned violent and been transferred from Blairerno's easygoing home for inebriates to Montrose's secure asylum for the insane.

Eleven months later, in November 1891, Arthur's more explicit story "A Sordid Affair" appeared in the weekly *People*, which had serialized his sensationalist novel *The Firm of Girdlestone* the year before. The new brief story featured another fictional incarnation of Charles Doyle. A dressmaker's husband, "a small man, black bearded and swarthy," is an amateur artist. Formerly a clerk, his "long course of public drunkenness had ended in a raging attack of delirium tremens, which could not be concealed from his employers, and which brought his instant dismissal from his situation."

Although exhausted by years of worry and trouble from her husband's drunkenness, the dressmaker, Mrs. Raby, believes that she can help him conquer his demons. "It was always with others that she laid the blame, never with him, for her eyes were blind to the shattered irritable wreck, and could only see the dark-haired bashful lad who had told her twenty years ago how he loved her."

Mrs. Raby makes a beautiful gray satin foulard dress on order for a customer—only to find it missing the next morning. Arthur was again drawing upon his own family's sad experience when he wrote the scene in which Mrs. Raby rushes to a nearby pawnshop to find her newly made work hanging on a hook.

"That's my dress," she gasps.

The pawnbroker says, "It was pawned this morning, ma'am, by a small, dark man."

Later, on the street, Mrs. Raby sees a crowd of boys jeering at "a horrid crawling figure, a hatless head, and a dull, vacant, leering face."

She hails a cab, and someone helps her pile her husband into it.

> His coat was covered with dust, and he mumbled and chuckled like an ape. As the cab drove on, she drew his head down upon her bosom, pushing back his straggling hair, and crooned over him like a mother over a baby.
>
> "Did they make fun of him, then?" she cried. "Did they call him names? He'll come home with his little wifey, and he'll never be a naughty boy again."

Arthur closed the story with an apostrophe to his mother (and possibly to his sisters and Touie): "Oh, blind, angelic, foolish love of woman! Why should men demand a miracle while you remain upon earth?"

* * *

Soon Arthur passed another literary milestone. Longmans, Green & Company published *The Captain of the Polestar and Other Tales* in England in March 1890 and the following month in the United States. Here Arthur's early attempts at sensational fiction could cavort together for the first time— the title story alongside "J. Habakuk Jephson's Statement," his fictionalized take on the *Mary Celeste* ship; his horror story "The Ring of Thoth" partnering with his horrific story "John Barrington Cowles" to produce chills. "The Parson of Jackman's Gulch," which D. H. Friston had illustrated two years before his drawings adorned *A Study in Scarlet*, was thus rescued from the ephemeral moment of magazine publication, as were five other stories.

"Dr. Conan Doyle appears to be equally at home," wrote *The Glasgow Herald* in its review, "with the eerie, the sensational, and the humorous. The *motifs* of all these stories are well selected and capitally worked out." The reviewer seemed unaware of revealing Arthur's carefully wrought surprises: "In 'John Barrington Cowles' the reader meets with a vampire or some similar gruesome monster disguised as a fascinating young lady. And this happens in Edinburgh!"

Arthur kept new short stories circulating, and many were accepted— most, of course, reflecting little about his father or other personal matters. As he looked around for new approaches, he thought of continuing his Sherlock Holmes cases in short form. He knew that readers were familiar with series of tales about a recurring character, from Dumas's several novels about d'Artagnan to numerous accounts in the 1860s by Scotland's first police detective, James McLevy. Arthur also understood that stand-alone tales with a recurring character would dodge the notorious pitfall in serializing longer works: the potential loss of interest from a reader who had missed one or more issues and had thus lost track of the narrative. A single recurring character of proven popularity would not only establish an author's loyal readership but also bind readers to the periodical in which his adventures appeared. This might be a selling point for a young author, to help him stand out from his many competitors who were equally eager to fill space in periodicals.

CHAPTER 28

Adventures in the Strand

I should at last be my own master. No longer would I have to
conform to professional dress or try to please any one else. I would be
free to live how I liked and where I liked. It was one of the great
moments of exultation of my life.

—ARTHUR CONAN DOYLE, *MEMORIES AND ADVENTURES*

The Strand, a historic thoroughfare in Westminster, ran for less than
a mile along the busy north shore of the Thames, from Trafalgar
Square to Temple Bar, the boundary between Westminster and
London. There the Strand became Fleet Street. Angling northward from the
Strand, crossing Exeter Street and emptying into Tavistock Street, was a
minor avenue called Burleigh Street. From there, in a tiny, cluttered room on
the top floor of an office building, in time for Christmas 1890 although
dated January 1891, the publisher George Newnes launched the first issue of
a new periodical dubbed *The Strand Magazine*.

Newnes and his colleagues had considered naming it *The Burleigh Street
Magazine*. The cover, beautifully drawn by a flourishing young painter and
designer named George Charles Haité—who was famed for his uncanny
recall of scenes and colors—showed a glamorized view looking eastward down
the Strand toward the eighteenth-century church St. Mary le Strand, with a
corner plaque on a building in the foreground reading BURLEIGH STREET.
When Newnes was planning the periodical, however, its actual address seemed
a mouthful, and the Strand was so close by that he settled on the shorter title.
Despite its parade in the 1890s of innocent shops that could not have looked

less cosmopolitan, the street was significant in English history. It evoked aristocratic palaces and ecclesiastical gatherings that could help create and sustain an identity in the minds of readers. Here John Evelyn had witnessed the Restoration of Charles II and had afterward written, "I stood in the Strand and beheld it and blessed God!" Burleigh Street held no such magic.

The youngest son of a Derbyshire Congregational minister, Newnes possessed more than his share of imagination and confidence. A decade earlier, in Manchester, he had launched *Tit-Bits*, an aptly named magazine filled with short and often sensational anecdotes distilled from many other popular sources. Newnes had famously hired Manchester's "Newsboys Brigade" to hawk his new publication on the streets, and within two hours they had sold five thousand copies of the first issue. Gradually it came to publish short articles, short fiction, and humor, and it had been hugely successful for him. He proved a genius at promotional gimmicks. The *Tit-Bits* Prize competitions had once awarded to a lucky reader an entire house in Dulwich, and Newnes had even masterminded an outrageous scheme whereby every issue of *Tit-Bits* contained an active railway accident insurance policy for the commuting reader. Soon his magazine left most other penny weeklies in the dust.

Newnes had been racing forward ever since, and had for several years been a popular Member of Parliament for Newmarket. Aware of the diverse and not always overlapping markets for periodicals, he had also founded *The Westminster Gazette*, a liberal political newspaper with modest circulation but wide influence, and *The Wide World Magazine*, which specialized in true-life adventure.

He was a few months away from forty when he launched the glossy, high-quality *Strand*. The technology of both printing and distribution had advanced greatly since the dense pages of Richard Steele's *Tatler*, issued thrice weekly in a single folio half-sheet in the early eighteenth century. From lithography to reliable mails to railway commuting, many factors were merging to support a flowering of new periodicals. Yet Newnes saw that British magazines were slow to take advantage of these advances. American magazines were developing an ever greater following in England—"because," wrote Newnes later, "they were smarter and livelier, more interesting, bright and cheerful." He resolved to launch a native magazine on the American model—a glossy, handsome journal that could compete with the established sixpenny monthlies, such as *Scribner's* and *Harper's* from the United States, as well as England's own *English Illustrated* and the long-established *Cassell's Family Magazine*.

Early on, he hired as editor Herbert Greenhough Smith, a Cambridge man and a former *Temple Bar* editor. Dark-haired, mustached, peering through round spectacles, Smith labored at a cluttered dusk in his tiny office on the top floor in Burleigh Street—a sanctum guarded by a phalanx of clattering typewriters, a recent invention that had caught on quickly, especially in publishing. Like Arthur, Greenhough Smith turned his middle name into a part of his surname. Born in Gloucestershire in 1855, he was only four years older than Arthur. To Newnes's dream of an eye-catching innovation—his uneconomical hope to publish an illustration on every page, to draw the browser's eye and keep the reader's active—Smith added his vision of a literate meeting of fiction and articles from at home and abroad. They planned to launch with only self-contained examples of both, rather than serializing longer work. Early issues included many translated stories by foreigners, such as the Frenchmen Guy de Maupassant and Alphonse Daudet and the Russians Alexander Pushkin and Mikhail Lermontov.

The Strand, with its attractive pale blue issues available at W. H. Smith's flourishing railway bookstalls for sixpence, was targeted at suburban and working-class readers. They soon learned that they could be assured of finding literate, intelligent entertainment without risk of moral or intellectual provocation. While supporting *The Westminster Gazette*, which was never financially independent, Newnes did not want politics and what he considered the indecencies of modern art to infect his popular magazine. The periodical quickly established a readership among the working class. The first issues sold two hundred thousand copies per month, roughly the same as the well-established *Cassell's* had managed during its heyday in the 1870s.

Just as *The Strand*'s encouraging launch embodied changes in the world of publishing, so did the manner in which Arthur's stories reached the magazine's office. When, in early 1891, an envelope containing Arthur's first two stories about Sherlock Holmes crossed Greenhough Smith's busy desk, it came via A. P. Watt, a prominent literary agent whose clients included the writer of the hour, the young Rudyard Kipling. Watt had recently taken on Arthur.

Like Arthur, Watt was a transplanted Scot, although a generation older—born in Glasgow in 1834. In earlier years, he had sold books in Edinburgh and read manuscripts for the London publisher Alexander Strahan, publisher of the periodicals *Good Words for the Young* and the

Sunday Magazine. He became a partner in a new incarnation of Strahan & Company, established himself as an advertising agent, and in the late 1870s added the representation of authors to his résumé.

By 1881 he was promoting himself as a full-time literary agent. During the long history of literature, other people had at various times represented or advised writers. But Alexander Pollock Watt seems to have been the first to establish himself as a respected professional who shopped manuscripts to editors and represented authors in contractual negotiations in return for a percentage of the monies received from publishers. By the time that he expressed interest in Arthur's career, his representation could immediately raise an editor's estimation of a new author. A manuscript submitted under Watt's name from his first-floor office at 2, Paternoster Square, received an editor's attention in ways that a mailing cylinder from Southsea did not.

"I really do not know how a busy man like myself," wrote one publisher to Watt, "could ever manage to publish serial stories at all were it not for your assistance, which entirely saves one the trouble of ploughing through rubbish, and at the same time enables one to ascertain, at a moment's notice, exactly to what extent leading novelists are available for the purposes of serial publication."

By the time he represented Arthur, Watt claimed that he did not advertise, but he cleverly exploited other methods of self-promotion. Whenever his office changed address, Watt ran many announcements as a form of advertising free of claims and self-promotion. In 1891, he publicized recent changes in copyright law as a form of notifying writers and publishers that he was conversant in these legal technicalities. His primary form of self-promotion was his shameless distribution of admiring letters by his clients to potential clients. And when an author who later became prominent left Watt for another agent, Watt retained the absentee's name on his ever-growing client list.

With the explosion of serial and reprint options, as well as translations and other foreign rights, publishing was becoming more complex, ever more a competitive business. When a publishing house or magazine was on the market during these unpredictable times, moreover, Watt and other agents served as legal assessor of the value of the firm's copyrighted materials and physical office and warehouse. Agents' position as assessors also further demonstrated the value of copyrighted materials—the kind of copyright that Ward, Lock had deprived Arthur of in 1886 when they insisted upon buying *A Study in Scarlet* outright, withholding the possibility of future royalties. Authors were demanding more agency and fairness in the publishing enterprise. Agents positioned themselves not only as savvy legal representatives brokering individual publishing contracts but also as protective partners in career growth. And not all Watt's clients were authors. Publishers knew that, for a fee, they could farm out to Watt the task of selling serial rights or other potentially profitable sidelines that for some reason they could not handle themselves.

When Smith opened the envelope from Watt, he found two new stories by Arthur Conan Doyle. He was already familiar with Arthur's work. By this time, the young man had published numerous short stories in a wide variety of magazines, as well as the novels *A Study in Scarlet*, *The Sign of Four*, and *Micah Clarke*. Probably Smith had already dealt with Arthur personally. In March 1891, in only its third issue, *The Strand* published Arthur's slight and gimmicky story "The Voice of Science," featuring a gramophone, a brilliant invention that had been conjured only fourteen years earlier by the American Thomas Edison. At a party, instead of playing the scientific speech expected, the instrument reproduces a recitation of a character's vices, as quickly recorded behind the scenes by another character. In a review of the March issue of *The Strand*, Arthur was identified as "Mr. A. Conan Doyle, a popular American writer," but the error appeared only in the *Whitstable Times and Herne Bay Herald*.

Both of the new stories submitted by Watt were far superior to "The Voice of Science." They featured a character that Smith knew had appeared in two novels but never before in a shorter adventure—a cocksure young consulting detective named Sherlock Holmes. The author's handwriting across these neat pages was crisp and clear, as legible as print, and Smith thought that Arthur's writing voice now held a similar limpid clarity. Amid the usual tide of mediocrity flooding an editor's desk, Smith decided that this young Conan Doyle fellow was writing precisely the sort of tale that *The Strand* had been hoping to publish. Smith claimed later that immediately after reading the stories he rushed into Newnes's office and held them out to his boss with a dramatic flourish.

Arthur's first experience with a literary agent went well. Before the first issue of *The Strand* appeared, Watt had asked £4 per one thousand words for "The Voice of Science" and had received it. Smith and Newnes were so enthusiastic about the new Sherlock Holmes stories that Watt negotiated an agreement with them under which Arthur would produce a total of six Holmes stories, one per month, for £200. In terms of both editorial enthusiasm and professional remuneration—entwined, as usual—Arthur had arrived.

CHAPTER 29

Deerstalker

All the drawings are very unlike my own original idea of the man.

—ARTHUR CONAN DOYLE, *MEMORIES AND ADVENTURES*

To illustrate the new series of Sherlock Holmes stories, George Newnes turned first to a young man named Walter Paget. He had drawn for *The Sphere* during the Boer War of the early 1880s, with the job of producing finished magazine illustrations from the rough front-line sketches sent by artists in the field. Walter was the youngest of three artists in a talented family. His eldest brother, Henry, painted technically good if uninspired portraits and historical scenes, with occasionally more exotic fare, such as "The Lady of Shallott," in the manner of the Pre-Raphaelites.

But it was the middle brother, Sidney, who wound up illustrating the Sherlock Holmes stories. Born in London, a year Arthur's junior, Sidney Paget drew marble busts at the British Museum for two years before studying at Heatherley's School of Art in London and then enrolling at the Royal Academy for several years. He had been exhibiting in annual Academy shows since the age of eighteen. Instead of illustrating Arthur's work himself, Walter Paget served as model for Sidney's drawings and watercolors.

With his brother as inspiration, Sidney Paget conjured a more handsome figure than Arthur had envisioned. Arthur saw Holmes as over six feet tall but scarecrow thin, thus looking even taller, with a large aquiline nose jutting between close-set eyes. Walter Paget was better-proportioned, with a ruggedly handsome profile, and Sidney metamorphosed him into Holmes, from dimpled chin to high cheekbones and receding hairline. Like Arthur, Walter was in his late twenties at the time.

In the fourth story, "The Boscombe Valley Mystery," Paget portrayed Holmes and Watson riding in a train carriage, en route to the scene of a murder near the real town of Ross on the river Wye in Herefordshire. By this time, trains provided quick and easy access to the countryside for urban residents, but the journey was accompanied by soot and ash. Thus, even in warm weather, train passengers tended to equip themselves for travel much as their horse-drawn ancestors had, in sturdy traveling cloak and headgear. When Arthur wrote a scene in which Watson arrives at Paddington Station to meet Holmes for the journey to Boscombe Valley, he described his detective as "pacing up and down the platform, his tall, gaunt figure made even gaunter and taller by his long grey travelling cloak and close-fitting cloth cap." In Paget's drawing, Holmes and Watson are framed by the window, Holmes in profile and wearing one of the illustrator's own favorite hats—a deerstalker.

Whether or not Paget saw the illustrations of Holmes wearing a deerstalker in the *Bristol Observer*'s serialization of *The Sign of Four* the year before, he often wore a deerstalker himself, a habit picked up in the country during his youth. Unlike the artist in Bristol, Paget understood the rules of fashion and did not assign the deerstalker to Holmes until he started out for the countryside. In the first stories for *The Strand*, Paget portrayed Holmes in a top hat—de rigueur for an urban gentleman—or in a bowler when wearing his Inverness cape. He might wear a tattered bowler when disguised as a drunken groom, or he might posture before Watson in a wide-brimmed hat when personating a clergyman. But soon, thanks to the high quality of Paget's illustrations and the popularity of the series in *The Strand*, the deerstalker came to be associated with Sherlock Holmes.

In December 1890, eight and a half years after his arrival in Portsmouth, Arthur locked the doors of his Southsea medical practice. He had resolved to give up general medicine and become a specialist instead. With Touie, he moved briefly to Vienna, Austria, where he studied ophthalmology. By the end of March 1891, they were in London, where Arthur opened a new small practice at 2 Upper Wimpole Street.

Patients were few, and Arthur found time to write six Sherlock Holmes stories in quick succession. On the tenth of April, within a week of mailing in the first story, "A Scandal in Bohemia," he had finished a second, "A Case of Identity." Ten days later he rolled up and mailed "The Red-Headed League." Another week saw him completing "The Boscombe Valley Mystery." He mailed "The Five Orange Pips" on the eighteenth of May.

The first story, "A Scandal in Bohemia," appeared in the July issue, which went on sale on the twenty-fifth of June. Having wound up married after the romantic end of *The Sign of Four*, Dr. Watson visits Holmes in their old flat and participates in a charming adventure slight in detection but rich in atmosphere. In concept it bore a clear kinship with Poe's "Purloined Letter," but Arthur swept away the Gothic trappings and the disquisitions on logic and replaced them with humor and vivid scene-setting. In a daring move, he also provided a glimpse of an intriguingly smart foe—a woman who outwits Holmes in his very first short adventure.

The story opened with Watson's comments on his friend's analytical mind:

> To Sherlock Holmes she is always *the* woman. I have seldom heard him mention her under any other name. In his eyes she eclipses and predominates the whole of her sex. It was not that he felt any emotion akin to love for Irene Adler. All emotions, and that one particularly, were abhorrent to his cold, precise, but admirably balanced mind. He was, I take it, the most perfect reasoning and observing machine that the world has seen; but, as a lover, he would have placed himself in a false position. He never spoke of the softer passions, save with a gibe and a sneer.

The masked King of Bohemia consults Holmes in his rooms at Baker Street, offering a fortune in return for a compromising photograph of him held by his former romantic interest, the American actress and opera singer Irene Adler. Through disguise and subterfuge, Holmes learns Adler's hiding place for this memento. By the end of the story, however, he reveals himself as far more romantically minded than Watson had realized, and indeed emerges as not only a modern-sounding, science-minded hero but something of a gallant.

Sidney Paget drew ten illustrations to accompany "A Scandal in Bohemia." He portrayed Holmes and Watson in their Baker Street sanctum, interacting with the king both early and late in the case, and out on the street. He also showed Holmes in disguise, as both a pious cleric and a bewhiskered, bibulous groom. Again Arthur had followed in the footsteps of Gaboriau. As early as *Monsieur Lecoq*, Gaboriau had described the theatrical artistry of his young detective:

"And do you suppose he wouldn't discover this surveillance?"

"I should take my precautions."

"But he would recognize you at a single glance."

"No, sir, he wouldn't, for I should disguise myself. A detective who can't equal the most skilful actor in the matter of make-up is no better than an ordinary policeman. I have only practised at it for a twelvemonth, but I can easily make myself look old or young, dark or light, or assume the manner of a man of the world, or of some frightful ruffian of the barrieres."

"I wasn't aware that you possessed this talent, Monsieur Lecoq."

"Oh! I'm very far from the perfection I hope to arrive at; though I may venture to say that in three days from now I could call on you and talk with you for half an hour without being recognized."

In a later novel, *The Mystery of Orcival*, Lecoq remarks, "I have been a detective fifteen years, and no one at the prefecture knows either my true face or the color of my hair."

In "A Scandal in Bohemia," Arthur wrote explicitly of his own detective's talents in this field: "It was not merely that Holmes changed his costume. His expression, his manner, his very soul seemed to vary with every fresh part that he assumed. The stage lost a fine actor, even as science lost an acute reasoner, when he became a specialist in crime."

Strand readers responded with great enthusiasm. Clearly they were pleased to see the new hero return the following month, August, in "The Red-Headed League." Built upon the absurd premise that a criminal might lure a pawnshop owner out of the way of a bank burglary by hiring him to go somewhere else and copy an encyclopedia by hand, the story was nonetheless filled with action and witty dialogue. With his usual disregard for details, Arthur jumbled the dates cited by characters, resulting in a misalignment of about six months.

Four more Holmes stories followed, one each month: "A Case of Identity," "The Boscombe Valley Mystery," "The Five Orange Pips," and "The Man with the Twisted Lip." The public's response was everything that Arthur could have daydreamed about when he was sending his early manuscripts on what he had called "the circular tour."

In "The Five Orange Pips," which appeared in *The Strand*'s November issue, Arthur returned to his scientific forebears who had drawn inspiration from Voltaire's Zadig and who had themselves inspired Thomas Huxley and Arthur himself. He was demonstrating yet again that he saw Sherlock Holmes as a kind of scientist, in the manner of his real-life inspiration, Joseph Bell. But in doing so, he let Holmes fall into the logical, generalizing tone of Auguste Dupin. The scene merged Arthur's inspirations:

> Sherlock Holmes closed his eyes and placed his elbows upon the arms of his chair, with his finger-tips together. "The ideal reasoner," he remarked, "would, when he had once been shown a single fact in all its bearings, deduce from it not only all the chain of events which led up to it but also all the results which would follow from it. As Cuvier could correctly describe a whole animal by the contemplation of a single bone, so the observer who has thoroughly understood one link in a series of incidents should be able to accurately state all the other ones, both before and after. We have not yet grasped the results which the reason alone can attain to. Problems may be solved in the study which have baffled all those who have sought a solution by the aid of their senses."

Copies of the magazine seemed to leap off shelves. Many newspapers and magazines reviewed even short stories and articles published by their colleagues and rivals, and soon "A Scandal in Bohemia" was garnering attention from Exeter to Hull, from Sheffield to many venues in London. In Portsmouth, the *Evening News* of July 18 reported, "The many friends in Portsmouth of Dr. A. Conan Doyle are noting with pleasure his steady rise in literature. Dr. Conan Doyle is now one of the most attractive of modern writers, not only in the eyes of readers, but in the keener eyes of publishers and critics."

With financial security, Arthur and Touie were able to invite his sister Conny to retire from working as a governess. She returned from Portugal and began living with her brother and sister-in-law, busily typing up Arthur's stories on a newfangled typewriting machine. Dr. and Mrs. Conan Doyle hosted dinner parties. They rode their new toy, a tall two-seater tricycle, to visit friends. Touie was never as robust as her husband. Riding in Surrey with Arthur, Connie, and Innes, she had to admit she could not bear the pace of cycling—but rather than end the journey, Arthur sent his wife home via train.

Meanwhile, all signs indicated a flourishing literary career for Arthur. A. P. Watt settled with Greenhough Smith that the magazine would pay the impressive price of £300 for a second half dozen Holmes adventures, regardless of their length. Arthur set to work with the confidence of an acclaimed and well-paid writer. While writing the new stories, however, he was knocked off his feet by a fierce bout with influenza. Three years earlier, the disease had taken the life of his sister Annette, and for several days he wondered if it might steal his as well. After a week of misery, he emerged from delirium to find his mind clear of distractions and his road ahead clearly visible. He resolved to no longer spend time on any aspect of medicine as a profession, to renounce it completely and devote himself to writing.

Soon he was selling his medical instruments.

Born in Ireland, Samuel Sidney McClure moved to the United States at the age of nine when his mother immigrated after the death of her husband. By the time he encountered Arthur's work, McClure (usually known by the initials S. S.) was in his early thirties and had long since founded the first newspaper syndicate in the United States. His network made available to many periodicals a steady stream of news stories, feature articles, cartoons, comic strips such as *The Katzenjammer Kids*, and opinion columns. Of more interest to Arthur's career, McClure's syndicate was also well-known for seeking out novels and story series for serialization.

After a working trip to London in 1889, McClure traveled north to visit with Andrew Lang at St. Andrews University. Lang informed McClure that the venerable firm of Longmans, Green & Company, founded as Longman in 1724, was about to publish *Micah Clarke*, by a relatively new author named Arthur Conan Doyle. Having recently reviewed *A Study in Scarlet*, Lang was still full of enthusiasm for it, and he told McClure that this "shilling shocker" was also good. As he traveled south to England, McClure found the tale of Enoch Drebber's murder on a newsstand and read it on the train. He resolved to get this new author to write something for the McClure syndicate.

Two years later, when Arthur's Sherlock Holmes stories began appearing in *The Strand* in 1891, McClure read them and judged them by the personal standard that had served him well: Did the story exert a pull on him—hitting him in his solar plexus, as he liked to say, rather than in his brain? He claimed to work by the rule of three: Each story that he considered buying had to survive three readings within a single week. Those that passed this test would garner his agency's support. He often found himself, while commuting homeward on a Philadelphia train after a long workday, missing his station because he had yet again been drawn into a story that he had already read.

The Holmes adventures passed McClure's test with flying colors, and he bought them for £12 apiece—a good price for reprints. When his syndicate began to distribute them in the United States, however, many magazine editors responded with less enthusiasm than had McClure himself. For one thing, editors complained that the stories were too long for syndicated work—eight or nine thousand words instead of the usual five or so. Thus editors had a difficult time placing them in newspapers and magazines. The stories were also slow to gain reader enthusiasm in the United States. Most of the first dozen had been reprinted there before readers began to sway editors. The gradually accumulating reader response, and a blossoming affection for the character himself, finally wooed editors to share McClure's view of Arthur Conan Doyle and Sherlock Holmes.

CHAPTER 30

To My Old Teacher

Mediocrity knows nothing higher than itself; but talent instantly recognizes genius.

—ARTHUR CONAN DOYLE, *THE VALLEY OF FEAR*

In October 1891, four months after "A Scandal in Bohemia" launched the Sherlock Holmes stories in *The Strand*, and after the series had demonstrated broad popularity, Ward, Lock asked Arthur to write a preface for their new edition of *A Study in Scarlet*.

Still resenting the exploitative contract that Ward, Lock had offered for his first Sherlock Holmes novel, Arthur refused. He had money in the bank and a growing reputation.

They replied begging permission to use a subtitle for their new edition that would mention the now well-known name of Sherlock Holmes.

He refused.

The new year of 1892 was exciting for Arthur. Eleven years after leaving college in Edinburgh, he was tasting the fruits of success. The January issue of *The Strand*, which appeared in December 1891, featured the seventh Sherlock Holmes story, "The Adventure of the Blue Carbuncle," a lighthearted Christmas tale rich in wintry London atmosphere. It was followed by "The Speckled Band," "The Engineer's Thumb," "The Noble Bachelor," "The Beryl Coronet," and "The Adventure of Copper Beeches." The run finished in July.

Arthur was also still writing nonfiction. The January issue of *The Speaker*, edited by influential journalist Wemyss Reid, carried his essay on British humor, which highly praised the comic novel *Three Men in a Boat* by Jerome K. Jerome. The same month, he met Jerome at a party of the informal Idlers' Club hosted by Robert Barr, a loudmouthed but kindhearted editor who was about to launch a new monthly, *The Idler*. There Arthur also met other young writers, including James Barrie, who had graduated from the University of Edinburgh in 1882, a year after Arthur, and who had since written three novels about his native Kirriemuir (disguised as Thrums), Scotland, and was making a name for himself as a playwright. Barr had grown up in Canada and built a reputation there and in the United States through his writing for *The Detroit Free Press*. Barr would later create Eugène Valmont, a vainglorious French sleuth who would serve as one of the inspirations for Agatha Christie's pompous Belgian detective, Hercule Poirot.

In May 1892, *The Idler* published its editor's own parody of Sherlock Holmes, "Detective Stories Gone Wrong: The Adventures of Sherlaw Kombs." With a parenthetical apology to his friend "Dr. Conan Doyle, and his excellent book, 'A Study in Scarlet,' " Robert Barr (under his old American pen name Luke Sharp) launched into a gentle skewering of this character so colorful and larger-than-life that he irresistibly invited burlesque:

> I dropped in on my friend, Sherlaw Kombs, to hear what he had to say about the Pegram mystery, as it had come to be called in the newspapers. I found him playing the violin with a look of sweet peace and serenity on his face, which I never noticed on the countenances of those within hearing distance.

On the last day of May, Charles Doyle was transferred to Crichton Royal Hospital in Dumfries, southwest of Edinburgh, almost to the coast across from the Isle of Man. Diagnosed as a dipsomaniac, he was also described as afflicted with dementia; shortly after a visit by a physician, he could not recall it. "Facile and childish," one attendant said of him. He seemed unable to recognize even the staff he regularly dealt with. At sixty, he was gentle and quiet. "Certainly not dangerous to others," wrote a physician in Charles's file.

At first Charles became known as the patient who might praise the food or remark upon how well he slept. Gradually, however, he declined. Soon he suffered more epileptic seizures. By the following summer, Charles was noisy and incoherent. Although restless, he spent months in bed.

On the third of October 1893, an attendant noted that Charles seemed in a good mood and happy with his surroundings. The patient solemnly gave the attendant a folded paper, saying that it was in gratitude for excellent service, and that it contained gold dust gathered during the night from moonlight that had fallen onto Charles's bed.

A week later, tossing on the same bed, Charles Doyle died of an epileptic seizure.

Arthur's financial worries seemed to be over, at least for a while. With *Micah Clarke* selling well and drawing new readers to *The Sign of Four*, and with his series of stories in *The Strand* making the name of Sherlock Holmes known far and wide, he could take a deep breath. In December 1891, he, Touie, and Mary Louise settled in South Norwood, on the southern side of London almost to Croydon, in a three-story, sixteen-room redbrick house with gated wall and balconies, bargeboard gable and chimney pots. This new domain on handsome Tennison Road was a long way from the surgery at Bush Villas. Norwood was named for the Great North Wood's vast tract of oaks, which had supplied shipyard timber and charcoal for centuries. It had been the haunt of generation after generation of Gypsies, some of whom found their way into Samuel Pepys's diary in 1688.

Arthur was quick to credit Joseph Bell for his role in inspiring the unique abilities of the suddenly famous consulting detective in Baker Street. During the eleven years since his departure from Edinburgh, Arthur had stayed in touch with his former professor. In early 1892, only halfway through the run of the first dozen Sherlock Holmes stories in *The Strand*, Arthur was interviewed by Raymond Blathwayt, a travel writer and journalist, for the May issue of the recently launched London monthly *The Bookman*.

Blathwayt and Arthur sat in the study, which Arthur had decorated with Arctic trophies and with drawings and paintings by his father.

How on earth, the reporter demanded of Arthur, had he evolved out of his "own inner consciousness" such an extraordinary person as Sherlock Holmes?

Arthur laughed heartily. "Oh, but if you please, he is not evolved out of anyone's inner consciousness. Sherlock Holmes is the literary embodiment, if I may so express it, of my memory of a professor of medicine at Edinburgh University."

He provided anecdotes of Bell's diagnostic technique and concluded, "So I got the idea for Sherlock Holmes. Sherlock is utterly inhuman—no heart—but with a beautifully logical intellect. I know nothing about detective work, but theoretically it has always had a great charm for me."

Arthur was quick to cite his literary genealogy as well: "The best detective in fiction is E. A. Poe's Monsieur Dupin; then Monsieur Lecoq, Gaboriau's hero."

Bell wrote to Arthur, perhaps in response to this interview. On the fourth of May, Arthur replied:

> It is most certainly to you that I owe Sherlock Holmes, and though in the stories I have the advantage of being able to place him in all sorts of dramatic positions, I do not think that his analytical work is in the least an exaggeration of some effects which I have seen you produce in the out-patient ward. Round the centre of deduction and inference and observation which I have heard you inculcate I have tried to build up a man who pushed the thing as far as it would go—further occasionally— and I am so glad that the result has satisfied you, who are the critic with the most right to be severe.

In August, after concluding a year of monthly installments in the Sherlockian adventures, *The Strand Magazine* itself ran an interview with Arthur. They sent Harry How, a journalist known for his insightful interviews, to talk with their suddenly famous contributor.

How was effusive in his article:

> Detectivism up to date—that is what Dr. Conan Doyle has given us. We were fast becoming weary of the representative of the old school; he was, at his best, a very ordinary mortal, and, with the palpable clues placed in his path, the average individual could have easily cornered the "wanted" one without calling in the police or the private inquiry agent.

During their conversation, Arthur not only mentioned Joseph Bell but showed off a framed photograph of him, sharp-eyed and eagle-nosed— that immortalized him from a dozen years earlier, when Arthur studied with him.

After talking with Arthur, Harry How wrote to Bell in Edinburgh for more information from his point of view, and he received a typically modest reply.

2, Melville Crescent, Edinburgh, June 16, 1892.
Dear Sir, —

You ask me about the kind of teaching to which Dr Conan Doyle has so kindly referred, when speaking of his ideal character, "Sherlock Holmes." Dr Conan Doyle has, by his imaginative genius, made a great deal out of very little, and his warm remembrance of one of his old teachers has coloured the picture.

He went on to give examples of how he and other professors tried to encourage observation and deduction among their students. Then he added a disclaimer:

> Dr Conan Doyle's genius and intense imagination has on this slender basis made his detective stories a distinctly new departure, but he owes much less than he thinks to yours truly,
> Joseph Bell

Despite his disclaimers, Bell may have found the temptation to hold forth about his former student irresistible. Four months later, *The Bookman* followed up Blathwayt's interview with an essay on Arthur Conan Doyle and Sherlock Holmes written by no less an authority than Bell himself. Arthur was astonished when he saw a listing for it and was eager to read it when it appeared.

Again, rather than take any credit, Bell cited his own revered mentor, James Syme, as someone whose teaching legacy had "made a mark on Dr. Conan Doyle's method." Then he made several interesting points about the appeal of Arthur's detective stories.

> Dr. Conan Doyle's education as a student of medicine taught him how to observe, and his practice, both as a general practitioner and a specialist, has been a splendid training for a man such as he is, gifted with eyes, memory, and imagination. Eyes and ears which can see and hear, memory to record at once and to recall at pleasure the impressions of the senses, and an imagination capable of weaving a theory or piecing together a broken chain, or unravelling a tangled clue, such are implements of his trade to a successful diagnostician . . .
>
> Dr. Doyle saw how he could interest his intelligent readers by taking them into his confidence, and showing his mode of working. He created a shrewd, quick-sighted inquisitive man,

half doctor, half virtuoso . . . He makes him explain to the good Watson the trivial, or apparently trivial, links in his chain of evidence. These are at once so obvious, when explained, and so easy, once you know them, that the ingenuous reader at once feels, and says to himself, I also could do this; life is not so dull after all; I will keep my eyes open, and find out things.

In a later interview, Bell went further:

I should just like to say this about my friend Doyle's stories, that I believe they have inculcated in the general public a new source of interest . . . They make many a fellow who has before felt very little interest in his life and daily surroundings think that after all there may be much more in life if he keeps his eyes open than he had ever dreamed of in his philosophy. There is a problem, a whole game of chess, in many a little street incident or trifling occurrence, if one once learns how to make the moves.

George Newnes was not one to waste time or opportunities. Only four months after "The Adventure of the Copper Beeches," the last of the first dozen Sherlock Holmes stories, appeared in the June issue of *The Strand*, Newnes capitalized upon the phenomenal success of his new favorite author by publishing a collection, *The Adventures of Sherlock Holmes,* illustrated with more than one hundred of Sidney Paget's pictures from the pages of the magazine. Soon Harper & Brothers in the United States published an edition, which included fifteen illustrations and a frontispiece by Paget. The book was hugely popular, removing Arthur's last doubts about his potential to make a good living as a writer.

Now there were three books out in the world showcasing the fictional legacy of Joseph Bell. In fact, Arthur had modeled aspects of Sherlock Holmes upon Bell so clearly that readers who had known the medical professor immediately caught the resemblance. The next year Arthur received a letter from former Edinburgh University student Robert Louis Stevenson. He was now famous. His rousing pirate saga *Treasure Island* had been published to universal acclaim in 1883, and the dark science fictional novella *Strange Case of Dr Jekyll and Mr Hyde* in 1886. Stevenson had also written two historical novels of the kind that Arthur loved; *The Black Arrow* had been serialized in 1883 and *Kidnapped* in 1886.

Suffering from tuberculosis, Stevenson had traveled to the tropics and settled in Samoa. In a letter to Arthur dated April 5, 1893, he blended the praise of a reader and the condescension of a rival.

> Dear Sir, — You have taken many occasions to make yourself agreeable to me, for which I might in decency have thanked you earlier. It is now my turn; and I hope you will allow me to offer you my compliments on your very ingenious and very interesting adventures of Sherlock Holmes. That is the class of literature I like when I have the toothache. As a matter of fact, it was a pleurisy I was enjoying when I took the volume up; and it will interest you as a medical man to know that the cure was for the moment effectual.

Stevenson ended his letter with a question that hearkened back to his own studies at Edinburgh medical school: "Only the one thing troubles me: can this be my old friend Joe Bell?"

"I'm so glad Sherlock Holmes helped to pass an hour for you," replied Arthur on May 30. "He's a bastard between Joe Bell and Poe's Monsieur Dupin (much diluted)."

Stevenson could see through Holmes to the inspiration behind. And he knew from visceral personal experience the mountains of paper and rivers of ink that a writer must exhaust before reaching success. But he could not have known how much affection, experience, admiration, and debt were distilled into Arthur's words for the dedication on the first page of *The Adventures of Sherlock Holmes*. Although he was only thirty-three when he penned the brief tribute, Arthur well understood his own journey—from racing up the wide infirmary staircases in Edinburgh to peering anxiously through wooden blinds at Bush Villas in Southsea to being applauded by George Newnes and Greenhough Smith as he, they, Sherlock Holmes, and *The Strand* soared to fame. Sherlock Holmes had bought Arthur's home and enabled him to bring his sister Conny home from Portugal. So in the front of the book that brought him freedom and acclaim, Arthur inscribed simply:

To
my old Teacher
Joseph Bell, M.D., ETC.
of
2 Melville Crescent, Edinburgh

Acknowledgments

"Now, Watson," said Holmes, as a tall dog cart dashed up through the gloom, throwing out two golden tunnels of yellow light from its side-lanterns, "you'll come with me, won't you?"

"If I can be of use."

"Oh, a trusty comrade is always of use; and a chronicler still more so."

—ARTHUR CONAN DOYLE, "THE ADVENTURE OF THE MAN WITH THE TWISTED LIP"

My wife, Laura Sloan Patterson, once again proved smart, witty, encouraging, and supportive, as she has through fourteen books during fifteen years together. Every day she improves my life and work. Recently we heard our three-year-old, Vance, say to himself, "Daddy is working on Sherlock," which reminds me how much Laura has heard about the subject of this volume.

Thanks to my wonderful agent, Heide Lange, who has been guarding my career for two decades, and to her excellent assistants Stephanie Delman and Samantha Isman. George Gibson, my editor at Bloomsbury through seven books, helped me figure out my goals for *Arthur and Sherlock*, and then marched through various drafts. This book is dedicated to him as a token of appreciation for his talents and commitment as an editor, and of my admiration for his character as a gentleman. Thanks also to the rest of the crew at Bloomsbury USA: George's former assistant Lea Beresford, my former publicist Carrie Majer, assistant editor Callie Garnett, assistant editor Grace McNamee, art director Patti Ratchford, managing editor Laura Phillips, production editor Jenna Dutton, publicist Sarah New, copy editor Sue Warga, proofer David Chesanow, and indexer Kay Banning. At Bloomsbury UK I want to thank editor Alexa von Hirschberg, managing editor Imogen Denny, editorial assistant Callum Kenny, and art director and illustrator Paul Mann.

Many thank-yous go to Sherlockians. Leslie S. Klinger and Mike Whelan invited me to be Distinguished Speaker at the annual Baker Street Irregulars national party in New York City, where I met great people and learned from responses to my talk. Andrew Solberg was my Sherlockian sage on this book, answering all sorts of questions and encouraging the whole way. Both Les and Andy generously critiqued parts of the manuscript. Jacquelynne Bost Morris invited me to speak at the annual Baltimore gathering A Scintillation of Scions and explore some of these topics aloud among the faithful. Nancy Coble Damon at the Virginia Festival of the Book in Charlottesville and Serenity Gerbman at the Southern Festival of Books in Nashville also invited me to speak on these topics, which resulted in great conversations and connections.

In discussing the background of nineteenth-century detective fiction in *Arthur and Sherlock*, at times I drew upon my research and writing for anthologies I have edited on this topic. I would like to thank the excellent editors with whom I worked on those books: Michael Millman, the former editorial director of Penguin Classics who commissioned my first such collection, *Arsène Lupin, Gentleman-Thief*; Elda Rotor, the current editorial director of Penguin Classics, who commissioned my *Penguin Book of Gaslight Crime: Con Artists, Burglars, Rogues, and Scoundrels from the Time of Sherlock Holmes* and *The Penguin Book of Victorian Women in Crime: Forgotten Cops and Private Eyes from the Time of Sherlock Holmes*; and George Gibson, editor of all my books with Bloomsbury, who launched my Connoisseur's Collection series with them and thus edited *The Dead Witness: A Connoisseur's Collection of Victorian Detective Stories*. Elda also asked me to write an introduction to the Penguin Classics edition of Anna Katharine Green's novel *The Leavenworth Case*, the research for which further sketched in for me details of the genre and era.

Thank you to the invaluable crew at the Greensburg Hempfield Area Library, who track down obscure tomes with Sherlockian finesse: Sara Deegan, Jessica Kiefer, Christine Lee, and Aurea Lucas. Also many thanks to library director Linda Matey and to Diane Ciabattoni and Donna Davis. Perpetual gratitude to the former director and my ongoing pal, Cesare Muccari.

Gwen Enstam and Duncan Jones, with the Association for the Study of Scottish Literature, helpfully critiqued the Edinburgh chapters. Friend and historian John Spurlock discussed this book and other aspects of history and science many times. Jon Erickson, friend and science reference librarian at the Jean and Alexander Heard Library at Vanderbilt University, was essential, as usual. Jerry Felton, Robert Majcher, and Katherine Neely keep yours truly typing. Thank you, Brian and Sarah and Elliott Ferrell, for great conversations while dining and boating and beaching; and Elliott, come over soon and play with Vance's new cars.

Notes

OVERTURE: REMEMBERING

brass plate suspended from a wrought-iron railing: Stavert, frontispiece.

Patients wishing to consult Arthur strode along Elm Grove: Donald A. Redmond, 32.

number 1, Bush Villas: ACD, *A Life in Letters*, 160, tells when he moved and where; 161 reproduces ACD's labeled sketch of the street; Stavert, 16, shows 1880s advertisement for the hotel, with view of house, church, and hotel; an 1879 architectural plan of the church's renovations, plus a description of the neighborhood, appeared in the 21 November 1879 issue of the *Building News*, available at http://archiseek .com/2012/1879-elm-grove-baptist-church-southsea-hampshire/#.VG5TXN5_a2w; a mid-1880s photograph, and a close-up of 1880 street map of Portsmouth, are at www .conandoylecollection.co.uk/lancelyn-green-downloads/05-summer-ACD.pdf.

Bush Hotel: See newspaper advertisement for hotel in Stavert, 16.

Arthur enjoyed . . . billiards in the hotel and playing bowls: Stavert, 15.

the arched entryway on the left: ACD, *A Life in Letters*, 163; ACD's sketch, 161; photo of ACD at Bush Villas, 185

small waiting room: ACD, *A Life in Letters*, 183.

his hearty, infectious laugh: Blathwayt comments upon this trait himself, as do others among ACD's friends and interviewers.

wooden blinds: ACD, *A Life in Letters*, 167.

later he wrote it into one of his novels: ACD 1895, chap. 15. ACD asserted more than once that this novel was autobiographical, details of which have been confirmed by many scholars.

Only his name on the spine: ACD, *Memories and Adventures*, chap. 8.

Bell would have approached crime-solving: ACD, *Memories and Adventures*, chap. 8.

PART I: DR. BELL AND MR. DOYLE

"Physiognomy helps you to nationality": How, 188.

CHAPTER I: A SUPER-MAN

"So now behold me, a tall strongly-framed": ACD, *Memories and Adventures*, chap. 3.

crowded gaslit amphitheater: Liebow, 135.

how a Red Indian in North America might behave: ACD, quoted by Blathwayt.

"Well, my man": Details in this opening section not otherwise cited derive from ACD's own reminiscences, in his memoir *Memories and Adventures* (especially chap. 2, "Recollections of a Student," and chap. 11, "Sidelights on Sherlock Holmes"), and from his comments quoted at length in How. See also Harold Emery Jones, who attended Bell's medical classes alongside Conan Doyle, and who quoted only slightly different dialogue in a very similar account. Note, however, that both accounts were written after Sherlock Holmes's own approach was famous.

accent called "educated Edinburgh" . . . tanned, muscular: Scarlett, 699.

Bell's high-pitched voice: ACD, *Memories and Adventures*, chap. 3.

observant man ought to learn a great deal . . . Regarding female patients: Saxby, 23–24.

some mustached or bearded: Based upon numerous photographs of students from this period, including of ACD; e.g., portraits from 1880 made in the studio of James Howie Jr. at 60 Princes Street; see www.edinphoto.org.uk/0_C/0_cabinet_prints_howie_6_ edinburgh_medical_students_1880.htm.

Arthur would pay his four guineas: ACD, *Memories and Adventures*, 24; amounts and payment method confirmed in various contemporary university sources.

unusually kind figure: ACD, quoted in How.

especially to women and children: Liebow, 68, 85, 134.

appointed senior surgeon to the infirmary: Liebow, 125–126.

"extra-academical instructors": Liebow, 125–126, 140–141.

Tired-looking young men in black coats or tweed: ACD, *Red Lamp*, "His First Operation."

grand three-winged, U-shaped Royal Infirmary building: description of infirmary not otherwise cited derives from Grant, 4:297–300.

glassmakers had glazed . . . joiners had donated: Grant, 4:298.

trying to cram each year's classes into a half year: ACD, *Memories and Adventures*, chap. 3.

he scrawled countless notes: Bell, "Adventures"; Liebow, 130–131, 134.

the student asked the professor to repeat details: Bell's description of ACD's response, in Scarlett, 700; ACD's account, ACD, *Memories and Adventures*, chap. 3.

Joe Bell—as students and friends affectionately called him: Saxby, 13.

Rather short, with angular shoulders: Scarlett, 699; much of it echoed in Liebow.

His eyes, with their unusual two tones of blue: Stoker.

grades of Satisfactory in all classes: Miller, 60.

Bell came to consider him one of the most promising men: Saxby, 21–22.

Surgical outpatients might walk in: Liebow, 128.

during the next year fifteen thousand patients: Turner, 197.

Arthur and other efficient clerks interviewed patients: Liebow, 128, quoting ACD's former classmate, Dr. Clement Gunn

seventy or eighty per day: How, 186.

When Arthur began working as clerk: ACD, *Memories and Adventures*, 26.

He was proud of his reputation: Jones, vi.

"never neglect to ratify your deductions": Jones, v.

"What sort o' crossing did ye have from Burntisland?": *Lancet*, August 1, 1956. To conform with other quotations within my text, I have slightly modified the Scots dialect in this particular account to match the form of other quoted dialogue, without changing the wording.

"Quite easy, gentlemen": MacGillivray, 121.

"a super-man": Curor.

"We thought him a magician": Quoted in Wallace, 27.

CHAPTER 2: YOUR POWERS OF DEDUCTION

"It is no wonder that after": ACD, Memories and Adventures, chap. 1.

Škoda . . . guided Hebra: Finnerud, 225–226.

"This man is a tailor": Quotations by Hebra and examples of his method derive from a student, Fox, 103–106. Klauder pointed me to Tardieu and Fox.

Auguste Ambroise Tardieu: See Tardieu.

Dupuytren . . . mentioned in Gustave Flaubert's novel: Flaubert mentions Dupuytren in chap. 11 of pt. 2. The Balzac story is available in many editions; for background, see Moulin.

in the attic of the main building: Grant, 4:298–299.

polished deal operating table . . . a tin tub filled with sawdust: ACD, *Red Lamp*, chap. 2, "His First Operation."

the doctor simply threw him out of the clinic: Anecdote by ACD's contemporary student C. E. Douglas, quoted in Liebow, 134–135.

"What is the matter with this man, sir?": Jones, 14, is the source for this entire dialogue.

the life of a student instead of a patient: Jones, vi ff.

Joe Bell seemed irresistibly colorful: Some details (such as liveried coachman) from Scarlett, 699.

Bell mimicked his own revered mentor: Liebow, 129.

He also credited Syme: Harrison, *A Study in Surmise*, 234–235.

"Try to learn the features of disease": Bell, "Adventures."

Bell had served as house physician: Westmoreland and Key, 326.

he discovered in his late teens: See entry on Syme in *Encyclopedia Britannica*, 11th ed. (1911).

"My aim has been to describe": Bell, *Manual of the Operations of Surgery*, ix.

brilliant paper on epithelial cancer: Liebow, 51.

"Whilst discharging his duties": Liebow, 49–50.

Arthur too considered Bell kind: How, 186.

he traced both his love of the world: Liebow, 56–57.

his marriage in 1865: Anonymous, "Obituary, Joseph Bell, M.D.," 456–457.

"dedicated to God in his cradle": Saxby, 25.

His wife died in 1874: Anonymous, "Obituary, Joseph Bell, M.D," 456–457.

Water of Leith . . . a sewer: R. W. B. Ellis, from 1960 *Scotsman* article, quoted by Liebow, 68.

The disease produced gray mucus: Description of symptoms from Greenhow, 13.

"blankets of a bed": Hume, "Frances Home," 62.

promoted the local slang word *croup*: Moir, 506–507.

identical to illnesses known in the mid-eighteenth century: Greenhow, 12.

Speculations about its cause: Guilfoile, 25.

he drew the infected mucus: Saxby, 32–33.

Afterward he suffered from the disease: Bell, "Notes," 816–817.

he never lost the limp: Liebow, 135.

By January 1865, Bell was presenting: Bell, "Notes," 816.

CHAPTER 3: ART IN THE BLOOD

"Oh, Arthur," his mother exclaimed: ACD, *Memories and Adventures*, 11–12.

at times Arthur squirmed with embarrassment: ACD, *Memories and Adventures*, chap. 1.

Arthur, who could not have been more than four: ACD, *Memories and Adventures*, chap. 1; Thackeray died in December 1863.

Elegant, bearded, witty: ACD, *Memories and Adventures*, chap. 1.

"more in the class of a work of Art": Baker, xxi. Details about Matheson not otherwise cited derive from Baker.

grand windows of the Glasgow Cathedral: Beveridge, 265; Georgina Doyle, 31–32.

Our Trip to Blunderland: Jambon.

Rather than sell his infrequent watercolors: ACD, *Memories and Adventures*, chap. 1; Beveridge, 265, quoting Mary Doyle.

so drunk that he could neither recall his own name: Beveridge, 265, quoting letter from Mary Doyle to Dr. James Rutherford at the Crichton Royal Asylum, dated

December 3, 1892, and describing events "just thirty years ago—Decr. 62." Other details of Charles's behavior in this context not otherwise cited also derive from Mary Doyle, quoted by Beveridge. See also Baker, introduction.

"To know him was to love him": Beveridge, 265.

At no point could his annual salary plus artwork fees have surpassed £300: ACD, *Memories and Adventures*, chap. 1.

Office of Works placed him on half pay: Beveridge, 265, quoting Mary Doyle.

his superiors, Robert Matheson and Andrew Kerr: See letter from Mary Doyle, dated December 3, 1892, quoted in Norman, 128–130; also Georgina Doyle, 31.

"discharged his duties with diligence and fidelity": Baker, xxiv.

he asked innocently if his father had been unwell: ACD, *A Life in Letters*, 79.

He always remembered her stirring porridge: ACD, *Stark Munro*, chap. 3.

he read to his mother while she knitted: ACD, *Memories and Adventures*, chap. 2.

He first learned to read French: ACD, *Memories and Adventures*, chap. 2.

as the eldest son, he felt the burden: ACD, *Memories and Adventures*, chap. 3.

CHAPTER 4: SEVEN WEARY STEPS

"Stonyhurst, that grand mediaeval": ACD, *Memories and Adventures*, chap. 2.

one-eyed, pockmarked headmaster: Ibid., 11; Lycett, 26.

Father Francis Cassidy: Ibid., chap. 1.

tolley: Ibid., chap. 1.

Proud, defiant Arthur yearned for respect and affection: Ibid.

half-holiday (Wednesday and Saturday afternoons): Holden, 106–107.

Rapt students sat or squatted: ACD provides these details in "Juvenilia," although two and a half decades after the fact; they seem a bit too storylike.

Jimmy Ryan . . . classmate Patrick Sherlock: Miller, 110.

relative of Arthur's Irish aunt: Lycett, 122.

Macaulay, featured Sherlock prominently in his *History of England*: Macaulay, 1:248, 569, 582; 2:548; 4:passim; and other examples.

His weakest subject was chemistry: ACD, *A Life in Letters*, 32–33.

"Like pallid daisies in a grassy wood": ACD, *Memories and Adventures*, chap 2.

passing the matriculation exam . . . with honors: ACD, *A Life in Letters*, 73.

"Well, Doyle, you may be an engineer": ACD, *Memories and Adventures*, 17.

originally the Anglo-Norman name D'Oil: Ibid., 8.

helped steer Arthur away from Catholicism: Evolution of his attitudes discussed in ibid., chap. 2, "Under the Jesuits."

he stopped reading English books: ACD, *A Life in Letters*, 81 (letter to Mary Doyle, May 1876).

he might accidentally modify a neuter noun . . . Admiral Hyde Parker: ACD, *A Life in Letters*, 78.

the *Feldkirchian Gazette*: Miller, 40.

By the age of five, he was writing: ACD, "Juvenilia."

"each man carring a knife gun pistle": Only thirty words of this story, usually titled "The Story of a Bengal Tiger," survive, reprinted many places and visible in a scan of the original at https://www.arthur-conan-doyle.com/index.php?title=The_Story_of_a_Bengal_Tiger.

On the way home in August 1876: ACD, *Memories and Adventures*, chap. 2.

"I shall look to his development with great interest": ACD, *A Life in Letters*, 18–19 (letter from Michael Conan to Mary Doyle, April 11, 1864).

encouraged his obviously intelligent grandnephew to read . . . Poe: Cawthorne, 4–5.

Arthur had admired Poe since boyhood: ACD, *Memories and Adventures*, 74.

kept a copy of his *Tales* . . . at Feldkirch: Lycett, 481 n. 47.

to read Poe aloud: ACD, *A Life in Letters*, 93 (letter to Dr. Bryan Charles Waller, September 9, 1876).

CHAPTER 5: ATHENS OF THE NORTH

"Travellers who have searched the whole world round": ACD, *Firm of Girdlestone*, chap. 5.

two miles to the north and east: Black, *Black's Guide to Edinburgh*, 2.

It was rich in adjectives for the winds: Stevenson, *Edinburgh*, 95.

watcher gazing northeast across the Firth: Stevenson, *Edinburgh*, 1.

German Ocean: a common nineteenth-century English name for what is now called the North Sea; Stevenson uses the term in *Edinburgh,* 1.

towered four hundred feet: Campbell, 119.

its time gun could be heard: Stevenson, *Edinburgh*, 1879, 87–88; Gilbert, 132.

The castle stood so high that shepherds in Fife: Stevenson makes the point about the ship visible in Fife in *Edinburgh*, 14; the rest I pieced together from photographs.

"in one vast expanse": Black, *Black's Picturesque Tourist*, 26.

"Athens of the North": Ibid., 27.

a bustling market down in the city: Description of the Grassmarket in this paragraph derives largely from 1870s photographs by George Washington Wilson.

The drum and bugle . . . could be heard: Stevenson, *Letters*, letter of October 14, 1873.

bristling with turnpike stairs . . . since the fifteenth century: Ibid., 2:230.

Holyrood's crumbled abbey stood: Stevenson, *Edinburgh*, 3, 86.

Greyfriars Kirkyard: Stevenson, *Edinburgh*, chap. 1.

dark streets of Old Town: Description of Old Town derives primarily from ibid., chap. 2.

The view from many windows: ACD, "Southsea."

hovels and tenements were torn down: Ballingall, 82; Stevenson, *Edinburgh*, 17ff.

"Dr. Waller," as Arthur called him: ACD, *A Life in Letters*, 79 (letter from ACD in Feldkirch to Mary Doyle, April 1876).

"hard work getting up the subjects": ACD, *A Life in Letters*, 80 (letter from ACD to Mary Doyle, May 1876).

Bryan Waller's family manse in Yorkshire: ACD, *A Life in Letters*, 153.

paying the entire Doyle family's rent: ACD, *A Life in Letters*, 74–75.

a watercolor of many colorful skaters: See *Figures Ice-Skating*, by Charles Doyle, at www.artnet.com/artists/charles-altamont-doyle/figures-ice-skating-n1E0Pj_6_9oVJy2ITKItHw2; sometimes cited elsewhere as "Skaters on Duddington Loch."

Duddingston Loch: Stevenson, *Edinburgh*, 104–105.

Edinburgh Skating Club: Information on sports in Edinburgh at this time largely from Gerald Redmond, ch. 2, "The Traditional Sports of Scotland," esp. 54ff.

perhaps this change would permit Charles to complete his skating picture: ACD, *A Life in Letters*, 79 (letter from ACD in Feldkirch to Mary Doyle, April 1876).

CHAPTER 6: NO MAN OF FLESH AND BLOOD

"I do not think that life has any joy": ACD, "Juvenilia."

James Thin, Bookseller: ACD, *Memories and Adventures* recounts his threepence purchases but does not name the bookshop; however, scholars (e.g., Lycett, 57) agree that ACD's mention of the location and description of outdoor sale bins, etc., firmly indicate that it was James Thin, already a legendary shop beside the university. Full address in various contemporary publications, including *Publishers' Weekly*, and a store advertisement in *Bookmart: A Monthly Magazine of Literary, Library, and Bibliographical Intelligence*, August 1887, 116.

Thomas de Quincey: for description, see Anonymous, "Booksellers of Today"; Froude, 1:415 (letter from Thomas Carlyle to John Carlyle, November 29, 1827).

reminded one observer of Dominie Sampson: Anonymous, "Booksellers of Today," 83–84. Most of the description of Thin's shop derives from this article.

James Thin's siren call to impecunious Arthur: ACD, *Through the Magic Door*, chap. 1. Titles and reading details in this chapter derive largely from this source, esp. chap. 1, unless otherwise cited.

a treatise on warfare, written in Latin: Ibid., chap. 8.

he dived into books as a refuge: ACD, *Memories and Adventures*, chap. 1.

the nearby library informed his mother: ACD, "Juvenilia," seems to disagree with *Memories and Adventures*.

three-week Christmas holiday: ACD, *A Life in Letters*, 67. For descriptions of tombs, see *Westminster Abbey* (Radnor, PA: Annenberg School Press/Doubleday, 1972),

"His body is buried in peace": ACD, *Through the Magic Door*, chap. 1, says that he visited grave at age sixteen. For the inscription, see www.westminster-abbey.org/our-history/people/thomas-babington-macaulay.

It was the kind of antique diction: ACD remarks upon this point throughout "Juvenilia" as well as in *Memories and Adventures*.

Macaulay was typical of the *Review*'s commitment: Ferris, 1.

Macaulay had long since become: ACD, *Red Lamp*, chap. 1.

as a young man Arthur admired Macaulay's authoritative tone: Ibid.

he read them in bed by candlelight: Ibid., chap. 2.

He admired Scott's adventurous tales: Ibid., chap. 2.

John Ruskin and Thomas Carlyle argued: Chandler, 317.

"This must be the devil": Scott, *Ivanhoe*, chap. 13.

Arthur thrilled at such scenes: ACD, *Red Lamp*; ACD, *Memories and Adventures*, chaps. 2, 3, and elsewhere.

"whose novels have not only refreshed": *Black's Picturesque Tourist*, 38.

Arthur . . . wished that Scott had turned his imagination: ACD, *Red Lamp*, chap. 2.

Arthur also loved martial poetry: In ACD, *Red Lamp*, chap. 1, and many places elsewhere, ACD discusses notions of manliness and poetry.

"Unroll the world's map": Mayne Reid, 7, 12.

Arthur as a boy spent his time imagining hand-to-hand combat: ACD, "Juvenilia." All of the examples of his reading adventures in this paragraph derive from this source.

CHAPTER 7: ODE TO OPIUM

"Surrgeanis and Barbouris within": John Smith, 1. Other details about the college's early days in this paragraph derive from Smith, 2–5.

Oxford and Cambridge, where many influential faculty members still opposed: Lightman makes this point, 22.

William Rutherford: *Dictionary of National Biography*, 1901, 333–334. Biographical details not otherwise cited derive from this source.

250 students in his practical physiology course: obituary by J.G.M. in *Nature*, April 20, 1899, at www.nature.com/nature/journal/v59/n1538/abs/059590a0.html.

Henry Littlejohn: Anonymous, "Sir Henry D. Littlejohn," 648. Summary of Littlejohn's teaching style drawn mainly from this obituary, written by a former student.

appointed Littlejohn as Edinburgh's first Medical Officer of Health: Lycett, 26.

He studied in Paris: Christison, *Life*, 1:280ff. Much of the summary of his career derives from these two volumes.

Christison was legendary by the time: Anonymous *Scotsman* obituary, January 28, 1882.

Calabar ordeal-bean: Christison, "Properties," 193–204.

A fellow of the Royal Society, Garrod was renowned: Storey, 1189–1190.

Arthur signed the flyleaf: Billings, 37.

underlining items and making notes on almost every page: Billings, 38.

"Evaporate excess Colour between Calico": Quotations from and descriptions of ACD's copy of *Materia* not otherwise cited derive from Billings.

"I'll tell you a most serious fact": Miller, 59.

CHAPTER 8: DRINKING POISON

Several times in my life: ACD, *Memories and Adventures*, chap. 5.

"Third year's student": Ibid., chap. 3. The account of working with both Richardson and Hoare derive from this chapter.

"by mutual consent": Ibid., chap. 3.

"No woods, little grass": ACD, *Stark Munro*, chap. 5.

earnest payment of one shilling: Pulsifer, 327; ACD, *Memories and Adventures*, chap. 3.

He reminded himself that his mother had worked hard: ACD, *Memories and Adventures*, chap. 4.

he had worked three months without a chat: ACD, *A Life in Letters*, 111–12 (letter to Mary Doyle, October 19, 1878).

Arthur found himself gazing at a lump of iron: ACD, *Memories and Adventures*, chap. 5.

Arthur risked his life in a dangerous experiment: ACD first mentions administering gelseminum to himself as an experiment in a letter to Mary Doyle dated June 1879 (ACD, *A Life in Letters*, 117); an earlier letter to Mary noted that he arrived in Birmingham on June 2 (ibid., 113); thus the experiment must have occurred in June, although his account of it was not printed in the *British Medical Journal* until September. Description of effects derive from ACD, "Gelseminum."

an alkaloid pain depressant called gelseminum: Ringer and Murrell, various articles from 1875 through 1878, q.v.

toxic alkaloids of the strychnine family: Hare et al., 739–741, 1618. (Note that Hare uses the spelling "gelsemium," established as standard soon after ACD was writing; for rationale for name change, see *Druggists Circular and Chemical Gazette*, 1879, 179.)

"Though much used in America": Billings, 41; Ringer and Murrell, December 25, 1875.

influenza, ague, and menstrual cramps: Ringer and Murrell, December 25, 1875.

less accepted throughout Europe: James, *Guide*, 72–73; Billings, 41.

The Lancet **had been publishing a series of well-researched articles**: Ringer and Murrell, 1875–1878.

"In all these experiments": Ringer and Murrell, March 18, 1876.

"in doses sufficient to produce decided toxic effects": Ringer and Murrell, May 6, 1876.

Standards there were so lax: Ringer and Murrell, June 15, 1878.

a woman who died after receiving it as a painkiller following an abortion: Ringer and Murrell, June 15, 1878.

The minim had been introduced in 1809: Powell, 6–7.

CHAPTER 9: INTEMPERANCE

"Would you care to start next week": ACD, *Memories and Adventures*, 34. Most details of the whaling voyage, including ACD's observations and thoughts not other-wise cited, derive from this source, chap. 4. As apparent below, the other main sources were the journal and Sutherland.

Students at Edinburgh University were much freer: Ibid., chap. 3.

compiling a list of hosiery: ACD, *"Dangerous Work,"* 222, n. 11 (March 2).

dispensing tobacco: Ibid., 223 (March 4).

black eye raised the crew's estimation of their college-educated medico: ACD, *A Life in Letters*, 123.

"an addle-headed womanly fool": Ibid., 138 (letter to Amy Hoare, July 1881).

other girls he longed, at least in passing, to marry: Ibid., 140 (letter to Mary Doyle, July 1881).

off to the Isle of May to photograph birds: ACD, "After Cormorants."

Friends had long urged Mary Doyle: Beveridge, 265.

"INTEMPERANCE—Home for Gentlemen": Norman, 126. Kincardineshire is now part of Aberdeenshire.

comprehensive annual *Medical Directory*: http://search.wellcomelibrary.org/iii/ encore/record/C__Rb1349810__SThe+Medical+Directory__Orightresult __X5?lang=eng&suite=cobalt.

In early 1881 . . . Blairerno House gained a new inmate: ACD, *Memories and Adventures*, 23–24, says it was 1879, when ACD was "aged twenty"; Beveridge cites details from the 1881 census records.

the Habitual Drunkards Act of 1879: R. W. Lee, 243–246.

In the foothills of the Grampian Mountains, Blairerno: descriptive details from Georgina Doyle, 41–42.

he daydreamed about rescuing his mother: ACD, *Memories and Adventures*, chap. 7.

the storm that sank the SS *Clan Macduff*: ACD, "Slave Coast," mentions the ship; for wreck information, see www.wrecksite.eu/wreck.aspx?71808.

barely able to stand but feeling that he had won another battle: ACD, "Slave Coast."

He realized that he often acted out of bravado: ACD, *Memories and Adventures*, chap. 5. The shark anecdote is from this chapter also.

"This negro gentleman did me good": Ibid.

he could make more money . . . with his pen: ACD, *A Life in Letters*, 147 (ACD letter to his mother, January 1882).

CHAPTER 10: DR. CONAN DOYLE, SURGEON

"nearly frightened the immortal soul": ACD, *A Life in Letters*, 153 (ACD letter to Lottie Doyle).

Arthur liked to brag to his family: ACD, *A Life in Letters*, throughout, esp. letters to his mother and his sisters.

Capricious and volatile Dr. George Budd: ACD, *A Life in Letters*, 155ff.; ACD, *Memories and Adventures*, chap. 6.

He arrived in June: In ACD, *Memories and Adventures*, chap. 7, Conan Doyle says "June or July 1882"; Stavert, 19–22, argues convincingly for late June, even postulating Saturday, June 24.

he liked the holiday atmosphere . . . of Southsea: ACD, "Southsea."

bustled with yachts and men-of-war: Ibid.

Arthur bought a map: Stavert, 17.

He carried only his ulster: ACD, *A Life in Letters*.

probably a tin box: Stavert, 9, makes this reasonable assumption.

photographic equipment: Stavert, 9.

a large brass sign: ACD, *A Life in Letters*, 157.

Filthy urchins scuttled by: Sadden, entry for January 18.

Frequently Arthur stepped over tracks: See photo, Stavert, 11; Portsmouth city history at www.welcometoportsmouth.co.uk/portsmouth%20trams.html.

Bath chairs: Stavert, 10–11, and Portsmouth City Museum, www.geograph.org.uk/photo/1987460.

"At present the soldiers' wives": Quoted in Portsmouth City Council, "A History of Council Housing in Portsmouth," www.portsmouth.gov.uk/ext/documents-external/hou-100years-history-of-housing.pdf.

Arthur spent his first week locating: ACD, *Memories and Adventures*, 63.

number 1, Bush Villas: ACD, *A Life in Letters*, 160, tells when he moved and where; 161 reproduces ACD's labeled sketch of the street; Stavert, 16, shows 1880s advertisement for the hotel, with view of house, church, and hotel; an 1879 architectural plan of the church's renovations, plus a description of the neighborhood, appeared in the November 21, 1879, issue of the *Building News*, available at http://archiseek.com/2012/1879-elm-grove-baptist-church-southsea-hampshire/#.VG5TXN5_a2w.

The rent was £40: ACD, *Memories and Adventures*, 63.

Arthur bought a tired old bed: ACD, *A Life in Letters*, 161; ACD, *Memories and Adventures*, 63.

Arthur slept several nights wrapped in his ulster: ACD, *A Life in Letters*, 162, 184.

The portmanteau, in the back room with nothing but a stool beside it: ACD, *Memories and Adventures*, 65.

white curtains . . . knickknacks: ACD, *A Life in Letters*, 199.

downstairs the consulting room was fitted for gas: Ibid., 182–183.

"to get," he told his mother: Ibid., 166.

few patients dropped in during free hours: Ibid., 175–176.

William Roylston Pike: Ibid.

Kirton, a young dentist whose office was across the street: Stavert, 34–35; "young" determined from details in the *Dentists Register*, 132 (London: General Medical Council/Spottiswoode, 1904).

One Southsea dentist paid every week: Stavert, 34.

Realizing the irony in this transaction, he confided: ACD, *A Life in Letters*, 167.

"emerged from the fray without much damage": ACD, *Memories and Adventures*, 62–63.

Arthur counted upon this tradition: Ibid., 65.

"A man had the good taste": ACD, *A Life in Letters*, 180.

Fond of colorful characters: ACD, *Memories and Adventures*, 68–69.

Once he kept a pottery jug for his troubles: Ibid. he says of the jug, "I have got it yet."

Once a poor woman begged him to tend her daughter: Ibid., 69–70.

turn him away from the traditional religion of his upbringing: Ibid., 69.

CHAPTER 11: A WEALTH OF YOUTH AND PLUCK

I found that I could live quite easily: ACD, *Memories and Adventures*, chap. 6.

Arthur's brother, Innes, arrived in mid-July: ACD, *A Life in Letters*, 168–169.

"far healthier town": ACD, *A Life in Letters*, 165.

a physician lost face with patients: Ibid., 164.

he had grown a mustache: Ibid., 184–185.

volunteering to help fishermen on their boats: ACD, *A Life in Letters*, 167–168.

In the summer of 1877: Ibid., 97–100.

he had spent his spare time entertaining: Ibid., 120.

mailed home toy French foot soldiers: Ibid., 21.

"I am very happy to know that I have a little brother": Ibid., 52.

Founded in the twelfth century: Portsmouth City Council, "A History of Council Housing in Portsmouth," www.portsmouth.gov.uk/ext/documents-external/hou-100years-history-of-housing.pdf.

"a terrible little dayschool": Kipling, chap. 1; Green, 44–45.

From the beach he brought home crabs: ACD, *A Life in Letters*, 172.

"We have vaxenated a baby": ACD, *Memories and Adventures*, 67. The following dialogue derives from Innes's letter; wording is precisely as quoted, but punctuation has been altered to conform to contemporary dialogue format.

in letters to his mother he often itemized his parsimonious budgeting: Among countless examples in ACD, *A Life in Letters*, for example, see 162, 165, 170.

"Lord knows I am as poor as Job": Ibid., 161–162.

"There is nothing I put my mind to do": Ibid., 160.

his annual income would rise to £1,000: Ibid., 159.

To his mother he confessed that his indignation: ACD, *A Life in Letters*, 199.

he saw a "taxgatherer" coming: Ibid., 198 (letter to Charlotte Drummond, n.d.)

Most unsatisfactory: ACD, *Memories and Adventures*, 70.

chained tomes of Renaissance Oxford: Streeter, xiv.

"We have become a novel-reading people": Trollope, 108. Griest quotes this line, 3, amid further context on this topic.

Charles Dickens and his primary rival, William Makepeace Thackeray: Griest, 4.

Mudie's Lending Library: Griest's is the most comprehensive book about Mudie and the hugely influential circulating libraries.

The library trade was dominated: Griest, 40ff.

"The work has been distended": Henry James.

Arthur's favorite novel, *The Cloister and the Hearth*: ACD, "My Favorite Novelist"; ACD, *Magic Door*, chap. 6.

"childish egotism": Quoted in Griest, 116, citing a Reade letter in the Berg Collection, New York Public Library.

Friends who visited included Claud Currie: ACD, *A Life in Letters*, 172–173.

One friend pronounced number 1, Bush Villas: Ibid., 173.

rolled them up, inserted them into mailing cylinders: ACD, "Juvenilia."

popular Welsh writer Rhoda Broughton: ACD himself makes this comparison; ACD, *A Life in Letters*, 151 (letter to Mary Doyle, March 1882).

"That Veteran" to *All the Year Round*: Ibid., 171, 174, 182; see *All the Year Round,* September 2, 1882.

CHAPTER 12: THE CIRCULAR TOUR

to whose pages Arthur had long aspired: ACD, *Memories and Adventures*, chap. 8.

Like Arthur, he had written many stories before venturing to tackle a novel: Payn, 15ff.

"*The Cornhill* this month has a story in it": ACD, "Juvenilia."

a two-year-old issue of *The Cornhill*: ACD, *A Life in Letters*, 170–171. "The Pavilion on the Links" was published in September–October 1880.

Arthur decided that only with publication of a novel: ACD, *Memories and Adventures*, chap. 8.

The book was more a series of sketches and miniature essays: ACD *Narrative of John Smith*. His partial rewrite, c. 1884–1893, was published in 2011.

plot somewhat resembled that of *A Lost Name*: Crawford makes this point, as do other scholars.

"I would need a private graveyard": ACD, *A Life in Letters*, 242.

"We know very well what that means": ACD, *Firm of Girdlestone*.

"fairly good as light literature goes nowadays": ACD, *A Life in Letters*, 270.

"the circular tour": ACD, *Memories and Adventures*, chap. 8.

CHAPTER 13: THE UNSEEN WORLD

earliest memory was the sight of his dead maternal grandmother: Georgina Doyle, 35.

feeble patient, who was twenty-five, only a month older: Ibid., 54.

"Both ladies thanked me a very great deal": ACD, *Stark Munro*, chap. 15. Actually a phrase precedes this quotation in the sentence.

he died on the twenty-fifth of March: Georgina Doyle, 54.

40 percent of the burials at Highland Road were of children: www.friendsofhigh
landroadcemetery.org.uk/history.htm.

God was ordering him to escape: Beveridge, 266. Descriptions of Montrose not otherwise cited, including quotations, derive from this essential article by Beveridge.

Founded in 1781 as the Montrose Lunatic Asylum: Poole, esp. 1–21.

the entire institution came to be called Sunnyside: See www.historic-hospitals.com/
gazetteer/angus/.

authorities took action even before notifying Mary or Arthur: See letter from Mary
Doyle, dated December 3, 1892, reproduced in full in Norman, 128–130.

"Has been weak minded & nervous": Beveridge, 266.

Mary began to worry that if Charles were free: See letter from Mary Doyle, dated
December 3, 1892, reproduced in full in Norman, 128–130.

"We must not . . . lose sight of the great principle": Beveridge, 265.

"of an overpowering presentiment": Ibid, 267.

"This morning took an epileptic attack": Ibid.

Petite, with childishly small hands and feet: See Touie's daughter Mary's memories,
quoted in Georgina Doyle, 101.

A. Conan Doyle, MD, wrote Arthur: Georgina Doyle, 55.

she received a larger share of her father's estate: Ibid., 62–63.

no hearse to convey his coffin: Ibid., 61.

£100 per year: Stashower, 70.

CHAPTER 14: THE METHOD OF ZADIG

"Why do you not worship Bel?": Quotations from Daniel stories derive from the 2011
Revised Edition of the New American Bible; I consulted the edition on the website of
the United States Conference of Catholic Bishops. I slightly changed some punctuation
to match the rest of the chapter.

"You mean her bitch": Quotations from *Zadig* derive from Voltaire, chap. 3, in a
nineteenth-century anonymous translation. I modernized some punctuation and
changed capitalized nouns to lowercase to conform to usage in the rest of this
chapter.

"This single track therefore": Coleman, 102.

CHAPTER 15: THE FOOTMARKS OF POE

"Edgar Allan Poe, who, in his carelessly prodigal fashion": ACD, "Preface," vi.

"It is not improbable": Poe, "Rue Morgue."

"The mental features discoursed of as the analytical": Ibid.

"The reader is disposed to believe": Reprinted in Walker, 132–133.

"Mr. Poe is a man of genius": Reprinted in ibid., 135.

Poe brought Dupin back: For bibliographical material, see the detailed pages on the website of the Edgar Allan Poe Society of Baltimore at www.eapoe.org/index.htm, esp. www.eapoe.org/works/editions/agft001c.htm.

Poe was taking to its limit his notion: Silverman makes this point, 172, and other critics do elsewhere.

"These tales of ratiocination": Poe, letter to Phillip P. Cook, August 9, 1846, LTR240/RCL654, on www.eapoe.org/works/letters/p4608090.htm.

Naturally Poe was himself drawing upon: Silverman, 149–150, re: "William Wilson."

"drew razor swift as he could pull it": Humphreys, 75.

"a strange chuckling hoarse voice" . . . **"a deep wailing and melancholy cry"**: Scott, chap. 16.

Eventually the ape kills a man: Scott, chap. 25.

CHAPTER 16: HOW DO YOU KNOW THAT?

"As to work which is unconsciously imitative": ACD, "Preface," vi.

"Un meurtre sans exemple dans les fastes de la justice": For details on French piracy of Poe's "Rue Morgue," see Wigmore, esp. 231–235, and Cutler, chap. 1.

Baudelaire began translating stories: See exhibition catalogue, "Baudelaire, Translator of Edgar Allan Poe," Brown University, www.library.brown.edu/cds/baudelaire/translations1 .html.

"You will, therefore, go there": Dumas, 20:226

CHAPTER 17: GAMES OF CHESS, PLAYED WITH LIVE PIECES

"king's peace": For general background on the evolution of official police forces in Britain, from Norman days through the end of nineteenth century, see W. L. Melville Lee; for a more recent and detailed analysis of Victorian detectives, see Shpayer-Makov.

Efficient policing required: W. L. Melville Lee discusses the issue of trust and coop-eration, 329ff.

"clean-shaven, farmer-like": Sala, 1:95.

"We are not by any means devout believers": *Household Words*, July 27, 1850. See Philip Collins, chap. 9, esp. 198ff.

"What he liked to talk about": Sala, 1:76.

"Dickens had a curious and almost morbid partiality": Ibid., 1:95.

"Any of the Detective men will do anything for me": Dickens, *Letters*, 6:380 (letter to Bulwer Lytton, May 9, 1851). For more on Dickens's attitude toward police officers and detectives, see Philip Collins, esp. chap. 9.

Inspector Jonathan "Jack" Whicher: Summerscale, 51ff.

"On the mat at the stair-foot": Wills, 104ff.

"Gaboriau had rather attracted me": ACD, *Memories and Adventures*, chap. 7.

PART 3: MR. HOLMES AND DR. WATSON

"No writer is ever absolutely original": ACD, *Memories and Adventures*, chap. 12.

CHAPTER 18: DR. SACKER AND MR. HOPE

"*A tangled skein*" . . . red marbled notebooks: Bergem.

"The difficulty is to seize at the beginning": Gaboriau, 45.

"There's the scarlet thread of murder": ACD, 1887, chap. 4.

He remembered his aquiline face: ACD, *Memories and Adventures*, chap. 8.

Faulds presented his idea to London's police department: Godfrey, 136–138; see also Donald Reid. I discuss the growth of fingerprint studies in Sims, *Adam's Navel*, 166–173.

Ormond Sacker [or Secker]—*from Sudan*: See illustration, ACD, *A Life in Letters*, 245.

Sacker or Secker . . . Stamford Street: Harrison, *Study in Surmise*, 33–37. Harrison postulates numerous possible roots for names that ACD used; I cite only those that seem reasonable, not far-fetched, and relevant to my story.

Belmont Street . . . William Rance: Donald A. Redmond, 33.

Charpentier . . . Cowper: Ibid., 32–33.

remembering Joseph Alexandre Lestrade: Ibid., 35.

Reverend J. Gelsen Gregson: Ibid., 33; Porter, 276.

not "Mr. Sharps or Mr. Ferrets": ACD, *Memories and Adventures*, chap. 7.

surnames, including Sherrington Hope: Stoker, 8.

Chief Inspector William Sherlock: *Home Chronicler*, March 2, 1878, 137, and February 25, 1878, 122; *Times*, November 3, 1877. Mrs. Meredith, "Juvenile Delinquency," *Transactions of the National Association for the Promotion of Social Science*, 1881, 375. Quail, 158 quotes Stavert.

The 1881 census listed Inspector Sherlock: www.archiver.rootsweb.ancestry.com/th/read/LONDON/2000-10/0970943447.

In February 1881, *The Portsmouth Evening News* reported: *Portsmouth Evening News*, February 16, 1881, available at www.kenthistoryforum.co.uk/index.php?topic=6163.0.

Inspector Sherlock was in court at Westminster: Booth, 107.

The Times reported another of Sherlock's exploits: *Times*, January 6, 1883.

The 1881 post office directory: Harrison, *Study in Surmise*, 38–39.

under the jurisdiction of Chief Inspector William Sherlock: Ibid., 39.

fame of Sir Thomas Watson: Ibid., 177–178.

the famed physician had also studied in Edinburgh: See the Royal College of Physicians site, www.munksroll.rcplondon.ac.uk/Biography/Details/4657.

The first Afghan War . . . again invaded Afghanistan: For general background information on the British view prevalent in ACD's time, see Hanna.

"Arthur borrowed a memorable image: ACD used the gouty knuckle image in the 1904 Sherlock Holmes story "The Adventure of the Missing Three-Quarter." For original source see Thomas Watson, vol. 2, 1067. For background see Klinger 1999, 28–29. Klinger alerted me to this borrowing.

a gigantic iron statue of a lion was erected in Reading: web.archive.org/web/20070928000734/http://www.readingmuseum.org.uk/collections/album/pdfs/maiwand-25.pdf.

Watson would have been an acting surgeon: Klinger 2006, 3:8 n. 3.

Chopin composed no pieces for solo violin: Baring-Gould 1:178, n. 111.

"neither kith nor kin" . . . "naturally gravitated": ACD 1887, Chapter 1.

CHAPTER 19: BOHEMIANS IN BAKER STREET

"Sherlock Holmes [is] a bastard": ACD, letter to Robert Louis Stevenson, 1893.

number 33, Rue Dunot: The street address is given in the third Dupin story, "The Purloined Letter."

Baker Street was not more than a quarter of a mile long: Baring-Gould, 1:86.

Upper Baker Street . . . dense with London history: Examples in this paragraph derive from Wheatley, 1:90–91.

The *B* in the street number: Baring-Gould, 1:85, 86.

"Underneath the table": Reade, 2:125–126.

"She became a perfect Bohemian ere long": Thackeray, chap. 44.

"As the phrase 'Egyptian' was once generally used": Anonymous, "Literature of Bohemia," 17–18.

CHAPTER 20: A LITTLE TOO SCIENTIFIC

"The fatal mistake which the ordinary policeman makes": Saxby, 23–24.

"Monsieur G——, the Prefect": Poe, "Rue Morgue." Although the Holmes story "The Adventure of the Second Stain" was published after the period my book concerns, it is Conan Doyle's most Poe-like story in its construction; it involves an indiscreet letter that has gone missing, the threat of blackmail, and a hiding place that isn't hidden—but then it was a reboot of "A Scandal in Bohemia." Note: All quotations and descriptions involving Dupin not otherwise cited derive from Poe's three Dupin stories.

"the same very rare and very remarkable volume": Poe, "Rue Morgue."

Robert Louis Stevenson and the American Bret Harte: ACD explicitly invokes Stevenson and Harte in numerous places; e.g., see Stoker and ACD, *Magic Door*, chap. 6.

attributed Arthur's own "J. Habakuk Jephson's Statement" to Stevenson: Lycett, 107–108.

Arthur saw himself as brave and indomitable: ACD demonstrates this view of himself in many letters to his mother in ACD, *A Life in Letters*, and later in a variety of autobiographical contexts, including his own account of the 1880 whaling voyage and his later comments about his volunteer work with the military.

"They ascended to the room in question": Lecoq, *Mystery of Orcival*, chap. 7.

When reading detective stories, he found it annoying: See filmed interview with ACD, (1927), available at www.youtube.com/watch?v=XWjgt9PzYEM.

CHAPTER 21: THE BOOK OF LIFE

"I began to think of turning scientific methods": ACD, in filmed interview (1927), at www.youtube.com/watch?v=XWjgt9PzYEM.

Holmes uses the term *deduction* instead of *induction*: Snyder makes this point, 105. A good introduction to Holmes's method is Konnikova, 155–208.

Bacon explicitly defined "inductive history": Bacon, "Advancement of Learning."

"'I ate minced pies on Monday and Wednesday'": Macaulay, 428.

"The patient, too, is likely to be impressed": How, 188.

CHAPTER 22: A BASILISK IN THE DESERT

"I had written in *A Study in Scarlet*": ACD, *Second American Adventure*, chap. 5.

convicted confidence artist Joseph Smith: See court record reprinted in Anonymous, "Original Prophet," 229–230 (see full article for context); Fawn Brodie, 121.

Joseph Smith became embroiled: for general background on Smith, see Fawn Brodie.

baptized forty-three thousand English converts: Tracy, 41–42.

Although polygamy had been forbidden in England: Wall and Ames, 2.

in part through accounts of virtuous women described: Arrington and Haupt, 244ff. General information about fictional responses to Mormonism not otherwise cited derives largely from Arrington and Haupt. Arrington was affiliated with the Mormon Church and apparently skeptical about criticism thereof, but this article serves as a guide into primary sources.

"His presence was that of the basilisk": Ward, 66.

"A Terrible Tale of the Danites of Mormon Land": Arrington and Haupt, 257. The novel was *Gold Dan*, by Albert W. Aiken.

"Latter-day Saints who are set apart": Twain, chap. 12.

The Washoe were a tribe: Tracy, 62, led me to the Washoe clue; it is his assertion, following his own extensive review of nineteenth-century representations of Mormons, that the word *Washoe* appears in no others.

"Washoe is a pet nickname for Nevada": Twain, 160.

CHAPTER 23: A BORN NOVELIST

"If the secret history of literature": ACD, *Narrative of John Smith*, p. 27.

Optimistically, he sent the manuscript to James Payn: ACD, *Memories and Adventures*, chap. 8.

Arthur sent the manuscript to J. W. Arrowsmith: Ibid.; details about Arrowsmith derive from www.discovery.nationalarchives.gov.uk/details/rd/387891c4-3179-43e8-8d76-4cdbcbceb70a. See also *The Bookseller*, January 24, 1908, 40.

Finally he thought to send it to Ward and Lock: In ACD, *Memories and Adventures*, ACD stated that he sent the book to Ward, Lock & Co. That was indeed the name of the publisher by the time ACD wrote his autobiography, but in 1886 it was still officially Ward and Lock. See www.wardlockredguides.co.uk/page/aboutWL.html.

He first self-published *The Mystery of the Hansom Cab*: Pierce, 114, 274.

"Being a detective, and of an extremely reticent disposition": Fergus Hume, chap. 4.

George Thomas Bettany: For background on Bettany, see Anonymous, "George Thomas Bettany"; for anecdote about Jeanie Gwynne Bettany "discovering" *A Study in Scarlet*, see Kernahan, from which derive most details in this scene.

She read through the pages written in Arthur's neat round hand: Kernahan.

Arthur replied immediately, on the first of November: ACD, *Memories and Adventures*, chap. 7.

"We regret to say": Ibid., chap. 7. Following details about ACD's thoughts derive from this source.

The son of a Cheapside publican: Bergem, 1.

Following a banking collapse in May: For general background on the financial crisis, see Collins 1992 and Elliott.

The company had been known as Ward and Lock: See Liveing.

Beeton turned in a new direction and included political satire: Bergem, 2.

"An Exciting Christmas Eve; or, My Lecture on Dynamite": www.arthur-conan-doyle.com/index.php?title=The_Boy%27s_Own_Paper.

"an old institution": Solberg.

Bell retired from the Edinburgh Infirmary: Liebow, 150–151.

"Lord," he wrote in his diary: Ibid., 151.

in January 1887, a group called upon him: Liebow, 151.

textbook for nurses . . . Royal Hospital for Sick Children: Liebow, 152–153.

"Mr. Bell's whole career": *Edinburgh Medical Journal*, June 1887, 1145.

diseased, handicapped, and wounded children . . . Birth defect: Bell, "Five Years' Surgery."

CHAPTER 24: THE PRETERNATURAL SAGACITY OF A
SCIENTIFIC DETECTIVE

"After weighing the evidence": ACD, "A Test Message," *Light*, July 2, 1887.

The issue went on sale in November for one shilling: Bergem, 3; also www.bestof sherlock.com/beetons-christmas-annual.htm.

was listed as R. André: Young, 199; and guide to the Richard André Papers at the University of Southern Mississippi, at www.lib.usm.edu/legacy/degrum/public_html/ html/research/findaids/DG0028f.html.

Hamilton had published three of her five novels: www.victorianresearch.org/atcl/ show_author.php?aid=2178.

David Henry Friston: Most information about Friston derives from Bergem, 4–6.

"JUST READY, IN PICTURE COVERS": From original advertisement in *The Graphic*, November 26, 1887, reprinted in Solberg.

An illustrated weekly, *The Graphic*: Bills; Korda, esp. 76–84.

"It is not at all a bad imitation": Quoted in Solberg.

CHAPTER 25: TRUTH AS DEATH

"His brush was concerned not only with fairies": ACD, *Memories and Adventures*, chap. 1.

The young woman blushed and asked for a copy of the drawing: Baker, 12. All descriptions of Charles Doyle's artwork in this passage derive from images reprinted in Baker.

told a physician that he had encountered his wife: Norman, 147, from a Sunnyside record dated October 6, 1887.

At this time Charles was worrying often about death: Beveridge.

"Has no memory for anything recent": Norman, 147, from a Sunnyside record dated March 23, 1888.

Charles produced six drawings for Ward, Lock: For images, see www.arthur-conan-doyle.com/index.php/A_Study_in_Scarlet#Illustrations.

"somewhat unfinished" . . . **"contented with his lot:"** ACD, *A Life in Letters*, 270.

"for Papa's drawings for the Study": Ibid., 251 (n.d.).

Henry Ball . . . create wood engravings: Ibid., 250–252.

"Ward & Lock are perfect Jews": Ibid., 251.

they owed him nothing beyond the amount they had already sent: Ibid., 255, 256.

Ward, Lock had bought the rights to publish *Smith's Select Library of Fiction*: Cox and Mowat, 20.

Conway sold outright to Arrowsmith . . . *Called Back*: Law, n.p. Most information on the publication of *Called Back* derives from this article.

Arrowsmith's Christmas Annual: More info on this annual at www.victorianresearch .org/atcl/show_journal.php?jid=130.

her gravestone read "Called Back, May 15, 1886": Habegger. Dickinson's bedroom in Amherst displays a copy of *Called Back*.

Conway had died suddenly of typhoid: Anonymous, *Truth*, May 21,1885.

Young Folks' Paper: The weekly appeared under a variety of different titles between 1871 and 1897. Some sources list *Young Folks* as the title during publication of *Kidnapped*, but that title had been enlarged to *Young Folks' Paper* in December 1884.

"A chemist on each side will approach the frontier with a bottle": ACD, *Memories and Adventures*, chap. 7. ACD's response to Wilde appears here as well.

"it is no part of the publishers' plan": Mott, 396–401.

CHAPTER 26: WATSON'S BROTHER'S WATCH

an error that he would write to J. M. Stoddart to correct: Klinger, 3:234, n. 50.

"It is a fullgrown book": Boström and Laffey, 27.

"Dr. A. Conan Doyle has gone at one stride": Ibid., 28.

The Scotsman **said that it was a fine book**: Ibid., 30.

"Very interesting and very readable": Ibid., 32.

"There is an Irish lilt in this shamrock": Baker, 28.

"I am certain if my many Vols": Baker, 56, and transcription 87; undated but from Charles Doyle diary entry surrounded by drawings dated June and July 1889.

At about the same time as these private complaints: Beveridge, 267.

CHAPTER 27: DREAD OF MADHOUSES

"I was now once more at a crossroads": ACD, *Memories and Adventures*, chap. 10.

"Is there anything being done with this?": Kernahan.

Arthur's contract with *Lippincott's* **gave the magazine three months of exclusivity**: Donald A. Redmond 14.

the *Bristol Observer* **... deerstalker hat**: Ibid., 1993, 87. You can see the illustrations reprinted at www.arthur-conan-doyle.com/index.php?title=The_Sign_of_Four #Illustrations.

Deer stalking: See MacRae; Scrope.

Charles was transferred to the Royal Edinburgh Asylum: Beveridge, 267.

"He has an intense dread of madhouses": ACD, "Surgeon of Gaster Fell."

"Dr. Conan Doyle appears to be equally at home": Boström and Laffey, 65–66.

A single recurring character of proven popularity: ACD, *Memories and Adventures*, chap. 10.

CHAPTER 28: ADVENTURES IN THE STRAND

"I should at last be my own master": ACD, *Memories and Adventures*, chap. 10.

George Newnes: Background information on Newnes derives from Jackson and Welch.

considered naming it *The Burleigh Street Magazine*: Newnes, 363.

"I stood in the Strand and beheld it and blessed God!": Quoted in Tames, xxiii.

"because," wrote Newnes later, "they were smarter": Newnes, 364.

Herbert Greenhough Smith, a Cambridge man: McDonald, 152.

To Newnes's dream of an eye-catching innovation: Ibid.

The first issues sold two hundred thousand copies: Ibid., 156.

When, in early 1891, an envelope containing: Herbert Greenhough Smith, 171–173.

Watt seems to have been the first to establish himself as a respected professional: In making this point I rely upon the extensive discussion of it in Gillies, "Watt." For background on Watt, see Gillies, *Professional Literary Agent*.

"I really do not know how a busy man like myself": Quoted within the Watt interview in *Bookman*, October 1892.

Watt claimed that he did not advertise: Gillies, "Watt," nn. 35, 36.

they could farm out to Watt the task of selling serial rights: Interview with A. P. Watt, *Bookman,* October 1892, 21.

"Mr. A. Conan Doyle, a popular American writer": Boström and Laffey, 102.

The author's handwriting across these neat pages: Herbert Greenhough Smith, 171–173. All details about Smith's early response to ACD's writing derive from this source.

CHAPTER 29: DEERSTALKER

All the drawings are very unlike": ACD, *Memories and Adventures,* chap. 11.

But it was the middle brother, Sidney: Anonymous, "Artists," 786.

he often wore a deerstalker himself: See Paget.

Arthur found time to write six Sherlock Holmes stories in quick succession: Composition and mailing details in this paragraph derive from Baring-Gould, 1;14.

"And do you suppose he wouldn't discover this surveillance?": Gaboriau, anonymous translation of *Monsieur Lecoq,* chap. 19.

"I have been a detective fifteen years": Gaboriau, *The Mystery of Orcival,* chap. 11.

"The many friends in Portsmouth": Boström and Laffey, 112.

McClure read them and judged them: McClure, 203–205.

CHAPTER 30: TO MY OLD TEACHER

Still resenting the exploitative contract: ACD, *A Life in Letters,* 312.

"Facile and childish": Details of Charles Doyle's death derive from extensive quotations from Crichton medical records, reproduced in Norman, 159–161.

evolved out of his "own inner consciousness": Blathwayt. I have slightly changed some of the punctuation within dialogue.

"It is most certainly to you that I owe Sherlock Holmes": Baring-Gould, 1:8.

Arthur was astonished when he saw a listing for it: ACD, *A Life in Letters,* 315 (letter to Mary Doyle dated November 1892).

"I should just like to say this about my friend Doyle's stories": Anonymous, "Original of 'Sherlock Holmes.'"

illustrated with more than one hundred of Sidney Paget's pictures: Baring-Gould, 1:14 n. 26.

"Dear Sir, — You have taken many occasions": Stevenson, *Letters,* 4:186–187 (letter to ACD, dated April 5, 1893).

"To my old Teacher": ACD, *Adventures of Sherlock Holmes.*

Bibliography and Further Reading

Anonymous. "Artists of 'The Strand Magazine.'" *Strand*, December 1895.

Anonymous. "Booksellers of To-Day." *Publishers' Circular*, July 25, 1891.

Anonymous. *Druggists Circular and Chemical Gazette: A Practical Journal of Chemistry as Applied to Pharmacy*, Vol. 41. New York: William O. Allison, 1897.

Anonymous. "George Thomas Bettany (1850–1891)." Obituary in *Times*, 4 December 1891.

Anonymous, "The Literature of Bohemia." *Westminster Review*, January 1863.

Anonymous. Obituary of Joseph Bell, M. D. *New York Times*, 19 October 1911.

Anonymous. "Obituary, Joseph Bell." *Edinburgh Medical Journal*. Vol. 7 (1911), 454–463.

Anonymous. "The Original of 'Sherlock Holmes': An Interview with Dr. Joseph Bell." *Pall Mall Gazette*, 28 December 1893.

Anonymous. "The Original Prophet, by a Visitor to Salt Lake City." *Eclectic Magazine of Foreign Literature, Science, and Art*, April 1873.

Anonymous. *Sewage Disposal*: Report of a Committee Appointed by the President of the Local Government Board to Inquire into the Several Modes of Treating Town Sewage. London: Eyre & Spottiswoode, 1876.

Anonymous. "Sir Henry D. Littlejohn, M.D., LL.D. Edin., F.R.C.S.E." Obituary in *British Medical Journal*, 10 October 1914.

Anonymous. "Sir Robert Christison, Bart., M.D., D.C.L., Ll.D., Physician In Ordinary To The Queen In Scotland: Vice-President Of The British Medical Association, Etc." Obituary. *Scotsman*, 28 January 1882.

Anonymous. "Sir Thomas Richard Fraser, M.D., F.R.S. . . ." [obituary]. *British Medical Journal*, 17 January 1920, 100–102.

Anonymous. *Westminster Abbey*. Radnor, Pennsylvania: Annenberg School Press/Doubleday, 1972.

Arrington, Leonard J., and Jon Haupt. "Intolerable Zion: The Image of Mormonism in Nineteenth Century American Literature." *Western Humanities Review*, Summer 1968.

Bacon, Francis. *The Physical and Metaphysical Works of Lord Bacon, including The Advancement of Learning and Novum Organum*. Edited by Joseph Devey. London: Bell & Daldy, 1872.

Baker, Michael. *The Doyle Diary: The Last Great Conan Doyle Mystery*. New York: Paddington Press, 1978.

Ballingall, William. *Edinburgh Past and Present: Its Associations and Surroundings*. Edinburgh: J. Moodie Miller, 1877.

Barwise, Sidney. *The Purification of Sewage: Being a Brief Account of the Scientific Principles of Sewage Purification and Their Practical Application*. London: Crosby, Lockwood and Son, 1899.

Bell, Benjamin. *The Life, Character, and Writings of Benjamin Bell, by His Grandson*. Edinburgh: Edmonston and Douglas, 1868.

Bell, Joseph. "The Adventures of Sherlock Holmes." *Bookman* (London), December 1892. Reprinted under the title "Mr. Sherlock Holmes" as introduction to Ward, Lock & Company's 1892 edition of *A Study in Scarlet*.

——. "Five Years' Surgery in the Royal Hospital for Sick Children." *Edinburgh Hospital Reports*, 1893.

——. *A Manual of the Operations of Surgery, for the Use of Senior Students, House Surgeons, and Junior Practitioners*. 2nd ed. Edinburgh: Maclachlan and Stewart, 1869.

——. "Notes on a Case of Paralysis Following Diphtheria." *Edinburgh Medical Journal*, March 1865.

——. "Tracheotomy in Diphtheria." *Edinburgh Medical Journal*, August 1864.

Bergem, Phillip George. "The 1887 *Beeton's Christmas Annual*: The Annual, the Author, and the Artist." Privately published catalog.

Beveridge, A. "What Became of Arthur Conan Doyle's Father? The Last Years of Charles Altamont Doyle." *Journal of the Royal College of Physicians of Edinburgh* 36, 2006.

Billings, Harold. "The *Materia Medica* of Sherlock Holmes." *Baker Street Journal*, 2006.

Bills, Mark. "Thomas, William Luson (1830–1900), Wood-Engraver and Newspaper Proprietor." *Oxford Dictionary of National Biography*.

Black, Adam and Charles. *Black's Guide to Edinburgh and Environs, Hawthornden and Roslin*. Edinburgh: Adam and Charles Black, 1868.

——. *Black's Picturesque Tourist of Scotland*, 14th ed. Edinburgh: Adam and Charles Black, 1859.

Blathwayt, Raymond. "A Talk with Dr. Conan Doyle." *Bookman*, May 1892.

Blumberg, Jess. "Abandoned Ship: The *Mary Celeste*." *Smithsonian*, November 2007.

Booth, Martin. *The Doctor and the Detective: A Biography of Sir Arthur Conan Doyle*. New York: Thomas Dunne/St. Martin's, 1997.

Boström, Mattias, and Matt Laffey, editors. *Sherlock Holmes and Conan Doyle in the Newspapers*. Indianapolis, IN: Gasogene Books, 2015.

Bower, Alexander. *The History of the University of Edinburgh, from 1756–1829*. Edinburgh: Waugh and Innes, 1830.

Brake, Laurel, and Marysa Demoor. *The Lure of Illustration in the Nineteenth Century: Picture and Press*. Basingstoke, Hampshire: Palgrave Macmillan, 2009.

Bramwell, Byrom. "The Edinburgh Medical School and Its Professors During My Student Days (1865–1869)." *Edinburgh Medical Journal*, April 1923.

Brewster, David. *The Kaleidoscope: Its History, Theory, and Construction*. London: John Murray, 1858.

Brodie, Fawn. *No Man Knows My History: The Life of Joseph Smith*. New York: Knopf, 1945; rev. ed., 1971.

Brodie, Robert N. "'Take a Wire, Like a Good Fellow': The Telegraph in the Canon." Quoted in Klinger, 3:65–66.

Brown, Curtis. "'The Commercialization of Literature' and the Literary Agent." *Fortnightly Review*, July 1906.

Bulwer-Lytton, Sir Edward George D. *Pelham; or, Adventures of a Gentleman*. New York: P. F. Collier and Son, 1892.

Byerly, Ann. "Sidney Paget: Victorian Black-and-White Illustrator." *Baker Street Miscellanea* 35, Autumn 1983.

Cawthorne, Nigel. *A Brief History of Sherlock Holmes: The Complete Guide to the World's Most Famous Detective*. London: Constable & Robinson, 2011.

Cep, Casey N. "Called Back." *Paris Review*, October 30, 2013.

Chadwick, Edwin. *Report to Her Majesty's Principal Secretary of State for the Home Department, from the Poor Law Commissioners, of an Inquiry into the Sanitary Condition of the Labouring Population of Great Britain*. London: W. Clowes and Son, 1842.

Chandler, Alice. "Sir Walter Scott and the Medieval Revival." *Nineteenth-Century Fiction* 19, no. 4, March 1965.

Christison, Robert. *A Dispensatory, or Commentary on the Pharmacopoeias of Great Pharmacy, Actions, Uses, and Doses of the Articles of Materia Medica*. 2nd ed. Philadelphia: Lea & Blanchard, 1848.

——. *The Life of Sir Robert Christison, Bart, Edited by His Sons*. Two volumes. Edinburgh: William Blackwood and Sons, 1885.

——. "On the Properties of the Ordeal-Bean of Old Calabar, Western Africa." *Monthly Journal of Medicine*, March 1855.

Clark, Michael, and Catherine Crawford, editors. *Legal Medicine in History*. Cambridge: Cambridge University Press, 1994.

Coleman, William. *Georges Cuvier, Zoologist: A Study in the History of Evolution Theory*. Cambridge: Harvard University Press, 1964.

Collins, Philip. *Dickens and Crime*. Bloomington: Indiana University Press, 1968.

Cox, Howard, and Simon Mowat. *Revolutions from Grub Street: A History of Magazine Publishing in Britain*. Oxford: Oxford University Press, 2014.

Crawford, Gary William. "A Tale Told Again: Le Fanu's 'Evil Guest' and *A Lost Name*." *Le Fanu Studies* 4, no. 1, 2009.

Cross, Whitney R. *The Burned-Over District: The Social and Intellectual History of Enthusiastic Religion in Western New York, 1800–1850*. Ithaca, NY: Cornell University Press, 1950.

Curor, A. L. "Dr. Bell Our Teacher." *Daily Express* (London), July 11, 1930.

Cutler, Edward S. *Recovering the New: Transatlantic Roots of Modernism*. Hanover, NH: University Press of New England, 2003.

Devine, T. M., and Jenny Wormald, editors. *The Oxford Handbook of Modern Scottish History*. Oxford: Oxford University Press, 2012.

Dickens, Charles. *The Letters of Charles Dickens* (The Pilgrim Edition). Edited by Madeline House, Graham Storey, and Kathleen Tillotson. Volume 6, Oxford: Clarendon Press, 1988.

Doyle, Arthur Conan. *The Adventures of Sherlock Holmes.* London: George Newnes, 1892.

——. "After Cormorants with a Camera." *British Journal of Photography,* 2 parts, October 14 and 21, 1881.

——. *Arthur Conan Doyle: A Life in Letters.* Edited by Jon Lellenberg, Daniel Stashower, and Charles Foley. New York: Penguin Press, 2007.

——. *"Dangerous Work": Diary of an Arctic Adventure.* Edited by Jon Lellenberg and Daniel Stashower. Chicago: University of Chicago Press, 2012.

——. *The Final Adventures of Sherlock Holmes.* Edited by Peter Haining. Berkeley, CA: Apocryphile Press, 1981.

——. "Gelseminum as a Poison." Letter to the editor. *British Medical Journal,* September 20, 1879.

——. "The Glamour of the Arctic." *Idler,* July 1892.

——. "Juvenilia." *Idler,* January 1893.

——. "Life on a Greenland Whaler." *Strand,* January 1897.

——. *Memories and Adventures.* London: Hodder and Stoughton, 1924. Reprint: Oxford University Press, 1989.

——. "My Favorite Novelist." *Munsey's Magazine,* January 1898.

——. *The Narrative of John Smith.* London: British Library, 2011.

——. "On the Slave Coast with a Camera." *British Journal of Photography,* March 31 and April 7, 1882.

——. "Preface to the Author's Edition." *The Adventures of Sherlock Holmes.* New York: D. Appleton, 1902.

——. *Round the Red Lamp.* New York: McClure, 1908.

——. *Our Second American Adventure.* London: Hodder and Stoughton, 1923.

——. "Some Personalia About Sherlock Holmes." *Strand,* December 1917.

——. "Southsea: Three Days in Search of Effects." *British Journal of Photography,* June 22, 1883.

——. *The Stark Munro Letters.* New York: Longmans, Green, 1895.

——. "Surgeon of Gaster Fell." *Chambers's Journal,* four parts, December 6–27, 1890.

——. *Through the Magic Door.* London: Smith, Elder, 1907. Serialized first in *Cassell's* from November 1906 through October 1907.

——. "The Truth About Sherlock Holmes." *Collier's: The National Weekly,* December 29, 1923. Reprinted in *The Final Adventures of Sherlock Holmes,* ed. Peter Haining. Berkeley, CA: Apocryphile Press, 1981.

——. "To the Waterford Coast and Along It." *British Journal of Photography,* August 17, 1883.

——. *The Uncollected Sherlock Holmes.* Edited by Roger Lancelyn Green. London: Penguin, 1983.

Doyle, Georgina. *Out of the Shadows: The Untold Story of Arthur Conan Doyle's First Family.* Ashcroft, B.C.: Calabash Press, 2004.

Dumas, Alexandre. *The Romances of Alexandre Dumas D'Artagnan Edition.* Translator anonymous. Boston: Little, Brown, 1888.

Durie, Alastair J. "Tourism and Commercial Photography in Victorian Scotland: The Rise and Fall of G. W. Wilson & Co., 1853–1908." *Northern Scotland* 12, 1992.

Eddy, Spencer L., Jr. *The Founding of the Cornhill Magazine.* Ball State Monograph no. 19. Muncie, IN: Ball State University, 1970.

Elliott, Geoffrey. *The Mystery of Overend and Gurney: A Financial Scandal in Victorian London.* London: Methuen, 2006.

Ferris, Ian. "The Debut of *The Edinburgh Review*, 1802." *BRANCH: Britain, Representation, and Nineteenth-Century History,* www.branchcollective.org/?ps_ articles=ina-ferris-the-debut-of-the-edinburgh-review-1802.

Finnerud, Clark W. "Ferdinand von Hebra and the Vienna School of Dermatology." *A.M.A. Archives of Dermatology and Syphilology,* August 1, 1952.

Flanders, Judith. *The Invention of Murder: How the Victorians Revelled in Death and Detection and Created Modern Crime.* New York: St. Martin's, 2010.

Foster, Michael [as "M. F."]. Entry on Emil Du Bois-Reymond. *Encyclopedia Britannica,* 1911.

Fox, George Henry. *Reminiscences.* New York: Medical Life Press, 1926.

Froude, James Anthony. *Thomas Carlyle: A History of the First Forty Years of His Life, 1795–1835.* 2 volumes. London: Longmans, Green, 1882.

Gaboriau, Emile. *The Mystery of Orcival.* Anonymous English translation. New York: Holt & Williams, 1871.

Geddie, John. *Romantic Edinburgh.* London: Sands, 1900.

Gerber, Samuel M., editor. *Chemistry and Crime: From Sherlock Holmes to Today's Courtroom.* Washington, D.C.: American Chemical Society, 1983.

Gilbert, W. M. *Edinburgh in the Nineteenth Century: Being a Diary of the Chief Events . . .* Edinburgh: J. and R. Allan, 1901.

Gillies, Mary Ann. "A. P. Watt, Literary Agent." *Publishing Research Quarterly,* Spring 1993.

——. *The Professional Literary Agent in Britain, 1800–1920.* Toronto: University of Toronto Press, 2007.

Godfrey, Barry. *Crime in England 1880–1945: The Rough and the Criminal, the Police and the Incarcerated.* New York: Routledge, 2014.

Grant, James. *Cassell's Old and New Edinburgh: Its History, Its People, and Its Places.* 6 volumes. London: Cassell, Petter, Galpin & Co., 1880s. Available in various editions online, including via www.edinburghbookshelf.org.uk.

Green, Roger Lancelyn. *Kipling and the Children.* London: Elek Books, 1965.

Greenhow, Edward Headlam. On Diphtheria. London: John W. Parker, 1860.

Griest, Guinevere L. *Mudie's Circulating Library and the Victorian Novel.* Indianapolis: Indiana University Press, 1970.

Guilfoile, Patrick G. *Diphtheria.* New York: Chelsea/Infobase, 2009.

Guthrie, Douglas. "The Rise of Medical Education in Scotland." In *Janus in the Doorway.* Springfield, IL: Charles C. Thomas, 1963.

——. "Sherlock Holmes and Medicine." In *Janus in the Doorway.* Springfield, IL: Charles C. Thomas, 1963.

Habegger, Alfred. *My Wars Are Laid Away in Books: The Life of Emily Dickinson.* New York: Random House, 2001.

Hale, Edwin M. *A Monograph upon Gelseminum: Its Therapeutic and Physiological Effects Together with Its Uses in Disease.* Detroit: Dr. Lodge Homeopathic Pharmacy, 1862.

Hanna, H. B. *The Second Afghan War, 1878–79–80: Its Causes, Its Conduct, and Its Consequences.* 2 volumes. London: Archibald Constable, 1904.

Hare, Hobart Amory, et al. *The National Standard Dispensatory: Containing the Natural History, Chemistry, Pharmacy, Actions, and Uses of Medicines.* Philadelphia: Lea & Febiger, 1909.

Harrison, Michael. *In the Footsteps of Sherlock Holmes.* New York: Frederick Fell, 1960.

——. *A Study in Surmise: The Making of Sherlock Holmes.* Bloomington, IN: Gaslight Publications, 1984.

Holden, Horace. *Young Boys and Boarding-School: The Functions, Organisation and Administration of the Sub-Preparatory Boarding-School for Boys.* Boston: Richard G. Badger/Gorham Press, 1913.

Holt, Henry. "The Commercialization of Literature." *Atlantic Monthly,* November 1905.

How, Harry. "A Day with Dr. Conan Doyle." *Strand,* August 1892.

Hume, E. E. "Francis Home, M.D. (1719–1813): The Scottish Military Surgeon Who First Described Diphtheria as a Clinical Entity." *Bulletin of the History of Medicine* 11, 1942.

Hume, Fergus. *The Mystery of a Hansom Cab.* Melbourne: Hume, 1886.

Humphreys, David. *The Miscellaneous Works of Colonel Humphreys.* New York: Hodge, Allen, & Campbell, 1790.

Jack, Thomas C. *The Waverly Handbook to Edinburgh, Comprising a Complete Guidebook to the City and Neighbourhood.* Edinburgh: Thomas C. Jack, 1876.

Jacobs, Edward. "Eighteenth-Century British Circulating Libraries and Cultural Book History." *Book History* 6, 2003.

Jambon, Jean. *Our Trip to Blunderland, or, Grand Excursion to Blundertown and Back.* Edinburgh: Blackwood and Sons, 1877.

Jackson, Kate. *George Newnes and the New Journalism in Britain, 1880–1910.* Aldershot: Ashgate, 2001.

James, Henry. "Hardy's *Far from the Madding Crowd,*" *Nation,* December 24, 1874.

James, Prosser. *A Guide to the New Pharmacopoeia.* London: J. & A. Churchill, 1885.

Johannsen, Albert. *The House of Beadle and Adams and Its Dime and Nickel Novels: The Story of a Vanished Literature.* Norman: University of Oklahoma Press, 1950. Available at www.ulib.niu.edu/badndp/beeton_samuel.html.

Jones, Harold Emery. "The Original of Sherlock Holmes." Originally published as preface to *Conan Doyle's Best Books.* New York: Collier, 1904.

Kadane, Joseph B. "Bayesian Thought in Early Modern Detective Stories: Monsieur Lecoq, C. Auguste Dupin, and Sherlock Holmes." *Statistical Science* 24, no. 2, 2009.

Kaye, Marvin. *The Game Is Afoot: Parodies, Pastiches, and Ponderings of Sherlock Holmes.* New York: St. Martin's, 1995.

Kernahan, John Coulson. "Personal Memories of Sherlock Holmes." *London Quarterly and Holborn Review,* October 1934.

Kerr, Douglas. *Conan Doyle: Writing, Profession, and Practice.* Oxford: Oxford University Press, 2013.

Key, Jack D. "Medical Writings of a Literary Physician: Sir Arthur Conan Doyle (1859–1930)." *Minnesota Medicine,* June 1978.

Kipling, Rudyard. *Something of Myself.* London: Macmillan, 1937.

Klancher, Jon. *The Making of English Reading Audiences, 1790–1832.* Madison: University of Wisconsin Press, 1987.

Klauder, Joseph V. "Sherlock Holmes as a Dermatologist: With Notes on the Life of Dr. Joseph Bell and the Sherlockian Method of Teaching." *A.M.A. Archives of Dermatology and Syphilology*, October 1953.

Klinger, Leslie S. *The New Annotated Sherlock Holmes.* Three volumes. New York, W. W. Norton, 2005, 2006.

——. "Those Gouty Knuckles. . . ." *Baker Street Journal*, September 1999.

Konnikova, Maria. *Mastermind: How to Think Like Sherlock Holmes.* New York: Viking, 2013.

Kopley, Richard. *Edgar Allan Poe and the Dupin Mysteries.* New York: Palgrave Macmillan, 2008.

Korda, Andrea. *Printing and Painting the News in Victorian London: The Graphic and Social Realism, 1869–1891.* Farnham, Surrey: Ashgate, 2015.

Law, Graham. "On Wilkie Collins and Hugh Conway 'Poor Fargus.'" *Wilkie Collins Journal.* Online; no date.

Lee, R. W. "Comparative Legislation as to Habitual Drunkards." *Journal of the Society of Comparative Legislation* 2, 1901.

Lee, Sidney. "Memoir of George Smith." *Dictionary of National Biography*, 1901 Supplement.

Lee, W. L. Melville. *A History of Police in England.* London: Methuen, 1901.

Liebow, Ely M. *Dr. Joe Bell: Model for Sherlock Holmes.* Bowling Green, KY: Bowling Green University Popular Press, 1982.

Lightman, Bernard. "Conan Doyle's Ideal Reasoner: The Case of the Reluctant Scientific Naturalist." *Journal of Literature and Science* 7, no. 2, 2014.

Liveing, Edward. *Adventure in Publishing: The House of Ward Lock, 1854–1954.* London: Ward Lock, 1954.

Lycett, Andrew. *The Man Who Created Sherlock Holmes: The Life and Times of Sir Arthur Conan Doyle.* New York: Free Press, 2007.

Macaulay, Thomas Babington. *Lord Macaulay's Essays (and Lays of Ancient Rome).* London: George Routledge and Sons, 1892.

MacGillivray, Charles Watson. "Some Memories of Old Harveians, with Notes on Their Orations." *Edinburgh Medical Journal*, January 1912.

Macintyre, I. M. C. "Scientific Surgeon of the Enlightenment or 'Plagiarist in Everything': A Reappraisal of Benjamin Bell." *Journal of the Royal College of Physicians of Edinburgh*, Number 41, 2011.

MacRae, Alexander. *A Handbook of Deer-Stalking.* Edinburgh: Blackwood, 1880.

Mann, Ruth J., and Jack D. Key. "Joseph Bell, M.D., F.R.C.S.: Notes on a Case of Paralysis Following Diphtheria." *The Pharos* (Alpha Omega Alpha Honor Medical Society), Spring 1982.

Martin, John H. "Saints, Sinners, and Reformers: The Burned-Over District Revisited." *Crooked Lake Review*, Fall 2005.

Marx, Karl. "The Aims of the Negotiations.—Polemic Against Prussia.—A Snowball Riot." In *Marx and Engels Collected Works*, 13:598–599. Moscow: Progressive Publishers, 1980. Online at www.marxengels.public-archive.net/en/ME0833en.html.

McClure, S. S. *My Autobiography*. London: John Murray, 1914. [Said to be ghostwritten.]

McDonald, Peter D. "The Adventures of the Literary Agent: Conan Doyle, A. P. Watt, Holmes, and the Strand in 1891." *Victorian Periodicals Review*, 30.1 (1997).

McNally, Raymond T., and Radu Florescu. *In Search of Dr. Jekyll and Mr. Hyde: The True-Life Origins and Cultural Impact of the Classic Horror Story*. Los Angeles: Renaissance, 2000.

Meigs, Charles D. *Obstetrics: The Science and the Art*. Philadelphia: Lea and Blanchard, 1849.

Meltzer, Charles Henry. "Arsene Lupin at Home." *Cosmopolitan*, May 1913.

Miller, Russell. *The Adventures of Arthur Conan Doyle: A Biography*. New York: St. Martin's, 2008.

Moir, John. "On Croup: Its Nature and Treatment." *Edinburgh Medical Journal*, November 1878.

Moore, Grace. "The Great Detectives: Dupin, Sergeant Cuff, and Inspector Bucket." *Strand*, in https://www.strandmag.com/the-magazine/articles/the-great-detectives-dupin-sergeant-cuff-inspector-bucket-by-grace-moore/.

Mott, Frank Luther. *A History of American Magazines*, vol. 3: *1865–1885*. Cambridge, MA: Harvard University Press, 1957.

Moulin, T. "Doctors in Balzac's Work." *Frontiers of Neurology and Neuroscience*, March 5, 2013.

Newnes, George. "The One Hundredth Number of 'The Strand Magazine': A Chat about Its History." *Strand*, April 1899.

Norman, Andrew. *Arthur Conan Doyle: Beyond Sherlock Holmes*. New York: History Press, 2007.

Orel, Harold, editor. *Sir Arthur Conan Doyle: Interviews and Recollections*. New York: St. Martin's, 1991.

Paget, Winifred. "Sherlock Holmes's Deerstalker." *Picture Post*, December 16, 1950.

Panek, LeRoy Lad. *The Origins of the American Detective Story*. Jefferson, NC: McFarland, 2006.

Payn, James. "The Family Scapegrace." In *My First Book*. London: Chatto & Windus, 1897.

Pierce, Peter, editor. *The Cambridge History of Australian Literature*. Cambridge: Cambridge University Press, 2009.

Poe, Edgar Allan. "The Murders in the Rue Morgue." *Graham's*, April 1841.

———. *The Works of the Late Edgar Allan Poe, with Notices of His Life and Genius*. 4 volumes. Edited by N. P. Willis, J. R. Lowell, and R. W. Griswold. New York: J. S. Redfield, 1856.

Poole, Richard. *Memoranda Regarding the Royal Lunatic Asylum, Infirmary, and Dispensary, of Montrose*. Montrose: J. & D. Nichol, 1841.

Porter, Andrew. *Religion Versus Empire? British Protestant Missionaries and Overseas Expansion, 1700–1914*. Manchester: Manchester University Press, 2004.

Powell, Richard. *The Pharmacopoeia of the Royal College of Physicians of London*. London: Longman, Hurst, Rees, and Orme, 1809.

Power, D'Arcy. Entry on William Rutherford. *Dictionary of National Biography*, 1901 supplement.

Pringle, R. V. "The George Washington Wilson Photographic Archive: A Postscript." Proceedings of the George Washington Wilson Centenary Conference at the University of Aberdeen, March 1993. Available online at www.rvpmp.talktalk. net/gww/gww.html.

Pulsifer, C. "Beyond the Queen's Shilling: Reflections on the Pay of Other Ranks in the Victorian British Army." *Journal of the Society for Army Historical Research* 80, 2002.

Quail, Sarah. *Foul Deeds and Suspicious Deaths Around Portsmouth*. Barnsley, South Yorkshire: Wharncliffe/Pen & Sword, 2008.

Rahn, B. J. *The Real World of Sherlock*. Stroud: Amberley Publishing, 2014.

Reade, Charles. *A Terrible Temptation: A Story of the Day*. 3 volumes. London: Chapman and Hall, 1871.

Redmond, Charles. *Sherlock Holmes Handbook*. Second edition, Toronto: Dundurn Press, 1993.

Redmond, Donald A. *Sherlock Holmes: A Study in Sources*. Montreal: McGill-Queen's University Press, 1982.

Redmond, Gerald. *The Sporting Scots of Nineteenth-Century Canada*. East Brunswick, NJ: Associated University Presses, 1982.

Reid, Donald. "Dr. Henry Faulds—Beith Commemorative Society." *Journal of Forensic Identification*, 53, no. 2 (2003).

Reid, Mayne. *The Scalp Hunters: A Romance of the Plain*. New York: G. W. Dillingham, 1891.

Richards, Jeffrey. *Imperialism and Music: Britain 1876–1953*. Manchester: Manchester University Press/Palgrave, 2001.

Ringer, Sydney and William Murrell. "On Gelseminum Sempervirens." *Lancet*, December 25, 1875.

——. "On Gelseminum Sempervirens." *Lancet*, March 18, 1876.

——. "On Gelseminum Sempervirens." *Lancet*, May 6, 1876.

——. "On Gelseminum Sempervirens." *Lancet*, June 15, 1878.

Robinson, Marilynne. "On Edgar Allan Poe." *New York Review of Books*, February 5, 2015.

Rodin, Alvin E., and Jack D. Key. "Doctor Arthur Conan Doyle's Patients in Fact and Fiction." *Medical Heritage*, March/April 1985.

Roggenkamp, Karen. *Narrating the News: New Journalism and Literary Genre in Late Nineteenth-Century American Newspapers and Fiction*. Kent, OH: Kent State University Press, 2005.

Sadden, John. *The Portsmouth Book of Days*. Stroud, Gloucestershire: History Press, 2012.

Sala, George Augustus. *Things I Have Seen and People I Have Known*. 2 volumes. London: Cassell and Company, 1895.

Scarlett, E. P. "The Old Original: Notes on Dr. Joseph Bell Whose Personality and Peculiar Abilities Suggested the Creation of Sherlock Holmes." *Archives of Internal Medicine*, November 1964.

Scrope, William. *The Art of Deer-Stalking*. London: John Murry, 1839.

Shpayer-Makov, Haia. *The Ascent of the Detective: Police Sleuths in Victorian and Edwardian England*. Oxford: Oxford University Press, 2011.

St. Clair, William. *The Reading Nation in the Romantic Period*. Cambridge: Cambridge University Press, 2004.

Sanders, Lisa. *Every Patient Tells a Story: Medical Mysteries and the Art of Diagnosis*. New York: Broadway Books, 2009.

Saxby, Jessie M. E. *Joseph Bell: An Appreciation by an Old Friend*. Edinburgh: Oliphant, Anderson & Ferrier, 1913.

Scott, Walter. *Count Robert of Paris*. Edinburgh: Robert Cadell, 1832.

——. *Ivanhoe: A Romance*. Edinburgh: Archibald Constable, 1820.

Sheehan, A. V. *Criminal Procedure in Scotland and France*. Edinburgh: HMSO, 1975.

Silverman, Kenneth. *Edgar A. Poe: Mournful and Never-Ending Remembrance*. New York: HarperCollins, 1991.

Simpson, Harold. *A Century of Ballads, 1810–1910: Their Composers and Singers*. London: Mills & Boon, 1910.

Sims, Michael. *Adam's Navel: A Natural and Cultural History of the Human Form*. New York: Viking, 2003.

——, editor. *The Dead Witness: A Connoisseur's Collection of Victorian Detective Stories*. New York: Bloomsbury, 2011.

——, editor. *The Penguin Book of Gaslight Crime: Con Artists, Burglars, Rogues, and Scoundrels from the Time of Sherlock Holmes*. New York: Penguin Classics, 2009.

——, editor. *The Penguin Book of Victorian Women in Crime: Forgotten Cops and Private Eyes from the Time of Sherlock Holmes*. New York: Penguin Classics, 2011.

Sladen, Douglas. *Twenty Years of My Life*. London: Constable, 1914.

Slater, Michael. *Charles Dickens*. New Haven: Yale University Press, 2009.

Smith, Herbert Greenhough. *Odd Moments: Essays in Little*. London: George Newnes, 1925.

Smith, John. *The Origin, Progress, and Present Position of the Royal College of Surgeons of Edinburgh, 1505–1905*. Edinburgh: Royal College of Surgeons, 1905.

Snyder, Laura J. "Sherlock Holmes: Scientific Detective." *Endeavour*, September 2004.

Solberg, Andrew. "Chair à Canon: In the Beginning." *Irene's Cabinet* (2010).

Sparks, Tabitha. *The Doctor in the Victorian Novel: Family Practices*. Farnham, Surrey: Ashgate, 2009.

Springfield, Lincoln. "London's Undiscovered Murders: A Serious Problem Carefully Considered." *Harmsworth Monthly Pictorial Magazine* 1, 1898–1899.

Stavert, Geoffrey. *A Study in Southsea: From Bush Villas to Baker Street*. Portsmouth: Milestone Publications, 1987.

Stevenson, Robert Louis. *Strange Case of Dr Jekyll and Mr Hyde*. London: Longmans, Green, 1886.

——. *Edinburgh: Picturesque Notes*. London: Strangeways and Sons, 1879.

——. *The Essential Dr. Jekyll and Mr. Hyde: The Definitive Annotated Edition of Robert Louis Stevenson's Classic Novel*. Edited by Leonard Wolf. New York: Plume, 1995.

——. *The Letters of Robert Louis Stevenson*. Edited by Sidney Colvin. New York: Scribner's, 1911.

Stoker, Bram. "Sir Arthur Conan Doyle Tells of His Career and Work, His Sentiments Towards America, and His Approaching Marriage." *New York World*, July 28, 1907.

Storey, G. D. "Alfred Baring Garrod." *Rheumatology* 40, no. 10, 2001.

Streeter, Burnett Hillman. *The Chained Library: A Survey of Four Centuries in the Evolution of the English Library*. New York: Burt Franklin, 1931.

Summerscale, Kate. *The Suspicions of Mr. Whicher*. New York: Walker, 2008.

Sutherland, Gavin. *The Whaling Years: Peterhead, 1788–1893*. Aberdeen: Centre for Scottish Studies, 1993.

Sweeney, Susan Elizabeth. "The Magnifying Glass: Spectacular Distance in Poe's 'Man of the Crowd' and Beyond." *Poe Studies/Dark Romanticism* 36, nos. 1–2.

Tait, Haldane P. *A Doctor and Two Policemen: The History of Edinburgh Health Department*. Edinburgh: Mackenzie and Storrie, 1974.

Tames, Richard. *London: A Cultural History*. Oxford: Oxford University Press, 2006.

Tardieu, Auguste Ambroise. *Mémoire sur les modifications physiques et chimiques que détermine dans certaines parties du corps l'exercice des diverse professions, pour servir à la recherche médico-légale de l'identité*. TK, 1849–1850. Anonymous translation.

Taylor, Roger. *George Washington Wilson, Artist and Photographer, 1823–1893*. Aberdeen: Aberdeen University Press, 1981.

Thackeray, William Makepeace. *Vanity Fair: A Novel without a Hero*. London: Bradbury and Evans, 1848.

Tracy, Jack. *Conan Doyle and the Latter-day Saints*. Revised edition. Bloomington, IN: Gaslight Publications, 1979.

Traill, Thomas, Robert Christison, and James Syme. *Suggestions for the Medico-Legal Examination of Dead Bodies*. Edinburgh: Scottish Record Office, 1836.

Trollope, Anthony. "On English Prose Fiction as a Rational Amusement." In *Four Lectures*, edited by Morris L. Parrish. London: Constable, 1938.

Tully, William. "Gelseminum Nitidum of Pursh." *Boston Medical and Surgical Journal*, October 3, 1832.

Turner, A. Logan. *Story of a Great Hospital: The Royal Infirmary of Edinburgh, 1729–1929*. Edinburgh: Oliver & Boyd, 1937.

Twain, Mark. *Roughing It*. Hartford, CT: American Publishing, 1873.

Tweedie, Major-General W. "'Bits' of Edinburgh Sixty Years Ago—and After." *Chambers's Journal*, June 1908.

Voltaire [François-Marie Arouet]. *Zadig, or The Book of Fate: An Oriental History, Translated from the French Original of Mr. Voltaire*. London: John Brindley, 1749.

Walcott, Mackenzie. *A Guide to the South Coast of England*. London: Edward Stanford, 1859.

Walker, Ian M, editor. *Edgar Allan Poe: The Critical Heritage*. London: Psychology Press, 1997.

Wall, Brian, and Sarah Ames. "Parallel Prosecutions: Mormon Polygamy and Evidentiary Doubt in *The Dynamiter* and *A Study in Scarlet*." Unpublished manuscript based upon Ph.D. dissertation.

Wallace, Irving. "The Incredible Dr. Bell." In *The Fabulous Originals: Lives of Extraordinary People Who Inspired Memorable Characters in Fiction*. New York: Knopf, 1955.

Ward, Mrs. Maria [pseud.]. *Female Life Among the Mormons: A Narrative of Many Years' Personal Experience. By the Wife of a Mormon Elder, Recently from Utah*. New York: J. C. Derby, 1855.

Watson, Thomas. *Lectures on the Principles and Practice of Physic*. London: Parker & Son, 1843.

Watson, William N. Boog. "An Edinburgh Surgeon of the Crimean War—Patrick Heron Watson (1832–1907)." *Medical History*, April 1966.

Weinreb, Ben, Christopher Hibbert, Julia Keay, and John Keay. *The London Encyclopedia*. 3rd edition. London: Macmillan, 2008.

Welch, Charles. "Newnes, George." Biographical entry in *Dictionary of National Biography*, 1912.

Westmoreland, Barbara F., and Jack D. Key. "Sir Arthur Conan Doyle, Joseph Bell, and Sherlock Holmes: A Neurologic Connection." *Archives of Neurology*, March 1991.

Wheatley, Henry B. *London Past and Present: Its History, Associations, and Traditions*. 3 volumes. London: John Murray, 1891.

Whewell, William. *The Philosophy of the Inductive Sciences*. London: John W. Parker, 1840.

Whipple, George. "Remarks on the Preparations of the Pharmacopæia." *Chemist*, May 1855.

Whitman, Walt. *The Collected Writings of Walt Whitman*, vol. 5: *The Correspondence (1890–1892)*. Edited by Edwin Haviland Miller. New York: New York University Press, 1969.

Wigmore, John H. "Did Poe Plagiarize the Murders in the Rue Morgue?" *Cornell Law Review*, February 1928.

Williamson, C. N. "The Illustrated London News and Its Rivals." *Magazine of Art*, 1890.

Wills, W. Henry. *Old Leaves: Gathered from Household Words*. New York: Harper & Brothers, 1860.

Woodhead, G. Sims. "Obituary" [for William Rutherford]. *Edinburgh Medical Journal* 5, 1899, 434–436.

Young, Timothy G. *Drawn to Enchant: Original Children's Book Art in the Betsy Beinecke Shirley Collection*. New Haven, CT: Yale University Press, 2007.

Index

Note: The abbreviation ACD refers to Arthur Conan Doyle.

POWER TALKING

OTHER WORKS BY GEORGE R. WALTHER

BOOKS
Phone Power

VIDEO TRAINING PROGRAMS
Phone Power
Power Talking
TeleMax

AUDIO TRAINING PROGRAMS
Phone Power (Multiple Editions)
Power Talking
Profitable Telemarketing
TeleMarkeTrends

POWER TALKING

50 Ways to Say What You Mean
and Get What You Want

GEORGE R. WALTHER

G. P. PUTNAM'S SONS
New York

*This book is dedicated
to my daughter, Kelcie Paige.*

*You will hear the sound
of one man clapping.*

G. P. Putnam's Sons
Publishers Since 1838
200 Madison Avenue
New York, NY 10016

Copyright © 1991 by George R. Walther
All rights reserved. This book, or parts thereof, may not be reproduced in any
form without permission. Published simultaneously in Canada

Library of Congress Cataloging-in-Publication Data
Walther, George R.
    Power talking : 50 ways to say what you mean and get what you want
 / George R. Walther.
        p.   cm.
    Includes bibliographical references.
    1. Business communication.   2. Oral communication.   I. Title.
    HF5718.W36   1991   90-29118   CIP
    658.4'52—dc20

ISBN 0-399-13606-1
Printed in the United States of America
1   2   3   4   5   6   7   8   9   10

Acknowledgments

THIS book is the direct result of enthusiastic feedback from clients, readers, users of my audio and video tapes, and audience members who asked for more of the "Power Talking" concepts introduced in *Phone Power*. Thank you all for inspiring me to write *Power Talking*.

It's a long trail from concept to finished book. Adrienne Ingrum got me started by encouraging me to "put it in writing." My agents, Arthur and Richard Pine, handled the publishing negotiations and allowed me to concentrate on creating my best work. Laurie Larsen's nimble fingers and sharp eyes helped with much of the word processing. My Putnam editorial team, Rena Wolner and Christine Pepe, provided superb support, expertly pared the manuscript, and helped me polish my writing.

Many colleagues in the National Speakers Association have provided priceless fellowship and professional support. I appreciate their abundant suggestions and assistance.

No author could ask for a better "home team." Thank you, Julie, for your contributions of ideas and time. I respect and appreciate your rare and marvelous combination of raw brainpower and levelheadedness. And most important of all, thank you for being such a wonderful mother.

Contents

Introduction

Two employees, in adjacent offices, each tell their supervisors that they haven't completed their monthly status reports on time:
Employee A says:

"Well, John, to tell you the truth, there were so many distractions this week that, I hate to say it, but I just couldn't finish the report on time. It's not my fault. I couldn't help it. You know what I mean. I'm afraid I can't complete it until around the middle of next week."

Employee B says:

"John, my monthly status report is not yet finished. We can review my outline of the highlights together now, and I'll have the completed report for you before Thursday morning. I take responsibility for the delay. I decided that some other projects warranted a higher priority."

Which employee has better career prospects?

You and a friend own identical cars, and they both start making peculiar squealing sounds somewhere in the engine compartment. First thing Monday morning, each of you takes your car to a different nearby dealer.
Dealer A says:

"Gee, I don't know what to tell you. Our service department won't be open until about 9:00 or so. It's Monday, you know. I couldn't help you myself. I'm only in the used car sales department. You'll just have to check back a little later. Sorry."

Dealer B says:

"I'll be glad to help you. The service department will be open by 9:00. Meanwhile, I can help you fill out the Work Order form. That way you'll be all set when they open in a few minutes."

Which dealership is likely to create satisfied customers who recommend it to their friends?

You decide to computerize your home finances. You visit two software stores to find out which personal accounting program will work best for you.

Salesperson A says:

"The problem is, there are so many different programs, it's almost impossible to figure out which one's right for you. I'd hate to see you get stuck with the wrong one. Let's see now, which might be the best program for me to sell you?"

Salesperson B says:

"Our challenge is to find out which program will best match your needs, and I'll be happy to help you with that. I want to be sure that we select the software that you'll be happiest with. Let's talk about what you want the program to do, and then I'll recommend the best choice."

Which salesperson will probably win your business?

In each case, A conveyed the same basic information as B. Yet, you, as the supervisor, or car owner, or software shopper, experienced a very different reaction to what each person said.

The big distinctions lie in how A and B expressed themselves. They both used common language; each said about the same number of words; neither spoke more intelligently than the other. Yet, the impact of what each person communicated differed dramatically.

All day, every day, people size **you** up based on the way you talk. In these examples, B is clearly going to move ahead faster and experience more professional success, make customers happier, enjoy stronger friendships, and generate higher sales than A.

This book shows you how to ensure that you're always in the "B" position. The Power Talking techniques you'll learn here help you create consistently positive impressions whenever others hear you. They apply equally well at home with family and friends, or at work with customers, supervisors, and peers.

Power Talking shows you how to speak the language of success. Use the words and phrases you read here, and you will experience greater professional achievements, more harmonious relationships with friends and colleagues, a happier family life, better emotional and physical health, and yes, you'll even make more money.

Learning to speak more powerfully isn't like studying Latin or taking German classes. There's no vocabulary quiz. You already know all the words and phrases you'll ever need to know. It's how you put those everyday expressions together and how you use them that counts.

This book presents simple ways to put positive thinking theories to work in your life. You don't even need to finish reading this introduction before you start reaping the benefits.

I've gathered 50 specific expressions you can use to help make sure things go your way, and covered each one in its own chapter. You can begin with any of the 50, start at the beginning or at the end. Or just keep flipping through the book, adopting phrase after phrase. When you spot a powerless expression that you recognize as part of your present daily speaking habits, read that chapter. Maybe you'll notice a familiar phrase like "I'll try," or "that could be a problem," or "I'll be honest with you," and say to yourself, "Hey, I say that all the time. What's wrong with it? How is my use of that expression holding me back? What should I be saying instead?" Read that chapter immediately.

The 50 chapters are grouped into sections, each focusing on one of the traits shared by successful, happy people. Power Talkers, for instance, rebound resiliently from apparent setbacks. Section III, "Rebound Resiliently," includes several examples of get-back-on-track phrases you can use when things aren't going quite the way you'd like.

Every chapter deals with a specific, all-too-common phrase, and includes personal anecdotes and stories about encounters with clients, audience members, friends or family. Then, each of the 50 chapters proceeds with the rationale behind the substitution I've recommended.

And finally, each chapter concludes with a "Quick Reference: What You Can Do Right Now" summary. There, you'll find common power*less* phrases that you may be using habitually and unwittingly, along with their recommended Power Talking replacements.

So, let's start! Flip through the book right now. Find a powerless phrase that you know you sometimes use. Maybe it's "I'll have to . . ." Read Chapter 1 and decide to banish that phrase starting *now*. Purge it from your vocabulary. Today, begin substituting the phrase "I'll be glad to . . ." and keep it up. Then, move ahead to another phrase that catches your interest. Don't worry about reading the chapters or sections "in order." Do read them all.

You're going to see immediate results. Creating long-term changes in your life by changing the way you speak isn't easy— and it's also not terribly difficult. Start with one phrase right now. Get those powerless phrases out of your vocabulary and start Power Talking.

POWER TALKERS . . .

I. Project Positive Expectations

THE most noticeable characteristic of Power Talkers is that they project positive expectations, both for themselves and for others. You're probably familiar with the concepts of positive thinking as detailed in Dr. Norman Vincent Peale's classic, *The Power of Positive Thinking.* As he put it, "When you change your thoughts, you change your life." But you can't just sit in a corner and think positively—that won't change your life. You need to interact positively with others. I agree with Dr. Peale's advice about positive thinking, and recommend that you take one more step.

Power Talkers go beyond **thinking** positively—they **talk** positively, too. Notice the big difference between a person who says, "I can never remember anyone's name" vs. the person who says, "I'm working to improve my memory."

I recently had my home remodeled, and I noticed that the contractors who said, "I'll try and get back to you by tomorrow" rarely did. Those who said, "I will have an answer for you before 5:00 tomorrow" followed through and lived up to their commitments. That's because the expectations they set didn't just influence me, the listener. They influenced themselves as well. When you set positive expectations for others, you're setting them for yourself, too. Making a commitment increases your reliability in the other person's eyes, and it also helps you program yourself to follow through.

One manager of a public utility company in San Francisco noticed that her people often revealed their gloomy morale through their routine daily greetings. She'd overhear co-workers passing in the hallways greeting each other with, "Hey, how's it going?" The most common responses ran along the lines of, "Oh, OK, I guess," and "Only four more days 'til the weekend." She suspected that these comments brought everyone's attitude down.

During her next staff meeting, she explained her theory and implemented a reward system to encourage positive responses. She designated individuals to serve as "mystery greeters," so other employees wouldn't know when their responses were being assessed. The greeters asked co-workers how they were, and noted those who offered positive responses. Those who the "mystery greeters" felt contributed most to a positive atmosphere were recognized and rewarded with a small prize at the end of the day. The result?

"It made a huge difference almost overnight. Once people became aware of the effect their greetings and responses had on each other, I heard them saying things like: 'Great!' or 'I'm doing really well today, how 'bout you?' and so on. They all started believing each other, and really did feel much better. You could easily gauge the difference in morale."

In the following chapters you'll meet people who focus on affirmative language and action, who set optimistic expectations for themselves and others, and who think, speak, and behave positively. They use their own language to help create success for themselves. You can, too.

1. *I'll Be Glad To!*

YOUR CO-worker went to lunch without arranging for phone coverage. You're working through lunch so you can go home a little early. Her phone, on the desk beside yours, rings and rings and rings. Annoyed, you finally decide to answer it.

Say out loud to yourself:

"I'll have to take a message and she won't get it for another hour or so."

Now, say:

"I'll be glad to take your message and make sure she gets it before 1:30."

Which will give the caller the more favorable impression? Which will make you feel better about taking the message?

"Good Evening, thank you for calling the GE Answer Center, I'm Miss Cooley, how may I help you?"

The GE Answer Center uses my Power Talking techniques for its employee training program. I like to call in anonymously from time to time and check to see how consistently the Center's employees apply their training.

When my wife and I had decided to buy a freezer, I called (anonymously, of course) the Answer Center late one Sunday night for product information before visiting a dealer. I started by asking about energy consumption:

"Which type of freezer is more energy efficient: upright or chest style?"

17

Miss Cooley didn't sound old enough to have purchased many freezers herself, and I was a little skeptical about her firsthand knowledge.

"That's a good question. I'm in training now, and I'd like to compare the efficiency ratings of several models for you."

She'd LIKE to? I'm used to people saying something more along the lines of,

"Well, I'm still only a trainee, so I couldn't tell you for sure. What I'd have to do is look up some different models and see if I can figure that out."

Rather than making it sound like a burden, I got the feeling that Miss Cooley was actually looking forward to finding out the answer herself.

GE markets a line of freezers under the Hotpoint brand name, so I asked for information about those models as well. "I'll be glad to check on the Hotpoint models for you," Miss Cooley said.

What was with her? It was 2:00 A.M. in Louisville, where she was answering my call. How could she be so GLAD to help me?

She talked me through the various features, and then she offered to look up a nearby dealer where I could compare several models.

I know that GE makes fine products, and I appreciate being able to get information whenever I want it, even if that's late at night. The icing on the cake is the extremely congenial way Miss Cooley and her colleagues respond to callers' questions.

The GE Answer Center is one outstanding example of a company's commitment to providing customers with complete, accurate information and friendly human contact. One of General Electric's original reasons for establishing the Answer Center was to "put on a friendly face" for consumers who might perceive GE as a gigantic, cold, bureaucratic corporation.

What struck me most during my conversation with Miss Cooley was something very simple: her consistent use of phrases like "I'll be glad to check that . . ." and "I'll be happy to get that information." In each case she communicated not just that she had or would get the information I needed, but that she'd do it with pleasure. Imagine working an eight-hour shift beside Miss Cooley. If you handle twelve calls an hour, and each one includes, on average, three requests for information, you have the opportunity to choose between saying, "I'll **have to** look that up" and "I'll be **glad to** look that up," 288 times each day. After hearing yourself say "I'll have to" 288 times in a single workshift, how are you likely to feel? Exhausted, cranky, weary, put-upon? Would it make a difference if you kept hearing yourself say, "I'll be glad to" instead?

Indeed, it can make a big difference, as the training staff and management at GE can attest. Even after answering thousands of calls, GE staffers there are remarkably enthusiastic, cheerful, and at the same time entirely professional. One reason for the excellent morale is the training department's focus on Power Talking. From their first day in training, new employees are coached to deliver accurate information in an upbeat manner.

In the course of an average day, we all respond to many requests for information. A simple word substitution changes the whole tone of the response. Saying "I'll be **glad to** check those dates for you" not only projects a pleasant, cooperative attitude; it also makes you feel better.

Whether you're responsible for employee training programs in your organization or are interested in making your own dealings with friends, supervisors, or customers more rewarding, take advantage of the benefits that result from substituting positive phrases like "I'll be happy to" for burdensome ones like "I'll have to."

QUICK REFERENCE

What you can do right now:

Each time you begin to say "I'll **have to**," substitute a phrase that shows you'll be **glad to.** Notice the difference it makes in your own mood and in others' attitudes about cooperating with you.

Instead of saying,

"I'm afraid I'll have to check that and call you back."

Say,

"I'd like to check that and call you back."

Instead of saying,

"I'm gonna have to pull your file."

Say,

"I'll be glad to pull your file."

Instead of saying,

"I'll have to do it."

Say,

"I'll be glad to do it."

2. Will You Try, or Will You DO It?

YOUR garage has been a mess for months. Tools are jumbled on the workbench, the recycling bins are overflowing, and the floor is filthy. Your spouse asks you (again) to clean it up this weekend.
Say out loud to yourself:

"OK, OK, I'll try to do it before the ball game on Sunday."

Now say:

"I will have it cleaned up by Sunday afternoon."

Which promise will motivate you to follow through with action?

Jeff Salzman is the co-author of *Real World 101* and *CareerTracking*, both valuable guides for accelerating your success in business. He told me about an encounter with a lawyer that dramatized the difference between "I'll try" and "I will."
Early in Jeff's advertising career, one of his clients was sued. The

plaintiff's lawyer wanted Jeff to give a deposition. "The game," Jeff points out, "is to make yourself as unavailable as possible so as to avoid helping the other side build its case." The lawyer asked if Monday would be convenient for Jeff to meet with him. Jeff was busy. How about Tuesday? Oh, gosh, meetings all day. The lawyer quickly realized that Jeff was being cagey, so he switched gears, asking an open-ended question: "So, Jeff, when will you give your deposition?" Jeff couldn't maintain that he was "too busy" forever, so he suggested, "I'll try for two weeks from Friday." The lawyer's response was to ask for a firm commitment: "Do I have your word that you **will** give your deposition two weeks from Friday?" Jeff thought to himself, "He's got me! Once I've made a commitment and given my word, he's won the game." Of course, Jeff honored his commitment. And he also learned a lesson. Ever since that phone call, whenever he detects an indefinite "I'll try . . ." in somebody's statement, he counters with, "Do I have your word that you **will**?"

The person who benefits most when you say "I will" is *you*. When you hear yourself making a firm commitment, you are more likely to follow through with action than if you say "I'll try." That's merely an abbreviated form of "I'll give it a shot but I'm not making any promises—we'll just wait and see what happens." Or, as Drs. Ken Blanchard and Norman Vincent Peale wrote in *The Power of Ethical Management*, "Trying is just a noisy way of not doing something."

QUICK REFERENCE

What you can do right now:

Tell yourself and everyone else what you **will** do, not what you'll **try** to do.

Instead of saying,

"I'll try to finish up the market research analysis by the middle of the week."

Say,

"I will complete the market research analysis no later than Wednesday afternoon."

Instead of saying,

"I'll try to practice my pitching three times a week to get ready for the softball league playoffs next month."

Say,

"I will practice my pitching three times a week and be ready for the softball league playoffs next month."

Instead of saying,

"I'll try to do it."

Say,

"I will do it."

3. Say What You Want to Do

WHILE handling your arrangements for a last-minute business trip, your travel agent suggests guaranteeing the hotel room with a credit card.

Say out loud to yourself:

"I'd hate to see you lose your reservation if the flight is delayed and the hotel assumes you're a no-show."

Now say:

"I want to guarantee that your room will be held for you even if you arrive a little later than expected."

Which version sounds more helpful? Which suggests a more optimistic outlook?

*   *   *

You hear some interesting excuses when you're an Accounts Receivable collector. I was coaching a seasoned collector named Sharon at Ford Motor Credit's Detroit branch office when we encountered Leon D. This customer insisted that he was deceased, and had even personally signed a letter verifying his own demise!

Sharon showed me the extensive records of her previous conversations with Leon D., and his case was very sad indeed. He had purchased a new Ford pickup truck and financed it through his dealer. Soon after his loan was approved, he developed a severe brain tumor that clouded his thinking. Sharon had verified his diagnosis with the Veterans Administration hospital and learned that his condition was life-threatening. Since it was impossible to reason with Leon, she called his wife and learned that he was on strong medication, and was drinking heavily and behaving irrationally.

I listened in as Sharon called Leon's wife at her workplace:

"Hello, Mrs. D., this is Sharon at Ford Motor Credit. I'm calling because we still haven't received the overdue payments for your husband's truck, and now his record in the computer shows that his insurance has been canceled for nonpayment. I hate to say it, but I see no alternative but to have the vehicle repossessed unless you're willing to help me."

Sharon had already threatened Leon with repossession, and his response was to hide the vehicle. Repo agents had been driving by his house looking for the truck, but were unable to locate it. If Mrs. D. wouldn't make the payments, Sharon hoped that she would at least reveal the truck's location.

Unfortunately, Mrs. D. wasn't helpful:

"Go ahead and do whatever you have to do. I can't talk with him. He's completely crazy. I have no influence over that man. Take the truck if that's what you want to do."

Sharon pressed on and described the likely consequences:

"Mrs. D., a repossession is going to look very bad on your credit record and will be part of your file for years to come. You don't want to have a default, do you?"

Mrs. D. knew that she wasn't legally responsible.

"Listen, young lady, I didn't sign that contract and I'm not accountable for Leon's irresponsible behavior. There's nothing I'm going to do to help you and I don't care what happens. Besides, the doctors say he's going to die any day. I have no money to pay you or anybody else. I'm barely able to make the house payments. But Leon does have an insurance policy. And when he dies, that's my only hope of keeping my home. I don't drive his truck, and I didn't sign for it, so why should I care what happens to it?"

Now, with all the cards on the table, Sharon didn't know what to say. She ended her conversation having made no headway at all:

"Mrs. D., it sounds like you have enough problems to deal with. I'd hate to see them get worse because of a repossession and default on your husband's credit records, but if you won't help me, that's my only choice at this point."

After the call, Sharon and I talked about the difference between an "I'd hate to . . ." and an "I want to . . ." approach. People don't care to hear about potential bad news—in fact, they'll screen it out. They reach a point where they think things simply cannot get any worse. Sharon's approach had this effect on Mrs. D.

She had been unsuccessful using the negative strategy: "If you don't act now, things will get even worse." I suggested that Sharon use the positive "I want to . . ." strategy rather than the negative "I'd hate to . . ." approach which hadn't been working.

The following week Sharon called Mrs. D. again:

"Mrs. D., I can understand the uncomfortable position you're in considering your husband's poor health and difficult behavior. My aim is to make things better for you, not worse. You're absolutely right, you have no legal responsibility to help me locate the truck for repossession. I can help you avoid a potential problem. Because of your husband's canceled auto insurance coverage, medical history, and drinking behavior, it's very likely that you would be sued if he injured or, heaven forbid, killed someone while driving the truck. **I want to** help you keep your home and make sure you receive your insurance proceeds. What I *can* do is ensure that Leon doesn't injure anyone. If you'll tell me where to find the truck, I'll have it quietly removed and will tell nobody about our conversation. I feel sorry about the terrible situation you're in, and I **want to** help make it better."

Mrs. D. hadn't thought of it that way. She quickly agreed to tell Sharon where Leon had the truck hidden and asked that she arrange to have it picked up as soon as possible.

As a precaution, Sharon phoned the local police department and explained that Ford was about to repossess the vehicle. The cops knew Leon well, and considered him extremely dangerous. The Chief of Police insisted on helping out by sending three of his patrol cars to rendezvous with Sharon and the repo agent. Ford avoided a "write-off" on the vehicle, and they may well have saved a good deal of grief for Mrs. D. and for potential innocent victims, too. The "I want to . . ." approach helped Sharon make the best of a bad situation.

Whenever you're motivating someone to do what you'd like them to do, focus on the desirable positive end result, not the negative potential. Tell people what you **want to** do for them, not what you'd **hate to** do to them.

You face many opportunities to make this simple substitution throughout your daily life. If you and your spouse are planning to attend the school play, and you're concerned about tight timing, you generate more positive attention by saying:

> "Let's both leave work a little early today. I **want to** be sure we're both there on time to **enjoy** Emily's performance in the school play,"

rather than,

> "You'd better leave work a little early today. I'd **hate to** have you get caught in traffic and **miss** Emily's performance in the school play."

If you're talking with a sales prospect about a special offer that expires at the end of the month, consider the more positive impact you will have by saying:

"**I want to** be sure we get your order processed before Friday so you can **take advantage of** the special bonus program running this month,"

instead of using the negative "hate to" approach:

"I'd **hate to** see you **miss** the special bonus program we're running this month, so you'd better be sure your order isn't late."

Whenever you use a phrase like "I'd hate to," you focus attention on the looming potential negative outcome you want to avoid. The image you project will be a positive one when you focus on the good results you are moving toward, rather than the bad ones you seek to avoid.

QUICK REFERENCE

What you can do right now:

Use "I want to" and describe the positive outcomes you envision, rather than saying what you'd "hate to" have happen.
Instead of saying,

"We'd better go to the airport a little early. I'd hate to miss the flight because we got caught in traffic."

Say,

"**Let's go to the airport a little early. I want to be sure we make the flight in plenty of time.**"

Instead of saying,

"I'd hate to see your credit ruined by having your car repossessed and your account shown as a default."

Say,

"**I want to help you keep your credit record strong and ensure that your account shows a positive rating.**"

Instead of saying,

"I'd hate to give you the wrong information."

Say,

"I want to give you the right information."

4. I Haven't Yet and I CAN

YOUR boss asks you to prepare a Lotus spreadsheet analysis and determine the company's present break-even production level. You're not proficient with Lotus 1-2-3 or any similar spreadsheet software.

Say out loud to yourself:

"I can't do a spreadsheet analysis and I can't even figure out Lotus 1-2-3."

Now, say:

"I haven't done a spreadsheet analysis before. I can start by learning to use Lotus 1-2-3."

Which sounds like the employee who's going to move ahead, learn new skills, and become an increasingly valuable asset to her company? Which lacks confidence, sounds stagnant, and probably faces a limited future in this position?

As Beth, my new hairstylist, began lathering up the peppermint shampoo, she started in with the usual get-friendly-with-your-new-client opening question:

"So, George, what business are you in?"

Most people don't know any professional speakers, so I wasn't surprised at her reaction when I told her about my work:

"What do you mean? You give speeches for a living? Oh gawd, I can't speak. Oh, I'm OK just one-on-one, but it would be impossible for me to give a speech. In fact, one of my teachers had me do all my oral book reports in writing because I just couldn't talk in front of the class. I even took a speech course once, but I got an F. I get all sweaty and my mind goes completely blank. No, I can't give speeches."

Each time the subject of speaking has come up since her first oral book report, Beth has repeated to herself and anyone listening: "I can't give a speech." Her mind has heard her own proclamation over and over again, and she's absolutely convinced it's true.

Beth talked (nonstop) through my shampoo, cut, and style, so I know she **can** speak. If there had been fifty other clients waiting for their haircuts, all within earshot but out of sight, Beth would have been giving a speech without even knowing it.

To be accurate, she should have said,

"I haven't ever liked giving speeches."

Or, even,

"I don't like giving speeches, have always done poorly in the past, and don't want to ever do it again. In fact, I feel scared stiff at the prospect of facing a group of people and giving a speech."

That might all be true, but for Beth to say she **can't** speak in front of a group is inaccurate and self-limiting.

There's very little that you or I absolutely can't do. I've never competed in Alaska's annual Iditarod dogsled race, don't like prolonged exposure to subzero temperatures, and do my best to avoid pain and suffering. I **can**, though, compete in a dogsled race across Alaska. Of course I'd need years of training, an extensive and demanding physical conditioning program, substantial financial backing, and lots of other preparation; and I **can** compete in the Iditarod race. I don't want to and guarantee that I won't. But I **can.**

Whenever people tell you—or themselves—what they **can't** do, they're slamming shut the door that leads to their untapped potential. As I wrote this book, I often caught myself saying what it seemed like I **couldn't** do. On many mornings I looked over my daily journal of writing progress and thought to myself,

"I can't squeeze out more than two and a half or three hours of solid writing each day. At this rate I can't possibly finish the manuscript before my publisher's deadline."

Well, you're reading the book and I did complete it on time. The correct statement would have been:

"I haven't yet exceeded three uninterrupted hours in my daily writing schedule. I am going to finish the manuscript on time, so that means I'll need to write for about six hours each day. Starting today, I can begin adjusting my personal schedule and free up more time for concentrated writing."

When someone says, "I can't do that," it's probable that he's placing an inaccurate and counterproductive limitation on what he can accomplish. The word "can't" acts as a self-fulfilling future predictor. If you say you can't accomplish something, that's like saying you never will. Since your mind likes you to be right, it works hard to ensure that you're correct when you say you "can't." It functions as a powerful saboteur, undermining your effectiveness so you do not reach your goals, even if you attempt to do so.

QUICK REFERENCE

What you can do right now:

When describing your capabilities to yourself or to someone else, eliminate "I can't" from your vocabulary.

Instead of saying,

"I can't even break par on that golf course!"

Say,

"I haven't yet broken par, and I'm working on it."

Instead of saying,

"There's no point looking at new homes. We can't even afford a condo! We'll be renting some lousy apartment for the rest of our lives."

Say,

"**Considering our present financial situation, we can afford a home in two to three years. As the market adjusts, we'll be saving toward our down payment. Meanwhile, we can fine-tune our budget.**"

Instead of saying,

"I can't do that."

Say,

"**I haven't yet done it and I can.**"

5. *Refuse to Be Helpless*

AFTER you've been feeling tired for months, your doctor discovers that you have a rare bone-marrow disease. Following an extensive course of treatment that includes hundreds of transfusions, the doctor tells you that there is nothing further medical science can do to prolong your life.

Say out loud to yourself:

"I guess that's it. If the doctors hold out no hope for me, I may as well quit. What's the point? I'm in pain and I'm going to die anyway. I give up."

Now, say:

"I don't accept that. My condition is not hopeless. I can and I will improve the quality, if not the quantity, of my life."

Which sounds like the patient who will see little improvement in his condition? Who has a fighting chance?

Michael Ballard's "new life" began when his doctor, George P. Konok, M.D., said,

"I'm going to start your treatment from the neck down. You're going to finish it from the neck up."

Michael was a successful account executive in Ontario, Canada, selling packaged goods through the network of Hallmark stores in his territory. He became ill and was diagnosed as having inflammatory bowel disease, commonly known as colitis. Some of the unpleasant effects are emotional: worry, panic, and embarrassment. It doesn't do much for your self-confidence to know that you could "have an accident" at any time. The worst part was hearing a well-intentioned medical professional tell him, "There is nothing that can be done for your condition."

Colitis can have a particularly sinister consequence: It is often a precursor to cancer. Soon, Michael was diagnosed with cancer of the bowel near his liver. The doctors warned that his lymph glands could be next, and for cancer patients, that's usually the beginning of the end.

Along with this new diagnosis came a blessing in the form of his new physician, Dr. Konok. He pulled a blackboard up to Michael's bedside and gave him a serious "chalk talk," diagramming the various organs that were affected, showing Michael what the surgeons would do and explaining how the chemotherapy was supposed to work. After a careful, factual explanation of Michael's current condition, he got around to the prognosis. He flipped the chalk up in the air and said,

"I can tell you the odds that are in the medical textbooks, but I want you to know that you make your own odds. I cannot guarantee that you can make yourself live any longer. I can absolutely guarantee that you can live a fuller life if you decide to. When you begin your chemotherapy, you will experience side effects. If you view this as a healing process, you will have a much better experience than if you view it as a sickening one. I will treat you from the neck down. Your job is to treat yourself from the neck up."

Michael's treatment proceeded, with three operations. After the third, supposedly final step in his course of treatment, he was informed that the operation had failed; the cancer was still proliferating.

Michael had always used positive language in his professional life. Now, though, facing the biggest "contest" of his life, he was using negative language, accepting the doctors' assessments that his situation was "hopeless." When they said, "You can't change things," he believed them.

At this point, Michael Ballard decided that the same techniques which had brought him success in his sales contests were his best hope for success in his life.

Home from the hospital between treatments, he bought a new pair of running shoes to use as he became well again. He played positive music including "The Rainbow Connection" and the theme from "Rocky." He paced around the house in his new running shoes, reading favorite quotations from *The Best of Success*. Michael's breakthrough came when he transferred the skills he had learned, mastered, and benefited from in business to his personal health.

Today his doctor describes Michael Ballard as "Dangerously fit. Able to leap tall buildings with a single bound, and very tall ones with a running start."

He has had no sign of cancer for eight years, and has chosen not to have any for the balance of his life.

Michael Ballard now has a new profession. He teaches seminars about using the power of language to help patients recover from their illnesses. He's intent on making doctors and nurses acutely aware of how damaging their language can be for worried patients—and how powerfully helpful it can be when used positively.

He explains that the techniques and specific words he used won't work for everyone. In his volunteer work, patients often comment,

"Michael, I can't say what you said. It doesn't feel right for me."

He answers,

"Fine, put it in your own words, but keep the spirit. Repeat the positive affirmations that feel right for you. If you say nothing else, say 'Oh, yes I can.' Don't let anyone, medical professional or not, tell you that your situation is hopeless. You can always improve the quality of your life, even if you don't change the quantity of it."

If you are already threatened by a serious illness, please do not give up. You can fight. Your positive expectations will improve the quality of your life.

QUICK REFERENCE

What you can do right now:

If you feel sick, supplement prudent medical attention with personal action. Use your language to promote a positive attitude and strengthen your body's natural disease-fighting powers.

Instead of saying,

"I can't fight this. My condition is hopeless. The doctor said so."

Say,

"I can improve the quality of my life, and I will. The doctor doesn't realize how strong I am."

Instead of saying,

"My condition is hopeless; I can't change it."

Say,

"I can improve the quality of my life."

6. *Better When Than If*

YOUR child is unenthusiastic about his French classes and has a hard time completing his homework assignment each night. Tonight you use a reward to encourage him to finish.

Say out loud to yourself:

"If you finish your French assignment tonight, you may have a big helping of that new French Vanilla ice cream I bought today."

Now, say:

"When you finish your French assignment tonight, we'll all have a big helping of that new French Vanilla ice cream I bought today."

Which sounds like you really expect him to finish his homework? Which shows that you aren't at all sure he's going to?

You've probably noticed merchants in your neighborhood becoming more environmentally conscious lately. Some of the supermarkets in our community post special tags indicating products that use recycled packaging, those that are biodegradable, and so on. Some of the stores offer a few cents off your total bill when you bring in your own shopping bag. Some have a small bin for depositing shopping bags to be recycled. All those shopping bags are menacing to our environment because they can last for centuries. Recycling also saves trees and oil.

As I began writing this book, our local Safeway store made no provision for recycling shoppers' bags. My wife decided to change that. She said to the checkout clerk, "I really appreciate the efforts you've made to be environmentally conscious. When will you begin a shopping-bag recycling program?"

Not, "do you think you could," not "would you consider," not "it might be a nice idea if you would." "WHEN WILL YOU?"

The clerk responded:

> "Good question. I'm going to talk to the manager myself before the end of my shift. We should have a bag recycling program. It won't take long to set it up."

The Coal Creek Village Safeway store now has a shopping bag recycling bin. If your supermarket doesn't yet, ask a "When Question," not an "If Question" next time you're shopping.

When Citibank, US West, Bank of America, and AT&T want to improve their bill collectors' effectiveness, they call in Bill Arnold, principal of the International Collection Training Institute. His job is to show people how they can project positive expectations onto others. Consider the difference between saying,

> "I'll tell you what: If you can pay this balance off by the end of the week, I'll waive the late charges."

and

> "Bring in your check for $67.50 before the end of the week, and I will waive your late charges. When before Friday will you come in so I can credit your account?"

Bill steps right beyond the typical question, "Do you think you could possibly pay this off by the end of the week?" He projects the positive expectation that the debtor will pay. His goal is to finalize the schedule for doing so, not to find out **if** it's going to happen.

If the debtor says, "Wait a minute, here. I didn't say I was going to pay by the end of the week," Bill backtracks to establish the basis for his positive expectation:

> "Richard, I'm sure you are an honest and responsible person, aren't you?"
> "Of course I am."
> "And you do want to honor your obligations, don't you?"

"Well, I do want to."
"So you'd like to settle this by the end of the week, wouldn't you?"
"Yes, but I don't have enough money right now."

Once again Bill steps past the "iffy" questions and projects a positive expectation. Rather than saying,

"Well, when do you think you might have enough to pay it off?"

he presumes that the debtor wants to make headway as quickly as possible. He asks,

"How much are you going to be short of the $_____ that's due on this week's payment?"

In other words, Bill doesn't take the approach of asking **if** the debtor will pay, he moves ahead to the next question, **when** will he pay? And if the debtor says he doesn't have enough to pay it all now, Bill doesn't ask when he will, he asks **how much** he **will** pay right now.

When you want someone to take a reasonable action, ask a logistical question. Not "if," but "when and how much?"

QUICK REFERENCE

What you can do right now:

When you hear yourself starting to ask a conditional "If . . ." question, rephrase it to incorporate your positive expectation.
   Instead of saying,

"We like the new park area you've provided for the homeowners in our development, but it's awfully rocky. We're wondering if it would be possible to have the rocks removed and the surface smoothed?"

Say,

"We like the new park area you've provided for the homeowners in our development. When will you have the rocks removed and the surface smoothed?"

Instead of saying,

"I know your repair people are probably really busy, but we need our phones fixed quickly. Do you think you could send someone over sometime today?"

Say,

"I know your repair people are really busy and I appreciate your help. Since these phones are our crucial link to customers, we need them repaired fast. What time this afternoon can you have someone here?"

Instead of saying,

"I was wondering if you can . . . ?"

Say,

"When will you . . . ?"

7. *It's No Problem!*

YOU'VE just been informed that you were "volunteered" to act as a chaperone for the Youth Activity Program offered in conjunction with your spouse's professional association convention next month.

Say out loud to yourself:

"Sixty teenagers in one room, and I'm going to be responsible for maintaining order? That's going to be a terrible problem!"

Now, say:

"Sixty teenagers in one room, and I'm going to be responsible for maintaining order? That's going to be an interesting challenge!"

Which version presupposes that things will go poorly? Which suggests that you'll work out a creative way to handle the situation?

The Master of Ceremonies introduced Sonny Hendrix as he wheeled himself to center stage to deliver his commencement address. Everyone in the audience could see that Sonny's body was somewhat asymmetrical, his arms and legs positioned oddly as he sat in his wheelchair. He didn't hold his head up quite straight, and there was something unusual about the way he spoke. Many in the audience must have been thinking, "And I thought I had problems. Sonny's entire existence in that wheelchair must be one big problem."

Sonny doesn't see it that way.

I met him at the most inspiring graduation ceremony I've ever attended. It took place at the Resource Center for the Handicapped, or R.C.H., near my home in Seattle. A former elementary school facility, deemed unnecessary several years ago, has been converted to a learning center dedicated solely to the needs of people with special physical challenges.

R.C.H. students are not content to receive public assistance and idly waste their lives. They decide to be active, contributing members of the work force and enroll in rigorous business and vocational courses with the aim of securing employment and becoming self-sufficient. The program is supported entirely by corporate sponsors and volunteers.

The Commencement Program began with guest speakers representing a few of the corporations that support the Center: The Boeing Company, John Fluke Manufacturing, GTE, Digital Equipment Corporation, and so on. Not one speaker during the entire evening's program used the word "problem." It would have been so easy to describe these students as people beset with multiple problems: limited mobility, public ignorance, stares and scrutiny, and many forms of prejudice.

Nobody mentioned "problems." They all talked about "challenges." Frank Shrontz, Chairman and CEO of Boeing, noted that his company employs 10,000 people with "medical challenges" rather than "disabilities." Instead of referring to the graduates as people whose "problems" entitle them to pity or special considerations, he pointed out that Boeing's hiring policies have been formulated to address the company's own best interests. "When we find individuals like these people, who have overcome significant challenges, we see people who have courage and perseverance. They make great employees."

Sonny Hendrix was one of the student speakers. He had completed the Center's "TeleProfessionals" curriculum, emphasizing telemarketing and customer-service telephone skills. Addressing his fellow graduates, speaking into the microphone that was being held for him beside his wheelchair, he said:

> "Our disabilities are only equal to the barriers or doors we allow to be placed in front of us. We are responsible for our challenges."

Sonny wasn't willing to accept the notion that a handicapped person faces problems and that most doors are closed to him. After the ceremony I phoned him for an interview and we talked about "problems" and "challenges." He made a very distinct differentiation:

> "A problem is something you hate. A challenge is something you want to overcome."

One of my clients is a midlevel manager at a large telephone company. She noticed that her first-level supervisors brought their "problems" to her, asking for her solutions. This practice wasn't helping to prepare them for career advancement, and left her with little time to handle her other responsibilities. She wanted to maintain her "open door" policy, and she noticed that when she was very accessible, she'd often reach the end of the day feeling that she'd been "dumped on" all day long and had accomplished little except for extinguishing many small fires.

Her solution for this "problem" was to meet with all the supervisors who reported to her and institute a new "solution policy." She reaffirmed her desire to talk with supervisors individually whenever they felt the need. However, she asked that they change their dialogue. Supervisors were forbidden to use the word "problem," and were also prohibited from starting the discussion until they had at least one solution in mind.

The old way:

"Excuse me, Kathryn, I need to talk with you. I have a problem with Dennis Swall. He's been late for three days in a row now, and he's setting a very bad example for others. What should I do about it?"

The new way:

"Excuse me, Kathryn, I'd like to tell you about a situation I'm handling. I've had a challenge improving Dennis Swall's punctuality, and I have an idea for how to handle it. Please tell me if you can suggest an even more effective approach."

The result? Kathryn did her supervisors a great service by encouraging them to be self-reliant. She was still able to ensure that the solutions they wanted to implement were appropriate, and everyone felt less depressed. Rather than being inundated with burdensome "problems," Kathryn and her supervisors used their meetings to discuss the relative merits of various positive solutions.

The same problem/solution substitution will work in your personal life, too. When friends or family members start talking about "problems," help them by shifting the discussion toward solutions. This keeps you focused on challenging opportunities rather than on depressing problems.

QUICK REFERENCE

What you can do right now:

Substitute "challenge" or "opportunity" for "problem" and concentrate on exploring solutions.

Instead of saying,

"Now that Jason is a teenager, we're having all kinds of problems with him."

Say,

"We face some new challenges, now that Jason is a teenager."

Instead of saying,

"The recent international crises have disrupted the currency exchange markets and caused all kinds of problems."

Say,

"These recent currency fluctuations have opened up lots of new opportunities."

Instead of saying,

"I'm afraid that's going to be a problem."

Say,

"That sounds like a challenging opportunity."

8. *Self-Fulfilling Prophecies Come True*

AFTER finally becoming adept with the telephone system used in your division, you're transferred to another building, where a totally different system is used.

Say out loud to yourself:

"Oh no! I'm terrible at learning all these phone features. It'll probably take me months to get up to speed, if I ever do. It was bad enough retrieving voice mail and making transfers from my old phone. I'll never learn a whole new system of commands."

Now, say:

> "I became proficient with the phones we used before, and I know I can do just as well with the new system. I'll get some coaching from my co-workers, and pick up one of those quick-reference cards to keep handy."

Which sounds like someone who is doomed to cutting off callers and bumbling transfers with his new phone? Who's going to apply himself and learn the new system quickly?

Somehow, over the last few years, I have convinced myself that I'm terrible with directions. The curious thing is that I've traveled extensively throughout much of the world without ever getting lost. I've hitchhiked from Nairobi to Cape Town, trekked into the Highlands of New Guinea, and hiked ancient unmarked Inca trails in the Andes. I always reached my intended destination without problems.

Yet I've recently become notorious for getting lost right in my own hometown. Our friends Lou and Vanna Novak recently invited us to dinner at their home, just 25 minutes away from ours. Before leaving the house, I called Vanna and said,

> "I realize we've been to your place twice before, but I think you'd better give me the directions again. You know how I'm always getting lost."

As I went through the motions of writing down her instructions, I didn't take the trouble to verify the details, expecting that I'd get lost anyway. Sure enough, half an hour after we were due for dinner, I called on the car phone.

> "Lou, we're lost. I have no idea what happened. I watched for the Magnolia Street Bridge, just like Vanna said, but somehow we ended up on the Ballard Bridge, and now I'm not even sure which side of the canal we're supposed to be on. I always get lost coming to your house."

I felt so foolish. Our infant daughter was screaming in her car seat, and my wife, Julie, was in the backseat, tending to the baby and chastising me for garbling Vanna's instructions. We finally arrived (45 minutes late) only after Lou "talked me in" on the car phone as I drove. It was like one of those old-fashioned movie scenes where the pilot of a small plane has a heart attack and his passenger guides the plane in for a landing by listening to radioed instructions from the tower.

On the way home, Julie pointed out that, right from the start, I had set myself up for getting lost. There was no way I **wouldn't** get lost. I'd programmed Lou and Vanna **and myself** for the eventual outcome by saying, "I'm always getting lost."

I have a compass in the van, I'm smart, I carry a detailed map, and I'm a skilled communicator. There's no logical reason for me to ever get lost. Why create artificial limitations on my own abilities? As of right now, I've decided to stop saying, "I always get lost." Instead, I'll listen carefully to instructions, make clear notes, and say, "I'll find it easily."

What are your self-imposed limitations? What have you convinced yourself you're not good at? What myths do you perpetuate by telling others you lack certain talents?

"I'm all thumbs when it comes to fixing things."
"I can't cook worth a darn."
"Study French? I can't even pronounce the names of California wines. I'm terrible with languages."

I have decided today, as I write, that I'm unlocking my talent for finding my way anywhere. I invite you to decide, today, as you read this page, to unlock more of your talents, too. Stop telling yourself and others that you're "not good at" something, and find out how good you truly are.

QUICK REFERENCE

What you can do right now:

Replace habitual self-limiting phrases with empowering assertions.

Instead of saying,

"I've always had trouble with math. I'm just not good with numbers. I can never figure out percentages, even with a calculator."

Say,

"I do lots of mathematical things well. I'm going to stop at the library and refresh myself on some basic calculations I've forgotten, like figuring out percentages."

Instead of saying,

"I'm no good at that."

Say,

"I'm getting better at that."

9. *Get a Return on Your Investments*

You sell advertising space for a leading nature magazine, and are meeting with an entrepreneur who has decided to market a special high-tech birdfeeder. Hers is a shoestring operation, and the potential advertiser has just started her business, operating from her kitchen table.

Say out loud to yourself:

"I realize that spending $500 on a magazine ad is a big commitment. It's hard to tell, of course, but you could get hundreds of orders."

Now, say:

"This ad represents a $500 investment. Let's look at the return that will generate even if the response is only one-half of one percent of our readers."

Which approach is most likely to catch the entrepreneur's interest? Which sounds like the wiser allocation of funds?

Since I recently became a father, I've been advised by many other parents to "spend as much time as possible" with my child while she's still very young. Sometimes, major parts of my day pass when I've done nothing except play with, talk to, adore, and love our little baby. My wife does the same. I don't think of it as "spending" time with her. We're "investing" our time. I enjoy a big return: I know I'm a happier, more productive person when I take time out to enjoy Kelcie, and I also believe that for her whole lifetime, she'll benefit from getting a high quantity of high-quality attention from her parents.

There may be times as you read this book when you think I'm making too big of a deal about semantics. This could be one of those times. Consider the important influence your words have on your thinking.

Let's start with *Webster's Ninth New Collegiate Dictionary*:

spend: 1: to use up or pay out : EXPEND 2a: EXHAUST, WEAR OUT 2b: to consume wastefully : SQUANDER 3: to cause or permit to elapse : PASS 4: GIVE UP, SACRIFICE

My goodness, is that what I'm doing when I take a break and play with Kelcie for an hour? Waste, squander, sacrifice? Now, let's flip back to the "I"s.

invest: 1: to commit (money) in order to earn a financial return 2: to make use of for future benefits or advantages

That's more like it. When I use my time to be with my daughter, I'm doing it because I expect benefits and advantages. I get to feel good and so does she.

Are you investing enough time with your family? Would the "payoff" be worth increasing your stake?

In business, when you decide to commit your limited funds to buy computers, hire people, or pay rent, you do it because you expect the company to get a return on its investment. You don't spend on advertising, promotion, health care programs, and company vehicles—you invest.

Consider substituting "invest" for "spend" in your personal life. I've found there are quite a few times when "spending" is appropriate. If I go to the State Fair and purchase some cotton candy, I'm not making an investment. I do buy things just because I like them for the moment. However, when it comes to buying a car, or choosing which washing machine to buy, or adding to my wardrobe, I like to think of my purchases as "investments."

Thinking—and talking—about "investing" creates a consciousness of plenty rather than scarcity. If you're always spending, you're continually depleting limited resources. When you invest, you apply some of your resources with the expectation that you'll create more of them.

When you describe how you'll use your time, money, and energy, talk in terms of investing. Use your resources in a wise way that will generate a payback, whether that means short-term satisfaction, long-term financial rewards, or a deep sense of having done the right thing.

QUICK REFERENCE

What you can do right now:

Substitute "invest" for "spend" when you talk about how you'll use your time, money, and other resources.

Instead of saying,

"We're going to spend more money on our house and add a greenhouse enclosure outside the kitchen windows."

Say,

"We're going to invest in a greenhouse enclosure to make our home more enjoyable. When we move, it'll be an attractive selling feature, too."

Instead of saying,

"We just cannot spend any more money on furniture right now. Your department is going to have to make do with the desks and chairs we already have."

Say,

"We're not going to purchase any new furniture at this time. While investing in more ergonomic chairs and tables could result in higher productivity, some other investments will provide a better return for us right now."

Instead of saying,

"With fall approaching, it's time to spend another bundle on clothes. I need a new coat, new shoes, and while I'm at it, I'll have to buy some new slacks, too."

Say,

"I'm going to invest in a new wardrobe for fall and winter. I'll choose a good coat to keep me warm and comfortable, and some shoes and slacks to help me look my best at work."

Instead of saying,

"I'm going to spend some time and money taking night classes."

Say,

"I'm going to invest some time and money taking night classes so I'm ready to move ahead in my career."

10. *Nothing's Impossible*

You've already had a terrific sales record and your performance is nearly 20% ahead of the same period last year. The Regional Manager compliments you on your performance and informs you that your quota for the next quarter has just been increased by 25%.

Say out loud to yourself:

"That's impossible! I'm cranking at top speed already, and I got lucky on a few big orders in the first quarter. That's why I'm 20% ahead of quota right now. There's no way I can close the year with a 25% increase."

Now, say:

"That's going to be a challenge. A combination of circumstances has helped to make my 20% gain possible so far. You can continue relying on my total commitment for the second half of the year. I'll do my best to meet the new quota, and I don't believe that the 25% increase is realistic."

Which sounds like the person who has a shot at hitting 25%?

You may be familiar with one of Reverend Robert Schuller's many books, or perhaps you watch his television broadcasts from the Crystal Cathedral in California. I was fortunate to be among the architecture buffs who toured the Cathedral when its designer, Philip Johnson, officially unveiled his gem to the architectural community. I later learned the "inside story" behind the construction of this impressive edifice.

When he first called Philip Johnson, Dr. Schuller explained that he wanted to build a dramatic cathedral constructed entirely of glass, with outstanding acoustics and an unobstructed view of the pulpit from every single seat. This kind of building had never been constructed before, and required vast amounts of special glass and innovative construction techniques. On top of that, the Southern California site is located in one of the world's most active earthquake zones. As he explained his vision of the Crystal Cathedral to Mr. Johnson, Dr. Schuller added one special challenge: He had no money.

Mr. Johnson looked at him and said,

"Wait a minute, let me get this straight. You want to erect a huge building the likes of which the world has never seen. You want it to be constructed using materials and techniques never before employed, and you have absolutely no money to work with? That's impossible!"

Smiling, Reverend Schuller asked Philip Johnson to open the large dictionary atop a pedestal in his office and look up the word "impossible." Mr. Johnson walked across the room, began flipping pages, and after a moment of confusion, the famous architect looked up and said, "There's no 'impossible' in this dictionary."

There was Dr. Schuller, standing beside his desk wearing an impish grin and holding an X-Acto knife in his uplifted hand. He explained to the puzzled architect that he uses his blade to remove that negative word from any dictionary that crosses his path.

"Anything is possible," says Dr. Schuller.

There are very few things you may set out to accomplish that are truly "impossible." Difficult, demanding, challenging, never-before-achieved, sure—but not impossible. Why prejudice your own expectations by labeling a lofty pursuit as "impossible"?

Most of the great figures in history have had little use for the word "impossible." Did Columbus say it was impossible to sail to another continent? Did Kennedy say it was impossible to put an American astronaut on the moon? They faced daunting initial challenges and many setbacks along the way. And they decided to not label their goals as "impossible."

The single worst effect of deciding that something is "impossible" is that you don't even give your efforts a chance. The principle of "cognitive dissonance" applies to the use of the word "impossible." Your mind likes to make sure you're right. When you've convinced yourself that a thing is so, you set about to prove it.

If you tell yourself that it's impossible to awaken an hour early and work on setting up a realistic family budget, it is. You sleep a little too long, you feel groggy rather than alert, and you decide to put off working on the budget until some other time. Cognitive dissonance is at work. If you did awaken bright and early, and got right to work producing a realistic budget, you would have proven your earlier self-assessment wrong. Your mind doesn't like you to be wrong, so it goes to work proving you were right all along.

When you tell yourself,

"I will wake up refreshed, an hour ahead of schedule, and use that quiet time to start setting up a realistic family budget," your mind, again, sets out to prove you are right.

When you eliminate "impossibility thinking," you open doors to achieving goals you never thought possible. Let your mind get busy proving you're right about what you decide is possible, instead of setting about to validate your assessment of what you've deemed impossible.

QUICK REFERENCE

What you can do right now:

Banish the word "impossible" from your vocabulary. Substitute a more accurate and positive phrase to describe what appears infeasible.

Instead of saying,

"I realize that you want to earn enough money to buy yourself a car this summer, but it's impossible. Insurance costs for you would be outrageous."

Say,

"I know you'd like to have your own car, and it will take a lot of money to buy one and then make sure you have adequate insurance coverage. Let's work on a realistic plan and discuss

it with your father tonight. If this summer doesn't seem realistic, let's see about aiming for Christmas."

Instead of saying,

"Get promoted to Account Executive before the end of the year?
That's impossible! I'd need at least twelve months of experience
and there are already two other Sales Assistants in line for the
next opening."

Say,

"As far as I know, nobody has yet been promoted to Account
Executive in under a year. I want to be the first. I'm going to
work as hard as I can to build a really outstanding performance record."

Instead of saying,

"This is impossible."

Say,

"This is going to require some special effort, and it can be
done."

11. Kids Are All Ears

YOUR hefty teenager joins in with some younger children down the
street as they play on a slip-'n'-slide toy stretched across their front
lawn. When your large boy runs and slides down the vinyl run-
way, his mass and momentum combine and he shoots past the end
of the strip, wrecking the plastic pool, leveling the neighbor's
gladiolus, and snapping off one of the automatic sprinkler system's
riser pipes.

Say out loud to yourself:

"John! What's the matter with you? Now look what you've done, you stupid kid. You've wrecked the Tates' front yard. You never act your age. You're going to get in trouble all your life, aren't you?"

Now, say:

"John! Looks like you're going to be doing some gardening. I know you mean well, and you're getting too big to play with young children's yard toys."

Which sounds like a parent who'll encourage his child to use good judgment and grow gracefully into young adulthood? Which will steer his child to a future of self-esteem problems?

When little Julie was only six years old, she had a very short attention span. She had little interest in school and failed third grade. By the fourth grade, her performance had improved very little, so her teacher conferred with her understandably concerned parents. She informed them, "You might as well face it, Julie will never be any more than an average student."

It's amazing how perceptive young children are. Although Julie doesn't remember her teacher ever directly telling her of her discouraging assessment, she somehow got the message.

Julie performed at an average level all through elementary and junior high school. Always insecure about her mediocre scholastic performance, she formed most of her friendships with people who didn't excel in much of anything. They expected little of her, and that's what she delivered.

In ninth grade, Julie contracted mononucleosis and stayed home in bed for nine weeks. With few distractions, she threw herself into catching up on the schoolwork that she was missing by being out of class. For the first time she discovered that with some hard work she could be an A student and not an average one.

Twenty years later, a veterinarian noticed how Julie, at age 33, loved caring for horses. He told her she had a gift for diagnosing diseases and encouraged her to go to college, saying she was too smart not to. For some reason she believed him. Enrolled in some of the nearby college classes (and no longer burdened by the belief that she is destined to be "nothing more than average"), she's doing much better. Her G.P.A. is 3.82!

Julie had an unusual last name that you may have heard before: Ziglar. Her father is Zig Ziglar, one of the best-known professional sales trainers and speakers in the world. I first heard Julie Ziglar Norman's story over lunch with Zig and his wife, Jean. My wife and I had our then 3-month-old baby, Kelcie, with us and I asked Zig for some advice about what messages we should be giving our little girl every day during her most formative stage of life. Zig is the author of *Raising Positive Kids in a Negative World*, an outstanding book that every parent should read. In it, Zig cites an anonymous quotation:

Your Home Is Bugged!
In every home there are two microphones per child—one in each ear. These highly sensitive instruments pick up the table prayers, the songs sung, ordinary conversation, and all types of language. These all-hearing microphones transmit all they hear to highly impressionable minds. These sounds then become the vocabulary of the child and the basis for action.

I know from personal experience that children are highly susceptible to negative messages. I was told I had Dumbo ears as a kid, and even though the rest of my body eventually caught up, I saw myself as an ugly person right up until my late 20s. Whenever I looked in a mirror, it was as if the image was peculiarly distorted— like a weird fun-house mirror with two convex bulges—all I could see were those two huge, unbecoming ears.

What you say, and what others say, has a very powerful influence on your child's self-image. A bruised self-image will take years to heal, if it ever does.

Dr. Wayne Dyer, in his wonderful book *What Do You Really Want for Your Children?*, reminds all parents that they may be inadvertently lowering their children's self-confidence and self-worth. One common mistake is to tell kids that they are bad children, when the truth is that they are good children behaving badly. It may sound like there's not much difference between:

"You bad girl! You ruined the wallpaper when you drew on it with those crayons. Why are you so destructive?"

and,

> "Drawing on the walls is bad. Now you've ruined our wall-paper. That was very destructive."

While there is a huge difference in the psychological effects those two admonitions create, children are not yet able to grasp such subtle distinctions. We adults must take responsibility for making our approval of the child, and disapproval of the action, ultraclear.

Kids also shape their futures with their own language. When you hear your child say,

> "I always goof up my arithmetic. I'm dumb with numbers. I don't want to take the test. I have a tummyache,"

nip that powerless language in the bud:

> **"Jenny, you're very good with numbers. You're quite smart at figuring out how much change you should get when I give you a dollar to buy some fruit. You can do super well on the arithmetic quiz. Let's practice together right now."**

I take Zig Ziglar's and Wayne Dyer's advice seriously. Though my little Kelcie doesn't talk yet, I'm sure she understands my feelings, if not my words. I will never let a half a day pass without reminding her that she is a good, smart, beautiful person with a wonderful and rewarding life ahead of her.

Teaching your children to be Power Talkers is one of the most wonderful gifts you can give. Show them by your own example that you project positive expectations, for them and for yourself. And keep in mind that any children you interact with, whether they're relatives, neighbors, or kids you talk with for a few minutes while standing in line at the supermarket or sitting on an airplane, are weighing every word you say. We reap what we sow.

QUICK REFERENCE

What you can do right now:

Be especially conscious of Power Talking whenever you are around youngsters. Set an example and help shape kids' futures by speaking positively to and about them.

Instead of saying,

"You bad boy! You knocked over Mommy's vase and broke it."

Say,

"When you run in the house, it's easy to accidentally break things. Please don't. Keep on being such a good runner, and always run outside."

Instead of saying,

"Oh, kids, I'm sorry we can't go to Disneyland, but we can't afford it. Daddy's not very good at keeping jobs, so he got fired again."

Say,

"Kids, we're going to shift our plans and go to Disneyland next year, when you're a little bigger and you can go on more of the rides. Daddy's going to make an exciting change and get a new job he'll like better than his old one. We're going to save up the money and really look forward to an even better vacation."

Instead of saying,

"You're a bad child and you're always getting into trouble."

Say,

"You're a good child, and that behavior is not acceptable."

POWER TALKERS . . .

II. Give Credit Where Due

POWER Talkers give credit wherever credit is due. They don't hesitate to applaud others when they succeed, and they also give themselves credit whenever they create positive events in their own lives.

The effect your manner of speaking can have on your life has been carefully researched, and the results are dramatic. Dr. Martin Seligman, a psychologist at the University of Pennsylvania, has done outstanding work on the subject. The results of his research are reported in his book, *Learned Optimism*.

Dr. Seligman identified three main scales of optimism and pessimism in a person's common daily language, or "explanatory style." When faced with positive events, optimistic Power Talkers describe them using "universal," "internal," and "permanent" terms. Powerless pessimists tend to attribute positive events to "specific," "external," and "temporary" factors.

"Universal" means that you notice your success not just in one particular instance, but in all aspects of your life. "Specific" explanations mean that you see positive situations as isolated events.

"Internal" terms connote that you take personal responsibility, that you recognize your own role in bringing about positive outcomes, and give yourself credit for it. An "external" explanatory style means that you attribute the success to something beyond your control—to "a lucky break."

"Permanent" descriptions identify positive events as continuing evidence of your regular pattern of success. A "temporary" description says it's a fluke, a once-in-a-while happening.

When a Power Talking mother sees her son hit a home run that helps his Little League team win their game, she later tells him,

> **"I'm so proud of you, son. You really did a great job, and all that batting practice is really paying off. You hit well in the last game, too, and I'll bet you'll do even better during the playoffs. Your schoolwork is improving, you've been getting your chores done on time, and you've cut way down on junk food. I'd say you're hitting all kinds of home runs."**

You can easily detect her universal, internal, permanent explanation.

A mom who's not tuned in to the importance of what she says to her children might say:

> "You sure got lucky that time. That pitcher gave you a ball that only a farm leaguer could miss. And it's a good thing the wind was blowing out toward left field. Too bad you don't hit like that more often. You'd better enjoy the glory while you can. You've got that science test tomorrow, and you know it's your worst subject."

The powerless parent uses a specific, external, temporary description for the same event. The home run is an isolated event, due to external factors, and certainly not something that will continue. Which parent do you suppose has the more successful, happy child?

In business, the most effective leaders are those who publicly credit members of their teams when they succeed. If you want to develop loyal workers who keep on getting better and better, make sure you give them credit for their accomplishments. The same is true in personal relationships—great friendships are built on mutual admiration. Think about how much it means to you when someone you respect, trust, and perhaps love gives you heartfelt recognition for your personal accomplishments.

In the chapters ahead, you'll meet people who benefit from taking credit for their own accomplishments. You'll also see the beneficial results of acknowledging the credit others deserve for their achievements. Be a Power Talker; give credit wherever it's due.

12. *What's Your Excuse?*

You offer your colleague a ride home and when you arrive, she invites you in for a cup of coffee.

Say out loud to yourself:

"Oh, you'll have to excuse the mess. I left in a hurry this morning and the place looks terrible."

Now, say:

"Welcome to my home."

Whose home will appear neater to you? Where will you feel more comfortable? Who sounds like the more confident, secure person?

What a good hypnotist can do with a group of otherwise serious, reserved business executives attending their company's annual banquet is utterly amazing—and hilarious. Gil Eagles is one of the world's finest. He's hired by IBM, AT&T, and other top corporations when they want a world-class performance for their most important events. He can bring a group of corporate leaders up onstage, and within a few minutes, have them impersonating Elvis, reeling in fighting marlins, or behaving like demanding drill sergeants. Sitting in the audience, you just can't believe it when you see good old Joe, the mild-mannered, rather shy Senior Accountant you've known for years, up there wildly clicking imaginary castanets and performing a spirited flamenco dance in front of a thousand employees who've hardly ever heard him make a peep.

Gil is quick to debunk the misconceptions popularized by old-school hypnotists: He does not put his subjects into a trance or

59

induce a state of suspended consciousness. What any hypnotist really does is help his subjects create and live out a mental image.

If he suggests that they'll be embarrassed and look like fools, they won't cooperate. Instead, Gil brings his group of volunteers up onstage and paints an elaborate and reassuring mental picture so they can see themselves succeeding. As they sit—eyes closed—in a row of chairs facing the audience, he tells them that they'll feel **relaxed** and emphasizes that the whole purpose is **entertainment.** He says, "*You* will be the **stars**, and I will get to share in the credit." He asks the watching audience to "Give these **brave** people a round of applause."

With these statements, Gil creates a mental picture in his subjects' minds: They will be relaxed, brave, and entertaining star performers. Then he helps them act out those images.

Gil's success as a hypnotist is founded on one basic premise: People act out the pictures in their head. After more than 4000 masterful performances, he's very conscious of the images he creates onstage. Offstage, we all unconsciously project images we really don't intend. Gil and I both learned something about creating unintended pictures when I visited with him and his family.

After giving a speech in New York City, I called Gil and he offered to pick me up in Manhattan and drive me out to his home in New Jersey. From there, we'd head north to relax with his family at their weekend home in the Poconos. "All right, I'll pick you up at 1:00 in front of the hotel. You'll have to excuse my car, it's an old battered-up Cadillac."

Sure enough, he pulled up at the hotel in a marvelous classic Caddy and we drove to his home in Short Hills, N.J. His is a very exclusive, affluent community of corporate executives, doctors, and lawyers. Many of the residences are million-dollar mansions. As we walked into Gil's large, beautiful, antique-filled home, he said, "You'll have to excuse the mess; the dog has absolutely devastated the whole downstairs."

Soon we were all seated in the roomy Cadillac, cruising north through Pennsylvania to enjoy a weekend at the Eagles' lakefront cottage. As we pulled into the driveway, dozens of deer grazed along the roadside, the view over the small lake was serene, and their lovely house on the shore looked very inviting. Gil's welcoming comment was, "You'll have to excuse our little shack."

I've never enjoyed a more relaxing, comfortable weekend, or appreciated better friendships. There was absolutely no need for Gil to offer any excuses for anything. His home, car, and cottage were all delightful.

Unintentionally, though, Gil had "programmed" me to notice the slightly worn leather upholstery in his car and the teethmarks his magnificent Husky had left on the sofa's legs.

When I called it to his attention later, Gil couldn't believe he'd created those images. He's tremendously successful and is anything but insecure, yet he had unconsciously painted mental pictures that could make him appear ashamed of his home and car and cottage.

The whole point of Power Talking is this: The first step in using more powerful language is to become conscious of your negative habits so that you catch yourself right after using a powerless phrase. Then, you learn to catch yourself just *before* using the powerless version, and make the Power Talking substitution. And finally, you develop the unconscious habit of speaking powerfully all the time.

If you're ever fortunate enough to visit Gil, I expect you'll now hear him saying, "You can't miss me, I'll be driving a classic white Cadillac. You'll feel completely at home with my family. We're not stuffy or pretentious, as you'll see when you notice how comfortable our dog feels gnawing on the furniture. And you'll love our cozy cottage in the Poconos."

When I'm onstage delivering a Power Talking seminar, I often catch myself letting a powerless phrase slip out. I may say "but" rather than "and," or "I'll have to check on that," rather than "I'll be glad to check on that." To my live audience, and to you, my reader, I emphasize the critical point: Power Talking isn't a destination, it's a journey. Every day, I'm aware of my language and working to improve it. You can do the same.

When you say, "You'll have to excuse my . . . house/car/cooking/performance," your apology has two effects: First, you call attention to a condition **you're** uncomfortable about—and the other person may not otherwise have noticed. Second, you make yourself appear insecure.

Have you noticed that people who offer excuses rarely need to? As soon as they say, "You'll have to excuse my messy house," you're probably thinking, "What's she apologizing for? It's a lot neater than mine." Or, "She's right. Now that I'm scrutinizing, I can see that those knickknacks need a good dusting."

If people are going to be offended by the appearance of your home, or messy office, or dirty car, let them. It's their loss. In reality, most won't notice what you're uncomfortable about—if you don't call attention to it. And those who do shouldn't concern you. Now, if you've invited your boss to dinner and are genuinely concerned that your tiny apartment or orange-crate furnishings will make a negative impression, meet at an appropriate restaurant instead.

In short, don't apologize for something you feel insecure about. Fix it or forget it. Given the choice of meeting someone who's insecure and uncomfortable—with good reason or not—and someone who seems content and happy, I'd much rather be around the relaxed person.

QUICK REFERENCE

What you can do right now:

Stop making excuses and apologizing for some imagined short-coming. Either change it or forget it.

Instead of saying,

"You'll have to excuse my messy apartment. I just haven't had time to clean it up this week."

Say,

"Welcome. I'm glad to see you."

Instead of saying,

"Please pardon the piles of junk in my office. I've been so busy lately, I'm afraid it looks like a shambles!"

Say,

"Come into my office, I'll move some of these things out of your way."

Instead of saying,

"We could take my car if you can put up with the old clunker. I'm planning to get a new one, and meanwhile this one's going downhill fast."

Say,

"Let's take my car."

Instead of saying,

"You'll have to excuse my car/mess/hair/house."

Say,

Nothing!

13. It's Just My Opinion

THE executive whose phone you're answering is unavailable, and the caller asks when he should call back.
Say out loud to yourself:

"I'm afraid I wouldn't know that, I'm just a receptionist. I could be wrong, but maybe in the morning. That's only my guess, I really can't say for sure."

Now, say:

"My name's Bob Wilkins, and I'm the receptionist. Please tell me a little about your call, and I'll confirm when she'll be available to talk with you."

Which sounds like someone who's proud of his work? Who has low self-esteem, represents his boss poorly, and is unlikely to go very far in his career?

One of my clients asked me to participate in panel interviews of two finalist candidates being considered for a senior management position. Both possessed superb technical skills for the job; each had demonstrated an excellent ability to lead a department similar to that he or she would manage if chosen to fill this position.

While other interview panelists asked specific questions about the candidates' experiences and career accomplishments, I concentrated my attention on how each one spoke.

The first candidate began by saying:

"I'm Gwen Moss, and I'm here to present myself to you as a candidate to manage your Call Center. Two days ago, I received my packet of background materials and the set of six formal questions you're asking each candidate. I'll begin this morning by answering each of them for you."

The second began by saying:

"I'm Brian Bayer. Unfortunately, I only got your information and questions a couple of days ago, so I must confess that I haven't really had much of a chance to go through them in detail. I've taken a guess at some of the numbers and what I think you want to know. I could be way off, but after all, it's just my opinion."

One of the formal questions asked the candidates to "Please describe your philosophy regarding Customer Service processes from each of several perspectives." This question was broken down into important areas including hiring staff, training them, measuring quality vs. productivity, and so on.

The first candidate said,

"I firmly believe that . . ."

and she went on to explain some of her beliefs about Customer Service, including:

"Front-line employees must be empowered to solve, not pass the buck."
"If you're in doubt—DON'T HIRE!"
"If you're not moving ahead, you're falling behind."

The second said,

"I made up a little handout for you on my home computer. You'll have to excuse me, but I couldn't do it on a more powerful machine with a laser printer, so it doesn't look too good. Unfortunately, I only have access to an old dot matrix printer. As you'll see, I included some of the things I like to say about Customer Service. They're just some of my little slogans."

And they were listed in his handout:

"Service should be worth waiting for."
"Motivate employees to welcome difficult callers."
"Marketing is a philosophy, not a department."

As the hour-long panel discussion concluded, each candidate was given a few minutes to summarize.
Gwen said:

"I feel ideally suited to manage this department, and I want to work with you. In the words of your CEO, which I read in your most recent annual report, 'I can't think of a more exciting place to work.' I can see why he said that. This is where I want to be. Thank you for your consideration."

Brian said:

"Well, I don't really have much to add at this point. It's pretty much up to you, now. I'm sure I'm just one of the people you're considering. I saw where your CEO said, 'I can't think of a more exciting place to work.' I thought that was kinda neat, and I'm only hoping I'll get the opportunity to work here."

Aside from the candidates' phrasing, they were a toss-up. Both had very strong skills, backgrounds, and technical competence.
The dramatic differences in their levels of self-esteem were evident in their speaking styles. The first candidate confidently presented her answers to each question. The second (who'd had the

same amount of preparation time) apologized for not having had enough time to prepare more thoroughly. The first stated her analyses with conviction; the second excused his by characterizing them as "only my opinion."

When it was time to summarize, the first postured herself as the ideal choice, though she did not arrogantly proclaim herself a shoo-in. The second lowered himself to "just one of the people you're considering" when in fact he was one of the two finalists.

The substance of what each said carried equal value. Their styles of saying it were polar opposites. Consider their two lists of Customer Service philosophies, for example. They could easily have been swapped; both made sense and summarized important principles. Prefacing Gwen's list with an "I firmly believe" statement added importance to them. Prefacing Brian's with the denigrating phrase, "They're just some of my little slogans," devalued them.

My recommendation was to hire the first qualified candidate. What's yours?

Kay White is responsible for Pacific Bell's telemarketing training throughout California. She believes that our words reveal how we really feel about ourselves. They serve as a barometer that indicates our self-esteem levels. A poor self-image becomes a self-fulfilling prophecy. She says, "How you're treated depends on the way you behave. If you say you're 'only' a Customer Associate, you're saying you don't think much of your position, and customers treat you as someone with little authority."

Kay teaches her trainees to avoid belittling language. The Customer Associates listen to each others' self-descriptive language and tell each other if they hear diminishing terms. Her "nickel-in-the-jar" technique is particularly effective. Rather than just keeping a stroke tally of their verbal slips, trainees actually deposit five cents in the kitty each time they put themselves down. Each "plink" reminds them to think about the value of self-supporting language.

Kay also recognizes that her middle managers play an important role. They help shape an employee's self-image with every comment they make. She seeks to rid managers of such comments as,

"Considering your performance last month, I'm not at all surprised that you failed to reach quota this month. I just never can
count on you, can I?"

You may react to those phrases by saying, "But what manager
would ever be so stupid (and cruel) as to say things like that?"
Well, plenty do. Maybe you've worked for one.

One of Kay White's important goals is to show her managers
how to commend and reprimand employees. When someone performs well, she reminds managers to avoid personality-oriented
praise, and instead offer specific behavior-oriented compliments.

Rather than saying:

"You're really an asset to my department. You're delightful and
I'm pleased to have you here,"

say specifically what you notice:

**"Jolene, you did an excellent job of handling that customer's
question. Your answer was perfectly accurate, and you also
provided it in a friendly, caring way. Your word choice and
tone of voice were both very supportive. I really appreciate
your good work."**

Kay reminds her managers that such praise must always be
sincere and honest. If it's not, the listener's red flag raises and he
discounts what he hears, thinking to himself:

"I can tell when someone's trying to manipulate me. I can figure
out what you **really** think of me."

Of course, the result of insincere praise would be a counterproductive undermining of the employee's self-image. This low
self-esteem then leaks out whenever the employee talks with customers.

When it's necessary to reprimand an employee, a manager's
goal should be to change an unacceptable behavior, not diminish
the person's self-image. Kay recommends using the "Criticism
Sandwich" technique. Sandwich the negative information between two positive messages:

"Terry, you've really been improving with your customer contacts. For example, your answer to that last caller's question was completely accurate. Your tone of voice could have been friendlier, and I'd like you to work on that in the next call. Keep up the good work with your accuracy. I can see that you've really mastered the technical material from your training course."

Whether talking to yourself, describing your accomplishments, or commenting on another person's performance, avoid diminishing language.

QUICK REFERENCE

What you can do right now:

You're not "just" or "only" anything. Describe yourself, your beliefs, and your accomplishments positively and proudly.
Instead of saying,

"I've just been here for a few months, but the way I see things . . ."

Say,

"I've been carefully observing for the last few months, and the way I see things . . ."

Instead of saying,

"Well, it's only my opinion, of course, and I could be wrong about this, but I would say . . ."

Say,

"I believe . . ."

Instead of saying,

"I'm just the receptionist, so I probably wouldn't be able to help you very much."

Say,

"I'm the receptionist and I'll be happy to help you."

Instead of saying,

"I'm only just the . . ."

Say,

"I am the . . ."

14. Is "Luck" Getting the Credit for Your Hard Work?

A project you spearheaded has just received significant recognition at your firm's parent company. Your boss tells you that you're being talked about at headquarters as an up-and-comer. He asks, "How did you do it?"

Say out loud to yourself:

"Well, I'm not really sure. I guess I just got lucky. I've handled dozens of projects like that one and I guess someone just happened to notice this one."

Now, say:

"I worked hard! On that particular project, I incorporated the feedback I've received from the last several reports, and I'm pleased to see it really hit the target. I have an excellent support staff and they contributed a great deal, too."

Which sounds like the employee with the brighter future? Whose good work is likely to be repeated on the next big project?

*   *   *

If you don't have a strong relationship with a personal physician, and you suddenly need a doctor, where do you turn? You can contact a referral service such as the successful Ask-A-Nurse program, available to nearly half of the U.S. population. You can phone Ask-A-Nurse 24 hours a day, free of charge.

You wake up at 3:00 one morning with a throbbing left foot. Nothing shows—there are no cuts or bruises—but it hurts so much you can hardly get out of bed. Should you try to sleep and then limp in to work and see if it feels better later? Soak it in warm water? Should you see a doctor? What could it be?

A call to Ask-A-Nurse puts you in touch with a friendly, professional Registered Nurse who asks you about your symptoms. She uses a computer program that prompts her to ask the appropriate questions, and follows strict medical protocol. As you answer, it becomes clear to her that you should have the condition investigated further, right away.

The nurse directs you to a nearby hospital's emergency room, provides driving directions, and alerts them to expect you. After the visit she calls you back to check up and ensure that you were well cared for at the hospital. If you need to see an orthopedic physician, or another specialist, she'll recommend one that's convenient and meets your criteria. Of course, if all you need is an aspirin and an Ace bandage until you can contact your own physician, she'll say so during your initial call.

The Ask-A-Nurse program is a terrific hospital marketing and public relations tool. Not only does it bring in new patients, it also forms the basis for a long-term relationship between the hospital and the patient. The program is also a tremendous benefit to the community. Without charge, anyone can receive a Registered Nurse's confidential, professional assessment. (Only physicians provide diagnoses.)

As you can imagine, the success of this program rests squarely on the shoulders—or voice, actually—of the nurse who answers your call. Is she technically competent? Does she ask the right questions? Is she pleasant and understanding? Does she give the right answers? If she sounds vague or wishy-washy, or seems unsure of her assessment, you're not likely to trust or follow her advice.

Hospitals that offer the Ask-A-Nurse program in their communities are very particular about whom they hire. Interviews are extensive, and begin with a telephone screening. After all, if the nurse can't handle a pressured situation like a job interview over the phone, how will she do when a frantic mother calls to explain that her child faces a serious medical emergency?

When the program manager asks an applicant about her strengths and weaknesses, she'd better not hem and haw. Wrong answer:

"Oh well, I'm not really sure what I'd say my strongest points are. I guess, uh, well, it's hard to say. I was pretty lucky when I got a job at Bellevue in New York City. You get everything thrown at you there, you know. So I guess you could say I've been involved in a pretty wide range of situations."

Right answer:

"My two greatest strengths are what make me feel confident about pursuing this opportunity with you. First, I really enjoy relating to people in need. That's why I entered nursing in the first place. Being able to talk with and help 30 to 50 patients on the phone each day, compared with 15 or 25 on the floor, is appealing. Second, I have experience in a wide range of medical situations. Early in my career I set my sights on the most diversified institution I could find, and that was Bellevue Hospital in Manhattan. We built an outstanding nursing program there, and I'm pleased to have played a major role in reorganizing the department."

In the words of Pat Stricker, Ask-A-Nurse Program Manager at The Toledo Hospital in Ohio,

"I like it when people aren't afraid to tell me what they're good at. If they say, 'Well, gee, I don't know,' they probably lack the self-confidence we're looking for. On the other hand, if they're egotistical or boastful, I know they won't fit in well with the team."

Life is like one long series of interviews. People are sizing you up constantly—before you're hired, when you're considered for promotions, at significant milestones, and during normal daily conversations. When you deserve credit, give it to yourself. People whose opinions can help you succeed want to believe in people who already believe in themselves.

There are two big reasons for giving yourself credit whenever you're proud of your own accomplishments: (1) Others respect you for it, and (2) You deserve and benefit from it.

Don't write off your accomplishments as "lucky." People don't respect that kind of response. What you really should say is,

"Thank you. I worked hard and I'm very grateful for this recognition. My support team helped a great deal, too."

The way you react to praise helps others size you up as one who is either boastful, falsely modest, or appropriately appreciative.

The second reason for accepting credit when you deserve it is even more important. We all respond to rewards, and those that carry the most weight may be the rewards we give ourselves. When you say to yourself,

"I feel so good about winning this award. I worked hard and this makes it worthwhile,"

you've reinforced your own successful behavior.

In other words, giving yourself credit results in immediate and satisfying ego gratification, and it also promotes repeat performances.

When screening candidates during job interviews, I've noticed that their overuse of "I" phrases is a real turnoff. When a candidate says,

"I accomplished this and that, I won such-and-such an award, I turned our department around, I brought about a 22% revenue increase . . ."

the interviewer may feel cautious about this person's ability to work well with a team, and may also question the individual's professed 100% responsibility for departmental achievements. It's much more effective to share in the credit without hogging it all for yourself:

"Our department made some very significant improvements during my leadership. Together we generated a 22% revenue

increase, and as a result I was awarded the **Manager of the Year plaque. It feels great!"**

Take credit for your accomplishments. When others ask, let them know—modestly—that your success is a direct result of your diligent work plus the support of the others who helped. And when you talk to yourself, be sure that you reward and reinforce your own role in creating your successes.

QUICK REFERENCE

What you can do right now:

When you succeed, modestly acknowledge your own role in attaining your accomplishments, both to yourself and to others. Instead of saying to yourself,

"Gee, I can't understand why they picked me for this award. I haven't really done anything special to deserve it. I just got lucky."

Say,

"I don't always give myself enough credit. This award is proof that my talents and hard work are appreciated by others. It's time I recognized more of my own accomplishments."

Instead of saying,

"A lot of things just kind of went my way. I was lucky enough to guess right on the forecast for next year, and, what do you know, it just all came out pretty much like management was hoping it would."

Say,

"I drew on my past experience to forecast for next year, and incorporating management's views, the results were very accurate."

Instead of saying,

"I got lucky."

Say,

"I planned well and worked hard."

15. *What They Don't Know Won't Hurt Them*

WHILE visiting friends, someone suggests that you play bridge. Mary asks if you'll be her partner.

Say out loud to yourself:

"Well, I'll be your partner, all right, but I'm really not too good at cards. You'll have to forgive me if I make some stupid mistakes. I hope I don't make us lose."

Now, say:

"Great, let's play."

Which sounds like Mary will regret having asked you to play with her? Which leaves the door open for a fun, challenging game?

There are so many instances where people "cover themselves" by building a safety net of excuses, anticipating that they'll fail. Chances are if you say nothing people won't realize you're insecure about your abilities. The only person being supercritical of your performance is . . . you.

Last summer I set a personal goal of joining in on three open beach volleyball games. That may not seem like much of a goal to you, but for me it was an important accomplishment. I wasn't very athletic as a boy. I didn't voluntarily join in any athletic events, and in high school was able to secure my letter in sports only by serving as manager of the gymnastics team. As a result, I've felt insecure about participating in sports.

Still, there's no good reason why I couldn't be a fine athlete. I'm tall, well-proportioned, and have good coordination. My only shortcoming has been my attitude of athletic insecurity.

Sure enough, I did achieve my modest goal and joined in those three volleyball games. I enjoyed them thoroughly and played creditably. During the third game a brother and sister approached and asked if they could play. The sister, Stacy, a young woman about 25 years old, joined our team. She walked onto the court and said, "Gee, are you sure you guys want to have me on your team?" Sure enough, she did miss most balls coming toward her, but her lack of skill was exceeded by her lack of self-esteem. Every time she missed the ball, she'd say, "Oh, I'm sorry, I'm so bad at this. If you want me off the team just say so." It became embarrassing to play with her because all of us could just imagine what torment she was feeling, knowing that she'd probably flub the next volley.

Soon it was her turn to serve. She immediately prepared us all by saying, "This is going to be terrible. I can never even get the ball over the net." And of course she didn't. It was obvious that no one had ever shown Stacy how to serve, so I called for a time-out and gave her a quick lesson. The other team, being good sports, gave her another chance. On her next try, Stacy made an excellent serve which the opposing team did not return. Twice more she served very well, gaining points each time.

I could identify with Stacy because I know that of all the few times I've been coerced into some kind of athletic encounter, I've begun by apologizing for my expected poor performance and repeatedly beaten myself up for playing without skill. Stacy would have been much better off—as would I—had we simply played our best. Nobody in our volleyball game was an expert player, and her lack of skill would have been hardly noticed had she not called attention to her own ineptitude. Her performance would have been much better if instead of deriding her own serving ability she had simply said, "Would one of you show me how to hold the ball when I serve? It's been awhile."

Do your best without telling people that you think your best isn't very good.

QUICK REFERENCE

What you can do right now:

You're probably far more critical of yourself than anybody else will be. Go ahead and enjoy doing as well as you can.

Instead of saying,

"Well, I'm certainly no artist, but I'll try to sketch out a drawing of how this new process would work. I hope you'll be able to figure out what I mean despite all this horrible scribbling."

Say,

"I'll diagram this new process to make it clearer."

Instead of saying,

"I'm just terrible in the kitchen, but, well, I gave it a shot. I tried to make Fettucine Alfredo. I hope you can gag it down without getting too sick."

Say,

"I hope you'll enjoy eating my Fettucine Alfredo as much as I enjoyed preparing it for you."

Instead of saying,

"I'm really not too good at this."

Proceed to do your best without excuses.

16. *Ken and Spencer Were Right!*

You're talking with a peer about your department's tidy appearance. He comments that your area always appears well looked after—much neater than his own.

Say out loud to yourself:

"Well, that's the way I like it. I'm always telling the admin people around here that I expect this place to look shipshape. They do pretty well. They'd better."

Now, say:

"You know, you're right. My people really are good about keeping this area looking sharp. Mind if I tell them you said so? I'd like to let 'em know that I'm not the only one who notices and appreciates their good work."

Which sounds like the manager whose people will continue keeping the area neat and putting in a little extra effort? Which one probably has a morale problem, high turnover, and people who don't really enjoy working with him?

While vacationing with my family, I had my only firsthand encounter with a professional wrestler. Hawk, a member of the Road Warriors professional wrestling team, stayed in the condo development we were visiting. Within hours of his arrival at the resort, every kid and most of the adults staying in the complex knew he was there. He was immense and muscular and certainly caught everyone's attention the first time he stretched out to lounge beside the pool in his leopard-patterned swim shorts.

After observing a steady stream of autograph seekers and picture takers approach him by the pool, I settled into a lounge chair beside Hawk's and began to read. I probably wouldn't have chosen to stake my claim so close to him, but it was one of the few vacant chairs available. There was a kind of "clear zone" around Hawk. I guess most people felt as self-conscious as I did about sitting there and attempting not to stare.

It was impossible to ignore his conversations, considering his very loud, gravelly voice. It was understandable that very few adults approached Hawk to talk, because he certainly had an imposing physical appearance. Many children, however, walked right up to him and conversed quite comfortably. Most were young boys, and I imagined that many had probably said to their parents, "Someday I want to be a big, strong muscleman like him."

I was surprised to hear how Hawk talked with these children. He spoke in entirely positive terms. He didn't tell the boys, "You're a little pipsqueak, but if you work really hard, maybe someday you can be big and strong like me." Instead he told them that they were already growing strong. Even when skinny, underdeveloped kids came up to ask for his autograph, he'd find something positive and complimentary to say. "Your arms are really long. I'll bet you're a terrific basketball player."

After overhearing many such conversations, I got up the nerve to start talking with him myself. I told Hawk how impressed I had been with the way he handled kids, and it was then that I realized he was doing so totally by design. He said, "It's such an easy thing to do, and it can make such a big difference to these little guys." Not only was there a heck of a nice person underneath all the flesh and muscle, he was consciously guiding those kids to think highly of themselves.

Hawk was genuinely moved when I complimented him on his positive behavior with the kids. I'm sure that he hears no end of praise and admiration for his physique, but I suspect that very few people stop to tell Hawk they admire anything deeper than his physical appearance.

That conversation with Hawk completely changed my uneducated view of professional wrestlers. I've never before intentionally watched a professional wrestling match on television. If all those other big lugs are as sensitive, caring, and positive as Hawk, I may become a fan.

Ken Blanchard and Spencer Johnson were right! When they took the business book market by storm with *One Minute Manager* and its many spin-off books, they advocated "Catching People Doing Things Right." They correctly asserted that this was one of the most underused and most effective management tools around.

Power Talkers give credit wherever it's due, especially when it's unexpected. This whole book emphasizes two major audiences for your language: you, and the other people who hear you. Everyone benefits when you give credit to others for their accomplishments, even when it's just something little.

I live in a lovely wooded neighborhood near Seattle. The approach to my street is a long, steep hill with a center planting strip that extends for nearly a quarter of a mile. Throughout the year, the plants are trimmed, pruned, and rotated. After the azaleas' brief glory of intense, fiery red blossoms, somebody plants pansies in great numbers. When they wither, marigolds and lobelia appear. Somebody goes to a lot of trouble keeping that planting strip looking good. It's not automatic. The "somebody" is Susan. Every now and then I've noticed this woman digging and clipping and pruning and planting.

I'm sure most of my neighbors have commented to themselves about how beautiful and well-tended that strip is. One day I thought it was about time Susan found out how much her work is appreciated. I pulled over to the curb as I drove down the hill, lowered my window, and said,

"You do very nice work. I see you out here often, making sure the plants look good. Your efforts really pay off; they always look great. Thank you for being so conscientious about your work. I enjoy seeing it every time I drive up or down the hill."

Her face blossomed as beautifully as any of the annuals she had been planting. With a big smile, she said,

"I'm really glad you enjoy my work. I like doing it, too. Thank you for stopping. It makes me feel really good to know that you notice."

She's not the only one who felt good. Offering someone a compliment can make the complimenter feel just about as good as the one who's complimented. With Susan the gardener, that moment of seeing her smile and feel appreciated was well worth pulling over for. And, what's more, I feel extra good every time I drive by her handiwork, knowing that she probably thinks about my comment from time to time. When I see another round of fresh flowers coming into bloom, I know I haven't taken them or her for granted.

Since much of my speaking and consulting work is dedicated to fostering professionalism on the telephone, I'm especially attentive to people who do a great job handling my phone calls. When a secretary answers the phone in a clear, friendly manner, I take a moment to comment. When a Customer Service representative deals with my question professionally, I let that person know he

did a good job. I especially enjoy complimenting telephone operators who handle my calls well. Hotel operators, in particular, seem
shocked that a guest would take an extra moment to offer a com-
mendation. I end up feeling just as good as they do.

Invest a moment, every day, to "catch people doing things
right," as Ken and Spencer suggested. Tell them what you notice
and why you appreciate it. You'll both feel great about it.

QUICK REFERENCE

What you can do right now:

Go out of your way to compliment people and give them credit for
doing things right, especially when they don't expect it.
Instead of saying to yourself,

"Someone sure does a nice job with the lettering on those signs
at the drugstore. It must be someone who studied calligraphy."

Say to the store manager,

**"Who makes those signs I see all over your store? They do a
darn good job, and I'd like to tell 'em so, myself."**

Instead of saying,

"Her kids sure are quiet and well-behaved."

Say,

**"You've obviously given your children a lot of positive atten-
tion. They interact with everyone so politely and intelligently."**

Instead of saying,

"That daughter of mine is a big help around the house."

Say,

**"Darling, you are a big help around the house, and I appreci-
ate it."**

17. *You're About as Old as You Say You Are*

YOUR grown children invite you to join them for their annual trip to the family's country cabin.

Say out loud to yourself:

"I'm not a kid anymore, you know. I'm too old to enjoy that kind of thing."

Now, say:

"That'll be fun. I'd enjoy a change of scene, and of course, I like to be with you."

Which sounds like someone who'll live out his years in happiness, surrounded by people who enjoy his company? Which is likely to become a bitter, depressed, lonely old man his children won't really want to visit?

An audience member asked Dr. Norman Vincent Peale, author of *The Power of Positive Thinking*, why, at age 92, he continued to give speeches rather than quietly retiring to enjoy the life he'd made for himself.

"Why? . . . I'll . . . tell you . . . why. Because, . . . despite all the speeches . . . I've given . . . over the years, . . . and despite . . . the many books, . . . there are still a few negative thinkers out there!"

The audience rose in unison and roared with approving applause.

As a member of the National Speakers Association, I've had the opportunity to meet, hear, and work with many of the world's most celebrated speakers. At the Association's 1990 Awards Banquet in the Atlanta Marriott's Marquis Ballroom, my wife and I sat with Dr. and Mrs. Peale at dinner. This isn't normally a celebrity-hungry group, but the members sure went crazy over Dr. Peale.

After dinner Dr. Peale was called to the stage so he could announce that his friend and one of our colleagues, Michael Frank, had been selected to receive the Council of Peers Award of Excellence, the highest award accorded for speaking skills and professionalism. As Dr. Peale's name was announced, all 1500 tuxedoed and bejeweled professional speakers present for the banquet rose and applauded.

After his presentation, another speaker and I carefully helped the venerable gentleman down off the platform. As the audience prolonged its applause, the nonagenarian turned to me and my partner and quietly said with a chuckle, "You look like you're practicing to be pallbearers!" It was the only reference I heard him make to his age that whole evening, and he certainly meant it jokingly.

Later, I asked Dr. Peale for his prescription for enjoying life at such an advanced age. He said, simply, "Live your life and forget your age."

Many people hex their happiness by talking about how old they are. It seems that hitting their 40th birthday triggers a stream of "I'm getting old" exclamations that continues for the next 40 or so years. Why do many celebrities conceal or falsify their ages, as if acknowledgment of their years would lower their esteem in their fans' eyes? It's not a person's chronological age that matters, it's his attitude toward aging that makes all the difference.

Webster's Ninth New Collegiate Dictionary defines "youthful" as: "Having accomplished or undergone little erosion." Losing youthfulness is a process of erosion, and we do much of it to ourselves. We wear away our own self-images by commenting disparagingly about our advancing age. We send supposedly funny birthday cards that deride our friends as they mark the anniversaries of their birth. The collective effect of all these comments is to erode our feelings of youthfulness.

Just as there's no point in hastening your own erosion, why contribute to anyone else's feeling of "getting too old"? I recommend boycotting the greeting cards that make disparaging jokes about aging. Although meant in jest, they merely contribute to a collective consciousness that sees aging as a negative condition. Even if they're hard to find, scan your greeting card shelves and look for those cards that help buoy your friends and relatives as they get on in years.

QUICK REFERENCE

What you can do right now:

Use neutral or positive phrases in reference to advancing age. Don't erode vitality by speaking negatively about aging.

Instead of saying,

"I'm going downhill, my hair is graying, wrinkles are showing, and I look like an old bag."

Say,

"I keep myself in shape and I look good."

Instead of saying,

"At my age, you know, it's just too hard to have any fun anymore. My old body is giving out on me."

Say,

"At my age, I enjoy different kinds of fun. What did you have in mind?"

Instead of saying,

"I feel worse and worse. I'm getting too old."

Say,

"I feel good."

POWER TALKERS . . .

III. Rebound Resiliently

POWER Talkers rebound resiliently. Sure, they experience setbacks, and they bounce right back from them. They learn from their experiences and emerge stronger than they were going in. Ever notice how many truly wealthy people have been flat broke or even bankrupt at one or more times as they accumulated their wealth? They didn't give up. They learned, and rebounded resiliently.

In Section II, I discussed Dr. Martin Seligman's research dealing with the "explanatory styles" and language characteristics of optimists and pessimists. There, we examined how Power Talkers describe *positive* events. When things go *badly*, the Power Talker uses the opposite explanatory style. He concentrates on specific, external, and temporary explanations. The power*less* talker sees problems as being universal ("Not only is this situation not working out, but everything in my life is awful"), internal ("It's all my fault, I'm a loser"), and permanent ("Things never go my way, and this is just another example that proves it").

As a Power Talker, when you experience negative situations in life—when you lose a job, or your promotion doesn't come through, or your child has a difficult time in school—you consciously replace universal, internal, and permanent explanations with those that are specific, external, and temporary. When a Power Talker doesn't get that big promotion, he says,

"I missed out on that promotion, and I understand why. I haven't yet mastered the new inventory forecasting software, and it's really vital that I learn to use it well. I know I can, once I go through the training tutorial. I've had plenty of career successes in the past, and more great things are right around the corner for me. I'm certainly glad that I'm doing so well in the other areas of my life. My health is superb, my family relationships are great, and I have excellent job skills. I know that I'm ripe for career advancement, and will begin now working toward that next big jump."

It's entirely natural to respond negatively when things go wrong; I often do it myself. Don't expect the Power Talking principles to come naturally. Work at them.

In the chapters ahead, you're going to meet people who have rebounded from disastrous situations. They've changed bankruptcies, personal failures, alcoholism, depression, and smaller setbacks into positive experiences. You may be confronted with a variety of setbacks today, yourself. When they happen, use the Power Talking phrases in the following chapters and you'll come out ahead.

18. *Does Your History Repeat Itself?*

You get fired from your job. You're two payments behind on your mortgage. Your spouse walks out.

Say out loud to yourself:

"I know why this is happening to me: I'm a failure."

Now, say:

"I know there's an important lesson in all of this. What can I learn?"

Which sounds like the person who will go down for the count? Which is the winner who will learn valuable lessons from these circumstances and emerge wiser and stronger?

How would you feel if, at age 40, after 20 years of abundant business success, you had to call your father and ask him to loan you $400 . . . so you could afford to file for personal bankruptcy?

In the mid 1970s, Michael McCafferty left his position as a successful salesman at IBM in order to start his own business. He did very well with the Philadelphia-based computer service bureau he founded, and operated it profitably for seven years. It was acquired by a larger firm, and the President of the new parent company reached a handshake agreement with Michael that would make him a very rich man.

But first, the President died. It was then that Michael realized his agreement had never been put in writing. The new corporate officers decided not to honor it, and Michael was cheated out of his promised stock.

Humiliated, he packed up and left for Chicago, where he successfully ran another service bureau three times larger and "cashed out" after two years. Chicago's winters were just too much for him, so Michael, in his mid-30s, headed for San Diego, got a place at the beach, bought a vintage Ferrari, and lived a wonderful, carefree life. It got boring. That's when an old business associate approached him about starting a new venture.

Michael was intrigued. He coupled his mastery of computers with a recognition that people will always want convenient access to more information. He created the first Electronic Yellow Pages system and perfected the technology that is today still the basis for a growing industry.

Then his partner got cold feet and pulled out. Michael had no doubt that the business would be a big success and decided to invest further, on his own. He sold the Ferrari and bought a battered 1972 Vega. Then he gave up his place at the beach. And before long, every dime he had was invested in the failing business.

While Michael was reeking of desperation, a shark caught his scent. A fast-talking moneyman offered to rescue the company and get Michael back on his feet . . . for a 51% share of the company. Other partners were brought in and Michael's business crumbled.

Michael McCafferty quit working and sank into a deep depression. He had no income and lived off his credit cards. Bankruptcy was his only way out, but he couldn't afford the court filing charge! So his dad bailed him out one last time.

For a full year Michael repeatedly said to himself,

"Why me? What happened to my money, my Ferrari, my carefree early retirement? How come that fast-talking moneyman wound up with everything?"

His all-consuming thought was, "Why did this happen to me?" After a year of destitution, desperation, and depression, the answer dawned on him: "Because I let it." It was that simple. The world hadn't victimized him, he had invited his misfortune. He had trusted the wrong people, he'd behaved naively, he didn't get important agreements in writing, and he gave up authority.

He had conceded control. Not just financial ownership of the company, but control of his fate, too. He gave up control of everything by thinking that things were "happening to him."

Once he realized what the lesson was, he got to work. He read Og Mandino's classic, *The Greatest Salesman in the World*, and wrote out its affirmations on a 3 x 5 card:

> "Today I begin a new life.
> I will persist until I succeed.
> I will live this day as if it is my last.
> I will act now."

He read them aloud first thing in the morning, last thing before bed, and several times during the day.

Michael looked back on his "failures" and drew lessons from them. He distilled them into "The Ten Commandments for Managing a Young Growing Business," and he made a commitment to obey them. On St. Patrick's Day, 1983, he founded a new company and named it Remote Control (of course). As I write this book, Michael's company has grown at an average annual rate of 133% over the last seven years. Based on the lessons he learned from his multiple "failures," he created the top-selling software package in its category, "TeleMagic." It helps hundreds of thousands of sales professionals around the world become more organized, more profitable, and maintain control. Finally, Michael McCafferty is the multimillionaire he deserves to be. From his perch at the edge of the ocean in Del Mar, California, he watches the dolphins and pelicans and is grateful that he learned his lessons.

Power Talkers consciously recognize that failing is a vital part of succeeding. When they say "I failed!" it has an exclamation mark after it, and is closely followed by, "And here's what I learned." Losers just say, "I failed." It's followed by a period. As Vince Lombardi said,

> **"It's not whether you get knocked down. It's whether you get up again."**

Michael McCafferty got up again and drew invaluable lessons from his mistakes.

Don't fear failures, welcome them. May you have many, and learn important lessons from them all.

QUICK REFERENCE

What you can do right now:

When you're confronted with a "failure," look for the lessons you can learn and grow from the experience.

Instead of saying,

"What a stupid move. How could I have scraped together my entire life savings and spent it to build a spec house, only to discover that the market was already turning sour? I'm a complete failure."

Say,

"Putting all my eggs in one basket didn't pay off, and this investment has not produced an acceptable profit. I've learned some valuable lessons, though, and I'm not going to take an uninformed risk like that again."

Instead of saying,

"That's the fourth job interview I've had and again they didn't even call me back or send a letter. I must be a failure."

Say,

"My approach to these job interviews hasn't been working. One thing I've learned is that the interviewers don't call me back. Maybe that means I should take the initiative and follow up with them. After the next one, I'm going to immediately send a thank you note."

Instead of saying,

"I failed."

Say,

"Here's what I learned . . ."

19. *Half Empty, or Half Full?*

You've been working closely with an influential Director in your organization for the last five years. Your current major project is critically important to your future, and the Director has been your "coach" and prime backer. She calls you into her office and announces that she's accepted another position with a leading organization in your field.

Say out loud to yourself:

"Now what'll I do? She believes in me and fully supports me on this project, but she's leaving. Now I'm high and dry. I'll have to start over with someone new. This is a major setback for me."

Now, say:

"Now that she's leaving, I'll continue our association and keep her as a good contact outside our company. And I'll be able to develop a strong new relationship with her replacement. This is an interesting change."

Which sounds like the person who's going to feel depressed and go into a career "holding pattern"? Who's going to eagerly dive in and capitalize on a new set of circumstances?

In the publishing world, an author's most important contact is the editor. This is the person who believes in the writer and supports the book project right from the start. The editor negotiates the author's book advance and many other critical elements of the contract. Once the publisher has committed to producing the book, the author relies on the editor as the internal spokesperson; the editor orchestrates publicity, promotion, and sales support.

The editor who championed my first book, *Phone Power*, also initiated this one. With the *Power Talking* manuscript half finished, she called to tell me she had accepted a position with another publisher.

My immediate reaction was:

"That may be a great career move for her, but what a setback for me! Now I'll have to start all over at the bottom and work with an editor I've never even met. Maybe that person won't even like my book. What if she abandons it and lets the sales force ignore it?"

You know the old saying about the glass: It's either half-empty or half-full, depending entirely on how you look at it. I was looking at my glass and seeing risks, downside potential, and nothing but problems.

I hope you don't think that Power Talking comes easily or automatically for me or for anyone else. It requires concerted, constant attention and effort. Five minutes after hearing this "bad news," I got up from my computer keyboard, walked to the window of my writing office and, looking out at the stream and woods, forced myself to say,

"What great news! Now I'll have a strong advocate at another publishing house. When I meet my new editor, I'll get to 'sell' her on *Power Talking* so she's full of enthusiasm right from the start. Instead of presenting a half-formed idea, I can show her exactly what the book's about. And, with her fresh perspective, she'll probably offer plenty of new promotional ideas."

As I look back now, I can see that my editor's departure opened many new opportunities for me. The glass was half-full—and filling.

When confronted with any situation that represents a change in what we're accustomed to and planning on, most of us naturally see the negative side first. I do it often myself. The trick is to recognize that seeing the negative "half-empty" aspect first doesn't mean that's the only way you can, or will, look at it.

Seeing that the glass is half-full is a learned skill. Don't feel discouraged if it doesn't come immediately or naturally. Do use the power of your language to turn things around.

Be on the lookout. Whenever "this is bad news because..." crops up in your comments to yourself or others, stop and replace that line of thinking with, "This is good news because..." You can't exploit opportunities if you don't see them. Train yourself to see the good side by using a fill-in-the-blanks technique. Force yourself to complete the sentence: "There's a good side to this situation, and it's what I choose to focus on. This is great news because..."

QUICK REFERENCE

What you can do right now:

Rephrase negative reactions to unexpected changes and say, "This is great news. It means that...," and then start looking for the positive result that can follow.

Instead of saying,

"I didn't get the promotion; that's terrible news."

Say,

"I didn't get the promotion, and that's good news because it means I can expand my horizons. I'm going to make a few calls and see what my talents are worth to some other companies. Then I'll have a better idea of how well off I am right here."

Instead of saying,

"Darn, our house sale fell through. Now we have to start all over again."

Say,

"OK, that buyer backed out. I'm glad it happened now instead of at the last minute. This means we can reappraise the market conditions and be sure our pricing strategy makes the most of this present situation."

Instead of saying,

"The car repairs won't be completed by noon, as the dealer promised. That screws up my whole schedule."

Say,

"Since the car won't be ready by noon, I'm going to take this opportunity to walk over to the branch library down the street from the dealership. I haven't been there for ages. It's a good thing that my plans have changed."

Instead of saying,

"I see some very negative consequences resulting from this turn of events."

Say,

"I see some very positive consequences resulting from this turn of events."

20. *If Only I Had . . .*

You attend your trade association's annual convention and, upon reading the program carefully, realize that tomorrow night's Awards Banquet is a black-tie event. Your tux is hanging in the closet at home.

Say out loud to yourself:

"If only I had read the program more carefully before I packed. Why don't I ever plan ahead for these things? I'm going to look completely out of place."

Now, say:

"I'll check with the concierge and see about a last-minute tuxedo rental. Next time I'll be sure to carefully read the

**program materials several days before attending my conven-
tion."**

Which sounds like the person who's bound to have a miserable
time at the Awards Banquet and may well repeat the experience
next year?

A coronary bypass operation can really make you stop and think.
For a friend of mine, it also prompted a host of "If only I had . . ."
regrets. In his early 40s, this young man had concentrated on his
career, dedicated far too little attention to his family, and ignored
common nutritional guidelines.

From his hospital bed, Jerry kept talking about his regrets: "If
only I had spent more time with my kids." "If only I had avoided
all those high-cholesterol foods." "If only I had led a more balanced life."

To hear him talk, you'd have thought he was writing his own
epitaph. Despite the successful surgery, Jerry was still heading
down the wrong path. He was dwelling on his regrets and wishing
for what might have been, rather than concentrating on mending
his ways and aiming for an improved quality of life.

Jerry's turnaround began when his "If only I had . . ." statements ended. He agreed to delete the powerless phrase from his
vocabulary, and his family and friends helped reinforce the point
by interrupting whenever he started to say, "If only I had . . ."
Soon Jerry was saying, "I haven't enjoyed my family as much as I
deserve, and I'm changing that, starting now." "I haven't been
sensible about my eating habits, and I'm now beginning a healthy,
nutritious diet." "I've been out of balance, and now I'm consciously working toward a balanced life."

Today Jerry is like a new man. It wasn't just the arterial operation that did it. His verbal surgery played an important role, too.
You don't need a doctor's help to begin surgically removing your
own "If only I had . . ." regrets.

When you hear someone using the phrase "If only I had . . . ," you
can usually be sure that his gaze is fixed on the past. He's flounder-

ing in regrets, preoccupied with what can't be changed. The appropriate time to talk about a regrettable past is when you're conducting a retrospective analysis of what went wrong so you can fix it.

In my travels I've occasionally had my checked luggage lost or delayed and once even went onstage wearing tennis shoes and jeans. When that happened, I wished I had taken my luggage on board with me. I've also hand-carried my bulging garment bag, lugged it from gate B-1 to gate E-32 while running for a close connection, and wished that I had carried on nothing but my briefcase. In each case it would have been easy to get bogged down in "If only I had . . ." thinking.

Rather than dwelling on the past and regretting my actions, I've used these experiences to focus on the future: "When I pack and check all of my business clothing, I risk losing it; when I carry it on, I'm bogged down. So starting now I will find a better answer." My solution has been to check all of my luggage, including the fresh suit I plan to wear onstage. I fly wearing another suit that I could use for my presentation if my bags are lost. For footwear I choose comfortable black Reebok sneakers and carry a black marking pen. In a pinch I can ink over the white logo and my shoes will "pass."

If a salesperson just barely misses winning the regional sales contest, you can easily assess her likelihood of triumphing in the future based on how she describes her loss. If she says, "If only I had sold 5% more, I could be in Acapulco next January. What a bad break," her prospects are poor. If she says, "I was just 5% short of winning, and I'm sure I can be 5% more effective by qualifying my sales prospects more carefully. Next time I'll be more productive," you're hearing a winner.

The same "If only I had . . ." phrasing is common to managers, negotiators, and other professionals who consistently fall short of their potential. In fact, most anyone who says "If only I had . . ." is probably holding himself back from more fully succeeding in any endeavor from selling to parenting.

Help yourself eliminate negative, regret-filled retrospecting by doing away with the phrase "If only I had . . ." Replace it with a positive, forward-looking statement like "Starting now, I will . . ."

QUICK REFERENCE

What you can do right now:

Focus your attention—and your language—on what you will do to positively shape your future. Don't dwell on the unalterable past by talking about what might have been.

Instead of saying,

"If only I had held on to my Mustang for a few more years, I could have sold it for a lot of money as a classic."

Say,

"Next time I buy a car with appreciation potential I'll check the outlook before I sell it."

Instead of saying,

"Maybe we could have had a family if only I had been more family-oriented before my wife's hysterectomy. Now it's too late."

Say,

"I'd still like to have a family. We can look into adoption agencies or find out about becoming foster parents."

Instead of saying,

"If only I had."

Say,

"Starting now, I will."

21. Bottoming Out

Your life has slipped downhill. First you were demoted, then you started drinking, then your marriage crumbled.

Say out loud to yourself:

"I shouldn't have to go through this mess. I know things should be better for me, I just don't know where or how to start."

Now, say:

"I will change my life. I will start making things better today, right now. Nobody else will do it. I will take action."

Which sounds like the person who will wait and wait for something to happen, and later wonder why it never did? Who will start taking action and begin moving in the right direction?

For "Tom," it all boils down to a single truth:

"You can act yourself into right thinking, but you can't think yourself into right action."

When you hit bottom, you can't think your way out of it. You must **do something.** And for Tom, the most effective action was to change his language.

I met Tom while I lived at Venice Beach, California. Most who've heard of it think of Venice as an artsy, chic community. Movie producers, famous artists, and Beverly Hills rebels move there to be offbeat.

There's another side to Venice. Hippies who never quite moved out of the 60s live in ramshackle bungalows and drive psychedelically painted Beetles. They coexist with a violent community of hard drug users. It was there that Tom hit bottom. He was unemployed, broke, living in a slum neighborhood, stumbling along to the next bottle of wine, the next pill. He didn't realize he was an alcoholic until he totally burned out physically and emotionally.

Tom's life began to turn around when he met an Alcoholics Anonymous member who dragged him to his first meeting. By all outward appearances, Tom was indisputably a loser when he began the 12 steps of recovery procedure that's common to AA programs around the world.

His new sober friends helped him with support and faith. They encouraged him to adopt an attitude of Positive Expectancy. They told him to visualize what he wanted his life to be like, and he did. He concentrated on seeing himself as a successful, sober person. He wasn't sure *how* he would become successful; he just had faith that the way would become clear if he concentrated on the end rather than the means.

Then Tom's liver failed. Admitted to St. John's Hospital in Santa Monica, he lay in bed and reflected. He knew he wanted to be successful, he held an attitude of Positive Expectancy, he was thinking himself toward his goal, but he wasn't seeing any action. Looking back now, Tom views his hospital stay as a blessing. He had the time—sober—to really figure out his feelings. He concluded that there was a saboteur at work inside him. He'd visualize a goal, and then his lifetime of angry feelings took over and prevented him from reaching it.

It hit Tom with a flash: "Affirmations are worthless without action."

So, he began to **do**, not just think. He began writing out his affirmations:

"I, Tom, dare to be prosperous."
"I, Tom, relentlessly visualize success in every endeavor—and I act to make it so."
"I, Tom, reject, nullify, void, and veto all thoughts of failure."
"Failure will never overtake me if my desire to succeed is strong enough, and I act on that desire."

Then, there in the hospital, he began repeating them to himself, over and over again. Soon after his release, Tom landed a new job. A new friend who was a great salesman encouraged him to pursue a career in the sales profession, so Tom went to work for a small company that sold computer printer ribbons by phone. He applied himself, took action, and—one day at a time—became the top salesman.

Tom eventually left to start his own company.

Still repeating his affirmations, he lay on Venice Beach and visualized a room with 40 people, all producing profitable sales, all working for him. He started small, rolling out of bed, eating a bowl of cereal, and making the sales calls himself from his small apartment.

Today Tom is president of a company that sells computer ribbons to half of the Fortune 500 companies, manufactures a line of top-quality computer products in its 30,000-square-foot production facility, and employs 130 people. Annual sales exceed $15 million. Tom has a talented, loving, supportive wife (whom he met through the AA program), a young son, and a balanced life. When work pressures mount, he rewards himself by taking his family to a remote area of Idaho, where they own a rustic log cabin originally hand-built by a famous movie star. As Tom says, "It's not where you start, it's where you finish."

Tom's story isn't unique. Tens of thousands live lives as rich as his, and have rebounded from circumstances as dismal as his, too. They all have one thing in common: They didn't just decide to turn their lives around—they took action.

If you are at a low point in your life, take action. Begin by saying—not just thinking—what you want to be true. Use the power of affirmations and spoken words to move yourself toward the success you deserve. Lao-Tzu didn't remind us to think about taking steps, he wrote, simply:

"A journey of a thousand miles begins with one step."

QUICK REFERENCE

What you can do right now:

When you're at a low point, write out your affirmations, using positive language, and say them aloud to yourself. Don't just think, act.

Instead of saying,

"I'm failure-prone. Look at what a mess I've made of my life already."

Say,

"Failure will never overtake me if my desire to succeed is strong enough, and I act upon it."

Instead of saying,

"I'm visualizing myself as a successful person, putting my troubles behind me. But nothing is changing."

Say,

"Today, I am taking action. I am moving toward the success I deserve to make of myself."

Instead of thinking to yourself,

"I'm a loser."

Say,

"I am a winner."

22. *Bouncing Back*

YOU'RE managing a department that's threatened with extensive layoffs. Just when your workers need strong emotional support and effective representation, they discover that the union official representing their local has skipped off to Barbados with a big chunk of the retirement fund. A "workers' committee" asks to meet with you to discuss what the future holds.

Say out loud to yourself:

"I don't know what to tell you people. It looks bad, and I just don't see how things are going to turn around."

Now, say:

"I understand how uncertain you must be feeling, and I know we're facing big challenges. We've overcome hurdles before, and we'll make it out of this present situation, too. We are a strong team, and we will bounce back. I know we'll be able to come up with a good plan for turning things around by working together."

Which sounds like the manager whose team will get busy and start thinking of solutions? Which is about to face a worsening situation with morale declining and productivity sinking?

At 3:00 on a Friday afternoon, the movers arrived with empty cardboard boxes. The locksmith walked toward the VP's office with a drill and began changing the lock. Word spread quickly.

Barbara Grego was the Telemarketing Manager for House of Almonds, then a wholly owned subsidiary of Tenneco. She led her department to grow from four people to 27 in one single season. The company had discovered that salespeople could phone corporate gift buyers and secure very profitable orders for Almond Gift Packs. They weren't selling nuts so much as convenience. Companies that traditionally sent gifts to their customers during the holiday season could bypass shopping, gift wrapping, and shipping by turning to House of Almonds. They'd mail or fax their customer address lists, indicate which ones should get which category of present, jot out what the gift cards should say, and House of Almonds took it from there.

The prime selling season spanned just a few months, from August through November. The pressure was intense during this time; tension and stress plagued the department. Facing some critical challenges over internal funding, and undergoing the normal growing pains any department would experience during a 500% expansion, Barbara called me in as a consultant to advise her on management issues and train her rapidly growing telemarketing team. One of the telemarketing department's prime assets within the organization was a vice president who believed in Barbara's management. Then, at the peak of the crunch, he was given his walking papers.

As her mentor's office was cleared out, Barbara's reaction was to plaster the word "Buoyant" throughout the department. She thumbtacked banners to the wall and had key chains made for every employee. They all said just one word: "Buoyant."

Barbara Grego wanted to remind her staff—and herself—that they were buoyant. Life has its ups and downs, and if there were no challenges or upsets, it would be mighty dull.

Power Talkers recognize that during the tough times they grow stronger. Sure, circumstances seem to conspire and push us briefly underwater from time to time. When they do, it's easy to feel as if we're drowning. The key is to remember that adversity tests our mettle, giving us an opportunity to surface again, stronger and wiser.

The bleakest circumstances often precede a promising change of events. It's crucial to picture yourself, and the team you lead—whether that's your family or a work group—rising above the storm, getting your head back above water. Picturing it isn't enough. Talk about it. Let the words you use reflect your determination to hang in there with the expectation that things will improve.

QUICK REFERENCE

What you can do right now:

When you hear yourself describing a setback situation as a terminal disaster, rephrase your description to recognize that you will bounce back and move ahead.

Instead of saying,

> "My department's been slashed, my mentor has been fired, and my career's going into a nosedive."

Say,

> **"I'm buoyant enough to surface from this turbulent situation. Experiences like these are what strengthen my talents as a manager."**

Instead of saying,

"Since my best friend moved to the West Coast, I feel at a loss. I just don't see how I'll ever get past this loneliness."

Say,

"I really miss Nicole since she moved. Now I'm going to call Judy and start getting to know her. I know I'll make new friends."

Instead of saying,

"I've damaged the tendons in my foot and the doctor says I'll never play racquetball again."

Say,

"I'm going to really take care of myself so my foot will heal quickly. Then I'll find a sport that won't be so hard on my feet."

Instead of saying,

"I'm going under."

Say,

"I'm going to bounce back."

23. *It's Over!*

YOU'VE just returned home from a two-week vacation. Unlocking the front door, you find that your home's burglar alarm has been deactivated. You're sure you set it before leaving and fear that someone may have broken in sometime while you were away.
Say out loud to yourself:

"Oh no! What if we've been burglarized? They've probably stolen my jewelry! And what if they've taken the computer with all my records on the hard disk? If they've got my Daytimer, I'm in a real jam. What am I going to do?"

Now, say:

"We may have been burglarized, so let's carefully check all through the house. If valuables are missing, insurance will replace most of them. Let's do a thorough inventory."

Who's the best candidate for an ulcer? Which person do you want to be around when a real emergency occurs?

Stew Leonard approached the woman at the airport's Hertz counter and asked, "Have you seen a giant yellow chicken wandering around here?" The rental agent laughed and said, "No, as a matter of fact, I haven't." So Stew asked, "Which way to the escalator?" The rental agent replied, "Escalator? There's no escalator at this airport."

Stew Leonard founded and built the world's largest dairy store, according to Ripley's Believe It or Not. Tom Peters made him famous around the world when he extolled Stew's brand of customer service in his "Excellence" books and video. Tom Peters said, "I've searched the world over looking for excellence in every nook and cranny. One of the best examples I found was a dairy store in Norwalk, Connecticut . . . Stew Leonard's."

Stew was en route to be the keynote speaker at a conference on quality presented by Frank Perdue of Perdue Chicken. Frank holds an annual conference with notable guest speakers and invites his most important customers, suppliers, and key staff members to attend. This particular conference was being held at Amelia Island, an exclusive resort off the coast of Florida near Jacksonville.

In confirming the arrangements, Frank had said, "Stew, don't worry about a thing. As soon as you step off the plane, I'll have someone in a giant yellow chicken costume waiting by the escalator to meet you. The chicken will escort you right to the limousine. The island resort is connected to the mainland by a bridge and it's only an hour's drive from the Jacksonville airport."

But when Stew stepped off his plane, there was no chicken waiting to greet him. So he proceeded to the baggage claim area.

After watching all the other passengers claim their bags and leave, the carousel came to a stop, and Stew thought, "No chicken, and now no luggage! My clothes, my slides, my notes, everything I need is in my suitcase."

He finally decided to rent a car on his own, head out to the island, and make arrangements for lost luggage later. When he asked the Hertz agent how long the drive would take, she advised him it would take several hours. "Several hours? But Frank Perdue told me that the island is less than an hour away from Jacksonville!" She replied, "That's true, but we're not in Jacksonville, Florida. This is Savannah, Georgia!"

Stew suddenly realized that he had gotten off his one-stop flight to Jacksonville prematurely, at the intermediate stop. His luggage had gone on along with the plane to Jacksonville without him.

Stew paused for a minute and considered the situation. Within the hour his plane would be landing in Jacksonville without him; the passengers would stream off and notice a man in a chicken costume in the arrival area. The limousine driver would be faithfully waiting at the bottom of the escalator as Stew's unclaimed luggage circled on the carousel.

Stew followed his own prescription for dealing with setback situations: He laughed for a moment and said to himself, "It's over!" There was no point in dwelling on the situation or circumstances; it would help nothing at all to beat himself up for having gotten off the plane too soon. Instead he used his time and energy to contact Frank Perdue to be sure someone picked up his luggage in Jacksonville. He then made his way directly to the island via chartered airplane.

As Stew told me the story, he said: "My policy is that whenever there's absolutely nothing to be gained by dwelling on the stupidity of a situation, whenever something really bad happens and it seems like all my plans are ruined, I just say to myself, 'It's over.' That's my secret for making the best of the situation. In this way I save my energy to make things better. As it turned out, the plane I chartered got me to the island in plenty of time. My bags were delivered to the hotel, I had a great new story to add to my talk, and the program was a success."

*   *   *

Stew Leonard's advice reminds me of the most helpful book I read in high school. It was Dale Carnegie's classic, *How to Stop Worrying and Start Living*. In it he suggests a simple three-step process for ending fears and worries. It goes like this:

1. Identify exactly what it is that you're worried about and answer this question: What is the very worst thing that could happen as a result of this situation?

2. Accept "the worst" as if it were a reality. Visualize that it has already occurred. Having now accepted your worst fears, there is no need to expend any of your energy worrying about having them come true. They have come true!

3. Redirect the energy that you had been using to worry about your worst fears coming true, and now, instead, do something useful that will help prevent them from materializing.

I've used that simple formula in a wide range of situations and have found that it never fails. Let's put it to work in Stew's predicament.

1. *What's the very worst that could happen?* Well, Stew could have found that there were no charter flights available and realized that it was impossible for him to reach the island in time for his program. He could have missed it altogether and disappointed his friend Frank Perdue. The audience would also have been disappointed. Stew would not have been able to accept his professional speaking fee for the engagement and might well have suffered some financial penalty. He would have returned home to Connecticut knowing that he had disappointed his friend and his audience. If that had happened, Frank would probably have seen the humorous side of the situation, entertained the audience himself, and the conference would have gone ahead with an altered agenda.

2. *Accept "the worst" as if it were true.* In his mind's eye, Stew would visualize Frank Perdue walking onstage the following morning and announcing to the audience that Stew had gotten off the flight one stop too soon and wouldn't be able to give his talk. They would have muttered in disappointment and probably also laughed about the circumstances. Although unlikely, Stew might also have gotten a phone call from Frank chewing him out for missing the engagement.

Would Stew be in physical pain? No. Would his career be threatened? No. Would his personal fortunes be ruined? Of course not.

He would have disappointed his friend and the audience and suffered a financial loss. That's all. Accepting this, Stew would still want to carry on—and leave this mistake in the past.

3. *Now use the energy that you might have fretted away and do something constructive.* This is exactly what Stew did. He got on the phone, made the charter flight arrangements, notified Frank, and everything turned out just fine.

In this situation the complexities of the backup arrangements were such that a few minutes' delay could have made all the difference. The charter aircraft might not have been available a short while later. The pilot could have gone home for the day. The small, unlit airport at Stew's island destination might have shut down for the night. Had Stew paced around the airport bemoaning his situation and berating himself for making a stupid mistake, the "worst that could happen" might well have actually happened.

Think of how many times you've seen people drain their energy by constantly rehashing the details of a negative situation they're in. This cannot make things any better, and may well make them a lot worse. At the very least, the worrying and moaning makes everyone involved feel lousy. When you're in a predicament, accept circumstances as they are and use your energy to move ahead in a positive direction.

QUICK REFERENCE

What you can do right now:

When things seem to be headed for a disastrous outcome, stop and ask yourself, "What's the very worst thing that could happen?" Accept that eventuality as if it were true and say, "That's all; it's over." Then, get to work applying your energy to create a more positive outcome.

Instead of saying,

> "It looks like I won't be able to finish the report on time, and I just dread having to face my boss if it's not done. I can just imagine what he's going to do if I don't finish on time."

Say,

"I may not be able to complete the report on time. The worst that could happen is the boss will be disappointed and ask me to stay here late until it's finished. He's not going to fire me, he'll just be upset. That's all; it's over. Now, I'll work on outlining the remaining sections of the report so I have a good structure to show him."

Instead of saying,

"What rotten luck! I cut my hand just before the volleyball championships. Now I can't play and my team will probably lose. It'll be all my fault."

Say,

"With this cut on my hand, playing volleyball is out of the question. I'm the best spiker on the team and without me, we may lose. That's all. Since I can't play, I'm going to coach Ron so he'll improve his spiking."

Instead of saying,

"This is terrible, and it could get a lot worse."

Say,

"Even if the worst happened, I could live with it. So there's no point worrying. That's all; it's over. Now I'm going to work on making things better."

POWER TALKERS ...

IV. Accept Responsibility

Power Talkers eagerly accept personal responsibility. They put themselves on the line. Rather than blaming others and holding them accountable, Power Talkers see themselves as being in control of their fate. They're not victims and they don't talk as if they're casualties of circumstances beyond their control.

Power Talkers shape their circumstances. When they're not optimal, they get busy and change them. When a situation is truly not changeable, the Power Talker actively manages his own reaction to the circumstances.

In these coming chapters, you'll meet people who guide their own fates, who are masters of their own ships. They apply Power Talking language to very significant situations, like a crippling motorcycle accident, and to seemingly insignificant situations, like being "too busy" to relax with a good book. You're about to see how Power Talkers show others—and themselves—that they are responsible.

24. *Watch Where You Point That Thing!*

You're breaking in a new employee who shows excellent potential. He still seems confused about a few of the office procedures you've explained several times during training.

Say out loud to yourself:

"You make me so frustrated! I've explained this job over and over and you just can't seem to get it right."

Now, say:

"I feel frustrated when we don't understand each other. What areas shall I explain a little more clearly?"

Which statement is more likely to encourage cooperation? Which will result in changes that improve the situation?

My mother, Edith, used a lot of homespun adages that still make sense. In my mind's eye, I can see her smiling and pointing. As a kid, when I made an excuse for not completing my homework assignments on time, she'd extend the index finger of her right hand, curl back the other three fingers, and point at my imaginary excuse. If I said I couldn't complete a book report because my typewriter was jammed, she'd break into her radiant smile and, with a twinkle in her eye, emphatically point at the poor old Smith-Corona and wiggle her other three fingers. This was her way of reminding me that my attention should be concentrated on those other three fingers because they were pointing back at *me*. My index finger identified only the object of *imagined* responsibility.

Her pointing motion cued me to rephrase my description of the predicament. Instead of saying,

"The typewriter is jammed, and I can't use it, so I can't complete my report on time,"

I'd look at the other three fingers and remember to redirect my attention back to myself, and my role, by saying:

"I didn't plan ahead and check the typewriter. Since it's jammed, I'll be hand-writing my book report tonight and will get the typewriter fixed tomorrow."

Salespeople tend to gripe about customers who don't buy:

"That cheapskate can't see past the purchase price. He can't even understand that in the long run our equipment is less expensive to own and operate and will serve him better."

Where's that salesman's index finger pointing? At the customer. When he redirects his attention to the other three fingers, the scene changes:

"I still haven't convinced my prospect that the long-term operating costs are a more important consideration than the up-front price. I'll use another approach and make it more clear."

If he stays focused on his index finger, there's not much else he can do but look for another prospect. He discards the first non-buyer after declaring him defective. What he's really saying is:

"If that prospect can't see beyond the purchase price, it's his own fault. He's not smart enough and doesn't deserve to become my customer anyway!"

Paying attention to the other three fingers is much more productive. We can't really change our prospects or customers. We can alter our own behavior. If we set out to change others, we're likely to become more and more frustrated and disgusted about short-sighted prospects. When we concentrate on changing ourselves, we improve our own sales techniques and become more and more effective.

The old finger-pointing routine is especially relevant to emotional proclamations:

"You're driving me crazy!"

Really? The other person is forcing you, against your will, to lose control and go insane?

I've taught many seminars for Customer Service professionals who deal with a steady stream of emotional callers. It's tempting for them to say,

"Those rude callers make me so mad! They raise their voices, they swear, and they imply that I've loused up their accounts, even though I had nothing to do with it. They make me furious."

The reality is, some callers do raise their voices, curse, and make inaccurate accusations. But they don't make anybody mad. Mad people make themselves mad by reacting to stimuli. It's not the other person's fault.

Redirecting attention to where the other three fingers are pointing—to yourself—changes the situation:

"When callers raise their voices and say certain words, I become upset. I need to depersonalize those situations. Some specific words and behaviors trigger those reactions in me. I'm going to work on managing my reactions when I face those conditions in the future."

When you meet someone who's superb at handling upset people, notice how they concentrate on their own reactions to stimuli. They're paying attention to the other three fingers. Emotional confrontations result not so much from what other people do as from how we react to them.

Whether your goal is to manage your own emotions or communicate an important idea to a student, employee, or customer, focus on the three fingers that are pointing back to yourself. Changing the person or situation your index finger is pointing at is much more difficult and frustrating. You can always modify your own behavior.

QUICK REFERENCE

What you can do right now:

Be on the alert for that pointing finger! Whenever you hear (or see) yourself directing blame or responsibility elsewhere, focus on the three fingers that point back at you.

Instead of saying,

"He just doesn't seem to understand."

Say,

"I haven't yet made it clear."

Instead of saying,

"These customers just can't get it through their head that our price increase is reasonable and justified."

Say,

"I need to do a better job of explaining the justification for our price increase."

Instead of saying,

"You make me upset when . . ."

Say,

"I feel upset when . . ."

25. *Use the Time You Have*

THE boss asks if you saw the article about your leading competitor in an industry trade journal. You've been working at full steam on an important analysis project and have fallen way behind on your reading.

Say out loud to yourself:

"No, I didn't see it. In fact, I never have enough time to do any of my industry reading when I'm working on a big project. I just can't seem to get through all my work and I'm constantly getting more and more behind. I don't know what I'm going to do."

Now, say:

"No, I haven't scheduled time to read the industry journals since I've been concentrating on the analysis project. I'd like to talk with you about our priorities and make sure that I'm scheduling my time in sync with your expectations."

Which sounds like someone who's in control of his time? Who is flailing about, using time inefficiently?

It doesn't take a time management expert to verify that you have available 1440 minutes every day and 525,600 minutes each year. How you use that time is purely a matter of choice. Some people are phenomenally productive and continually accomplish the many ambitious goals they set for themselves. Others achieve very little and when asked why, say, "There just isn't enough time."

When you say, "There isn't enough time," or, "I just haven't had the time," what you're really saying is that it's out of your control. You could accomplish more if you were given a few extra hours each day, but you haven't been granted that extra ration, so you can't get everything done. It's not your fault, you're a victim of time shortage!

Power Talkers accept responsibility for what they do accomplish, and for what they don't. Your achievements are a reflection of your choices about how you use time. Don't blame a failure to reach your goals on a lack of time.

I once shared the speaking platform with a medical doctor whose specialty is treating overstressed business executives. We were both addressing a conference of Sales and Marketing Executives in Buffalo, New York. The people in that audience were definitely stressed. They create ad campaigns, answer to their officers' (often unrealistic) sales goals, and implement and administer quotas.

In his 45-minute presentation, the doctor revealed that there's only one effective way to handle stress. Actually, he used 44 minutes to tell entertaining stories and one minute to prescribe his stress cure-all:

> "I'm often called on to present a full-day seminar on stress management. Sometimes, though, the group has a tight schedule, so I can also cover it in a half-day version. If a client's budget is limited, I can do a two-hour program. Even a one-hour keynote speech is no problem. I've been studying and treating stress for many years and I have no doubt that I've found the answer. Since we have just a few minutes before my program ends, would you like to hear the ultracondensed version? In fact, would you like to know the one-sentence, surefire, cure-all technique that never fails to cure stress-related syndromes? *If you want to have less stress in your life, lower your expectations.* That's it. That's all there is to it."

As blasphemous as this prescription sounded to his audience of high achievers, he confirmed that it was the only prescription that really works. Destructive stress results from setting unrealistic expectations. If we would all align what we want to accomplish with what we're realistically able to do, we'd have much less destructive stress.

Don't wish for more time. Take responsibility for how you use your available time and recognize that what you do and don't accomplish is a reflection of your choices. Remind yourself of that choice by talking about your time in terms that acknowledge your role in managing it.

QUICK REFERENCE

What you can do right now:

Purge phrases that suggest time is out of your control—that there's not enough of it. Acknowledge your personal responsibility with your language.

Instead of saying,

> "I just haven't had enough time to finish it. I'm trying to get to it, but I just haven't been able to. I need more time."

Say,

"I haven't yet finished it. I'm following my priorities, and that particular task is something I've scheduled for next week."

Instead of saying,

"This job is driving me crazy! They expect me to get twice as much done as I can possibly hope to accomplish. I can't say no when they give me a new assignment or they'll think I'm not really dedicated. Meanwhile I'm really burning out."

Say,

"I work better when I'm not feeling so stressed. My manager may not even realize how hard I'm working. I'm going to list the projects I'm working on and ask him for some help in setting priorities. I'll explain what I can realistically accomplish and suggest that the lower-priority items be reassigned."

Instead of saying,

"I just can't get caught up; I don't have enough time."

Say,

"I can get caught up by managing my time and eliminating low-priority projects."

26.   It's Not What Happens to You, It's What You Do About It

YOU'RE working on an important project that's right up on a deadline. One key element isn't ready, and the project may not be finished on time.

Say out loud to yourself:

"It's not my fault."

Now, say:

"It's my responsibility."

Which statement sounds like it's coming from someone who will take charge of his situation and make the best of it? Which comes from someone who's going to sit around blaming others for the situation he's in and do little to change it?

I'd never shaken a fingerless hand until I met W Mitchell. I first saw this unusual person at a National Speakers Association convention in San Antonio. I felt uncomfortable as soon as I noticed him across the hotel lobby. Confined to a wheelchair and grossly disfigured with extensive burns and scars, he was the kind of person who, because of his appearance, many of us choose to avoid.

When I saw him again, months later, at another convention, I still didn't summon the courage to approach "Mitchell," as he likes to be called. I consider myself a friendly, outgoing person, but just kept thinking how awkward I'd feel reaching out for his scarred hand. Thankfully, he wheeled over and shook mine. I now know one of the most beautiful people on this planet.

In the early seventies, Mitchell's motorcycle collided with a laundry truck in the middle of a busy San Francisco intersection. Passersby gasped as the cycle's gas tank burst open and Mitchell became a human fireball. Today, the only parts of his face that aren't scarred are thin strips of skin his helmet strap had protected.

After reconstructive surgery that included numerous grafts onto the stumps of his burned-off fingers and extensive physical therapy (not to mention months of excruciating pain), Mitchell bounced back. He qualified for his multiengine pilot's license; cofounded Vermont Castings, Inc., a highly successful metal-casting company employing over 400 people; ran for Congress; met with U.S. Presidents and Cabinet members; served as Mayor of a Colorado town; and enjoyed an active social life.

Then, while taking some friends up for a sightseeing flight, the small plane he was piloting crashed. As a result, Mitchell's burned, scarred, disfigured body was now also paralyzed from the waist down.

You'd think he would have just given up after this second disaster. Instead he's gone on to become an extremely successful professional speaker. Mitchell wheels himself onto the stages of America's biggest sales meetings and conventions. He has appeared on the "Today" show, "Good Morning America," and "NBC Nightly News," and has been featured in *Time*, *Newsweek*, *Omni*, *Parade*, and *The New York Times*.

Mitchell is cheerful and productive, travels the world, manages extensive real estate investments, is happily married, and has a positive impact on a great many lives. How can he lead such a healthy life when he has so many handicaps, or "problems"?

"I have no problems," Mitchell says. "That's a foolish word. I do have many instances where unusual, challenging circumstances confront me. I am fully responsible for my present situation. Sure, the laundry truck driver was legally liable for the accident—and I'm responsible. I don't mean I'm guilty, or at fault. I am responsible—able to respond."

Mitchell sheds a whole new light on the concept of "blame." Many of us fall far short of achieving our potentials in life, and we often blame others. Can you think of friends who blame their parents, the educational system, a crooked business partner, or a multitude of other reasons for their situation? Do you do the same?

Power Talkers acknowledge that they are responsible. When we blame others, we weaken ourselves. Instead of improving our situation, we step backward. Other people and circumstances aren't what hold most of us back. *We* hold *ourselves* back because of the way we react to them.

Accepting responsibility means taking control of your life and the language you use to describe it. As Mitchell says, "It's not what happens to you, it's what you do about it."

QUICK REFERENCE

What you can do right now:

Accept personal responsibility for your present situation and decide to move forward rather than wasting energy by blaming your current condition on past circumstances.

Instead of saying,

"My parents couldn't afford to send me to college like yours did, so I wasn't lucky enough to get a degree. I had to go out and work while you got a free ride in school. Nobody will hire me for a really good job. I can't help it."

Say,

"I haven't gone to college yet, and I have gained a great deal of practical experience in my various jobs. I plan to take night courses and work toward a degree starting this summer. Meanwhile I'm looking into job opportunities that will take advantage of my diverse practical background."

Instead of saying,

"I couldn't meet my quota this month because my car broke down and I just couldn't get to many appointments. It was in the shop for a whole week. It's not my fault. I couldn't help it."

Say,

"I had unexpected car trouble, so I used one full week to telephone all of my longstanding customers whom I haven't talked with in a while. In the long run, I believe this effort will pay off. In the short run, it means I did not make enough appointments to meet my quota this month."

Instead of saying,

"I can't help it; it's someone else's fault."

Say,

"It's my responsibility to change things."

27. *You Can Count on Me*

It's Saturday morning and you're at your job, working in the Paint Department of a large home-improvement center. A customer calls because his garage-door opener isn't working.

Say out loud to yourself:

"Sorry, I can't help you. The Hardware Department won't be open until 10:00. You'll have to call back later."

Now, say:

"The Hardware Department will be open at 10:00. I'll be happy to help you myself by taking your message and getting it to them. What is your name, please?"

Which sounds like the more responsive, helpful organization? As a customer, which would you rather encounter?

By the eighth ring, I felt impatient. The Marriott organization has a reputation for outstanding service, so I was annoyed when the operator at their Atlanta Marquis property took so long to answer. Finally, after the eleventh ring, an operator answered and transferred me to Reservations. I heard some clicking, and there was silence. I had been cut off!

I called again, waited nine rings, asked for Reservations, heard the clicks and . . . drat!

The third time, my call was answered quickly. Rather than a reservation agent, I asked for the Hotel Manager. The operator placed me on hold while she paged him. After leaving me on "silent hold" a little more than a minute, she came back on the line to tell me he was unavailable. So I said she could transfer me to Reservations. You guessed it. Click.

You've no doubt experienced similar frustrations yourself. Since writing *Phone Power*, I'm on the alert for examples of excellent, as well as poor, handling of phone calls. I often count the rings and time the holds.

On my **fourth** attempt, the operator did connect me with the manager. He listened attentively as I described my experience. When I told him that I wanted to reserve a suite for my family, and was afraid that I would be cut off if I were transferred again, he said,

> "Mr. Walther, I'm not going to transfer you. I will handle your reservation myself. Then I'll investigate the phone system and find out why you've been getting cut off. When will you be arriving in Atlanta?"

The manager could have transferred me, and hoped I would be connected smoothly. He could have offered to take my name and number and have someone call me back to take my reservation. But instead he took responsibility and did it himself.

In his best-seller, *Swim With the Sharks Without Being Eaten Alive*, Harvey Mackay identifies many of the phrases that he's used throughout his incredibly successful career. When I interviewed him for *Power Talking*, he said,

> "There's a place in this world for anyone who will say, 'I will take care of it.'"

When you deal with people who say, "I will take care of it myself," you know that they are taking personal responsibility for the outcome. That doesn't mean they'll do the tasks themselves, it means they'll be accountable. The hotel's manager didn't walk over to the computer terminal at the Marriott and type in my reservation request. He did personally ensure that it would be handled properly.

QUICK REFERENCE

What you can do right now:

Even though you may not be the person who'll actually perform the tasks, accept personal accountability when you offer to help someone.

Instead of saying,

"I can't help you with that, you'll have to talk with the Customer Service Department."

Say,

"Customer Service can give you the best help with that question, and I'll stay on the line while I transfer you."

Instead of saying,

"Only the Regional Director can authorize a change in the rules. You'll have to call her yourself."

Say,

"The Regional Director has authority in the area you're asking about. I'll be glad to give you that number myself so you can call her directly."

Instead of saying,

"That's not my area. You'll have to get someone else to help you."

Say,

"I'll help you myself by getting your message through to the right department."

28. Do You Choose to Lose?

You work in a position that's well beneath your capabilities. You want time with your family on the weekends, and you don't want to schlep a bulging briefcase home each night. A friend asks why you haven't actively sought career advancement.

Say out loud to yourself:

"I just haven't been able to, what with the family and all. I could be doing a lot more with myself, but unfortunately someone has to be around with the kids on the weekends. Marge doesn't get out much during the week, and she insists on playing tennis every single Saturday. I really don't have much choice."

Now, say:

"I've chosen to dedicate myself to my family right now. I'll concentrate more on my career three or four years from now. Plenty of job opportunities will always be open to me, and now is the only time when I can be with my kids while they're preschoolers. I like giving Marge some freedom on the weekends. She sure works hard during the week while I'm at the office."

Who's happy? Who thinks of himself as a victim of circumstances?

One of the worst vacations I've ever endured was a two-week holiday in paradise with my family. We stayed at luxurious resorts, the weather was perfect, the beach was ideal. How could it have been so miserable?

My wife has two children from her first marriage, both teenagers. Except during summer vacations and alternating holidays, they live with their dad, so I'm a part-time stepfather. For this trip, we invited each of my stepchildren to bring one of their teenage friends along for two weeks in Hawaii. In addition to the four teenagers, we took our three-month-old infant, Kelcie, who had not yet reached the "sleep-all-night" stage in her development.

The result was that for those two weeks I slept poorly every night. Then I awoke each morning and spent the day reminding four teenagers to close the refrigerator doors after taking out their food, that they should turn off the lights before they go to bed, and so on. Rarely did they heed my instructions.

As the trip progressed, I became more and more grouchy and, in the end, blurted out to my wife that I had never experienced a worse two-week period in my life. I blamed the four teenagers for ruining our trip. The truth is that those four kids are swell young people who behaved well within the bounds of normalcy for thirteen- and fourteen-year-olds. Kelcie is a terrific baby and slept as well as you would expect any three-month-old infant to. Those four teens and a baby did not ruin my vacation. I ruined my vacation.

One challenge I face in writing this book is living up to my own advice. Whenever I complained to my wife about how the kids were wrecking the trip and making me miserable, she reminded me that the decision to enjoy or detest our holiday was completely in my hands. I "chose" to have a bad time. She got even less sleep than I did and was equally inconvenienced by the kids' messiness and lack of consideration. Julie, though, chose to have a good time, and she did.

The children's behaviors were completely predictable. Before ever planning the trip, I could have anticipated what it would be like. When I started feeling resentful, I could have said to myself,

"Four teenagers are not going to be thinking about turning off lights and cleaning their rooms. Our baby will probably wake us up a couple of times every night. I'm going to take those circumstances into account and choose to have a good holiday with my family."

Since I didn't choose to have a good time, the bad time I did have was also my own choice and my responsibility.

*   *   *

One consistent characteristic of winners is that they claim responsibility for their circumstances. They don't play the "victim" role. They don't draw the line at claiming credit and accepting responsibility when things go well. They also embrace the concept of personal responsibility when things aren't perfect. That way they reserve the power to change them.

Powerlessness, the inability to change what you don't like, is a lousy feeling. Ask anyone who's been a hostage in the Middle East or a POW.

Actually, though, there's very little that we can't change. OK, so you're not going to alter the course of a tornado that's bearing down on your home. Those truly unchangeable circumstances, though, are relatively rare.

"There are two big forces at work, external and internal. We have very little control over external forces such as tornados, earthquakes, floods, disasters, illness and pain. What really matters is the internal force. How do I respond to those disasters? Over that I have complete control."

LEO BUSCAGLIA

Winners see the distinction. We've all heard the old prayer:

"God grant me the serenity to accept the things I cannot change, change the things I cannot accept, and the wisdom to know the difference."

The key is in knowing the difference. Most of what most people identify as things they can't change are in fact changeable. And our reactions to the few things that truly can't be changed are, in themselves, matters of choice. I could not change my baby's sleeping patterns, and could not "control" those teenagers and instantly change them into gracious little adults. I could have changed my reaction to the circumstances. I could have **chosen** to enjoy myself despite the kids' behavior.

Recognize that most of what you like and don't like in your life is changeable. And even with the few things that you can't change, you can choose to react positively or negatively. Take responsibility, acknowledge your choices, and use the word **choose** when you describe the situations you're in.

QUICK REFERENCE

What you can do right now:

Avoid "victim" language; acknowledge your responsibility by using the word "choose." When you're unsatisfied with the way things are, choose to change them.

Instead of saying,

"I hate my job, but there's really nothing I can do about it. I'm stuck in this dead-end position, working for a boss I don't really like or respect."

Say,

"For now, I've chosen job security over professional challenge. I could work with more inspiring people, and one day I will. I'm going to start polishing my career skills and check into other opportunities. Meanwhile I'm glad I've created a secure role for myself right here."

Instead of saying,

"Sure, I'd love to get a new car, but we can't afford one. I know it's embarrassing to drive that beat-up junker, but there's just nothing we can do about it."

Say,

"Yes, I'd like a new car, and one day we'll have one. Right now, though, we're making a choice to keep the old one so we can have vacation money and go out for a nice dinner whenever we want to."

Instead of saying,

"I can't change things, I didn't get myself into this fix."

Say,

"I choose to make the best of this situation."

V. Encourage Cooperation and Reduce Conflict

Zıg Ziglar says:

> "I believe that you can get everything in life you want if you will just help enough other people get what they want."

Power Talkers are masters at working **with** other people and helping them get what they want. The most successful people are those who ensure that their "partners" also come out ahead.

Power Talkers use their language to encourage cooperation and defuse potential conflicts. They use "win-win" phrasing and form partnerships with others. Their aim is to ensure that both sides in all negotiations win—that there isn't a loser.

One of my consulting clients is a very successful resort developer who has acquired major properties around the country and developed them into profitable condominium and time-share projects. Today Mark is the Director of Marketing for a beautiful resort nestled in the gorgeous countryside near the Wisconsin Dells. Not only has he had a very successful career, he's also guided a whole team of telephone professionals to work together toward impressive mutual successes.

When I asked him what techniques he uses, I heard a lot of

Power Talking phrases. He explained that every member of his team starts the year by writing out his or her personal goals, which are reviewed with managers each week. Some new employees have a tendency to write, "Here's what I hope to do," or "Wouldn't it be great if . . ." Mark made it very clear that employees' goals are always rewritten to use the positive expectation language of "I will achieve . . ."

He also pointed out that the goals don't just relate to individuals, they pertain to the organization as a whole, as in, "This is what we will accomplish together." Using Power Talking, conflict-reducing language, is more effective than if he were to gather his employees together and say, "Here's what you have to do to make my resort a success."

In the following chapters you'll meet people who have succeeded in selling ideas and generating cooperation among others, who are good at stimulating group creativity, and who are extraordinarily successful at getting others to do what they want them to do. We are all "salespeople" every day. We "sell" our ideas to others and encourage them to agree.

You'll also learn the techniques employed effectively by talented "peacemakers" whose area of expertise is calming people who have already become upset and hostile. Power Talking leads to increased cooperation and decreased conflict. If you need to work with other people, you'll find these techniques very helpful.

29. Get That "But" Out of Your Mouth!

YOUR daughter has just passed a proficiency test after completing her first series of computer programming classes. She's working toward a promotion at her company.

Say out loud to yourself:

"You did a good job, Suzanne, **but** you'll need to do more to be ready for that promotion you want."

Now, say this:

"You did a good job, Suzanne, and you'll need to do more to be ready for that promotion you want."

Which sounds more encouraging? Which statement will stimulate Suzanne to move forward in pursuit of her goal?

Every real estate market has its ups and downs, including California's. In the 1980s, Southern California seemed blessed with prosperity. My friend Peter Schweizer and I both invested in California real estate throughout the 80s.

In 1990 Peter came up north to visit me in Seattle. As we walked in the woods, talking about our "California days," he reflected on our properties, saying,

"Yeah, my condo at Mammoth was a good investment, but it's so far away from L.A.; I just don't use it much. You sold your Venice Beach apartment building for a good price, but if you'd only waited another two years, you could've sold it for even more."

Peter still owns his very comfortable condo at a premier California ski resort. He bought it in the early 1980s for less than $20,000. He skis there five or six times a year, often loans it to friends, and also enjoys steady rental income. His investment has paid off superbly, and he could easily sell it for many times his original purchase price.

Yet, as we talked, Peter's concentration was on the negative aspect: "but it's too far away." His attention focused on the phrase following "but."

I am delighted to live in Seattle and I'm glad I moved away from L.A. when I did. My real estate investments in Washington have performed particularly well. Yet, again, Peter's focus was on the negative. The phrase following "but" got the emphasis:

"but . . . you could've sold it for even more."

I may have gotten a better price by selling my California property two years later. However, I wouldn't have been able to buy in Washington just before that market started getting hot.

The effect of the word "but" is to put two viewpoints in opposition to each other and to devalue one of them.

"It was a good investment, **but** . . ."

makes you wonder if it was such a good investment after all.

"You sold at a good price, **but** . . ."

takes away the compliment I was beginning to feel. In the first half of the sentence, my mind heard,

"You did well, George. You have a good sense of timing, anticipated the market well, and made a smart deal."

As soon as **"but"** rolled along, I stepped back and heard,

"Well, maybe you weren't **that** astute. If you'd only waited awhile, you'd have been much smarter."

Peter and I sat down on a boulder overlooking the Seattle skyline and sparkling Puget Sound and I explained that a simple substitution of one word makes a tremendous difference in the impact his statements have on others, and on himself.

"Yeah, my condo at **Mammoth Ski Area** was a good invest-ment, **and** it's so far away from L.A. that I don't use it much. You sold your apartment building for a very good price, **and** if you'd waited another two years, you might have sold it for even more."

This way Peter gives himself credit for his good investment sense while recognizing that things have changed. He's no longer inter-ested in driving five hours to his ski condo. Both conditions, the condo being a good investment, **and** his unwillingness to travel five hours to use it, coexist at the same time.

He's also complimenting me on selling my property at a good price **and** acknowledging that the selling price might have been greater had I waited.

The mere substitution of **and** for **but** reduces conflict by suggest-ing that two ideas can exist at the same time without one overrul-ing the other. Peter's original statement has a much more positive, powerful impact when he uses "and" rather than "but."

Sometimes "but" is what you really mean.

"It's a very expensive house, but there's no view, the rooms are small, and the school district has a terrible reputation."

Most of the time, though, we say "but" out of habit, when "and" would be a much better choice. Unless you really want to devalue the prior thought ("It's expensive, but a bad value") you're better off substituting the conflict-reducing "and."

When I conduct training sessions for sales professionals, one subject that's often requested is Objection Handling. For example, "What can I do when the customer says, 'But your price is too high'?" The very first step is to rephrase and repeat the customer's objection using "and" rather than "but."

One of my first sales training clients was Xerox. Their Business Products Division sells copier paper, toner, and other supplies. It's common for prospects to point out that they can buy paper much less expensively if it doesn't carry the Xerox brand. New salespeo-ple instinctively say,

"It may seem like our paper is more expensive, **but** . . ."

As soon as a salesperson utters "but," the prospect "hears" him trying to contradict her belief and she stops listening. People don't like to be told they're wrong. They immediately start to resist.

So instead I trained the salespeople to agree with their prospects:

"Yes, our paper seems more expensive, and the cost of making copies includes much more than the paper itself. Cheaper paper, for example, has a tendency to curl and jam in the machine. That means your expensive staff resources are pulled away from important projects to clear paper jams."

The customer isn't being told she's wrong; she's simply being provided with more complete information on which to base her buying decisions.

Replacing "but" with "and" creates a more cooperative atmosphere in sales situations, negotiations, family discussions, and any other time when you want to reduce conflict. Don't say "but" unless your true intent is to devalue a thought.

QUICK REFERENCE

What you can do right now:

Make a conscious decision to replace "but" with "and" as you talk to yourself and to others. Notice that your thinking "opens up" as ideas coexist instead of conflict.

Instead of saying,

"I'm getting the hang of my new job, but there are a few things I don't really understand."

Say instead,

"I'm getting the hang of my new job, and there are a few things I don't really understand."

Instead of saying,

"I know you want to expand the sales meeting to three full days, **but** consider the budget impact."

Say instead,

"I know you want to expand the sales meeting to three full days, and consider the budget impact."

Instead of saying,

"I can see that it's a good product, **but** it's expensive."

Say instead,

"I can see that it's a good product, and it's expensive."

30. *Let's Do It!*

DURING a brainstorming/feedback session with your sales team, it becomes clear that there are several sore points the group is concerned about. One member complains that supervisors in her department ring a bell when incoming calls are backed up, and she finds it distracting. She suggests eliminating the bell.

Say out loud to yourself:

"Well, I'm sorry you don't like hearing it, but it's the only way supervisors can let everyone know that it's time to get back to work. Without the bell, they'd have to constantly walk around gathering up their people. It's the only practical way to do it."

Now, say:

"I can understand how that would be distracting. Let's find another way to let everyone know when the department is very busy. How about a series of lights up on the wall? If the bell hurts more than it helps, we'll experiment with other techniques."

Which sounds like the reaction that will encourage more brain-storming ideas, quite possibly leading to innovative break-throughs? Which will "shut down" the participants' creative thinking?

Market researchers often use "Focus Groups" to sample cus-tomers' feelings about a company's products and services. A dozen or so customers are invited to an informal discussion in a research company's facility and are observed through a one-way mirror. They're told up front that company representatives will be watch-ing them, and they're encouraged to say whatever they have on their mind. A moderator gently guides the discussion, carefully holding back any of his own opinions to avoid influencing the participants' views.

Right after I completed my graduate studies, I was employed by a major advertising agency as an Account Executive. I handled sev-eral multimillion-dollar accounts, including Continental Airlines, McCulloch Chain Saws, and Van de Kamp frozen foods. Hearing what customers really thought about our ads and the clients' prod-ucts in Focus Group sessions was often very revealing. (It was kind of fun playing peeping Tom behind that mirror, too.)

Recently, Stew Leonard, owner of the world's largest grocery store, told me about a Focus Group session involving several of his store managers interacting with 16 women who had been asked to talk about buying fish.

One woman in the group said,

"I won't buy fish from your store because I only buy fresh fish, and yours isn't."

The Fish Department manager shot to his feet and responded,

"What do you mean it's not fresh? I handle the purchasing myself. We buy fresh fish every single day at Fulton Market."

The woman responded,

"If that were true, then why would you put it in those plastic packages like the frozen fish at the supermarket? I like to buy my fish nice and fresh, right off the ice."

The store was already selling 15,000 pounds of fresh fish every week, so it would have been understandable if the fish buyer had set out to convince the woman that she was wrong. Instead, Stew said,

"So she likes her fish on ice. If she thinks it makes such a big difference, let's do it."

The very next day, store personnel began building a fish display with a bed of ice. The week after installing the "fish bar," sales doubled! The interesting thing is that sales of the regular packaged fish did not decline at all. The extra 15,000 pounds of fish sold each week was all new sales, apparently purchased by customers who shared that woman's feelings.

It would have been very easy to be closed-minded about the fish situation—and lose out on more than three-quarters of a million pounds of fish sales each year.

Power Talkers definitely have strong opinions and aren't afraid to express them—when appropriate. Convincing the other person that your point of view is right can sometimes help you win the battle but lose the war. As a Power Talker, you want to make other people feel comfortable about expressing their ideas and encourage them to think creatively. Only after evaluating the merits of various approaches can you determine the best course to follow.

One of my clients in the resort development business has been very successful selling memberships in a national network of private campgrounds. For them, as for most sales organizations, new sales prospects who are referred by existing customers have the very best potential for becoming satisfied customers. The cost of finding them is low, their conversion rate is high, and they tend to be happier with their purchases than are other nonreferral new customers. Referred prospects have already been influenced by the most powerful form of advertising, word-of-mouth publicity from a satisfied customer.

I observed as my client gathered her employees together and presented them with the goal of brainstorming a dozen new ways to increase the flow of referrals. She didn't promote her own ideas and she didn't criticize any of the suggestions. In less than 30 minutes, the team had come up with 15 excellent approaches.

This manager was a conscientious user of Power Talking language, an encouraging cheerleader rather than a domineering critic. Her role was to keep saying, "That's good. I like it. Let's do it. Wow, that can work. Let's get some more ideas. Keep 'em coming. Who sees a way to connect these two?"

And when someone else in the group pooh-poohed an idea, she reminded them to keep an open mind.

Encourage other people to cooperate by inviting their input and ideas. Welcome unusual suggestions rather than quashing them. Get all involved parties to throw their ideas out on the table so creative solutions can result.

QUICK REFERENCE

What you can do right now:

Whenever you seek others' input and suggestions, stimulate a free flow of ideas, no matter how crazy some might seem.

Instead of saying,

"I want to give everyone a chance to suggest one or two approaches on this project. Please keep our limited budget in mind."

Say,

"Let's get lots of ideas going. Don't worry about how much they may cost. We'll consider practicality later. For now, anything goes."

Instead of saying,

"Your suggestion just won't work. Believe me, I've personally seen it fail at two other companies."

Say,

"Good suggestion. Let's keep going and come up with some more."

Instead of saying,

"That's not practical, it'll never work."

Say,

"That's an unusual approach, let's go with it and see where we end up."

31. *Do ME a Favor for a Change*

A fund-raiser for your local PBS station phones you at home. After introducing himself, he explains that he's hoping you'll make a donation.

Say out loud to yourself:

"I was wondering if you could do me a favor and make a contribution to the station. We have this contest going on for the phone reps, and I'm really close to winning a Disneyland trip for my family."

Now, say:

"We want to continue offering fine educational programming for you and your family. With your contribution, you'll receive our informative monthly newsletter and, of course, you'll have the good feeling of knowing that you're helping to provide your family with quality television programs."

Which approach will motivate you to open your checkbook?

There are lots of reasons that motivate people to do business together. Often, they're selfish ones. These can be counterproductive when it comes to encouraging cooperation. Only one reason really counts: The other guy must believe that he'll be better off by doing what you suggest.

I'm surely not against helping out a friend. When it comes to a business proposition, though, there's only one party I'm really watching out for: ME! It's amazing how many salespeople tend to concentrate on why **they'll** be better off if they get you to buy something. As a customer, it's completely irrelevant to me—unless we have a friendship—that you're "just this close" to meeting your quota for the month, or about to qualify for some kind of prize.

When I began presenting sales seminars in the early 1980s, many sales trainers used a popular acronym: WIIFM. The explanation went like this:

> "Whenever you're scripting a sales presentation, designing an ad, or writing copy for a direct mail campaign, only one thing matters: WIIFM! *What's In It For Me*? That's what customers want to know; that's what they're asking themselves as you present your case for what you want them to do. They don't care about a salesperson's company, product features, or personal situation. They care only about themselves. They want to know how the action you're suggesting will make them be better off."

A hospital information operator in one of my seminar audiences recently asked me a question following my presentation.

She said,

> *"When I ask callers for their insurance information, they often get huffy and indignant. Some of them don't have insurance, and I think they're afraid I won't help them if I find that out. When I tell them I have to get the information for our internal call reporting statistics, they still seem uncooperative. What can I say to make them feel like cooperating?"*

I wanted to help her figure that answer out for herself, so I just stood there with my arms crossed and said,

> *"Why should I want to give you my insurance information?"*

She seemed confused, and didn't immediately recognize that I was role-playing with her and taking the stance that her callers adopted. I continued,

> *"I don't care about **your** statistical project or your hospital's requirements. Just tell me why **I** should want to give you the information."*

She caught on. My point was that she should assume that any caller is constantly asking himself, "What's In It For Me?"

It took her only a few seconds to come up with the caller-oriented benefit:

> "Once I know a little about your insurance coverage, I can make sure I'm referring you to the best medical option for your circumstances. If you don't have insurance, I can make arrangements to talk with a public health facility. And if you do, I can determine which of our physicians already use direct billing plans with your particular insurance carrier, and that can make things much simpler for you when it comes to minimizing paperwork."

She got it! Her callers don't care about the hospital at all. They only care about themselves. She was really setting out to "sell" them on the value of cooperating with her information request.

Now when she wants to get insurance information from a caller, she can "sell" them on the benefits of cooperating with her question by saying,

> "In order to make sure I'm referring you to the physician or facility that's best for your situation, please tell me who your insurance carrier is. That way if one of the hospital's doctors has a direct billing arrangement with your company, your paperwork will be minimized later on."

When you want someone to cooperate, to follow your lead, to do something for you, take off your shoes. Get in the other guy's shoes. Look at the scenario from his standpoint and show him how he'll benefit by taking the action you recommend.

QUICK REFERENCE

What you can do right now:

When you need someone's cooperation, figure out why his participation will benefit *him*, not *you*. Emphasize the benefits he'll realize by following your suggestion.

Instead of saying,

"My son's Boy Scout troop is selling firewood, and if you could just do me a favor and buy two or three sacks, he'll be able to go on the campout next month."

Say,

"My son's Boy Scout troop is selling firewood, and it's an excellent value. The price is right, and you'll find it's good, long-burning hardwood. How much would you like to buy?"

Instead of saying,

"Look, when you interrupt me several times a day with your questions, it's almost impossible for me to get any serious work done. Would you do me a favor and save them up so I don't have to keep breaking my concentration?"

Say,

"You deserve my full attention when I'm answering your questions. The best way to get it would be to meet with me once or twice a day. That way I'll be able to really concentrate on helping you and cover several questions in depth each time."

Instead of saying,

"Will you do me a favor?"

Say,

"Here's why this will be good for you."

32. *You Get What You Ask For*

You meet with an important customer because you've heard that he's been talking to one of your competitors. Fearing that you could be about to lose his business, you decide to find out if there's something he's unhappy about.

Say out loud to yourself:

"John, you've been happy with our service, haven't you?"

Now, say:

"John, you're a very important customer and my aim is to constantly improve the way we serve you. What two or three areas would you like us to improve upon?"

Which question will encourage your customer to provide complete, candid feedback? Which will open a dialogue that leads toward a stronger relationship?

> "Hello, Mr. Walther, this is Debra in Room Service. I'm calling to find out if you were pleased with the pizza we delivered to your room this evening."

Nobody from any hotel's Room Service department had ever called me before. Debra asked if my pizza had been warm enough, spiced about right, and delivered on time. I answered that it had been fine. I was surprised at her call and wondered if she had some ulterior motive. Was there some sort of pizza recall? I dismissed the call, got some sleep, and presented my first training seminar for Ford Motor Credit the next morning.

The following month I returned to present another seminar for Ford and again stayed at the same hotel. I rarely leave my room the evening before a presentation. Most of the time I order from Room Service, review my program notes, and get to bed early so I'm fresh for my audience the next morning. I ordered the local chicken dish and enjoyed it. Once again my phone rang after finishing my meal.

> "Good evening, Mr. Walther, this is Debra calling from Room Service. I'd like to find out if your chicken was prepared to your liking."

The same young woman had called again. I answered her questions and asked her a few myself. I wanted to know more about why she was calling. Debra explained that she calls every single guest half an hour after their Room Service meals are delivered to ensure that things were just right.

I was struck with the simplicity of her approach. Of course! If you want to find out how to improve Room Service, or any other service, the best thing to do is ask your guest or customer directly. Very few people take the time to fill out those "guest comment cards" propped up on most hotels' bedside tables. But if you phone guests in their rooms, they'll probably talk to you.

By the time I'd presented my seventh training seminar for Ford, Debra and I had become quite friendly. I autographed a copy of *Phone Power* and delivered it to her office so I could observe her in action as she made her calls soliciting guest feedback. Later that evening I listened for two hours in her dingy cubicle right by the service elevators in the sub-basement, where the hotel's kitchen is situated.

Think of all the times you've been served an overpriced, mediocre meal in a restaurant and commented to your companions that the service was poor to boot. Invariably, when the maître d' asks, "Was everything satisfactory? You enjoyed your meal?" you smile and say, "Oh yes, thank you, it was fine." Why didn't you tell him the truth? Perhaps you could sense that he didn't really want to know. His question was a habitual routine—a hollow nicety.

As I sat beside Debra and listened in on her calls that evening, I noticed that guests were all quite surprised to hear from her, yet very few offered any really helpful suggestions. Were they really 100% satisfied, or did Debra's questions themselves need improving?

Most calls went about like this:

"Hello, Mrs. Hightsman, this is Debra in Room Service. I'm calling to find out if you were satisfied with the soup and salad we delivered to your room earlier this evening. Was everything OK?"

The guests nearly always said something like this:

"Well, how nice of you to ask! Yes, everything was fine. Thanks for calling."

After hearing several of these brief conversations, I asked Debra,

"Do you really just want to know if they were satisfied? Or are you looking for suggestions to help you improve? If you want more helpful feedback, let's ask a question that gets at the heart of what you're after.

*Instead of asking IF THEY ARE HAPPY, let's ask guests HOW WE
CAN MAKE THEM HAPPIER. If we've already made them as happy
as they can possibly be, they'll say so.''*

So, on the next call, Debra changed her question:

*''Good evening, Mr. Blackstone. This is Debra calling from Room
Service. I hope you enjoyed the prime rib dinner we delivered to you
tonight. I'd like to find out what one aspect of your meal could have
been a little nicer.''*

This took Mr. Blackstone by surprise.

*''Oh, my, it was very nice. Let's see, how could it have been a little
better? Well, the entrée was just right, but I noticed that my dinner roll
was rather hard. You could check up on the freshness. It's just a small
thing. Everything else was fine.''*

Debra zeroed in on the dinner rolls, and other guests reported
that theirs were also a little stale. She contacted the bakery chef,
arranged for a new batch, and continued with her calls to help her
hotel set the pace for constantly improving its service.

The best way to reinforce and improve any relationship is to stop
and take stock. Whether it's with a customer, a colleague, a spouse,
or a friend, find out exactly where you stand and make improvements where needed. When you want to improve any kind of
relationship, you must take the time to ask for sincere, candid,
complete feedback about how you can make things better.

Frequently, feedback comes your way without even asking for it.
It may be of a critical nature, and may be couched in harsh terms.
When you hear criticism, it's important to immediately let the
other party know that you welcome the comments. That doesn't
mean that you will necessarily agree with them or find them valid.
The important thing is to keep the communication channels open
and show the other person that you respect his viewpoint.

I recommend a two-step dialogue. First, say something like,

**''I'm really glad you're telling me this, and I do want to know
how you feel. Thanks for being comfortable enough to tell me
what's on your mind.''**

Then follow up by asking for specifics. Don't dismiss the criticism after hearing the generalities. Instead ask for more.

"Please help me understand why you feel that way. What did I do to cause your reaction? I want to be able to watch for it myself in the future."

Customer service mavens, employee productivity counselors, and family therapists constantly remind us to ask how we can improve our relationships. That's good advice. **How you ask** is almost as important as asking. Presume that you could do a better job in some area of your relationship and then ask exactly what that area is. Don't ask if things are OK; ask how you can make them better.

QUICK REFERENCE

What you can do right now:

Make it a habit to ask at least one relationship-improving question every single day.

Instead of saying,

"Are you feeling pretty good about our marriage these days?"

Say,

"What's one thing I can focus on to be a better marriage partner for you?"

Instead of saying,

"Are you happy with our service?"

Say,

"How could we improve our service for you?"

Instead of saying,

"Have you been pleased with my accomplishments since you promoted me?"

Say,

"I feel good about my accomplishments since my promotion, and I want to do even better. What are two or three things I can focus on to exceed your expectations?"

Instead of saying,

"Was everything satisfactory?"

Say,

"How can I do a better job for you?"

33. So, What CAN You Do?

You work at an airline ticket counter. An upset woman approaches and explains that she is on her way to visit an ailing grandparent but has lost her ticket. She asks you for a refund.
Say out loud to yourself:

"No, I can't issue you a refund for the ticket. You'll just have to fill out a lost ticket application and wait. You probably won't get an answer for three to four weeks."

Now, say:

"What I can do is issue a new replacement ticket and charge it to your credit card. Then I'll help you with the lost ticket application and forward it to our research department."

Which approach is likely to make your agitated passenger feel that you are working cooperatively toward a positive solution? Which will make her feel even more upset?

One morning while my wife and I were visiting a resort, we decided to have lunch a little early and headed down to the poolside terrace restaurant shortly before noon. The place was empty. No one else was seated, and a busboy was arranging silverware on the tables. The hostess saw us waiting at the entryway and approached with a smile, saying, "We'll be open and ready to begin serving lunch in just a few minutes. I can seat you then."

The first thing that ran through my mind was, "If you're going to be open in just a few minutes, why don't you just let us go in and sit down at one of those empty tables and wait?" I probably would have argued the point with her had she used the approach I'm more used to hearing: "The restaurant is closed now and we won't be open for a while. I can't seat you until then."

What she said carried the exact same meaning as the more common negative version. Her approach, though, informed us in a completely positive manner, stressing what she **could** do rather than what she couldn't. Instead of arguing or creating a conflict, Julie and I went to wait in the lounge and enjoy a drink. A few other couples had been greeted with her smile and positive statement, and they had also headed for the lounge to enjoy tropical drinks. That one hostess had used Power Talking—a positive rephrasing of a negative statement. The end result was that we were all happy to wait, her busboys and other staff members were able to prepare for lunch without interference, and the bar did some extra business!

For every "can't" statement, there's a "can." The negative "can't" version immediately erects a roadblock and creates a conflict with the listener. Compare the effect of "We won't be open this weekend and I'm afraid I can't get your order ready until Monday afternoon" with "We will be open again on Monday and I'll be glad to have your order ready that afternoon." The positive version is easier to understand. It also projects a much more friendly, cooperative, helpful impression.

I noticed how a flight attendant described entree choices on a recent flight to Chicago. To passengers in the front of the cabin, he offered lasagna, chicken, and beef tips. When he reached my row, the beef was gone. He said,

"Mr. Walther, I can offer you the lasagna entree, which gets lots of compliments, or the chicken dish, which I particularly like myself. Which do you prefer?"

What he didn't say is, "Oh, I'm so sorry, we're all out of beef, I can't offer that to you." By positively describing the alternatives he *did* have available, I felt happy about the choices.

Always choose to use the positive version of a negative statement. Tell people what you *can* do, not what you *can't*. They'll understand you more easily and feel better about what you've told them.

QUICK REFERENCE

What you can do right now:

Whenever you start telling someone what you can't do, change your focus and substitute a statement indicating what you can do.
Instead of saying,

"I can't give you a riverview room tonight; I'll have to put you in a city view for tonight and move you tomorrow."

Say,

"I can give you a city view room tonight and then have you moved into a riverview room tomorrow. That way you'll get to enjoy both views."

Instead of saying,

"I can't answer that question for you myself. I'll have to go check with one of our customer service people and get back to you later."

Say,

"I can help you with that question by talking to our customer service department and getting a definite answer. I'll contact you this afternoon to let you know exactly where things stand. What time would you like me to call?"

Instead of saying,

"Here's what I can't do."

Say,

"Here's what I can do."

34. Breaking the Language Barrier

ONE of your customers is very upset about a recent order. In a highly emotional state, he calls you and starts spouting off.
Say out loud to yourself:

"Well, Chris, it looks like you have a problem. What do you expect me to do about it?"

Now, say this:

"Chris, it's clear that we have a challenge here. Let's work together and solve it."

Which approach is likely to move you toward a solution and create a cooperative atmosphere with Chris?

Part of my training work involves showing organizations how they can do a much better job when dealing with upset customers. One of my assignments involved the elite team of US WEST Cellular's Customer Service representatives known as the Retention Group. Their job is to "save" customers who are so unhappy that they've threatened to cancel their cellular phone accounts. I "met" Chris B. on my first day of monitoring calls with my new client.
Everyone in the Customer Service Call Center had either been

yelled at by Chris B. or had heard animated stories about his tantrums, demands, and verbal abuse. Almost everyone hoped to avoid handling Chris's calls because he was totally unreasonable.

Then along came Mary Hatcher. Her tone of voice, demeanor, and superb language skills reassure you that everything's going to be OK. Mary makes things right.

By the time his call was transferred to Mary, Chris B. had already been complaining (vigorously!) for two years about US WEST Cellular's service. She'd heard plenty of stories about him and decided to make him her "special person." Mary determined that one of her professional challenges would be to turn this irascible customer around.

The first time Chris was transferred to her, Mary got personal:

"Chris, I'm familiar with your situation, and I am going to help you. Here's what I've been wondering: How could our service be so horrible, and yet you still keep doing business with us? Perhaps there's something else that you feel unhappy about. If you're having troubles in other areas, the last thing I want to do is contribute to your discomfort."

He was taken by surprise. She had immediately cut through the usual business façade to uncover the root of the problem.

Chris opened up and explained that his business life was a mess. He had problems in his relationships with employees. He wasn't getting along with his partner. Chris was doing poorly on many fronts. His favorite outlet was his car phone, where he could call Customer Service and unleash a toll-free tirade at someone he'd never have to face.

Chris was a specialist at erecting dividing barriers. His approach was:

"I'm the poor mistreated customer, you're the big rich company making money off me, and you don't understand what it's like to be on my side of the table. What are you gonna do to make up for my mistreatment?"

Mary is a specialist at dissolving barriers. Her approach is to get on the customer's side. In fact, she describes her position as being a Customer Advocate. Her language is filled with impediment-dissolving, team-building phrases.

"We do have an uncomfortable situation here. **Let's work together and solve this."**

Instead of permitting a verbal barrier to separate her from the customer, she dissolves it. Rather than trying to convince the customer he's wrong, she validates his feelings and moves ahead.

"I understand why you feel that way. You have a right to expect superior service. Let's find out what's going on so we can fix it."

Mary's approach works. With her words alone, she showed Chris B. that there was no barrier dividing them. She aligned with him, on his side, and he calmed down. Other Customer Service reps started reporting that he was actually sounding nicer when he called them. Mary succeeded in turning Chris B. around by deciding to dissolve the barrier that he imagined was dividing them.

Most conflict situations involve imagined barriers. When people are working together, on the same side of the table, there's no confrontation. The first challenge in reducing conflicts is to dissolve those barriers. You must show you aim to be a partner, not an adversary.

Be careful to avoid pronouns that contribute to the me/you schism. Use "we" and "us" rather than "you" and "I" to show that you view your relationship as a partnership.

Be sure to point out any common ground you share with your counterpart. Help the other person see that you truly are empathetic. Once you establish common ground with someone, they're much more likely to treat you as a problem-solving partner instead of an adversary.

Peacemakers like Mary Hatcher are masters at using conflict-reducing language. The principles they use are easy to master, and you'll most likely have an opportunity to use them today. Use words that show your counterpart that you want to dissolve barriers and work together.

<u>*QUICK REFERENCE*</u>

What you can do right now:

When you're involved in a conflict, use your language to show that you're intent on working **with**, not **against** the other person; show that you and your counterpart are on the same side of the table.

Instead of saying,

"It's your problem, what do you expect me to do about it?"

Say,

"We share this challenge, let's solve it together."

Instead of saying,

"Here's what you'll have to do."

Say,

"Here's what we can do."

Instead of saying,

"I understand what you want. But I must adhere to my policies."

Say,

"We share some important common goals. Let's see how we can work together."

35. *You're Invited!*

A group of neighbors has decided to contest a local landfill operator's request to extend his operating permit and triple the site size. You want the dump closed. It's going to take money. Your neighborhood association meets to decide how you will proceed.

Say out loud to yourself:

"This is going to cost a lot of money and you'll all have to make donations. You're also going to have to get others in the neighborhood to contribute, too, unless you can come up with a better idea."

Now, say:

"We're going to need a lot of money to succeed. We can ask everyone for cash contributions or we can hold some kind of fund-raising event like a big garage sale and invite the whole neighborhood to participate. Or we can do something else altogether. What are some other approaches we can consider?"

Which sounds like the tactic that will generate the most cooperation? Which is almost sure to fail?

One challenge I regularly face as a speaker is getting my audience back in the room after each coffee break. Typically, the seminar organizer or the client's Meeting Planner schedules 15 minutes for coffee at some point during the program. This usually drags out to 25 or 30 minutes, until I remind the client that we have a lot of ground to cover and suggest that he reassemble the audience.

Then the Meeting Planner goes into the foyer, where everyone is munching sweet rolls and guzzling coffee. He tries unsuccessfully to get the crowd moving back in, and finally stands on a chair and shouts, "We're running late. You'll have to return to your seats now."

I've found a much more effective Power Talking approach. Just before it's time to begin a break, I say to my audience:

"Everything is set for our coffee break now, and I'd like you to decide how we'll handle it. We can make it a long break that drags out to 25 or 30 minutes, or we can get right back to these Power Talking techniques and resume our program in exactly 15 minutes. Please raise your hand if you prefer . . ."

My audiences always choose the shorter break. They didn't come to drink coffee; they want ideas and strategies that they'll be able to put to work—and benefit from—right away. I also make a point of saying, "My watch reads 12 minutes past 10:00 right now, so we'll start again at 10:27. Enjoy the refreshments, and we'll resume at 10:27." (My experience has shown that for some reason people pay more attention to odd times. If you schedule a meeting to resume at 10:27, you'll have more people there on time than if you schedule it for 10:30.)

Still, human nature seems to include a herding instinct. Everybody waits for someone else to start moving back into the presentation room. At my seminars I've found that I'm the best person to play that role. At about 10:25 I move out to the foyer and start the herd moving. Instead of calling out, I approach four or five different clusters of people who are talking to each other and say, "I invite you to bring your coffee back into the ballroom; we're just about to resume."

There are two key elements of my audience-assembling technique that make it effective. First, the participants "own" their course of action. I don't dictate what they'll do, I let them choose. Second, I consciously use the word "invite." Nobody likes orders or mandates. Everyone likes an invitation. If I were using the more common audience reassembling techniques, people would be thinking,

"Oh, gee, do we have to go back in already?"

Instead, these same people look back at me and say,

"Oh, how nice. An invitation. We accept!"

This approach works every time. After all, the audience did come to get as many ideas as possible. I'm using Power Talking techniques to help ensure that they get maximum value from the program.

Think of the situations you face in your work and daily life. When you want to encourage cooperation, give the other person a role in choosing among options, and then "invite" him or her to follow through.

Isn't it odd that we so often use the phrase "have to" when we're inviting somebody to cooperate with us? Those words suggest that the other person has no choice, that the action we're about to describe is mandatory and quite possibly unpleasant.

Friends of ours recently said,

"You'll have to come over for dinner sometime soon."

We like them, and do want to join them, but it sounded more like a command than a gracious invitation. Soon after, I caught myself saying to other friends,

"We'll have to get together one of these weekends."

There again, an indication that socializing is more of an unwanted obligation than a preference. It's a lot more inviting to say,

"We'd like to get together with you next week. How 'bout going out for a movie and late dinner on Friday or brunch at our place on Sunday?"

To encourage cooperation, don't mandate that people do what you want them to. Invite them to choose among options, so they "own" their preference.

QUICK REFERENCE

What you can do right now:

When you want others to cooperate with you, "invite" them to do so and give them a choice about what they'll do.

Instead of saying,

"To be considered, you'll have to take this form, fill it out completely, and then bring it back in the morning."

Say,

"You can take this form home overnight and complete it at your convenience. Then I invite you to come back and drop it off in the morning."

Instead of saying,

"You'll have to send the whole unit back to the Regional Service Center to get it repaired."

Say,

"**You can either send the unit to the Regional Service Center or take it to a dealer. Which is more convenient for you?**"

Instead of saying,

"Here's what you'll have to do."

Say,

"**I invite you to choose the approach that will work best for you.**"

36. *I Recommend*

You sell life insurance and are talking with a young couple about their needs. Their first child is due in a few months, and the husband plans to buy a substantial term-life policy. You believe that he should also carry a term policy on his wife.

Say out loud to yourself:

"One other thing you might possibly want to consider is buying a policy to cover your wife. Although her health is excellent right now, you never know what might happen to her during childbirth."

Now, say:

"**It's wise of you to provide protection in case you personally aren't able to generate income for your family. Considering the possibility of complications during childbirth, I recommend that you secure temporary protection covering your wife as well.**"

Which approach is more likely to catch your prospective customer's interest and show that you are genuinely concerned for his welfare? Which is more likely to result in a sale?

That was no hypothetical example; it's exactly what my insurance agent said to me when I recently bought my first insurance policy. I'd always been dead set against buying insurance—until we learned that our first child was on the way.

When I was a kid, my dad offered simple advice (to anyone who'd listen) for dealing with life insurance salespeople. He'd say,

". . . and I always tell them I'll buy whatever they suggest, in the amount they think is best, so long as they pay every single premium, including their own commissions."

After hearing Dad often repeat his "funny" strategy at dinner gatherings as part of his party repertoire, I learned a clear—and erroneous—lesson about life insurance salespeople: "Don't ever buy anything from them. They're just after commissions."

I felt a lot different when Julie and I found that we were about to become parents. I decided it was finally time for me to have insurance protection for her and our baby. I reluctantly made the big jump and actually asked for an appointment with a life insurance salesman! I hadn't considered buying a policy for Julie, too, but did so after hearing the salesman's recommendation.

After buying the two policies, we decided to have our yard landscaped to include a nice play area for the baby. The salesman, after "closing" our landscaping sale, said,

"It's a very small additional investment, and I do recommend that you have us install landscape fabric underneath the ground-cover plantings and decorative mulch. That will prevent 95% of all weeds and will make sure that you're able to enjoy this landscaping without having to pull weeds every weekend."

We bought the landscaping fabric.

My life insurance salesman and the landscaper both used a common approach: They "recommended" a course of action.

*   *   *

"Recommend" is an amazingly powerful word. Whatever your occupation, you sell ideas to others all day long. Whenever you're selling, make strong use of the word "recommend."

I was hired to train a group of sales professionals at Resort Condominiums International in Indianapolis, a company that arranges for time-share vacation exchanges. One of their goals was to encourage callers to renew their memberships early and for longer terms. As I began the training sessions, I noticed that the phone reps commonly used an approach like:

> "Oh, and say, incidentally, while I've got you on the line, I notice that your membership will be expiring in another few months, so you might want to start thinking about getting that renewed. And while you're at it, one thing you might possibly want to consider is the cost savings from getting a three- or five-year extension instead of just a single year. Would that perhaps be of interest to you?"

I urged them to stop being so tentative and instead use the C.P.R. sales formula, a sales-closing technique I wrote about in *Phone Power*. Many readers have reported that it works wonderfully and helps them establish positive relationships with their customers.

First, *C*onsult with the customer and ask about his future plans. Does he enjoy using his exchange privileges? Does he have lifetime ownership of his time-share condo? Does he like to cut down on paperwork and save money?

Next, the reps *P*ersonalize the benefits of a multiyear renewal for that individual caller. They show the member that, considering his personal situation and interests, a multiyear renewal is a better way to go.

Finally, the rep uses the word *R*ecommend to "close the sale."

> "Mr. Volwiler, in your situation I recommend the five-year renewal plan. You mentioned that you do plan to continue using your exchange privileges, and that you don't want to be bothered with the annual mailings and calls reminding you that your membership is about to expire. With the five-year plan, you'll be renewed, with exchange privileges, for five full years. There's no annual paperwork to bother with and you can't possibly forget to renew each year. I recommend

that we put that through now. Which credit card shall I charge it on for you?"

Soon after the training session, one of the R.C.I. telephone reps called my office and exclaimed,

"It works! It's magic. I've been making sure I say 'recommend' in every call, and my sales closing rate is up by 25%."

"Recommend" isn't magic. And it does work. It works because it's a behavioral trigger. In the case of a salesperson, it's easy to get off track and focus on your own needs rather than the customers'. You may start thinking about the sales contest, your product training, your commission checks, and everything except what matters most: your customers' needs.

Using the word "recommend" reminds salespeople that their role is to act as the customers' partner. The R.C.I. rep's success didn't stem from his use of a magic word. It was a result of focusing on the customer, asking about his needs, and matching them with the benefits of R.C.I.'s long-term renewal plan by recommending.

Make "Recommend" an important part of your closing argument when selling a product, service, or idea. By practicing the C.P.R. approach and emphasizing the "recommend" step, you will be putting your concentration right where it belongs: on the other person's welfare.

QUICK REFERENCE

What you can do right now:

Whenever you set out to "sell" an idea, service, or product, focus on the benefits to the other person and use the word "recommend" to close the sale.

Instead of saying,

"Would you be interested in renewing?"

Say,

"Based on what you've told me, I recommend that you renew now and avoid the September 15 dues increase."

Instead of saying,

"I want to sell you . . ."

Say,

"I recommend that you purchase . . ."

Instead of saying,

"One thing you might possibly want to consider is to . . ."

Say,

"I recommend that you . . ."

37. *What Sounds Fair to You?*

YOUR neighbor has two large cedar trees on his side of the property line that separates your two houses. One tree looks like it's dying. Since it provides privacy for your deck, you want to keep it alive. He's shown little interest in taking action, so you call in a tree service and are told that a deep-root fertilizer injection will cost $150. You think your neighbor should pay, since it's his tree.

Say out loud to yourself:

"Look, you don't seem to care much about saving your cedar tree. It's pretty obvious that it's about to die. I called a tree service to get their advice. They say it'll cost $150 to fertilize it and I think you should take responsibility to keep it alive."

Now, say:

"I've noticed that the big cedar tree isn't doing very well. I know you're busy, so when I saw all the brown needles, I went ahead and called in a tree surgeon to find out if it can be saved. They say it'll cost about $150. The tree is on your property and we both benefit from the privacy it provides. What do you think would be a fair way to handle the expense?"

Which sounds like the approach that will promote a favorable outcome you're both going to be happy about? Which will make your neighbor think about putting up a tall fence and suggesting that you keep your nose on your own side of it?

Donna, a manager at a well-known Japanese office copier company, called my office to inquire about purchasing *Phone Power* audio and video tapes for all of her dealers. She wanted to help the independent retailers use effective telemarketing to sell copiers and supplies. This is an excellent strategy for many companies that rely on a network of independent dealers and distributors. When you help your dealers become more profitable, they buy more of your products as they succeed and their business grows.

From our first phone conversation, I felt that Donna would be difficult to deal with. She was intent on getting a special price on everything. I respect people who want to get the best possible value, but in her case there was something overly pushy about her approach. I explained that she would receive a 30% discount if her order totaled 250 or more individual tapes. She wanted 225, which qualified her for a 25% discount. She eventually placed an order for 250 items. I felt confident sending her the tapes along with an invoice, since the company is a very large and reputable one.

Three months later the invoice remained unpaid, though Donna had advised me repeatedly that it was "in the process" of being handled. Then along came a box containing 25 of the tapes. Her handwritten note said,

"I'm returning these 25 tapes for credit. Please reissue the invoice and it will be paid promptly."

My first reaction was to think to myself:

"What a con. She really only wanted 225 in the first place. She sat on the bill for three months, sent back the 25 that had qualified her for the lower price break, and now she expects me to give her a full credit for them so she'll still get the 30% discount on her 225. She's not going to get away with this!''

Here I was, getting all worked up over her attempt to take advantage of me. I thought of writing a "What kind of fool do you think I am?" letter. Then I thought of confronting her on the phone and telling her she wouldn't get away with her cheap tricks. And then I stopped for a minute and calmed down. The total amount of money at stake was a little less than $200. And I didn't really know that she wanted to take advantage of me, I just assumed it based on my reading of her personality.

I realized that the $200 wasn't my concern, I just wanted to be treated fairly. She was holding all the cards, though, since she hadn't yet paid a cent. Was the extra money my top priority? No. My real objectives were to: (1) Feel good about the transaction, (2) Keep the door open for a future relationship with the company, and (3) Get paid. All of those objectives were contingent upon her feeling good about working with me. Rather than writing a nasty letter or having a telephone confrontation, I decided to use a Power Talking approach. In situations like this one, good questions get you a lot further than strong statements.

I called Donna the next morning and said:

"Hello, Donna. I got the 25 tapes you sent back. Thanks for packing them up so carefully. They were in fine condition. I also got your note asking for a corrected invoice. I'd like your advice. Your original invoice included a 30% discount, based on 250 tapes. If you had ordered only 225 in the first place, you would have earned a 25% discount. I don't charge any restocking fee or other penalty for handling your return, and I have been waiting for three months to get your payment. Please tell me what you think would be the fairest way to handle this."

Presented with these facts, she considered for a moment and said,

''Well, I'd like the 30% discount, of course, but I guess the fairest thing would be for you to re-invoice me at the 25% discount.''

If she had insisted that the 30% discount was fair, I would have issued the new invoice without quibbling. As it was, I sent her a bonus gift with her invoice since I felt good about working with her.

The point is this: Almost everyone will treat you fairly if you give them a chance. Power Talkers keep the big picture, long-run view in mind. They don't sweat the small stuff. They think of the relationship. What counts in the end is feeling good. If you win the extra $200 and create an unhappy customer who feels she's been treated unfairly, it's not worth it. If you trade one minute of happiness for a minute of thinking mean, nasty thoughts about someone, you lose. Instead of confronting other people, work with them.

QUICK REFERENCE

What you can do right now:

Whenever you feel that people are about to treat you unjustly, appeal to their own sense of fairness. In the few cases where they proceed to act unfairly, forget about it.

Instead of saying,

> "You people replaced my brakes three weeks ago and now they've developed a new squeaking sound. Don't try to tell me that it has nothing to do with your work. I expect you to repair it."

Say,

> **"You did a nice job replacing my car's brakes three weeks ago. Now I've begun noticing a squeaking sound that wasn't there before I brought it in. What would be the fairest thing to do about it?"**

Instead of saying,

> "I lost my receipt, but I bought this lawn trimmer from your store less than a month ago. Now it's already broken. I still have the box it came in, with your store name on it, and I demand that you give me a refund."

Say,

"A month ago I bought this lawn trimmer from your store, and unfortunately it's already broken. I do have the original box with your store name on it and I don't have the receipt. What do you think would be the fairest way to handle this?"

Instead of saying,

"I know my rights, and I demand that you take care of this my way."

Say,

"Considering the facts, what would be the fairest way to handle this?"

38. Let's Look at This Another Way

As Sales Manager, you're given the task of selecting a new office furniture system for your Sales Department. After evaluating several suppliers, you decide that a movable cubicle design is best, and you select one with four-foot-high partition walls. Before signing the purchase order, the Facilities V.P. asks that you review your recommendation with her. She says, "It all looks fine except I disagree with your choice of partitions. Those short ones just don't give enough privacy. We should definitely go with the six-foot-high walls."

Say out loud to yourself:

"Cynthia, I disagree. The six-foot-high partitions cut people off from each other, and that creates a less cohesive feeling in the department. With all that isolation, productivity is bound to fall."

Now, say:

"I understand that you favor higher partitions, Cynthia, and I'd like to consider another point of view. True, the taller partitions create a more private atmosphere, and that can be good in many situations. Other Sales Managers have reported that their Supervisors find it more difficult to lead when they're cut off from their employees. In other words, the privacy of higher walls can lead to lower productivity. With our profit goals in mind, we need to consider that factor, too."

Which approach will lead to more cooperative dialogue? Which will result in each party digging in her heels and defending her own choice?

As Co-chair of a major convention's planning committee, one of my jobs was to promote innovative thinking from committee members. One of them, Jason, had a reputation for zany, inspired brainstorms.

This particular convention has always begun with a Friday-afternoon opening "Welcome" speech, followed by a brief cocktail reception, and then "Dinner on Your Own." Participants are supposed to have an early dinner, get a good rest, and then wake up alert and ready to roll when the program starts early Saturday morning.

In past years the Friday-night activities have created lots of complaints. The early arrivals at the cocktail party think of the fancy hors d'oeuvres as their dinner. Late arrivals find long lines and empty hors d'oeuvres trays. So good old Jason said,

"I know! Since the convention is in L.A., right near the beach, we'll have a beach party. We'll serve hamburgers and beer, play Beach Boys tunes, and everyone will get plenty to eat. It will cost a lot less than those fancy canapés, too."

The committee agreed that Jason had a wonderful idea, and he immediately went to work making the arrangements. Two months later, the Association's President heard about it. My Co-chair and I both received urgent messages on our answering machines:

"I totally disagree with this Beach Party thing. It's got to be stopped. I don't want everybody out partying late and then stumbling in, all hung over, for our Saturday-morning sessions."

I felt resistant as soon as I heard the third word of his message. I thought to myself,

"He appoints a committee, gives us a job, and we do it beautifully. Then he comes along two months later and tells us that what we've done is all wrong. He can plan his own convention!"

My Co-chair, Janet, acted as peacemaker. I don't think she knows the word "disagree." She doesn't use it, and as a result, people listen to her.

"George, I understand what he's concerned about, and this is another point of view we need to consider. He has a good point about the drinking and late partying. We don't want people to feel fuzzy when they come in to that kickoff session first thing in the morning. Still, Jason's idea sounds like a lot of fun."

We realized that the President didn't object to the Beach Party itself; he was concerned about promoting late-night rowdiness. Our real challenge was to find a way to have fun Friday night, let Jason know that we appreciated his creativity, and ensure that everybody would be fresh in the morning.

It didn't take Janet long to come up with the solution: Have the Beach Party, issue each person two drink tickets rather than hosting an open bar, and close it all down at 10:00. That plan would meet every objective.

When she talked with the President, Janet didn't say,

"The Committee disagrees with your idea of canceling the Beach Party."

Instead she began,

"We understand your concern about late-night partying, and we agree that that's not what we want. Instead of just canceling the Beach Party, let's consider some other options."

It looked like we were all going to have a good (but not too good) time . . . until the local chapter's liaison said he **disagreed** with the revised plan.

Nobody wants to be condemned or judged unfavorably; they stiffen, resist, and become combative when told that you "disagree" with them. It's a good term to avoid if you want to promote cooperation with other people.

Tune in "Mr. Rogers' Neighborhood" on PBS, and notice how Fred Rogers promotes nonjudgmental thinking in children. He actively fosters the idea that many people can have different viewpoints and interpret facts uniquely. Taking his "friends" (young viewers) on a museum tour, Fred says,

> **"And what do you see in that painting? It looks like some kind of chicken to me. You might see a dove, or some other bird, or something else altogether. Everybody has different ideas."**

You'll never hear Mr. Rogers criticize anybody else's idea or put it down. Unfortunately most of us aren't naturally in Mr. Rogers' frame of mind when it comes to negotiating or settling a dispute. It's best to avoid "disagree" and similar terms. Though you may not mean it that way, the other guy is likely to "hear" that you are judging him and labeling his way of thinking as wrong.

Validate others' views and let them exist alongside your own. Instead of saying, "I disagree with you," you'll find people much more cooperative when you say, "I understand your view, and I have another interpretation I'd like to discuss."

QUICK REFERENCE

What you can do right now:

Rather than suggesting that someone else's viewpoint is less valid than your own, accept new ideas and let them coexist alongside yours. Then tap the merits of both approaches and come up with an even stronger alternative.

Instead of saying,

"I disagree with your selection of our official rental car company. Your choice is too expensive."

Say,

"I understand your preferred selection of our official rental car company. Considering our budget constraints, let's talk about some of the other options, too."

Instead of saying,

"I think you're wrong about that paint color. A black bathroom is nauseating."

Say,

"I understand that you like the idea of a really 'different' color scheme for the powder room. Black paint would be one way to do it, and there are some other approaches that could get similar results, too."

Instead of saying,

"I disagree with you."

Say,

"I understand, and I'd like to consider some more viewpoints."

POWER TALKERS . . .

VI. Speak Decisively

When you listen to a Power Talker, you hear someone who gets to the point, does away with unnecessary verbiage, and says exactly what he means. There's so much vague, beat-around-the-bush talk these days that it's a real relief to find someone who chops away wasted wordage and concentrates on communicating concisely and precisely.

Power Talkers are definite about what they say. They make commitments about what they **will** do, not what they'll see if they can perhaps possibly try and maybe do. They're always conscious of projecting an image of reliability.

Communication is a two-way street, and Power Talkers do a good job of listening actively in addition to expressing themselves well. They don't, however, trust that they understand everything just right the first time. They demonstrate their communication skills by taking the time to verify that what they understood is, in fact, what you think you said.

In this section you'll meet people who manifest their reliability with their language. They show their communication skills by confirming their understanding when they're listening, and by using words efficiently and effectively when they're speaking.

39. *You Should?—Or You WILL?*

WHILE vacationing in the Caribbean, you decide to order a package of fresh tropical fruits and have it sent to your friends back home. The sales clerk says to you:

"Your gift package should get to Iowa in about a week or so."

Notice the difference if the clerk says:

"Your gift package will arrive in Iowa within five working days."

Which sounds like your friends are definitely going to get their fruit before it rots? Which version leaves you feeling rather indefinite about its arrival?

The salesman returning my phone call said,

"Like I said when I took the order, your screens should be ready in two weeks."

But I had ordered them two and a half weeks ago! The more I deal with people, the more convinced I am that the initial impressions you gain during your very first meeting are pretty darn reliable.

The screen company's fliers had been posted throughout my neighborhood, advertising "Any size screen measured and installed, $14.95." I called for an estimate well before Seattle's brief and wonderful summer began. The answering service operator told me that "Ned should call you back by the end of the day." He didn't. The next day I called again. The operator said, "Well, I don't know what to tell you. He should get back to you right after lunch." I knew he should, but didn't have any faith that he would.

After three days I wrote Ned off as yet another unreliable flake and called a different screen company for an estimate. After I had scheduled my new appointment, Ned finally called! Though I explained that I'd given up on him and called a competitor, he said he'd be in my neighborhood the next day and told me he'd stop by at noon.

He didn't. But he did show up at 4:30 and quickly measured all the windows. Figuring that Ned's prices were about the same as everyone else's, and he had already taken all the measurements, I gave him the order. He said they should be ready in two weeks.

After two and a half weeks without a word, I called and left a message. No callback. Another message. No callback. My third message was, "My screens are late. Return this call today or cancel my order." Ned did call me back, apparently oblivious to his promised (and missed) delivery dates. His old standard "should be ready in two weeks" rang hollow since we'd already passed the two-week point. Time marched on. On the one-month anniversary of our order, I left my final message for Ned:

"Tell Ned he can do whatever he wants with our screens. I'm going to find someone who can keep a promise and place a new order."

Ned called back, promising to arrive by 1:00 the next afternoon. He eventually arrived at 4:45 and discovered that some of the screens didn't fit quite right, altered them with the tools in his truck, and asked for his check as he headed out the door.

I followed Ned out to the driveway and said,

"Ned, I'd like you to know what I think of your service. You took twice as long as you said you would. You ignored most of my repeated messages to call. And you didn't honor one single commitment you made to me. I don't feel that you've treated me well as a customer."

Hardly noticing my obvious frustration, Ned only said,

"Hey, I couldn't help it. With this heat wave, what do you expect? Ninety-nine percent of my customers are happy, and there's always one percent that won't ever be pleased, no matter what. What do you want? I'm not gonna grovel."

I then realized that I had been wrong. Ned hadn't broken any commitments; he had never made any. He never said he **would** do anything, just that he **should.**

QUICK REFERENCE

What you can do right now:

Commit to specific dates, times, and amounts. "Should" avoids commitment and sounds wishy-washy.

Instead of saying,

"That should run about 40 or 50 bucks."

Say,

"Your charge will be $49.95."

Instead of saying,

"You should get this in just a few days."

Say,

"I will mail this first thing in the morning."

Instead of saying,

"We should get this done by . . ."

Say,

"We will get this done by . . ."

40. *Give Your Word and Then Beat It!*

You work part-time in a local quick-print shop. A customer brings in a large copying job and asks when it will be ready for pickup.
Say out loud to yourself:

"Well, I'll probably be able to have it for you later today. I'll shoot for, oh, probably about 4:00."

Now, say:

"I will have it ready for you today before 5:00."

If you were the customer, which statement would you consider more reliable? Which version is more convincing?

I was surprised when the Room Service waiter said, "We'll have your breakfast delivered to you in 20 minutes." I admit that I felt a little irritable after my delayed flights, late arrival, and short rest the night before.

I awoke at 7:00 A.M. and immediately called in my Room Service order. The 20-minute delivery time I had been quoted allowed me just enough time to shower, get dressed, watch the 7:30 news headlines as I ate, and be down in the seminar room by 8:00 to set up for my 9:00 keynote speech.

By 7:35 I was showered and dressed but still hungry. I called Room Service and asked about my breakfast. "It's on its way, that's all I can tell you." By 7:45 I felt impatient and angry. They had already taken twice as long as they'd promised. My morning routine was thrown off and I didn't like it. Each minute that I waited seemed like ten. Finally, at 7:51, the waiter arrived with my tray. The delay probably wasn't his fault, but I didn't greet him very cheerily. I told him that he was terribly late and grumbled about how much I resent the mandatory tips added to Room Service charges.

Was my 46-minute wait for breakfast unreasonable? Not really, except that I'd been promised delivery in 20 minutes. If the person who took my order had said, "Mr. Walther, I'll make sure you have your breakfast before 8:00," I would have been pleased that it was delivered a few minutes early.

My displeasure stemmed from the gap between my expectations and the hotel staff's performance. The larger that gap—when it's in the negative direction—the greater my dissatisfaction. If they had promised 45 minutes and delivered in 46, I would hardly have noticed. If they had promised a "10-minute express service" and delivered in 46, I would have been even more unhappy than I was. If they promised an hour and delivered in 46 minutes, I'd be pleased.

One of the surest keys to making people happy is to deliver more than you promise. If you call a mail-order company and purchase a sweater, you'll be delighted if it arrives within 10 days—providing they promised delivery within three weeks. If they said you'd have it in a week, you'll be unhappy when it arrives in 10 days. The customers' level of satisfaction is a result of the expectations created by the serving organization.

People count on us to deliver at least what we promise. They react favorably when we beat our promises and unfavorably when we fall short. Most often, we set others' expectations by telling them what we foresee happening. When someone asks you for a commitment, there are three responses you can offer:

1. Don't make a commitment—be vague:

"Well, I'll see what I can do, but I'm not really sure when I'll be able to finish the job. Probably toward the end of the week. We'll just have to wait and see."

Obviously this isn't going to create much support for your image as a reliable professional.

2. Make a hopeful commitment that you may not keep:

"I'll shoot for Wednesday afternoon."

If you finish on Thursday, instead, you've just created dissatisfaction.

3. Make a commitment that you will at least keep, and may well beat:

"I will finish the job before the end of the day, Friday."

Now, when you finish up on Thursday, you're a hero!

Jimmy Calano cofounded the world's fastest-growing, most-successful seminar organization, CareerTrack. I got to know Jimmy early in the company's history when I served as a consultant to their burgeoning telemarketing department. One reason for CareerTrack's enviable success record is the leaders' commitment to delivering more than they promise. When he's planning to send correspondence, Jimmy always makes it a practice to say, "I'll send it tomorrow," even though he intends to send it the same day. That way, if there's an unexpected delay, he'll still be keeping his word. Most of the time, though, he beats it, taking the other person by (pleasant) surprise.

George Patton's formula for success was similar:

"Always do more than is required of you."

The bottom line is this: Whenever you establish expectations for others, be certain that you'll at least live up to them. For best results, exceed them.

QUICK REFERENCE

What you can do right now:

Add a "safety cushion" whenever you make a commitment. Then delight the other person by doing your best to exceed the expectation you've created.

Instead of saying,

"I should be able to finish that report by, oh, let's say the 15th or so."

Say,

"I'll definitely have the report finished before the 17th."

Instead of saying,

"Your order should ship by Wednesday, or maybe Thursday. It kind of depends."

Say,

"Your order will ship before the weekend."

Instead of saying,

"I may be able to get to it by around 2:00 or 3:00."

Say,

"I will get to it before 5:00."

41. *I Think I Understand What You Think You Said*

YOU'VE just taken an order from one of your customers, and it's more complicated than usual. He has requested a special shipping address for this one purchase, and the delivery instructions are complex.

Say out loud to yourself:

"OK, I'm pretty sure I've got that right."

Now, say:

"Let's verify those directions to be sure I understood you clearly."

Which version demonstrates to your customer that you really care about getting things right? Which order is more likely to go astray, get delayed, and ultimately lead to an unhappy buyer?

I really enjoy those General Foods International Coffee flavors that come in little 4.5-ounce cans and cost a lot. "Suisse Mocha" and "Café Français" are my favorites, and at our house, we go through many cans every month. I wish the company would sell the same stuff in larger cans at a lower cost per serving. It bugs me that a substantial portion of the small cans' price goes to pay for the container itself. If they sold the product in five-pound cans at my local warehouse store, I'd happily buy it.

You've probably noticed that many of the foods you purchase today, and many other products, for that matter, have a toll-free telephone number printed somewhere on the packaging. Companies like General Foods rely heavily on customer input so they can make product improvements, clear up confusion, and respond to rumors and crises. If you open a can of food and find flecks of metal inside, the manufacturer wants to know about it immediately. Prominently displaying their 800 numbers is a front-line defensive strategy for organizations that want to hear about—and solve—potentially costly problems before they escalate.

As I waited for the microwave to boil my last cup from yet another Suisse Mocha can, I called the General Foods 800 number to ask if the company had considered selling its coffee in larger containers. A very courteous young man named Jerry at the General Foods Customer Service Response Center answered and sounded genuinely interested in my views. He stressed that input like mine was exactly what helps the company decide how to change and improve its products.

After explaining why only small cans are used (freshness!), and checking to see if there was anything else I wanted to comment about, he explained that his Marketing Department keeps track of which parts of the country call with what types of questions. He asked for my address and telephone number. After I told him, he said,

"Allow me to verify and make sure that I have this correct,"

and proceeded to repeat exactly what I had just told him.

His simple statement that he would verify my address showed me that he takes pride in performing his work professionally. General Foods must genuinely care about getting things right if they've taken the time to train their reps so carefully.

It's easy to think,

"Hey, what's the big deal? So the guy asked to verify an address. Why is that even worth mentioning in this book?"

The image you personally project to others and to yourself is a composite of many small elements. General Foods' image is built from advertising messages, the colors its designers chose for the coffee can labels, the way the Customer Response Center staff answers your calls, and yes, even the way Jerry verified my address. Each element contributes to the overall impression.

The technique Jerry used to confirm my address information also delivered a message to himself. He said he was verifying "... to make sure I have this correct." The message he sent to himself was:

"I'm a professional. I get things right because I take the time and trouble to double-check even something simple like a mailing address."

I also noticed that his phrasing eliminated any possibility of my "hearing" that he questioned my communication abilities. Had I spoken inarticulately and garbled my words while chewing gum, Jerry might well have said,

"Gee, it's so hard to understand you. I better verify to make sure you were saying what you meant to say."

He could have asked for verification in a way that I might interpret as an accusation that I wasn't speaking clearly. Jerry, however, took full personal responsibility for getting the address correct.

Professionals like Jerry inspire confidence and respect with everything they do, right down to the way they verify an address.

Take the extra step of verifying your communications with others to ensure that you also project that professional, follow-through image. And do it in a way that shows you acknowledge your responsibility for communicating clearly.

<u>QUICK REFERENCE</u>

What you can do right now:

Take an extra moment to verify that you have understood accurately. Do it in a way that shows you accept responsibility for getting the information correct.

Instead of saying,

"You're so hard to understand—I'm not sure I got that right."

Say,

"I want to verify that I understood you clearly."

Instead of saying,

"I think I've got that all straight. If I get lost along the way, I'll give you a call."

Say,

"Let's take a minute to be sure I have those directions all straight. That way I'll be sure to arrive right on time."

Instead of saying,

"I guess that about covers it. I think we understand each other."

Say,

"Let's verify that we're both in complete agreement by wrapping this up with a recap of our understanding."

42. Don't Take "No"—or "Yes"—for an Answer

Your neighbors have invited you over for a barbecue. The day before, you call to see what you may contribute.

Say out loud to yourself:

"Is there anything I can bring?"

Now, say:

"What's the best thing for me to bring?"

Which sounds like you really want to bring something? Which question is most likely to trigger the normal—though not necessarily true—response, "Nothing at all, just bring yourselves"?

One of the most challenging tasks any sales trainer faces is disciplining salespeople to stop asking Yes/No questions. Using multiple-choice and open-ended queries helps to uncover buying motivations.

One of my clients sells voice mail services for cellular phone customers. These portable phones are great, providing you're always available to answer calls. Most people who buy and use them do so because "being in touch" is vital in their business lives. While they are driving, mobile phone users are often talking on the phone, thus blocking incoming calls, unless they have a "call waiting" feature. In other words, people often don't get the constant availability they really want when they invest in a cellular phone.

That's where voice mail comes in. With this service, callers are always greeted in the cellular subscriber's voice. If he's already using the phone or has his phone turned off, the caller hears,

"Sorry, I'm either using my phone or am not available right now. Please leave a message after the tone and I'll get back to you shortly."

This service costs just a few dollars a month and tremendously increases the value of cellular phone service. Still, the Customer Service reps working for my client didn't do all that well selling voice mail service.

What were they doing? Asking Yes/No questions.

"Are you interested in signing up for voice mail service to go with your mobile phone?"

Of course most people said no without even understanding what voice mail is. Once they've heard a prospective customer say no, most salespeople get a little fainthearted, give up, and move on to the next call.

I was hired to train my client's telemarketing staff to do a better job of selling this valuable service. Our starting point was to focus on questions. After a short brainstorming session, we had two dozen good open-ended and multiple-choice questions scrawled out on flip chart pages, such as "How do you use the portable phone in your business" and "When people say they have trouble reaching you on your mobile phone, is it usually because you're away from the phone and don't answer, or because you're already using the phone, so they get a busy signal?"

After shifting away from Yes/No questions to the Open-Ended and Multiple-Choice varieties, sales statistics more than doubled. Many of the reps reported that once they asked the right questions, their customers quickly sold themselves on the benefits of using voice mail.

You ask questions to get information. Yes/No questions give you very little. When you want good information, ask good questions.

When your best friend comes home from the hospital after

minor surgery, you really want to know how you can help. If you ask a Yes/No question,

"Is there anything I can do?"

the answer will probably be no. To be a more helpful friend, use a different form of question:

"What's the one thing you'd most like me to do to help you get comfortable?"

Get in the habit of replacing Yes/No questions with multiple-choice and open-ended queries. They produce much more useful information for you to act upon.

QUICK REFERENCE

What you can do right now:

Whenever you ask someone a question, first ask yourself, "Is this a Yes/No question?" If it is, change it to the multiple-choice or open-ended variety.

Instead of saying,

"Is there anything I should get for you when I stop at the store?"

Say,

"What may I pick up for you when I stop at the store?"

Instead of saying,

"I'm considering hiring Mark for a position at my company. Does he have any particular strengths or weaknesses I should know about?"

Say,

"As I consider Mark for a position at my company, which of his personal strengths and weaknesses should I keep in mind?"

Instead of saying,

"Are there some features you really want in a new computer?"

Say,

"What are the features you really want in a new computer?"

Instead of saying,

"Do you have any questions?"

Say,

"What questions do you have?"

43. *Say It!*

YOU'RE being interviewed for a new job and the Personnel Director asks about your accomplishments at your previous employer.

Say out loud to yourself:

"Well, that's a really good question and I'm glad you asked it. First of all, one thing I'd like to say is that, generally speaking, my department was sort of a mess before I took over. Within six months, more or less, it ran fairly smoothly."

Now, say:

"My proudest accomplishment was reorganizing the department I led. It was very disorganized when I was promoted to the Manager position. Over the first six months we implemented a five-phase action plan that cut unnecessary paperwork by 30%."

Which sounds like the person you'd consider more seriously for any position? Who seems to be beating around the bush?

I sat in on one client's meeting with his attorney and was amazed at how little was said, and how many words it took to say it. The client wanted to know if it was legally permissible to tape record phone conversations between employees and customers. This is a complicated issue, as state and federal regulations may both come into play. Still, the answer should have come pretty close to "Yes" or "No."

Instead, the lawyer rambled on:

"Well, that's a very interesting issue you've raised, and I'd like to give you my views on it. Understand, of course, that these are just my opinions at this point in time. I would tend to think that—and keep in mind, of course, that this area is subject to a number of interpretations—it would be quite common to assume that certain legal considerations do color, or slant, an employer's ability to do so. Now, let me ask you something. What I would like to know is . . ."

I tuned out and so did the client. Why couldn't the lawyer just say, "Yes, if you have a beep tone on the line." Or, "No, not under any circumstances." Or even, "Yes and no: For calls to customers who are out of state, the more liberal federal regulations do permit taping; for intrastate calls, you may not record conversations under any circumstances."

I guess if you're paid by the hour—and thus by the word—it's advantageous to beat around the bush for a while. All those lawyer jokes must have sprung from clients' firsthand experiences. They're not all loquacious, of course. My own lawyer gets high marks for giving clear, concise answers. (Thank you, Scott!)

I'm not out to pick on lawyers; a lot of people talk a lot without saying much. I'll list some of my favorite pet peeves here, and you'll probably think of a dozen other examples to add.

At this point in time. Doesn't that mean "now"? I have a business associate who invariably uses this phrase. The only justification I can come up with is that he may think it sounds a little more fancy than "now." But it doesn't. It makes him sound self-important. For the phrase "at that point in time," substitute "then." Whenever you can say something in fewer, simpler words, do.

Can I ask you a question? You just did! Why make one question into two? When the time is right, go ahead and ask. You don't need to ask permission to ask a question.

Can I interrupt you? A poll of Americans' biggest communication beefs published in *USA Today* ranked unnecessary interruptions right at the top. The best strategy is always to hear the other person out and then respond. If someone is wandering away from the point, it's better to politely interject your comment without first asking permission.

I would tend to think that . . . Sounds wishy-washy. Say what you believe without first setting up a qualifying safety cushion to cover yourself in case your opinion proves unpopular or wrong.

I was going to say . . . This phrase adds nothing and may well undermine the impact of what the person proceeds to say. It's rather like "It was just a thought, and it may not be worth bringing up, but I guess I will anyway, so here's what I was going to say."

Kind of, sorta . . . There's a whole category of vague qualifiers that diminish the impact of what people have to say. These indefinite qualifiers add nothing to your meaning: dump them!

May I ask who's calling? Flying to a speaking engagement in Canada, I sat beside Gene Monroe, Vice Chairman of Huntsville, Alabama's, largest business-equipment dealer. He saw me working on the manuscript for this book and asked what it was about. As soon as I told him, he said,

> *"What I really hate is having someone ask if it's OK to ask who I am. I always say no. That really throws 'em. Why do they ask the question if they aren't prepared to deal with the answer?"*

Call screeners seem to give little thought to their questions about a caller's identity. If you're greeted with, "May I tell him who's calling?" and the secretary later returns to the line and advises you that he's in a meeting, don't you immediately suspect that you've been deemed Not Important Enough to be put through? A much more effective and courteous way to ask is to explain the benefit to the caller: "Please give me your name so I can prepare him for your call or schedule a callback."

I would say . . . Are you going to? Why not just say it? Is there an "if" upon which the statement is contingent? What does the conditional "would" contribute, anyway?

Can you spell your name? One of my favorites! I'm always tempted to answer, "Yes. In fact I learned how several years ago, and I've gotten quite good at it." What you really want to know is how the name is spelled, so I recommend asking your real question in a courteous fashion: "Please spell your name for me."

There's a great need for straight-shooting, get-to-the-point talk in business. Think of the phone charges, paper, postage, and computer time that we could save if people just said what they meant. And the meetings! I'm an advocate of standup meetings. I've heard waste-conscious managers say that all chairs should be removed before beginning routine staff meetings. It's just too easy to get settled in for a long session half-listening to people verbally wander. You can sit in a chair fairly comfortably for 60 to 90 minutes; you can stand on your feet for about half as long. People get to the point faster when they're on their feet.

Speaking economically and decisively doesn't just save time; it can also inspire confidence in your listener. When you use lots of unnecessary words, it can seem like you're trying to hide something, or like you're really not sure of what you're saying.

Customer Associates at Pacific Bell are trained to reinforce customers' purchase decisions with decisive, benefit-oriented statements. Rather than saying,

"I think it'll probably work out pretty well for you. Hopefully, that service should give you just about what you're after,"

trainers stress the importance of making unequivocal statements:

"This is going to be just right for you. I know you'll find the service to be exactly what you need."

The word, "hopefully," all by itself, undermines any chance of being heard as a decisive speaker.

"Hopefully this will change things,"

doesn't offer much hope. It's much stronger to say,

"This will improve your situation."

A Power Talker is not cold, unfriendly, stingy with words, or mechanical in his communication style. He's someone who does away with unnecessary verbiage, makes his point, and moves on.

There's a big difference between patiently comforting a friend who is in trouble and raising a question or making a point in business. A Power Talker is flexible and uses the communication style that's appropriate to the situation.

QUICK REFERENCE

What you can do right now:

Know what you want to say and say it!

Instead of saying,

"One thing I'd like to say is . . ."

Say it!

Instead of saying,

"Do you mind if I ask you a question?"

Ask it!

Instead of saying,

"Well, generally speaking, one thing I would sort of tend to think is . . ."

Say,

"I believe . . ."

POWER TALKERS . . .

VII. Tell the Truth

POWER Talkers prize integrity. People who are dishonest may feel that they get more rewards out of life than those who are always truthful. They may cheat to buy happiness. Though tangible wealth may contribute to happiness, material things are not the signs of true success. Many of the world's financially super-rich people are emotionally destitute. In the end, the good guys do win. Do you know any dishonest people who are truly happy?

Power Talkers let you know that they are 100 percent honest by eliminating integrity-busting phrases such as "To tell you the truth." When someone says, "Well, to be absolutely honest with you . . . ," don't you think to yourself, "Does that mean that he's usually not honest?"

In the chapters ahead, you'll be reminded of the powerful benefits of being consistently honest. You'll also see how difficult it is to conceal a streak of dishonesty. As a Power Talker, you constantly affirm your integrity with your choice of expressions and manner of speaking.

44. *To Be Honest with You*

YOU'VE just met an investment advisor who wants to win your trust and your business. You ask him about the performance of his own investment portfolio, and he responds,

> "Well, I have to tell you the truth, to be perfectly honest . . ."

Which way do you run?

In my first conversation with Mr. M., a promoter who booked me for a series of public seminars in Poughkeepsie, he said,

> *"We're working on booking the new Bardavon Opera House for your program. I have to tell you the truth, we could sell out all 1000 seats for each of the three seminars."*

I'm immediately wary when someone makes a point of prefacing supposedly truthful statements with phrases like, "I have to tell you the truth . . ." If a person is habitually honest, if his integrity is 100%, why would he need to make a point of explaining that he's about to tell the truth?

A month before the scheduled program date, he called me to explain that ticket sales were miserable:

> *"Well, to be completely honest with you, our marketing information in the computer was slightly off and we may have to start from scratch. Could we possibly push the date back a couple of weeks?"*

One peculiarity I noticed about this promoter was that he had no home phone number. In case of a last-minute flight interruption en route to an engagement, I want to be able to reach the meeting planner. Mr. M. said his home was his refuge; the phone rang enough during work hours. Later I learned that he didn't have a house. He lived in his parents' basement and used their phone! So much for this big-time promoter.

Each time I asked for a firm count of the audience size, his answer was evasive:

"Well, frankly speaking, anything could happen. There may be a last-minute surge of sales. Don't worry, we'll invite students at a local school to fill up all available seats."

Finally, the big day arrived! Julie and I flew to New York and were picked up at our Manhattan hotel in a somewhat shabby rented stretch limo. Mr. M. apologized,

"I'm sorry we had to pick you up with the car. Unfortunately, to tell you the truth, the corporate helicopter is taking one of our clients on a sightseeing trip today."

(Later it became clear that he and his company didn't even own a beat-up Ford Pinto, let alone a helicopter.)

"Well," I said, "the seminars begin first thing tomorrow morning. How many tickets did you end up selling?"

"Well, ah, to be completely candid, ah, I don't know the final figure, but ah, to tell you the truth, it looks like there may be only a couple of hundred."

"For each of the three seminars?"

"No, for all three seminars combined."

"Don't tell me that you've booked me into a 1000-seat opera house and we'll have less than a hundred people in each audience! It's going to look and feel like the program is a flop."

"Oh no, don't worry, we've moved the location to a nearby hotel's meeting room that'll be just the right size."

The next morning I walked into the meeting room, ready to set up my props and adjust the projector. There were only 25 seats. That turned out to be OK. Mr. M. had sold only 18 tickets!

Part of my agreement with the promoter was that the balance of my speaking fee would be paid before the program began. Standing outside the seminar room, he began patting his pockets when I asked for my check.

"Oh gee, to tell you the truth, I think I may have forgotten my checkbook."

My conversations with Mr. M. became interesting performances in themselves. I started to enjoy asking him for a simple, honest answer and then listening to him squirm and wriggle with some phrase that belied his innate dishonesty.

I did begin presenting the first of my three seminars without the promised payment, and explained that I would not begin the second one until he had visited the bank and secured a cashier's check.

I was surprised when, as I ended the first seminar three hours later, he returned with the strangest-looking check I've ever seen. Although it bore none of the customary pre-printed account information, it did have three different signatures scrawled on it, as well as a neatly affixed "certification label" in the upper left corner. It looked like a case of overkill, as if Mr. M. had said to some bank clerk friend:

"Look, to be perfectly honest, this speaker wants a certified check, but, well, to tell you the truth, I just won't have the funds until the end of the day. Could you maybe take one of those blank counter checks and stamp it a few times, and scribble some signatures on it, and stick some kind of label on it so it looks really official?"

The next morning, after completing the three seminars with a grand total of fewer than 100 in the combined audiences (just slightly shy of Mr. M.'s "honest" assurance of 3000), I went to three different branches of the bank on which the suspicious check had been drawn. Officers at each one looked at it skeptically and said they'd never seen a check quite like it. None would cash it.

It's sad, and true. Completely honest people are rare. Think of all the people you've known. There are a few who always do exactly what they promise, always tell the truth, and are completely trustworthy. And there are many whose honesty is well below 100%.

Even people who have a high sense of personal ethics use integrity-busting phrases. It's a habit that's easy to change—and well worth changing.

Be committed to complete honesty in your behavior and show it with your language. The rewards from establishing a reputation for 100% integrity last throughout your lifetime. Not only will others be much more willing to work with and trust you, you'll also enjoy the feeling of self-respect that results from knowing you are a person of unwavering character.

QUICK REFERENCE

What you can do right now:

When everything you say **is** totally honest, there's no need to alert anyone that you're about to tell the truth. Eliminate "integrity-busting" expressions that suggest you aren't always sincere and forthright.

Instead of saying,

"To be perfectly honest . . . ,"

BE perfectly honest.

Instead of saying,

"Well, to tell you the truth . . . ,"

ALWAYS tell the truth.

45. *Just Say No!*

A colleague at work asks you to pitch in and help him with a project. You're feeling pressured about your own workload and have no time to spare. Still, you don't want to disappoint your co-worker.

Say out loud to yourself:

"I'm awfully busy with my own work, John, but, well, I guess I could try to help you. I don't know if I can get to it, but I'll try and see what I can do."

Now, say:

"John, I'm completely committed to my own projects and cannot help with your assignment now. I suggest that you ask Tony. He's familiar with your department."

Which version are you likely to regret later on? Which is the more truthful approach?

My professional speaker colleagues don't generally like clients to videotape their presentations. When they do permit it, they normally charge a substantial fee. Speakers want to avoid the all-too-common nightmare of a client taping their presentations with poor-quality home video equipment, catching them on an off day, and then distributing the unedited tapes. Thousands may view them and conclude that a speaker isn't very good, based on that one bad tape.

In May 1990 I left my wife and our newborn daughter behind and flew to Detroit for a freebie. A member of my staff (since terminated!) had agreed to waive my fee for a seminar promoter, even though his was not a nonprofit organization—the only situation in which I'll give a free speech.

But I believe in keeping my word, and even though the client wasn't a nonprofit organization, he had been promised a free speech by my assistant, and I honored my employee's commitment. I didn't relish this engagement from the start, and I had made a commitment.

In the final week before the presentation, the promoter had called and offhandedly mentioned that he videotapes all programs for promotional use. Rather than asking for my permission, he used a ploy commonly attributed to slick, manipulative salesmen. "You don't have any problem with that, do you?" Instead of telling him how I really felt, I said it'd be OK. He agreed that I would be given the only master cassette of the tape and that brief clips from his copy would be used only for promotional purposes.

Immediately after hanging up, my inner voice said,

"Wait a minute, why are you agreeing to this? You don't want to go do this free speech in the first place; something smells fishy about the whole thing."

Upon my arrival at Detroit's Sheraton Southfield hotel, I found just what I had begun to suspect: a very low-budget operation. The promoter was arranging chairs, setting up tables, and attending to logistical details himself. At this point, though, I couldn't turn back. Once I'm on-site, my responsibility is to the audience. I knew that 650 people were looking forward to that evening's event.

An hour before starting time, a young man named Charlie walked in with his VHS camcorder. He was the promoter's long-time friend and had offered to tape all of the seminars in exchange for free tickets.

As it was, the program did go very well. The audience was attentive and responsive, the "video crew" unobtrusive, and I felt good about my performance. At the conclusion I received an enthusiastic ovation, autographed many books, and saw hundreds of happy audience members head for home, eager to put the seminar ideas into practice.

As the hotel staff began folding up the chairs and tables, I asked Charlie for my video master. He looked surprised and said it belonged to him, but offered to make me a copy. I firmly told him that the master copy was mine, and explained my agreement with the promoter. He said, "No, I keep the master. It's mine, but you may have a copy if you'd like."

Charlie was not a timid young man, and insisted quite firmly that the original master tape was his. I insisted that it wasn't.

Then Charlie came up with his hypocrisy jab:

"I've just been listening to your seminar, getting great ideas, and admiring you as a superb communicator. At this point, though, I feel that the way you're communicating with me is totally out of sync with what you've been saying during the speech."

And Charlie was absolutely right. After several minutes of our tense exchange, he "got me" with the truth. My communication behavior had been inconsistent with what I'd been saying on the platform. As a result, we were having a very uncomfortable exchange. Although we hadn't actually shouted, I had asked him to hand me the master so that I could stomp on it, thus ending the discussion about who would "own" it.

Our exchange turned the corner only after I responded to his hypocrisy charge:

"Charlie, you're right. I haven't communicated well with you. I haven't really been honest. Here's the truth: I feel taken advantage of. I didn't want you to tape me in the first place. I was advised just a few days ago that you would be here, and I should have insisted on adhering to my normal agreement that permits taping only with professional equipment, for payment of an additional fee. I haven't felt right about any aspect of your taping and should have denied permission right from the start."

Charlie's face relaxed and he smiled. "Now I understand," he said. "You should have told me that right from the start."

We finally agreed that he'd forward the original master to me after dubbing a copy for promotional use only. We called the seminar promoter over and reviewed our agreement together. And we ended up with a friendly understanding.

The lesson was an obvious one. When you don't want to say yes, don't. I had, and the result was a tense, charged atmosphere and temporary ill-will. Had I stuck to my convictions from the start, I could have avoided the entire confrontation.

When you halfheartedly agree to do something that you really don't want to do, you almost always regret it later. If you aren't sure you really want to do it, it's best to just say no.

While preparing the manuscript for this book, one of my neighbors called and asked me to help her with a "little project." She wanted help writing a letter to the real estate developer who's expanding our community. I'm concerned about the development issues she raised, and have already made many contributions to our neighborhood group. I was tempted to just go ahead and write the letter for her. By the time I'd have met with her, reviewed the draft, and so on, the "little project" would have taken away at least two hours from my much more important book-writing priority. So I said:

> "Sandy, my attention is fully dedicated to writing my new book right now. I know you'll do a fine job writing the letter on your own. No, I won't help you write it."

I felt so good about saying no! I didn't intend to be rude or uncooperative; I was simply drawing the line.

We all take on tasks and chores that we don't really want to do. The result is usually that we do them halfheartedly, feel bad about it, and regret that we said yes in the first place. It's much better to say no when that's what you really feel.

QUICK REFERENCE

What you can do right now:

Before you agree to do anything you're only half-sure you want to do, take a time-out. Decide if you'll be able to do a great job, enjoy doing it, and finish it without interrupting your other more important priorities. If you decide that you don't really want to do it, say no.

Instead of saying,

> "Well, I really don't have the time to help you, but I'll see if maybe I can squeeze in an hour or two for you."

Say,

> "No, I'm sorry. You'll be better off getting help from someone who can really get involved."

Instead of saying,

> "Gosh, it's an honor, and I don't know quite what to say. I'm not sure, but I guess I'll be able to serve on the PTA Board."

Say,

> "Thank you for honoring me with your invitation. I'll care-

fully assess my workload and other commitments and give you an answer by the end of the day."

Instead of saying,

"I don't really want to, but I guess I'll say yes."

Say,

"No, I won't. I do appreciate your asking."

46. *Never Say Always*

YOU'VE just purchased more plants for your living room after seeing yet another African violet wither away, just as the Boston fern did two weeks ago, and the philodendron before that.
Say out loud to yourself:

"Everything I try to grow always dies. I can't ever get any plant to stay alive for more than a month."

Now, say:

"Some of the plants I've been growing stay fairly healthy for a while, and then I'm not sure what happens. I'm going to find a houseplant book and figure out what I should be doing differently."

Which version sounds like you should just give up and buy silk flowers? Which shows you're going to improve on your track record?

I could see her paper plate tipping 10 degrees, then 15 degrees, then 20 degrees. The wedding was at a yacht club, which didn't explain her listing dish; we were ashore in the club's banquet hall. The sixtyish woman in front of me in the reception buffet line was attractive and vivacious. Her plate was heaped with shrimp, roast beef, macaroni salad, and, for some reason, a little pile of salted peanuts. She was waiting for—and concentrating on—the champagne-pouring bartender as her plate angled precariously. At 25 degrees, the first peanuts started to roll toward me, and I could visualize the whole melange slopping off the plate and onto my shoes.

"Excuse me, your food's just about to spill."

"Oh, don't mind me. I'm always spilling everything. Hah, I'm such a jerk! I'll spill anything. I'm probably going to spill this champagne, too! I always do."

Her self-denigration, though delivered jokingly, left me thinking that her self-esteem must be in pretty rough shape. She probably says that she always messes everything up—whether she's talking about cooking, playing the stock market, or anything else. Even though she seemed jolly, I felt sorry for this woman. She didn't think much of herself.

You know how uncomfortable it is to be around a couple that's having marital trouble. They have a couple of drinks, then start pouring out their mutual disgust.

"If she hadn't made us so late, I'd have helped with the barbecuing. She just never can get ready on time. She's always late."

"Me? He's the one who misplaced the car keys. He's always losing them. In fact he always loses everything. On our first date he even lost the concert tickets."

You want to stop them, but it's too late. They've already plunged into inaccurate universals: always, never, everything, nothing.

Universal statements are rarely true and they're hardly ever constructive. Is it possible that he **always** loses the keys, and **everything** else? Does the woman in line at the wedding reception **always** spill **everything**?

The most important place to start when eliminating universal terms from your vocabulary is with yourself.

"I can't believe I did it again! Every time I print something out on the computer, I always forget to switch from the dot matrix printer back to the laser printer. I never do get that right. What's the matter with me?"

This kind of self-abuse can't help change the situation. It's much more productive to replace the universals with more accurate modifiers:

"**Sometimes I forget to change the printer switch. I'm getting better about remembering, and I don't always get it right. Now I'm going to concentrate on setting the printer switch correctly.**"

Whether commenting on your own behavior or someone else's, eliminate untrue universal terms and replace them with accurate descriptions of what's really happening. You'll be doing yourself justice and encouraging others to cooperate with you, too.

QUICK REFERENCE

What you can do right now:

Be alert for and eliminate universal terms like "always," "never," "everything," and "nothing," especially when using them to criticize someone else's performance or your own.

Instead of saying,

"I can never remember your phone number."

Say,

"**Sometimes I have trouble remembering your number, so I'm going to write it down in my day planner book.**"

Instead of saying,

"You always pull in too far when you put the van in the garage. Can't you ever get it right?"

Say,

"When you leave me plenty of room in front of the van, it's much easier for me to get at my workbench. I appreciate it."

Instead of saying to yourself,

''Everything goes wrong every time I try to negotiate with him. I always end up on the short end and I never get treated fairly.''

Say,

"Sometimes my negotiating techniques haven't brought about a positive outcome. Next time I'm going to use another approach."

VIII. Get Back to Basics

I'VE been fascinated by Robert Fulgham's phenomenal success with his best-seller, *Everything I Need to Know I Learned in Kindergarten*. It's so true. Winston Churchill was right when he said, "All the great things are simple. . . ."

Having come this far in *Power Talking*, you've probably said to yourself many times, "These techniques are so simple!" And indeed they are. Power Talkers aren't particularly skilled at making things complicated; they don't employ any high-falutin' tricks. They are careful to speak positively, express appreciation, be optimistic, accept responsibility, be cooperative, say exactly what they mean, and tell the truth.

That's about all there is to it, except for three more basics: *Get people's names right, say "Please" and "Thank You," and when you're wrong, say you're sorry.*

This last section doesn't need any introduction. If you were spotty in your application of the preceding 46 techniques, and just made sure you remembered to always practice these last three without fail, you'd be way ahead of most folks. Power Talkers remember the basics.

47. *The Name Game*

WAITING to be seated at a restaurant, you vaguely recognize a diner who gets up from his meal and approaches you. His name doesn't come to mind.

Say out loud to yourself:

"I'm terribly sorry. I know I should remember your name, but I just can't think of it."

Now, say:

"It's nice to see you, I'm . . ."

Which is the more socially confident version? Which statement sounds more self-assured and which sounds weak?

I was shopping at one of those office supply warehouse stores, sampling the various felt pens, when a familiar woman approached and said, "Hi, there! I thought I recognized you."

I used to feel awkward when I didn't remember someone's name. I'd launch into the old standby "don't-hurt-their-feelings" excuses you hear all the time. Realistically, though, even a memory expert doesn't remember everybody's name. You and I definitely don't. When you've forgotten someone's name, do away with unnecessary verbiage, avoid belittling yourself, and always tell the truth.

I realized that I wouldn't remember this woman's name. As I opened my mouth, prepared to say,

"Please remind me of your name,"

she cut me off, saying,

"George, I'm Sandy Wilson, from PNSA. It's nice to see you."

Of course! I know Sandy and have talked with her on the phone and at meetings several times. She didn't leave me in the awkward position of having to explain that I'd forgotten who she was.

We skipped over the common social exchange about forgetting names and renewed our acquaintance quickly. I respected Sandy for taking the initiative.

When you deal with people, names are important. Fortunately, when you attend a convention, delegates usually wear badges proclaiming their names. You can discreetly glance down (as they do, too) and refresh your memory, maybe even appearing to have remembered on your own. But out in real life, you often have to ask.

One key to developing rapport with other people lies in knowing and using their names. Dale Carnegie reminded us long ago that the sound of a person's own name is the sweetest sound to anyone, in any language. We've all learned that developing a talent for remembering and using names can be a tremendous asset in business. You can easily excel in each of the three most common situations that come up when dealing with names: When you've forgotten theirs, when they've forgotten yours, and when you've first met (and not yet forgotten.)

1. Don't Lose Face Over a Forgotten Name.

The best way to handle forgetting a name is very simple. Accept it! You've forgotten a name—so what? Why worry about it? The other guy may have forgotten yours, too, and certainly has forgotten plenty of others'.

The next time you attend a party, bump into a long-forgotten colleague or customer at the airport, or end up in the Safeway line behind a new neighbor you've recently met, say,

"Please remind me of your name."

That's all. It's direct, courteous, and positive. It avoids that usual cumbersome, tucked-tail explanation: "Oh, I'm terribly sorry, but I just can't seem to remember your name, although it's right on the tip of my tongue." Leave out the embarrassment. There's no ignominy or disgrace about it. You've forgotten the name. You want to be reminded. Period.

2. And If You Suspect They've Forgotten Yours . . .

Self-assured, confident, powerful people announce their names when they see you. Even when chances are that you probably do remember theirs, they make it easy on you. They begin a conversation by reaching out for your hand, and as they shake it, say, "I'm Heather White. We met at the Nashville convention last year. It's nice to see you again."

Your best bet when seeing someone who may have forgotten your name is to say,

"Hi, I'm _____, nice to see you."

There's a built-in bonus to this approach: They'll probably respond with their own name, so if you've forgotten it you're already covered.

3. When You Hear It, Use It.

Most people don't really **forget** a name they used to remember, they just fail to remember it in the first place. Since names are vital in developing rapport and strengthening relationships, it's worth taking some simple steps toward improving your name memorizing techniques. The easiest thing to do is use a name right away once you've heard it.

A not-very-successful salesman once said to me:

"Yes, George, I've been very successful in sales. And you know, George, it's really not too hard to do very, very well once you've mastered the basics. One of the things I always try to do is use the other person's name during the conversation. And as you well know, George, that's especially important on the phone. It really grabs the other person's attention. But, George, you just can't please everyone. In fact, just the other day I talked to a guy from Iowa who, well, what he said, George, is, 'You seem slick when you use my name too much.' No kidding, George . . ."

Yikes! Screeching fingernails on a blackboard. I found myself counting how many times he said my name, wanting to interrupt and say, "You idiot! Why didn't you listen to that Iowan?"

Here's a simple guideline: *Use the other person's name three times in a conversation.* First, right after he says it. Second, sometime during the conversation, and third, as you end it.

Taking a couple of simple steps to ensure that you remember and use someone's name makes them feel good, and helps you feel good, too.

Your business life and personal life are both built around inter-personal relationships. Knowing and using people's names counts for a lot. Get in the habit of remembering and using them right from the start.

QUICK REFERENCE

What you can do right now:

Consciously use people's names three times during conversations. When you meet someone for the first time, immediately use his name and remember it. And when you see someone who may have forgotten your name, remind him right away. If you've for-gotten his, ask him to remind you.

Instead of saying,

"I'm sorry, it's right on the tip of my tongue, but I just can't seem to think of your name."

Say instead,

"Please remind me of your name."

Instead of saying,

"You probably don't remember my name, but . . ."

Say instead,

"Nice to see you again, my name's _____."

Instead of saying,

"Gee, I'm sorry, but I just can't remember your name."

Say instead,

"Hello again. I'm _____. Please remind me of your name."

48. What's the Magic Word?

It's Friday afternoon and your secretary has once again worked through lunch to be sure that your handouts are ready for the presentation first thing Monday morning.

Say out loud to yourself:

"I don't know how I'd get by without Christine. I wish the rest of the clerical staff were half as conscientious about deadlines as she is."

Now, say:

"Christine, I really appreciate you. Thank you for doing such excellent work on the handouts, and for giving up your lunch hour. I'm very grateful for your dedication, and I enjoy working with you."

Which version will ensure that Christine "keeps up the good work"?

A retired neighbor of mine devotes much of her time to fundraising for the American Cancer Society. She works tirelessly and has achieved great results that benefit many seriously ill patients. Recently, she called my wife in desperation.

"Julie, I'm in a terrible fix. Our biggest fund-raising event of the year is right around the corner and we don't have the tickets promised in our promotional literature for the auction. Do you know anybody who could make a big donation? One or two airline tickets would be ideal."

My mother died of cancer, so I definitely have a personal interest in wanting to help beat this disease. One of our best friends, Kevyn

Leiner, was at that time a Sales Manager for USAir. He's a great friend and a generous person, so he was our "target." Everything was right down to the wire, so the neighbor gave us a letter explaining the auction, and we faxed it to USAir immediately. Within 48 hours Kevyn came through with two unrestricted free tickets anywhere in the USAir route system, worth up to $3000. No strings.

When the auction took place, Julie and I were in England on a speaking tour. We returned home, expecting to find a Thank-you note and copy of the American Cancer Society's formal letter to USAir and Kevyn. We found nothing.

Although we saw the neighbor from time to time, we never really stopped to talk with her. I felt somewhat resentful that she hadn't thanked Julie, who was responsible for initiating the airline contact in the first place, and whose friendly persuasion convinced Kevyn to deliver.

Months later, I said to Kevyn,

"You know, that woman from the American Cancer Society never even had the courtesy to thank Julie for contacting you about the ticket you donated."

Kevyn's response:

"Oh, they never thanked me, either. It happens all the time. You'd be surprised how many charitable organizations ask for contributions, neglect to say please, and then never follow up in any way."

The point of the story is this: It's foolish, stupid, and ungracious to overlook simple courtesies like saying please and expressing appreciation. After all the neighbor's hard work, the lasting impression with us, and with USAir's Sales Manager, is negative. I presume the ticket fetched a good price, and that the ACS benefited. The neighbor, though, will find a cool reception if she turns to USAir or to us next year.

She didn't mean to be rude, I'm sure. She just overlooked one of the basics. She allowed her hard work to be overshadowed by a careless slip.

It's so easy, and so rare, to be genuinely courteous toward people who mean a lot to us—especially customers. And the payoff is phenomenal. One standard rule of thumb among sales professionals is that it costs at least five times as much to win an order from a new customer as it costs to win one from an existing customer. In my work as an advisor to Fortune 1000 companies, I've never found the figure to be that low. Organizations that have bothered to take a close look find it's at least ten times as costly to win new customers' business.

When I serve as a consultant to marketing organizations, I often begin by asking,

"What are you doing to let your existing customers know that you appreciate them?"

The answer is nearly always revealing and embarrassing.

Sales forces typically invest huge amounts of time, money, and personal energy chasing after new customers. And then they drop the ball.

One of my most popular speaking topics deals with reducing customer "churn." I use a visual analogy of a conveyor belt. Picture a long conveyor belt about 3 feet wide, moving away from you at a steady clip. You're standing at one end of the belt, alongside a salesperson, and the belt moves away from you, off into the distance. In my speeches, I show three slides depicting that conveyor belt.

The first shows the eager, enthusiastic salesperson lavishing attention on a new customer—let's call him Harry—helping him step up onto the belt. This corresponds to the most common, and most expensive, task in any marketing organization: *Winning new customers.* Using a combination of advertising, trade show exhibits, direct mail campaigns, telemarketing calls, and often, face-to-face sales appointments, we set out to convince prospects to buy something from us, to "get them on the conveyor belt."

My second slide shows the same conveyor belt scene. Now the salesperson is attentively schmoozing another prospect, hoping to convert him into a customer. Harry has now progressed in his relationship—moved along on the conveyor belt. He may even have made a couple of repeat purchases. The salesperson, though, is concentrating his attention on the new prospect, seeking to get him on the belt and convert him into a customer. Meanwhile, our friend Harry is glancing at his watch, thinking,

"It's been a while since I got much attention from my salesperson. I was very important to him just before my first purchase and now I'm feeling taken for granted."

The salesperson, of course, is hardly aware of Harry's feelings of being neglected. He's too busy winning new customers to pay much attention to the second big task in marketing: *Keeping customers on the conveyor belt.*

In the third slide, we see the same salesperson again. Sure enough, he's attentively convincing yet another new prospect to become a customer, to get on the conveyor belt. We see other customers who've recently begun their relationships with the company moving along into the distance, just as Harry did. And there's Harry, far down the belt, jumping off. He's on his way to jump onto some competitor's conveyor belt. They've begun making him feel important and appreciated again.

Most salespeople completely neglect the third task in marketing: *Find out why customers are getting off your conveyor belt.*

An organization's "churn rate" refers to the rate at which new customers become disenchanted and fall off the conveyor belt. In every business, a customer relationship may be thought of as a stream of expected future cash flow. That's especially evident for firms in the membership and subscription businesses. It costs them (and every other type of business) a lot to win a new customer. Take cable TV, for example. If a customer signs up for cable service and then cancels just a few months later, the company will lose money on the account. To stay in business, it has to actively seek new customers to ensure an adequate future cash flow to cover its fixed expenses. When one of these customers cancels his cable service, and the company has to replace him, it's dealing with churn.

A high churn rate is extremely costly. Think of what happens when you cancel your cable TV service. Several clerks are involved in closing your account and generating the paperwork to wrap things up. A service representative is dispatched to your home or apartment building to sever the cable connection. The computers are reprogrammed to delete your account number. But those are just the obvious costs.

We've got to consider the cost of winning another new customer—of getting him on the conveyor belt—to replace the missing cash flow represented by the unhappy customer who has just jumped off. For a cable TV company, that means more advertising, direct mail, telemarketing, special incentives, and even door-to-door sales calls.

Why does churn happen? One of the most oft-repeated statistics on the seminar circuits of the late 1980s came from the Wisconsin Restaurant Association. That study revealed that when a restaurant's patrons stop eating there and are asked why, they cite the following reasons:

1% Died
3% Moved away
5% Developed other relationships
9% Preferred a competitor
14% Were dissatisfied about the product (meal)
68% Felt an attitude of neglect or indifference

I know of no wide-reaching national research to determine why customers fall off conveyor belts, but those percentages look pretty accurate to me. I've had several clients conduct expensive studies to get their own answers. Top place always goes to the same reason: Customers feel taken for granted.

Once marketing executives grasp the true costs of customer churn, they want to know the most effective way to reduce it—to keep customers on the conveyor belt longer. The easiest way is ridiculously simple: Remember to say please and thank you.

It's so easy—and profitable—to improve the customer retention efforts in any business. You don't need to send expensive gifts or conceive a complicated customer appreciation campaign. A simple, sincere, personal thank you is all it takes.

Personal relationships can be a lot like customer relationships. Friendships and marriages can wither from the same tendency to neglect common courtesies. You can easily apply the same "conveyor belt principle" to your nonbusiness relationships. Your success at building and maintaining any kind of relationship depends on the same three skills: Initiating, Nurturing, and Recapturing. Whether it's your marriage, a close personal friendship, or a casual relationship with a neighbor, think in terms of getting 'em on the conveyor belt, keeping 'em on, and finding out what's wrong when they fall off.

Power Talkers remember the basics. They never fail to say please and thank you when it's the gracious thing to do. And they don't wait until it's expected. Every now and then they send a postcard, call a customer back, or drop in to thank a helpful neighbor. Parents who teach their children that "please" and "thank you" are magic words aren't exaggerating.

QUICK REFERENCE

What you can do right now:

Remember to exercise common courtesies in relationships with others, particularly those you may take for granted. Don't be stingy with "please" and "thank you."
Instead of saying,

"Those people at the dry cleaners sure do a nice job."

Say,

"Thank you for always treating me so well and taking good care of my clothes. I appreciate your excellent service."

Instead of saying,

"We've got to find a way to get 1000 new customers this quarter."

Say,

"I'm going to make absolutely sure our present customers know how much we appreciate them."

Instead of saying,

"My wife? Yeah, she's great. She feeds the baby, cooks good meals, keeps a lovely home and works hard. I'm lucky."

Say,

"Darling, I appreciate you. This weekend I'm going to do something special to let you know how much I mean it when I say, 'Thank you.' "

Instead of saying,

"They know I appreciate them."

Say,

"Thank you."

49. *Say You're Sorry*

FOLLOWING an audit of your expense account, the Branch Manager calls you to her office and asks about a meal receipt that doesn't appear to have been business-related. Sure enough, it turns out that you charged a family dinner to your company credit card three months ago.

Say out loud to yourself:

"With all the paperwork we have to do around here, I'm surprised there was only one incorrect charge. I'll bet everybody here has a few personal meals slip through now and then. You can't blame me for making a mistake once in a while."

Now, say:

"You're absolutely right, that was a personal meal and it should not have been charged to my expense account. I'm sorry I didn't catch it myself and I will be extra careful in the future. It's my mistake and I apologize."

Which sounds like the more trustworthy employee? Whose reaction do you respect? Who will the Branch Manager be more likely to recommend for promotion?

When you phone an airline to make a reservation, a pizza chain to place your order, or your bank's Customer Service center to inquire about a recent account statement, your call is handled by an

Automatic Call Distributor, or ACD, before you talk with an agent. Today, this type of electronic device is used in almost every large telephone center.

One major advantage of an ACD is that it helps callers connect with exactly the right person. The ACD analyzes each incoming call and quickly identifies which 800 number the caller dialed, what part of the country he's calling from, and in some cases, the specific telephone he's using. Then it directs his call to an agent who specializes in the questions he's most likely to ask. Telephone center managers rely on ACDs because they provide very helpful statistical analyses of representatives' performances. For every employee, supervisory group, work shift, or hour of the day, the manager knows how many calls were made or answered, how long the average call lasted, how much time the rep spent processing paperwork, and so on.

Managers pay careful attention to a key ratio called the "percent time available/unavailable." When an individual rep is clipping along, handling lots of calls with only a very brief pause between each one, his "availability" to talk with customers is high. When a rep is procrastinating, taking unnecessary time with his paperwork, chatting with co-workers, and avoiding customer contact, his ratio shows a high "unavailable" percentage.

One of my client's call center managers decided to post a report of all reps' individual statistics on the bulletin board. To avoid peer embarrassment, she substituted employee I.D. numbers for names. Two reps, Stanley and Stephanie, both checked the report and noticed that their ratios were unfavorable. They were handling fewer calls (and taking longer to do it) than their co-workers.

As a consultant to many call center managers, I have yet to discover a completely foolproof system for measuring performance (or allocating commissions, or fairly scheduling work shifts, or anything else). There's always someone who will outsmart whatever system management implements.

Stanley outsmarted the ACD in his call center. He figured out that the device counts how many minutes his phone is busy, how many calls he handles, and how long his conversations last. It doesn't "listen in" to see whom he's talking with or even if he's talking at all.

So Stanley began calling his home phone and letting it ring for three minutes, then hanging up and calling again, and then hanging up and calling again. The ACD counted each as a customer call. The next time statistics were posted in the lunch room, Stanley's numbers showed dramatic improvement! The average number of calls he handled each day soared from 47 to 92! According to the statistics, he was on the phone almost all the time. His average call length was right in step with the average for other reps. He appeared to be very productive.

Stephanie, a new employee, had been struggling to improve her performance statistics. Good ol' Stanley showed her how to do it. Overnight, her stats also showed amazing improvement.

Of course the manager noticed these dramatic changes and asked both employees what was going on.

Stephanie admitted her tricks, accepted personal responsibility for what she had done, apologized, and stopped doing it. Her performance continues to legitimately improve and her future with her employer is bright.

Stanley blamed his performance on the pressured environment. That ended his employment.

When I was in college at the University of California, Santa Barbara, I landed a dream job. I was hired to be the TWA Campus Sales Representative. The money wasn't much; the benefits, though, were incredible! As a 20-year-old student with an unlimited air travel pass, I asked myself each week:

"Shall I stay around campus this weekend, drop a couple of dollars at the theater, spend a few bucks on meals, and shoot a few games of Eight-Ball? Or shall I catch the polar flight to London, see two movies going over and two more coming back, enjoy four nice inflight meals, sightsee for a few hours in England, and spend zero dollars?"

I didn't spend many weekends on campus.

As an airline sales representative, you inevitably deal with some of your customers just after they've returned from a horror flight on your airline. I remember being verbally assaulted by the Men's Choir Director after he'd taken his boys on a European tour. I escorted them as far as Frankfurt, then bade the group farewell as they continued on to sing for some Austrian Countess and harmonize in several European capitals. I headed off to visit a friend in Berlin before returning home.

Two weeks later, back on campus, I was blasted by the Director:

"I'll never fly on TWA again! Your airline lost our entire group's luggage on the flight from Rome to Paris. You canceled our flight from Madrid to L.A. and instead sent us home via Lisbon, Philadelphia, and Kansas City. What have you got to say?"

My boss and mentor at TWA, Paul Oglesby, was a hulking giant who'd been a lineman for the Raiders before injuries forced him out of professional football. One of the most important lessons he taught me was:

"When you're wrong, make no excuses. Say sincerely, 'You are absolutely right and I don't blame you for feeling upset. I'm sorry we screwed things up for you.'"

After the Choir Director's tirade crescendoed, I followed Paul's advice and sincerely apologized without making excuses. Next year the Men's Choir again flew TWA on its European tour.

When the Chrysler Corporation was accused of resetting new car odometers back to zero after executives had driven them for personal use, what did Lee Iacocca do? He admitted the truth, made no excuses (in fact, he said Chrysler had been "dumb" to do it), apologized personally on the company's behalf, and offered settlements to the affected owners whose "new" cars really hadn't been unused. Dishonesty cost the company at least $26 million in penalties and settlements. Criminal fines alone could have exceeded $100 million if the Chairman had not chosen to be forthright. But he told the truth. As a result, the company's performance remained strong in the face of the potentially devastating publicity. The Chairman himself bolstered his respected image as an honest straight-shooter.

Follow Paul Oglesby's advice: When you are personally wrong, or when the organization you represent has mistreated a customer, it's always best to admit the mistake, accept responsibility, apologize, promise to do everything you can to correct it, and immediately begin following through.

QUICK REFERENCE

What you can do right now:

Whenever you make a mistake, admit it readily and say you're sorry. Defuse potential emotional flareups, avoid confrontations, and build others' respect for your character by facing facts, admitting the truth, and apologizing.

Instead of saying to yourself,

"With all these people drinking red wine, he'll never figure out that I'm the one who stained his new sofa. He probably won't even notice it until the morning."

Say,

"Wayne, I'm sorry, but I spilled wine on your sofa. Let's get some stain remover or soda water on it right away before it sets overnight."

Instead of saying,

"Don't blame me if the client files are out of order. Other people use them, too, you know."

Say,

"I'm sorry you had trouble locating the right client files. I'll go through and check them all before Friday."

Instead of saying,

"Look, it's just too bad. Don't blame me. I couldn't help it."

Say,

"I'm sorry; it was my responsibility."

IX. Share Their Pride

A true Power Talker is not content to bolster his own image and self-esteem, he makes sure that he's enriching others, too.

I began writing this book with an underlying mission. My drive welled up from a need I have experienced personally. Reflecting back, I now realize that many of my choices in life have been motivated by one common desire: to be acknowledged and applauded. I've found that I'm not alone.

This last chapter is my most important message to you.

50. *The Sound of One Man Clapping*

You've just read the draft of a long-term strategic plan for your organization prepared by an interdepartment project team you put together. It's outstanding.

Say out loud to yourself:

"Boss, this is the strategic plan my project team has developed. They did some fine work; it's the best plan we've had around here in a long time. They should be feeling pretty pleased with themselves."

Now, say:

"Team, I'm proud of every one of you who worked on this project. You've done an excellent job, and I'm going to make sure that the boss knows exactly how proud of you I am. After I've reviewed it with her, I'll give you point-by-point feedback. For now I want you to know your excellent and hard work is very evident. Thank you."

Which sounds like the leader whose team members will feel that their work was truly appreciated? Who's making a big mistake by assuming that his team feels appreciated?

My dad, Merle Walther, was born in 1908 and grew up in Sacramento, California. His large family—five children, of which my dad was the youngest—didn't have much money. Dad did have a penchant and talent for playing sandlot baseball. He was well known in the local leagues and was apparently a terrific first baseman. So good in fact that a scout from Detroit recruited him to play professional ball. Dad thinks of the afternoon when that scout came to his house as a near-religious experience. His dream was to play in the big leagues, and he imagined how proud his family would be as he became a famous baseball star.

Sitting in the humble front room my grandfather, John, had built in a converted barn, the scout asked for permission to take Merle back to Detroit so he could join the team. Dad recalls what his father said:

> *"I've heard about those baseball players. They drink. They smoke. They chase women. And after a few years, their careers are over. I won't hear of it. My son's going to go to college."*

Dad was heartbroken, but there was no arguing. After all, Grandpa John was a German "head of the household," and when he said NO, that was that. I'm sure Dad resented his father's decree all his life. He yearned to play baseball.

Sure enough, Dad went off to college and did quite well studying electronics. He got a good job with the Pacific Telephone and Telegraph Company and specialized in microwave transmissions.

When World War II broke out, he volunteered to join the Navy and became a radar officer on a destroyer escort in the South Pacific. I'm sure he played a lot of baseball on the Navy teams when they were ashore.

And then, after the war, I was born. What do you suppose Dad wanted me to do? Right. Play baseball.

As a kid, I remember Dad playing catch intensely with me in the front yard. For me it wasn't fun, it was torture. But Dad wanted to work me hard so I'd be the baseball star his father hadn't let him become. He forced me to sign up for Little League.

I showed an early inclination toward sales. Neighbors and family friends all said I had the gift of gab. I always sold the most Scout-O-Rama tickets and founded a succession of neighborhood sales enterprises peddling greeting cards, firewood, extension cords, trivets, used comic books, and Sno-Kones. I could succeed selling anything. Baseball just interfered with my sales activities.

I don't recall Dad ever congratulating me for being such a whiz-bang little salesman. He often pointed out that his son was a disappointing ball player.

Finally I summoned the courage to tell Dad that I would not join Little League the following season. So he joined, as the Chief Umpire. Poor Dad. He must have felt terribly ashamed when the other umps asked why his son didn't play on one of the teams.

Through my high school years, Dad continued to volunteer as a Little League umpire. I continued to avoid team sports. I was now active in the Junior Achievement program, winning sales contests and being chosen by my high school peers to head our model companies. Dad didn't acknowledge my business acumen, he just wished I would play baseball.

At high school graduation, I received many top academic and service honors, but none for athletics. Dad pointed that out, too.

In university, I majored in Rhetoric and Public Address, and graduated *summa cum laude*. Dad didn't say he was proud, only that he wished I had at least tried out for the college baseball team.

In graduate school I'd call Dad to tell him how well I was doing with my MBA program classes and he'd try to tell me how well the San Francisco Giants were doing. Finally he'd give up, saying, "Of course you don't give a damn about baseball. You never have. You're a zero in sports."

Years later, when I completed my first book, *Phone Power*, it struck me that of all the subjects I could have written a book about, I chose telephones. Dad had by now retired from a 40-year career with a telephone company. It seemed I was doing everything I could to win his approval. Except play baseball.

When the publisher sent me my first copy of the completed book, fresh from the printer, I inscribed it to Dad and sent it to him.

"Dad, you may never realize how much of my business success has been the result of striving to make you proud of me."

As I complete this book that you're reading, Dad still hasn't read *Phone Power*, and he hasn't once commented on my inscription.

A few years ago I presented a speech in San Francisco and invited Dad to be my guest in the audience. He'd had many opportunities before, but hadn't shown up. Even now, as a retired, lonely man (my mother had died some years earlier), he said that he probably wouldn't make it to my speech. Although he was in superb health, and the hotel ballroom was less than half an hour from his home, he complained that:

"Parking's impossible in San Francisco. And I'm sure as hell not going to pay some damned valet car parker fella three or four bucks just to park my car."

Well, Dad did show up. And I was in top form. As I ended my presentation, Dad stood up and began to applaud, biting his lower lip. I've enjoyed many wonderful ovations, but none was ever as loud as the sound of that one man clapping.

My eyes moisten, right now as I type, as I remember how I felt when Dad said the words I'd yearned to hear all my life:

"Son, I'm proud of you."

Whenever I share that story with my audiences, several people come up to the stage at the end of the program. Their eyes are red and they say,

"My mother/father was just like that. She/he never did say 'I'm proud of you,' though I wanted very much to hear it. What is it about our parents that makes it so hard for them to say it?"

Once I've opened up, others do. And it turns out that we're all pretty much alike. As I'm telling the story of my dad and his wish that I'd be something I'm not, I see many in the audience reacting emotionally. Instead of approaching me after the applause, I hope they proceed directly to the pay phones in the lobby and call the people they're proud of.

It's remarkable how common this striving for appreciation is. In Kirk Douglas's autobiography, *Ragman's Son*, he traces most of his life's achievements back to his struggle to be noticed and appreciated by his father. He never got the satisfaction of hearing his dad say that he was.

After 10 years as cohost of ABC's "Good Morning America," Joan Lunden recalled her life and career for an article in *Parade* magazine. Her father died piloting his small plane when Joan was 13.

"Up until then, I'd had a pretty comfortable life. But then all of a sudden the bottom dropped out, and my security was gone. I think that's when I first decided that I would always rely on my own strength and be in control of my own life."

The interviewer concluded by asking if, with a strong marriage, unpretentious life, three beautiful daughters, and a $10 million contract, she is content.

She paused and looked at her husband playing in the yard with one of their little girls and said,

"My biggest regret in life is that my father didn't live to see my success. If he's up there watching, I'm sure he's extremely proud of what I'm doing. And I don't just mean my job. I mean that I have a lovely family, that I live right and have the kind of values he would have wanted me to have."

After a decade of strained relations, my dad and I got together at last. The speech in San Francisco, when he finally said "I'm proud of you," was a milestone in our relationship. When I explained how much I wanted him to be proud of me, his response was,

"You must be kidding. Since the day you were born, I've been telling every friend I have how proud I am of you. Don't you know that?"

Well, now I know. And it feels great.

I've always thought my career choice is quite revealing. I stand onstage before hundreds or thousands of people, working hard to earn their appreciation. For years, their ovations helped compensate for my dad's failure to tell me that he was proud of me.

As William James said,

"The deepest principle in human nature is the craving to be appreciated."

You can be sure that most of the people you'll ever meet are striving to be noticed and applauded. It's a natural instinct, and one that goes unfulfilled in many. The people you know and work with are hungry for appreciation. They're probably not getting enough of it from the people they love.

If you do nothing else after reading this book, please call the people you love and tell them why you're proud of them. Do it now.

QUICK REFERENCE

What you can do right now:

Let the people you feel proud of hear about it.
Instead of saying,

"That daughter of mine is a wonderful student. Everyone likes her. And she's so beautiful. I'm proud of her."

Say,

"Sweetheart, I'm very proud of you. You're a wonderful student, you choose great friends, and you're gorgeous."

Instead of saying,

"That Gordon has a great future here. He's doing fine work in my department, and I suspect he'll be headed for the Home Office in a year or two. He should feel very proud of himself."

Say,

"Gordon, you are handling your career beautifully, and your work is very valuable to the company. I know you have an excellent future here. I'm proud of you."

Instead of saying,

"Our organization does a great job of putting on superb workshops that help a lot of people."

Say,

"Barbara, since you've been the Executive Director of our association, we've never had a finer management team. I want you to know that I'm proud to be a member of our association."

Instead of saying,

"I'm sure he knows I'm proud of him."

Say,

"I'm proud of you."

X. Do It Now

POWER Talking positively affects all areas of your life—**once you start using it.**

There are three critical steps in becoming a Power Talker: (1) Decide you're going to change, (2) Build a support system to keep you on course, and (3) Track your own progress to keep up the momentum.

1. Decide to Be a Power Talker.

Choose to project a more positive image for yourself, enhance others' cooperation with you, accelerate your career progress, and enjoy more positive, fulfilling relationships.

As you read the examples in this book, you notice that they're down-to-earth. You don't need to be some corporate big shot to benefit from using Power Talking in your life. These principles work whether you are a salesperson, a supervisor, someone who's just starting your career, or an established leader of your organization—and they're just as beneficial to parents, friends, consumers, and anyone else.

Are the Power Talking techniques difficult to master? Certainly not. There are no new words to learn and there's nothing tricky about applying the principles.

Once you make the decision, the action is easy.

2. Build a Support System.

Teaming up with a partner is the single most important action you can take toward becoming a Power Talker. Invite someone you work with, live with, or enjoy a strong friendship with to become a Power Talker, too. There's nothing like a companion who's tuned in and listening for power*less* phrases that may slip out during your conversations. Agree to help each other by remaining vigilant about each other's language. You could use a subtle reminder like winking or clearing your throat, or you could be a lot more conspicuous. Some Power Talkers write the powerless phrases they're purging on wide rubber bands and wear them around their wrist. When their partners hear them slip, SNAP!

For maximum results, form two or more partnerships covering your professional and personal lives. If you have children at home, help prepare them for the real world by sharing the Power Talking principles. It takes very little incentive to enlist their zealous support in cleansing your vocabulary. Offer a kid a quarter every time he catches you saying "but" instead of "and," and you'll soon break old habits.

Supportive "Power Talking" Quick Reference Cards and audio/video programs are also available to help reinforce these concepts. For ordering information, see page 251.

3. Keep Track of Your Progress.

You will notice the difference Power Talking makes in your own daily life, and you'll also become very aware of powerless talkers around you. Each time you hear someone say, "I'll be honest with you," or "I just got lucky," or "I'd hate to," or "I'll try," you'll notice the negative impression that phrase makes on anyone listening. And that will serve as a reminder to keep up your own steady progress.

All 50 Power Talking phrases are summarized in the "Quick Reference" section that follows. As you master each one, note your successes and reward yourself. Remember, though, that Power Talking isn't a final destination at which you arrive. It's a continuing journey, so enjoy your trip.

*   *   *

I've enjoyed my journey while writing this book for you, and have benefited tremendously from the process of listening for examples and translating them into principles. Thank you for reading.
More Power Talking to You!

George R. Walther

Quick Reference Summary

Use the following pages as a quick reference summary to remind you of the 50 Power Talking techniques.

Power Talkers . . .
I. PROJECT POSITIVE EXPECTATIONS

1. I'll Be Glad To!
Each time you begin to say "I'll **have to,**" substitute a phrase that shows you'll be **glad to.** Notice the difference it makes in your own mood and in others' attitudes about cooperating with you.
Instead of saying,

"I'll have to do it."

Say,

"I'll be glad to do it."

2. Will You Try, or Will You DO It?
Tell yourself and everyone else what you **will** do, not what you'll **try** to do.
Instead of saying,

"I'll try to do it."

Say,

"I will do it."

3. Say What You Want to Do
Use "I want to" to describe the positive outcomes you envision rather than saying what you'd "hate to" have happen.
Instead of saying,

"I'd hate to give you the wrong information."

Say,

"I want to help you get the right information."

4. *I Haven't Yet and I CAN*
When describing your capabilities to yourself or to someone else, eliminate "I can't" from your vocabulary.
Instead of saying,

"I can't do that."

Say,

"I haven't yet done it and I can."

5. *Refuse to Be Helpless*
If you feel sick, supplement prudent medical attention with personal action. Use your language to promote a positive attitude and strengthen your body's natural disease-fighting powers.
Instead of saying,

"My condition is hopeless; I can't change it."

Say,

"I can improve the quality of my life."

6. *Better When Than If*
When you hear yourself starting to ask a conditional "If . . ." question, rephrase it to incorporate your positive expectation.
Instead of saying,

"I was wondering if you can . . . ?"

Say,

"When will you . . . ?"

7. *It's No Problem!*
Substitute "challenge" or "opportunity" for "problem" and concentrate on exploring solutions.
Instead of saying,

"I'm afraid that's going to be a problem."

Say,

"That sounds like a challenging opportunity."

8. Self-Fulfilling Prophecies Come True

Replace habitual self-limiting phrases with empowering assertions.

Instead of saying,

"I'm no good at that."

Say,

"I'm getting better at that."

9. Get a Return on Your Investments

Substitute "invest" for "spend" when you talk about how you'll use your time, money, and other resources.

Instead of saying,

"I'm going to spend some time and money taking night classes."

Say,

"I'm going to invest some time and money taking night classes so I'm ready to move ahead in my career."

10. Nothing's Impossible

Banish the word "impossible" from your vocabulary. Substitute a more accurate and positive phrase to describe what appears infeasible.

Instead of saying,

"This is impossible."

Say,

"This is going to require some special effort, and it can be done."

11. Kids Are All Ears

Be especially conscious of Power Talking whenever you are around youngsters. Set an example and help shape kids' futures by speaking positively to and about them.

Instead of saying,

"You're a bad child and you're always getting into trouble."

Say,

"You're a good child, and that behavior is not acceptable."

Power Talkers . . .
II. GIVE CREDIT WHERE DUE

12. What's Your Excuse?
Stop making excuses and apologizing for some imagined short-coming. Either change it or forget it.
Instead of saying,

"You'll have to excuse my car/mess/hair/house."

Say,

Nothing!

13. It's Just My Opinion
You're not "just" or "only" anything. Describe yourself, your beliefs, and your accomplishments positively and proudly.
Instead of saying,

"I'm only just the . . ."

Say,

"I am the . . ."

14. Is "Luck" Getting the Credit for Your Hard Work?
When you succeed, modestly acknowledge your own role in attaining your accomplishments, both to yourself and to others.
Instead of saying,

"I got lucky."

Say,

"I planned well and worked hard."

15. What They Don't Know Won't Hurt Them
You're probably far more critical of yourself than anybody else will be. Go ahead and enjoy doing as well as you can.
Instead of saying,

"I'm really not too good at this."

Proceed to do your best without excuses.

16. Ken and Spencer Were Right!
Go out of your way to compliment people and give them credit for doing things right, especially when they don't expect it.

Instead of saying,

"That daughter of mine is a big help around the house."

Say,

"Darling, you are a big help around the house, and I appreciate it."

17. *You're About as Old as You Say You Are*
Use neutral or positive phrases in reference to advancing age. Don't erode vitality by speaking negatively about aging.
Instead of saying,

"I feel worse and worse. I'm getting too old."

Say,

"I feel good."

Power Talkers . . .
III. REBOUND RESILIENTLY

18. *Does Your History Repeat Itself?*
When you're confronted with a "failure," look for the lessons you can learn and grow from the experience.
Instead of saying,

"I failed."

Say,

"Here's what I learned . . ."

19. *Half Empty or Half Full?*
Rephrase negative reactions to unexpected changes and say, "This is great news. It means that . . . ," and then start looking for the positive result that can follow.
Instead of saying,

"I see some very negative consequences resulting from this turn of events."

Say,

"I see some very positive consequences resulting from this turn of events."

20. If Only I Had . . .

Focus your attention—and your language—on what you will do to positively shape your future. Don't dwell on the unalterable past by talking about what might have been.

Instead of saying,

"If only I had."

Say,

"Starting now, I will."

21. Bottoming Out

When you're at a low point, write out your affirmations, using positive language, and say them aloud to yourself. Don't just think, act.

Instead of thinking to yourself,

"I'm a loser."

Say,

"I am a winner."

22. Bouncing Back

When you hear yourself describing a setback situation as a terminal disaster, rephrase your description to recognize that you will bounce back and move ahead.

Instead of saying,

"I'm going under."

Say,

"I'm going to bounce back."

23. It's Over!

When things seem to be headed for a disastrous outcome, stop and ask yourself, "What's the very worst thing that could happen?" Accept that eventuality as if it were true and say, "That's all; it's over." Then, get to work applying your energy to create a more positive outcome.

Instead of saying,

"This is terrible, and it could get a lot worse."

Say,

"Even if the worst happened, I could live with it. So there's no point worrying. **That's all; it's over.** Now I'm going to work on making things better."

Power Talkers . . .
IV. ACCEPT RESPONSIBILITY

24. *Watch Where You Point That Thing!*
Be on the alert for that pointing finger! Whenever you hear (or see) yourself directing blame or responsibility elsewhere, focus on the three fingers that point back at you.
Instead of saying,

"You make me upset when . . ."

Say,

"**I feel upset when . . .**"

25. *Use the Time You Have*
Purge phrases that suggest time is out of your control—that there's not enough of it. Acknowledge your personal responsibility with your language.
Instead of saying,

"I just can't get caught up; I don't have enough time."

Say,

"**I can get caught up by managing my time and eliminating low-priority projects.**"

26. *It's Not What Happens to You, It's What You Do About It*
Accept personal responsibility for your present situation and decide to move forward rather than wasting energy by blaming your current condition on past circumstances.
Instead of saying,

I can't help it; it's someone else's fault."

Say,

"**It's my responsibility to change things.**"

27. You Can Count on Me

Even though you may not be the person who'll actually perform the tasks, accept personal accountability when you offer to help someone.

Instead of saying,

"That's not my area. You'll have to get someone else to help you."

Say,

"I'll help you by getting your message through to the right department."

28. Do You Choose to Lose?

Avoid "victim" language; acknowledge your responsibility by using the word "choose." When you're unsatisfied with the way things are, choose to change them.

Instead of saying,

"I can't change things, I didn't get myself into this fix."

Say,

"I choose to make the best of this situation."

Power Talkers . . .
V. ENCOURAGE COOPERATION AND REDUCE CONFLICT

29. Get That "But" Out of Your Mouth!

Make a conscious decision to replace "but" with "and" as you talk to yourself and to others. Notice that your thinking "opens up" as ideas coexist instead of conflict.

Instead of saying,

"I can see that it's a good product, but it's expensive."

Say instead,

"I can see that it's a good product, and it's expensive."

30. *Let's Do It!*

Whenever you seek others' input and suggestions, stimulate a free flow of ideas, no matter how crazy some might seem.
Instead of saying,

"That's not practical, it'll never work."

Say,

"That's an unusual approach, let's go with it and see where we end up."

31. *Do ME a Favor for a Change*

When you need someone's cooperation, figure out why his participation will benefit him, not you. Emphasize the benefits he'll realize by following your suggestion.
Instead of saying,

"Will you do me a favor?"

Say,

"Here's why this will be good for you."

32. *You Get What You Ask For*

Make it a habit to ask at least one relationship-improving question every single day.
Instead of saying,

"Is everything satisfactory?"

Say,

"How can I do a better job for you?"

33. *So, What CAN You Do?*

Whenever you start telling someone what you can't do, change your focus and substitute a statement indicating what you can do.
Instead of saying,

"Here's what I can't do."

Say,

"Here's what I can do."

34. Breaking the Language Barrier

When you're involved in a conflict, use your language to show that you're intent on working **with,** not **against** the other person; show that you're on the same side of the table, working as a teammate.

Instead of saying,

"I understand what you want. But I must adhere to my policies."

Say,

"We share some important common goals. Let's see how we can work together."

35. You're Invited!

When you want others to cooperate with you, "invite" them to do so, and give them a choice about what they'll do.

Instead of saying,

"Here's what you'll have to do."

Say,

"I invite you to choose the approach that will work best for you."

36. I Recommend

Whenever you set out to "sell" an idea, service, or product, focus on the benefits to the other person and use the word "recommend" to close the sale.

Instead of saying,

"One thing you might possibly want to consider is to . . ."

Say,

"I recommend that you . . ."

37. What Sounds Fair to You?

Whenever you feel that people are about to treat you unjustly, appeal to their own sense of fairness. In the few cases where they proceed to act unfairly, forget about it.

Instead of saying,

"I know my rights, and I demand that you take care of this my way."

Say,

"Considering the facts, what would be the fairest way to handle this?"

38. *Let's Look at This Another Way*

Rather than suggesting that someone else's viewpoint is less valid than your own, accept new ideas and let them coexist alongside yours. Then tap the merits of both approaches and come up with an even stronger alternative.

Instead of saying,

"I disagree with you."

Say,

"I understand, and I'd like to consider some more viewpoints."

Power Talkers . . .
VI. SPEAK DECISIVELY

39. *You Should?—Or You WILL?*

Commit to specific dates, times, and amounts. "Should" avoids commitment and sounds wishy-washy.

Instead of saying,

"We should get this done by . . ."

Say,

"We will get this done by . . ."

40. *Give Your Word and Then Beat It!*

Add a "safety cushion" whenever you make a commitment. Then delight the other person by doing your best to exceed the expectation you've created.

Instead of saying,

"I may be able to get to it by around 2:00 or 3:00."

Say,

"I will get to it before 5:00."

41. I Think I Understand What You Think You Said

Take an extra moment to verify that you have understood accurately. Do it in a way that shows you accept responsibility for getting the information correct.

Instead of saying,

"I guess that about covers it. I think we understand each other."

Say,

"Let's verify that we're both in complete agreement by wrapping this up with a recap of our understanding."

42. Don't Take "No"—or "Yes"—for an Answer

Whenever you ask someone a question, first ask yourself, "Is this a Yes/No question?" If it is, change it to the multiple-choice or open-ended variety.

Instead of saying,

"Do you have any questions?"

Say,

"What questions do you have?"

43. Say It!

Know what you want to say and say it!

Instead of saying,

"Well, generally speaking, one thing I would sort of tend to think is . . ."

Say,

"I believe . . ."

Power Talkers . . .
VII. TELL THE TRUTH

44. To Be Honest with You

When everything you say **is** totally honest, there's no need to alert anyone that you're about to tell the truth. Eliminate "integrity-busting" expressions that suggest you aren't always sincere and forthright.

Instead of saying,

"Well, to tell you the truth, . . ."

ALWAYS tell the truth.

45. Just Say No!
Before you agree to do anything you're only half sure you want to do, take a time-out. Decide if you'll be able to do a great job, enjoy doing it, and finish it without interrupting your other more important priorities. If you decide that you don't really want to do it, say no.
Instead of saying,

"I don't really want to, but I guess I'll say yes."

Say,

"No, I won't. I do appreciate your asking."

46. Never Say Always
Be alert for and eliminate universal terms like "always," "never," "everything," and "nothing," especially when using them to criticize someone else's performance or your own.
Instead of saying to yourself,

"**Everything** goes wrong **every time** I try to negotiate with him. **I always** end up on the short end and I **never** get treated fairly."

Say,

"Sometimes my negotiating techniques haven't brought about a positive outcome. Next time I'm going to use another approach."

Power Talkers . . .
VIII. GET BACK TO BASICS

47. The Name Game
Consciously use people's names three times during conversations. When you meet someone for the first time, immediately use his name and remember it. And when you see someone who may have forgotten your name, remind him right away. If you've forgotten his, ask him to remind you.

Instead of saying,

"Gee, I'm sorry, but I just can't remember your name."

Say instead,

"Hello again. I'm _____. Please remind me of your name."

48. *What's the Magic Word?*

Remember to exercise common courtesies in relationships with others, particularly those you may take for granted. Don't be stingy with "please" and "thank you."

Instead of saying,

"They know I appreciate them."

Say,

"Thank you."

49. *Say You're Sorry*

Whenever you make a mistake, admit it readily and say you're sorry. Defuse potential emotional flareups, avoid confrontations, and build others' respect for your character by facing facts, admitting the truth, and apologizing.

Instead of saying,

"Look, it's just too bad. Don't blame me. I couldn't help it."

Say,

"I'm sorry; it was my responsibility."

Power Talkers . . .
IX. SHARE THEIR PRIDE

50. *The Sound of One Man Clapping*

Let the people you feel proud of hear about it.
Instead of saying,

"I'm sure he knows I'm proud of him."

Say,

"I'm proud of you."

An Invitation from the Author

To arrange customized Power Talking or Phone Power presentations for your organization, I invite you to call my office 24 hours a day: 1-206-255-2900. I'm proud to personally present programs for leading corporations and associations worldwide. I am honored to hold the National Speakers Association's highest award for speaking skills and professionalism, the CPAE.

Many highly effective Power Tools are available to help you implement Power Talking throughout your organization and in your own personal life. They include audio and video cassette programs suitable for corporate training and individual use, plus easy-to-use quick reference cards and progress-tracking systems.

For a Fax Brochure describing Power Talking and Phone Power support materials, please fax your request to: 1-206-235-6360 and include a return fax number and address.

I'm now gathering ideas for *50 **More** Power Talking Techniques* and look forward to hearing your examples. I'll be pleased to credit you when they're used in the next edition.

George R. Walther
6947 Coal Creek Parkway, Suite 100
Renton, WA 98059
1-206-255-2900   Fax: 1-206-235-6360

Suggested Reading List

Blanchard, Kenneth and Norman Vincent Peale. *The Power of Ethical Management*. New York: Ballantine Books, 1989.

Blanchard, Kenneth and Spencer Johnson. *The One Minute Manager*. New York: Berkley, 1987.

Calano, Jimmy and Jeff Salzman. *CareerTracking*. New York: Simon & Schuster, 1988.

Carnegie, Dale. *How to Stop Worrying and Start Living*. New York: Simon & Schuster, 1984.

Davis, Wynn. *The Best of Success: A Treasury of Success Ideas*. Lombard: Great Quotations, Inc., 1988.

Douglas, Kirk. *The Ragman's Son*. New York: Simon & Schuster, 1988.

Dyer, Wayne W. *What Do You Really Want for Your Children?* New York: Avon, 1985.

Fulghum, Robert. *All I Really Need to Know I Learned in Kindergarten*. New York: Villard, 1989.

Hill, Napoleon. *Think & Grow Rich Action Pack*. New York: E. P. Dutton, 1988.

Mackay, Harvey. *Beware the Naked Man Who Offers You His Shirt*. New York: William Morrow, 1990.

_____. *Swim With the Sharks Without Being Eaten Alive*. New York: William Morrow, 1988.

Mandino, Og. *The Greatest Salesman in the World*. New York: Bantam Books, 1988.

Martorano, Joseph T., and John P. Kildahl. *Beyond Negative Thinking*. New York: Plenum Press, 1989.

Murphy, Joseph. *The Power of Your Subconscious Mind*. New York: Bantam Books, 1982.

Peale, Norman Vincent. *Positive Imaging*. New York: Ballantine Books, 1982.

_____. *The Power of Positive Thinking*. New York: Ballantine Books, 1990.

_____. *Why Some Positive Thinkers Get Powerful Results*. New York: Ballantine Books, 1988.

Schwartz, David Joseph, Ph.D. *The Magic of Thinking Big*. No. Hollywood: Wilshire Book Company, 1959.

Seligman, Martin. *Learned Optimism*. New York: Random House, 1990.

Seligson, Tom. "I Decided to Always Rely on My Own Strength" (Profile of Joan Lunden), *Parade* magazine, September 9, 1990.

Ziglar, Zig. *Raising Positive Kids in a Negative World*. New York: Ballantine Books, 1989.

About the Author

George Walther is in great demand as a consultant and speaker for leading corporations and associations worldwide. He shows business and professional leaders how to communicate more positively on the phone and in person.

He is the author of *Phone Power*, first published in the U.S. by G. P. Putnam's Sons in 1986 and now available in paperback, as well as foreign language, audio, and video editions.

George earned a B.A. in Rhetoric and Public Address, and an M.B.A. in Marketing from UCLA's Graduate School of Management.

He is one of fewer than 100 people worldwide to have been honored with the National Speakers Association's highest award for speaking skills and professionalism, the CPAE. He regularly addresses audiences around the world.

Corporate clients include Ford, Du Pont, Hewlett-Packard, GE, and numerous other Fortune 1000 companies. A wide range of associations including ASAE, Sales and Marketing Executives International, and the American Management Association also hire him to speak at their conventions.

George lives with his wife, Julie, near Seattle. Their first child, Kelcie Paige, was born while George completed the *Power Talking* manuscript. When not onstage delivering a speech, George can be found with his wife and daughter enjoying long walks in the woods.